TRACKING
THE BANISHED
IMMORTAL

P A U L A   M .   V A R S A N O

TRACKING THE BANISHED IMMORTAL

✥

The Poetry of Li Bo and
Its Critical Reception

UNIVERSITY OF HAWAI'I PRESS
Honolulu

03 04 05 06 07 08   6 5 4 3 2 1

Library of Congress Cataloging-in-Publication Data
Varsano, Paula M.
Tracking the banished immortal : the poetry of Li Bo and its critical reception /
Paula M. Varsano.
p. cm.
Includes bibliographical references and index.
ISBN 0-8248-2573-X (alk. paper)
1. Li, Bo, 701–762—Criticism and interpretation.
I. Title: Poetry of Li Bo and its critical reception. II. Title.
PL2671 .V37 2003
895.1'13—dc21
2003002470

Designed by Trina Stahl Design

Printed by The Maple-Vail Book Manufacturing Group

for my parents,
Sabe and Blanche

CONTENTS

ACKNOWLEDGMENTS

SETTING OUT UPON the path of a banished immortal is not something one does without a good, strong push, a large and detailed map, and the promise of a steady supply of nourishment. It was Yu-kung Kao who gave me that first push when he convinced me that it would not be pure impertinence to write my dissertation on Li Bo. His guidance and encouragement during my years at Princeton, along with the suggestions and support offered by Andrew Plaks, were essential to the completion of the thesis that—so many years later—inspired this book, transformed though it is. Stephen Owen's uncommon generosity in taking time to share his knowledge and insights as I worked through Li Bo's collected poems, along with his many published essays on Chinese poetry and poetics, continue to prove valuable to me today. During the early stages of my research, I also benefited greatly from regular discussions with Wang Yunxi and Yang Ming of Fudan University in Shanghai, who gently but firmly dissuaded me from many an interpretive error. Thanks are due as well, of course, to the now disbanded Committee for Scholarly Communication with the People's Republic of China, which provided the grant that enabled me to work at Fudan, and to the Foreign Students Office there, whose officers obtained a hard-won permission for me to follow the footsteps of the "Banished Immortal" into then restricted parts of Anhui and Zhejiang. Ably and warmly accompanied during that trip by my friend Tu Xiulan, I discovered how to go beyond merely studying Li Bo, to remembering him in his landscape and in the company of other present-day admirers. When I finally returned home to write, my late husband, Jacques Gagné, was there to sustain me with the humor and passion that were uniquely his.

When, more than a decade after the completion of the thesis, I returned to my old subject with new ideas and slightly grander ambitions, the advice and support of those mentors and friends continued to help me as I benefited from the tangible generosity of my colleagues at Smith College. Maki Hubbard, Daniel Gardner, Thalia Pandiri, Tom Rohlich, and Zhao Ling are foremost among those who, through their friendship and professional kindnesses, facilitated the completion of this manuscript. The Chiang Ching-kuo Foundation provided substantial financial support (allowing me to extend my sabbatical leave), as did the Smith College CFCD Fund. I thank Tian-yuan Tan for his work as my research assistant during the final stages of this book. An earlier version of what is now chapter 5 appeared in the *Harvard Journal of Asiatic Studies*. I am particularly indebted to the anonymous readers of the University of Hawai'i Press, who provided me with invaluable ideas (and corrections) in my revision of the manuscript.

To the members of my family—my brother David and his wife, Jill—to Michèle Magny, and to Dominique, Valérie, Mathieu, and Renaud Gagné—I owe a debt of gratitude for making sure I always had the "nourishment" I needed along the way.

Finally, I would like to recognize the inspiration and unfailing support of my parents, Sabe and Blanche, to whom I dedicate this book with love and gratitude; and of Alan Tansman, whose ideas and irreverence shed light on this path, and whose restless curiosity reminds me to keep the boundaries of the world wide open.

Introduction

Looking toward Heaven's Gate

From the middle of Heaven's Gate
    breaks forth the River of Chu,
Emerald waters' eastward flow touches
    north and then returns.
On either shore a mountain green,
    emerging face to face,
Beside the sun a lonely sail: one single
    sheet approaching.

天門中斷楚江開
碧水東流至北迴
兩岸青山相對出
孤帆一片日邊來

—Li Bo, "Looking toward Heaven's Gate Mountain" (望天門山)

THE PAIR OF mountains called "Heaven's Gate" marks the threshold between heaven and earth: the place that many readers will recognize as the dwelling place of the Tang poet Li Bo (701–762). Here, the edge of perceptible space becomes the center, and the massive solidity of the mountains serves, above all, to frame emptiness. As China's famed Banished Immortal, the poet fittingly portrays himself looking toward, but never passing through, the gate to heaven. His vision singles out the objects whose existence shapes the breadth and depth of the otherwise immeasurable void.

If this poem presents a vision of the world through the eyes of Li Bo, it also offers—not incidentally—a view of Li Bo through the eyes of generations of Chinese readers and critics. Just as he provided visual markers that enable us to "see" the invisible, critics have long been trying to establish the verbal means that would enable us to apprehend the "unattainable," inherently indescribable poetics that is said to be uniquely his. And just as readers of this poem understand that to cross the threshold into emptiness is to destroy that emptiness, critics have never tired of cautioning readers against venturing too close to the details that make up one of Li Bo's poems.[1]

Unfortunately, however, not all readers who complied with this warning did so out of respect for Li's poetry; not everyone was pleased by his penchant for the unreal or unfounded, the all-too-obvious pleasure he took in hyperbolic renderings of already dramatic landscapes, and his casual brushes with immortals. Depending on the critical focus of a given era and, of course, on the preoccupations of individual critics, Li Bo's stylistic and imagistic liberties provoked attacks on his moral fiber, his self-discipline, his grasp of literature and literary history, his perceptiveness regarding the so-called substantive world, or the overall nefarious effect that writings such as his might have on the continued development of poetry. The Northern (and, to a lesser extent, the Southern) Song dynasty (960–1279) is frequently cited as a particularly difficult one for Li's admirers. The charge of being all surface and no content—"all flowers and no fruit"—became a refrain among readers ranging from Li Gang (1083–1140) to Lu You (1125–1210) that was regularly revived throughout the traditional period by critics who feared seduction by virtuosity.

The charge was a serious one, implying that Li's poems were not the "articulations of intent" prescribed by tradition, but collections of words and images gratuitously arrayed with the sole and express intent of creating effect. His supposedly free-wheeling expressiveness was perceived by some as posing a threat to what has elsewhere been termed the ideal of expressive immediacy.[2] This ideal, which upholds poetic expression as the unmediated, untransformed verbal manifestation of emotion, is rooted in the "Great Preface" to the *Shijing*, a text widely read and studied by literati from the end of the Han dynasty through the Song (approximately the third through the thirteenth centuries), and whose influence upon the reading and writing of poetry extended through the end of the imperial era.[3] The ideal of immediacy conveyed in this text upholds the essential unity of the perceived world and the poem articulating that world, a unity that expresses itself as a work brought forth without forethought or artifice of any kind.

A poem perceived as having been thus produced, then, speaks to the poet's "authenticity," a shorthand term I use to connote the poet's capacity to give himself over to feelings produced by unimpeded contact with the real world, and naturally and spontaneously to convey the resulting feelings in words.[4] Li's exaggerated and invented vistas, however, did not correspond easily to the real world that readers recognized either from their own experiences or from the poems of the ancients. Partly for this reason, his work could and did strike some as the disruption of the ideal oneness of world and poem. In the evident mediation of his individual imagination, some perceived and decried the inauthentic or superficial poses of the pure performer.

Given the seriousness of these criticisms, Li Bo should logically have faded into the oblivion reserved for those poets deemed merely tantalizingly idiosyncratic. Quite to the contrary, however, Li Bo attained the status of a truly great poet during his lifetime, and his status has endured. In a critical tradition largely shaped by periodic discussions of its poets' rank and lineage, the "frivolous" Li Bo consistently emerges at the top of most lists, either on a par with his younger contemporary, Du Fu (712–770) as China's greatest poet, or in the slot just below him. Over the years, the intensity of critical partisanship rose and fell, but the gravity (and occasional vituperative tone) of the charges—and the passion and persistence of the debates they incited—stand as a measure of Li's perceived importance in the ongoing discussion of what poetry should be and, as he receded into the distant past, of how best to depict the overall landscape of Chinese poetry. The centuries of contention triggered by his disruption of the word-world continuum, by his propensity to explore the elusive, indescribable, or imaginary dimensions of human experience, ultimately revealed that his poetry possessed the power to transform the very standards against which he was being judged.

Li Bo was not just one of China's two greatest poets; he was the Chinese poet whose greatness was worth fighting for. This distinction, I believe, merits closer examination, not only for what it promises to reveal about Li Bo, but also for what it can tell us about the evolving values of the aesthetic tradition he ultimately helped shape. In this book I examine critical (and, on occasion poetic) writings from the period immediately following his death through the beginnings of the Republic (the early 1900s), and ask what exactly Li Bo provided that traditional readers of poetry felt compelled to protect and transmit, and what theoretical and rhetorical arguments were invoked by critics as they rose to the challenge.[5] In particular, I explore how and why this anointed guardian of all that is unlearnable and unattainable was gradually transformed, somewhat paradoxically, into a literary model, and offer some observations as to how this metamorphosis in turn effected the reception of Li Bo's poetry during the late imperial and early modern periods.

NEGATIVE RHETORIC AND THE EXPRESSION OF PLENITUDE

In "Looking toward Heaven's Gate Mountain," Li Bo marked the presence of the void, Heaven, by depicting it at the threshold: where a pair of mountains mark an otherwise invisible boundary line between heaven and earth, and where a single sailboat's progress marks a fluid passageway. The vision of the whole—of continuity in division—depends upon the steadfastness of the viewer's stance, and the critical language that has shaped and preserved the poetic territory occupied by Li Bo's works functions in a similar manner. Like the stolid, towering peaks, a host of critical terms name—and frame—all that Li Bo is not. Even during his lifetime and immediately afterward, readers both critical and admiring named his poetry as "not attainable" by mortal men, "not learnable" through the usual means of study and imitation, and "unrestrained" by the conventions and expectations of society and accepted literary practice. And, like the sailboat faring freely across that threshold, we meet with the intrepid, elusive names of the numinous: a series of otherworldly epithets and descriptive phrases associating Li Bo with the realm of deities and immortals, a realm where commonplace limitations of time and space hold no sway.

Delineation by negation, evocation by metaphor: the combination not only protects Li Bo's precious unlearnability against reduction by mechanical representation, but also preserves the existence of unlearnability as a legitimate category of poetic practice, carrying both the poet and his work safely through the critical skirmishes and transformations that would arise over the centuries. These two rhetorical approaches—the negative and the numinous—have been neatly encapsulated in the oft-repeated epithet, "Banished Immortal," which has been used to refer to Li Bo's supremely vivid and compelling persona during his lifetime and ever since.[6]

The question arises as to how negative rhetoric signifies within the traditional Chinese critical context. Today's readers, both Chinese and Western, when confronting a critical vocabulary largely composed of negative locutions, might be tempted to think in terms of Adorno's work on negative aesthetics or de Man's deconstructive readings. These theories of negativity, however, were fashioned in large part to account for the emergence of a fragmented, depersonalized modern poetics (informed by Kantian dialectical reasoning), and so conceive of a negative aesthetic primarily as an expression of resistance against dominant modes of discourse or artistic expression. Jonathan Culler summarizes this line of thinking as "a powerful strategy for interpreting even the most refractory poems: the most bizarre and disconnected images can be read as signs of alienation and anomie or of a breakdown of mental processes brought on by the experience in question."[7]

Although it is possible to demonstrate some superficial points of overlap between contemporary conceptions of negative aesthetics and the distant image of a rebellious, iconoclastic Li Bo, close scrutiny of the critical tradition that grew up around his poetry reveals that readers did not tend to focus on Li Bo as actively rejecting tradition. Nor did they think of him as having been affected by trauma (let alone as being in a state of alienation). A more accurate and historically more convincing context in which to situate the negative discourse associated with Li Bo is the rhetorical and epistemological construct that Andrew Plaks has termed "complementary bipolarity."

Plaks' model, derived from his structuralist reading of Cao Xueqin's (ca. 1715–ca. 1763) masterpiece, the novel *Hongloumeng* (Dream of the red chamber), elaborates the familiar yin-yang dualism expressed in such pairs of existential phenomena as hot/ cold, light/dark, true/false, and, especially pertinent to my discussion, substantial/illusory. According to this model, these pairs do not exist as absolute states standing in dialectical opposition, but reflect "the apprehension of experience ... in terms of the relative presence or absence of opposites." Plaks further specifies that these pairs are characterized by "ceaseless alternation towards and away from the hypothetical poles of each duality," so that "the ascendance of one term immediately implies its own subsequent diminution," and finally that "the endless overlapping of the axes of change ... eventually adds up to a convincing illusion of plenitude, and hence the perception of reality."[8] Of course, the unplanned unfurling of a line of critical discourse cannot be analyzed as though it were a deliberately constructed novel. But, as Plaks convincingly demonstrates, complementary bipolarity is not some random pattern imposed on one particular novel, but a defining paradigm forming the very basis of early philosophical thought and rhetoric. Whether the subject is society or literature, whether the form is lyrical or discursive, the drive to depict phenomenological plenitude—and the ubiquity of dynamic structures of complementary bipolarity—are familiar to all readers of traditional Chinese literature.

Both the numinous and the negative rhetoric of Li Bo criticism were conceived within the larger epistemological context of complementary bipolarity, as expressed in the overarching and enduring practice of Li Bo–Du Fu comparative criticism, a practice that forms the matrix for much of Li Bo criticism.[9] The "Li-Du" bipolar discourse, oft disputed but rarely analyzed, is almost as venerable as the poetry itself. Only a couple of generations after their deaths, the critic and author Yuan Zhen (779–831), in his funerary inscription for Du Fu, explicitly refers to the fact that Li and Du's contemporaries already referred to them as "Li-and-Du";[10] and the appearance of a shorthand reference to "Li-Du Excellence-Inferiority" (Li-Du youlie) in Du Fu's biography in the Jiu Tang shu (Old Tang history) indicates that, by the time of Five Dynasties (907–960), this practice had become a subject of discussion in itself.[11]

Many factors contributed to the initial formation of the Li-Du pair, not the least of which was their supposed friendship, characterized by some as rather one-sided, with Du Fu emerging as the more loyal, admiring, and, not surprisingly, sincere friend. But another force propelling this tradition was the urge toward the representation of aesthetic plenitude. This plenitude suggests more mutuality between the two poets than most readers might be willing to concede, given the nearly unquestioned and unabated dominance of Du Fu ever since the Song and the early characterization of Du Fu's self-sufficient wholeness. We often rely on positive or concrete experiences in order to comprehend or convey their necessarily elusive opposites, so it is not altogether surprising that Du Fu's reputed "learnability" and "earthboundedness" contribute in an obvious way to our ability to conceptualize Li's negative qualities of unlearnability and unfettered "immortality." But plenitude also dictates that readers' appreciation of Du Fu requires the presence of Li Bo—a requirement more difficult to grasp. What, after all, does Li Bo have to offer the poet who single-handedly integrated the disparate threads of the "ancient and modern" literary tradition, and whose sturdy footing in the world earned him the epithet "poet-historian"?[12] In effect, it is precisely Du Fu's self-contained perfection that necessitates Li Bo's promise of uncontainable infinity; it is this negatively rendered Li Bo who is deemed capable of lending true plenitude to the otherwise partial picture of Du Fu's perfection.

In order to make this argument, however, it is necessary to look again at the meaning of "plenitude" in this context. Plaks understood the depiction of plenitude in Dream of the Red Chamber as instrumental to producing an "illusion of reality," elsewhere described as "the sheer infinitude of existence—its all-ness."[13] Clearly, this explanation does not quite apply when the reality being rendered is the critically conceived topography of Chinese poetry. In this context, the all-ness being depicted is not that of human existence, but of a mode of its representation: plenitude as an aesthetic ideal. Just such a notion has been recently elaborated in the work of Elaine Scarry. In her book *On Beauty and Being Just,* she argues that beauty is experienced as a desire to go beyond the specific beautiful object we behold, perhaps through the urge to beget or reproduce it, or perhaps in "the search for something beyond itself, something larger or something of the same scale with which it needs to be brought into relation."[14] These impulses, she suggests, lead naturally to the frequent associations of beauty with immortality. Scarry concludes that, inevitably, "beautiful things ... always carry greetings from other worlds within them.... What happens when there is no immortal realm behind the beautiful person or thing is just what happens when there *is* an immortal realm behind the beautiful person or thing: the perceiver is led to a more capacious regard for the world. The requirement for *plenitude* is built-in."[15]

Although Chinese poetic discourse would never express this sentiment in terms of the platonic category of Beauty (present in Scarry's conception despite her removal of the capital letter) and although her insistence on immortality is a fortuitous coincidence, I find her description of the urge toward plenitude both compelling and helpful in concisely formulating the particular role that Li Bo played in the evolving conception of the lyric.

The desire for plenitude, thus explained, harbors a form of negativity that corresponds closely to the negative conceptualization of Li Bo's poetics, for it is a plenitude understood in terms not of completion, but of the impossibility of completion—or, to put it less negatively, in terms of the eternally fugitive, tantalizing dream of completion. Scarry's identification of the human need not for wholeness but for an elusive something more, although developed out of a tradition of Western philosophy, provides a concept that carries both the fundamental element of change and the motivating impulse of the reader's desire for certain types of aesthetic experience. It is in this sense, too, that Du Fu needs Li Bo, as it is in this sense that Li Bo's presence cannot be apprehended in the absence of Du Fu.

The bipolar plenitude mapped out by Li-and-Du is as multi-faceted as the works of the poets concerned, and as much in flux as the plenitude toward which readers yearn. The pair's characterizations as heaven-and-earth, immortal-and-sage, Daoist-and-Confucian, sage-and-historian, genius-and-erudite all suggest a stable binary unit. But that sense of stasis is not only theoretically in conflict with the rhetorical and philosophical tradition of bipolarity: its empirical existence proves to be illusory, shifting constantly as the search for a stable equilibrium between any two terms of a bipolar pair results in constant reformulation and constant redrawing of boundaries.

To be more specific, one of the most comprehensive and fundamental bipolar concepts applied to Li and Du is *xu* and *shi*, the literal (but misleading) translations of which are "empty" and "full." The earliest definition of *shi*, as found in the Han dynasty dictionary, the *Shuowen jiezi*, is "wealth," or material plenty, and the connotation of the material and the concrete carry through the word's varied usage over the centuries, ranging from sufficiency to inclusion in compounds denoting substance, reality, solidity, truthfulness, and the less directly related botanical connotations of seeds and fruit. Stephen Owen offers a helpful gloss for this term as it is used in literary criticism: "'solid,' 'actual.' Sometimes used in opposition to *xu, shi* refers to the fixity of definite form (as opposed to the 'plasticity' of *xu*) and to the external solidity of a ... 'scene' (as opposed to the 'empty' emotional coloring of the scene). A line is *shi* if it describes external things and has no 'empty' words that subordinate the description to the way the subject feels about it or interprets it."[16]

Owen's gloss indicates that *shi* carries strong connotations of the substantive, objective world, while *xu* embraces all that is elusive and modal, relating to the poetic subject's inner world. As he remarks elsewhere, this complex of meaning corresponds to the traditional linguistic distinction between lexically definable words and the grammatical function words, or particles, that join them in sentences, and "for the quality of subjective relation they imparted to an utterance."[17] This gloss also highlights the important fact that *xu* is not to be understood as a *lack* of anything, but as a recognizable quality of a significance equal to that of *shi*.

François Cheng, writing somewhat earlier, is insistent on this point. In warning his European readers away from the strong potential for misinterpretation across cultures, he inadvertently provides us with an excellent description of the elemental nature of the Li-Du pair in Chinese literary criticism, which is a motivating force in the maintenance of Li Bo's supremacy in the poetic pantheon: "For, in the Chinese view, Emptiness is not, as one might suppose, something vague or unreal, but a remarkably dynamic and active element. Linked to the notion of vital breath and the principle of alternation between Yin and Yang, it constitutes the site most propitious to the operation of the transformations whereby Fullness attains to true plenitude. It is [Emptiness], in effect, that, by introducing discontinuity and reversibility into a given system, allows the constituent components of that system to circumvent rigid contraposition of opposites and unidirectional development, and at the same time, that renders possible a unifying vision for man of the universe."[18]

Aside from the happy coincidence that led Cheng to think of *xu* as a "site,"[19] his description is also useful in confirming the traditional basis for an adaptation of Scarry's notion of plenitude, namely, the ideal condition in which the stable wholeness of the finite is activated by evocations of the infinite. This adulation of the category of Emptiness is fairly common in literary criticism from about the late Ming period through the founding years of the Republic. The following statement by the Qing critic Wu Qiao (1611–1695?) suggests that Cheng is not overstating the case, at least as things stood during the late imperial period: "Overall, writings that are *shi* are finite, while writings that are *xu* have no limits. The "Elegantiae" and the "Hymns" [of the *Shijing*] are comprised mostly of poetic expositions, and thus are *shi* works. The "Airs" [of the *Shijing*] and the *Sao* [e.g., Qu Yuan's "Encountering Sorrow"] contain many comparisons (*bi*) and stimuli (*xing*), and thus are *xu* works. Tang poems most often model themselves on the "Airs" and the *Sao,* and therefore are wondrous and subtle *(lingmiao).*[20]

Still, *xu,* and the nearly synonymous *kong,* did not always signify desirable qualities in literary writing, but also harbored nuances of falsehood, futility, and superficiality. In this derogatory sense *xu* made its first appearance in Li Bo criticism, when, in the thirteenth century, debates concerning the quality and depth of Li's knowledge of the classics were in full swing. By this time, a period when Song Neo-Confucian literati were broadening the philosophical and spiritual base of the Confucian classics in order to reestablish them as the basis for all learning, critics of Li Bo had already been divided into two camps: those who found his acquaintance with the classics superficial and flimsy, and those who discerned beneath the surface of "flowers and moonlight" a firm foundation in the *Shijing* or, at the very least, the *Sao.*

So, when the term "*xu*" first entered the vocabulary of Li Bo criticism, it was not as a means of praising the wondrously elusive worlds he evoked in his poems, but as a strong condemnation of his lack of learning. Readers pinpointed this lack not only in the relative dearth of direct references to the classics (a point that was hotly debated), but also in the disjuncture between the "*xu* tales about spirits and immortals"[21] presented in his poetry and the "real" world shared by all through the common medium of perception—the split between one person's hyperbolic imaginings and people's quotidian dealings with the social and political realities of the day. This disjuncture, evidence of what Owen has called Li Bo's "fictional imagination,"[22] challenged the ideal of immediacy (at least the way it was understood by the more traditionalist among Li Bo's readers), and cast doubt upon the substance and depth of the feelings Li articulated.

Xu, a central concept in the evolving criticism of Li Bo's poetry, presents certain difficulties to the translator. It has proven supple enough to embrace connotations from the damning to the laudatory. Its implicit pairing with *shi* ensures that, whatever the tenor of its connotations, it occupies the negative space of plenitude, while its strong suggestion of a foundation in worlds other than the tangible here and now lends it the air of the numinous. In an effort to evoke at least the possibility of this range of nuance and meaning, I gloss this term as "unfounded" or "unfoundedness." Morphologically, this translation captures the negative dimension of Li Bo rhetoric, and, in its opposition to things "founded" in perceived reality, it evokes the numinous dimension as well. As a derogatory term, it also bears witness to *xu*'s pejorative beginnings in the Li-Du critical debate. Like *xu*, the use of "unfounded" in clearly commendatory contexts should imbue it with the same slightly paradoxical air it carries when used to defend Li's particularities. As for *shi*, I have simply selected the word "substantive" for its evocations of solidity and empirical verifiability.

ATTAINING ANCIENTNESS: TWO NARRATIVES

Modern literary historians have observed that the Song emphasis on learning was the primary cause for Li's unpopularity relative to Du Fu during that dynasty, and that he recovered his high critical esteem when the Wang Yangming school of Neo-Confucian thought redirected the search for sagehood from the external sources of the classics and the material world to the internal resource of the essentially good "childlike heart."[23] According to this argument, this shift in thinking allowed for the recognition of the reality of the imagination and so facilitated legitimate appreciation of Li Bo's hyperbolic style and celestial imagery. Such an explanation bespeaks an admirable attempt to situate the critical discourse about Li Bo within larger historical and philosophical developments, and it is valid as far as it goes. But by oversimplifying the relationship between philosophical movements and literature (both theory and praxis), and by relying on the conventional dynastic periodization of monolithic politico-philosophical "movements," this view shortchanges both the complexity of ongoing debate and the importance of Li Bo to the evolving practice and reception of poetry.

Under what terms, then, was Li Bo's poetry first admitted into the ranks of poetic "greatness"—and how did his particular expression of greatness come to enter the poetic canon?[24] Tracing the evolution of critical discourse in two distinct but closely intertwined narratives will lead to a clearer understanding of these questions. One narrative chronologically traces the shifts in the internal makeup of key bipolar concepts as they present themselves in Li-Du comparative criticism; the other is the account of Li Bo's entry into the canon, and how that transformed reception of his work and transmission of his poetic persona. The movement of these intertwined stories is propelled by the desire of poetry readers (including Li Bo himself) to keep before them the promise of aesthetic plenitude, a promise that—by its nature—must not and cannot be fulfilled. As long as Li is endowed with the qualities that extend Du's perfect wholeness into the realm of the indefinable, and as long as Du stands as a reminder of Li's indefinability, their combined figure suggests both plenitude and its impossibility, sustaining bipolarity as a driving force in literary discourse.

Readers familiar with the literature will recognize that, in Chinese literary criticism, plenitude is never spoken of as such, but makes its appearance in the form of more specific (but equally unattainable) ideals—especially those composed of apparently irreconcilable oppositions. One such ideal taking form during Li Bo's lifetime, and rising to prominence as the ninth century began to wane, was that of *gu*—the "ancient"—codified in what be came known as the *"guwen"* (ancient style) movement.

THE BIPOLARITY OF ANCIENTNESS

It is not inconsequential that the seminal authors of the Li Bo critical tradition—those writers most often cited by subsequent critics—are Yuan Zhen (779–831), Bo Juyi (772–846), and especially Han Yu (768–824), renowned poets of the mid-Tang period. All three are commonly identified as among the founders of the *guwen* movement. Their comments contributed significantly to setting the terms for how Li Bo was to be considered and, most important, described.

And what were these critics' primary concerns in evaluating literature? The term *"guwen,"* when applied to the thought of Han Yu and his contemporaries, refers, in its narrowest literary application, to the promotion of *wen*, or "literary writing,"[25] that aspires to an "ancient," or *gu*, style of unadorned simplicity, and whose content reflects the writer's strong Confucian moral stance. In its broader sense, *guwen* encompasses a multifaceted, long-term attempt to establish and safeguard an integrated morality, based in the ancient Confucian philosophical and literary canon and expressed, sustained, and propagated in the literary writings of the latter-day ruling, writing elite. According to Peter Bol, *guwen*— especially as formulated by Han Yu—arose as an attempt to solve the paradox "between a conviction that men had to think for themselves and a belief that values had to be drawn from the cultural tradition."[26] The struggle to determine how writings might best manifest "ancientness"—alignment with the moral Way set forth by the ancients—can be understood as a quest for the perfect blend of two apparently contradictory modes of knowledge: shared wisdom gleaned from a socially unifying body of texts transmitted from ancient times, on the one hand, and the "ancient" practice of independently exercising one's own intelligence and moral judgment, on the other.

The fundamental bipolarity of the *guwen* movement thus construed embraces some of the central issues that arise as critics attempt to situate Li Bo in the tradition. Not the least of these is the conceptual pair *xu* and *shi*, or "unfounded and substantive," expressed in Li-Du comparative criticism. The semantic territory covered by each of these two terms, and the solidity of the boundary between them, shifted constantly as readers and writers responded to the many questions raised by *guwen*, for example, How does a poet articulate his natural response to the world in the face of increasingly clear-cut notions of what formal attributes such a natural response should exhibit? When does demonstrated knowledge of the ancients—in the form of allusion, adherence to generic and thematic convention, and repetition of well-worn moral anecdotes (three formally identifiable examples)—stop functioning as evidence of the writer's internalization of ancient values and start looking dangerously like obsequious imitation? What are the implications of deliberately avoiding recognizably ancient poetic features in the name of preserving authenticity? Conversely, when does a poet's vivid use of unusual phrases and images stop signifying a spontaneous response to the times, and start suggesting a performer more interested in creating a specific impression upon his audience? Finally, how can readers, often writers in their own right, discern the difference?

Partly in response to these questions—all of which attempt to navigate the bipolarity inscribed in the ideal of the ancient— writers transform the pairs of terms that, at various times, take center stage in the Li-Du debate: not only the comprehensive pair *xu* and *shi,* but also the more specific dualities of *cai* and *xue* (talent and learning), *shen* and *gong* (inspiration and craft), *wen* and *zhi* (pattern and substance), and *bukexue* and *kexue* (unlearn-ability and learnability), many of which antedate the self-conscious *guwen* movement by centuries. This constant transformation, as enacted in Li-Du criticism, is characterized by adjustments, and even reversals, in rhetoric and conceptualization. Over time, however, these changes reveal a pattern of cyclical movement from initial pairing, to extreme opposition, to a discourse that might best be called syncretic, and then back toward opposition. In the syncretic stage, each term of a bipolar concept is broadened to include many of its counterpart's defining attributes, gradually attenuating the pair's defining bipolarity. During the Ming dynasty, for example, this trend became most evident when such writers as Xie Zhen (1495–1575) and Tu Long (1542–1605) set about es-tablishing Li's work as *shi* within *xu,* and Du's work as *xu* within *shi.*

At such moments of equilibrium, Li's status is certainly safe, but such equilibrium is, by its very nature, the antithesis of the complementary bipolarity on which plenitude depends. Eventually, the cycle starts again, but on a slightly different track, because both the poets and the terms that had been used to qualify them have been significantly transformed by centuries of debate. Li Bo, like Du Fu, has become inextricable from the discourse that has grown up around him, and discussion of his work can hardly avoid being discussion of Li Bo criticism. When this happened, Li Bo truly acceded to ancientness, but an ancientness more expressive of his canonization than of his *xu* role in the bipolar picture of poetic plenitude.

CANONICITY AND ANCIENTNESS

Given the steady increase in scholarly interest in the nature and origins of canons and canonicity, it is no surprise that Western students of Chinese literature have begun in recent years to examine the formation of the Chinese literary canon. While such scholars as Adele Rickett and, more recently, Pauline Yu and Mark E. Francis have focused on the canonizing effects of poetry collections and their prefaces,[27] others have concentrated on the canonizing role played by hermeneutics. Notable among these is Steven Van Zoeren's book-length study of the history of *Shijing* hermeneutics, *Poetry and Personality: Reading, Exegesis, and Hermeneutics in Traditional China*.[28] Van Zoeren traces the development of the exegetical approaches that first identified the collection as a "classic" (*jing*) through centuries of transformations (inspired both by the discovery of shortcomings in exegetical approaches and by the changing values of the times) that ultimately worked to preserve that status. Van Zoeren follows Barbara Herrnstein Smith's[29] example and defines the classic in terms of its normative status as a prime repository of value, positing recognition of a work's classical status by the sustained hermeneutical effort it inspires: "We can say that hermeneutics comes into play when certain texts become authoritative within a culture and are treated as the privileged loci in which value is inscribed. Such texts become the centerpieces of their tradition, and they provide an ultimate justification and foundation for normative argument within that tradition. Studied, memorized, and explicated, their reading and interpretation are not of simply instrumental or historical interest, but rather are consequential both for the interpreter and for society."[30]

Van Zoeren is writing here about a body of texts whose inscribed value extended far beyond the belletristic, whereas Tang poems, for all the canonical status they eventually acquired, were never subjected to the intense hermeneutical scrutiny applied to the *Shijing*. Still, the elevation of Tang poets—most obviously Li Bo and Du Fu—to the status of "privileged loci" of value (both ethical and aesthetic), so that understanding them became consequential, becomes evident during the increasingly orthodox Song dynasty in the publication of anthologies and in the debates those anthologies inspired.[31] The practice of extemporaneous writings about poetry, in the form of *shihua,* also played an important role in consolidating the role of certain Tang poets, providing "justification and foundation for normative argument within the tradition."

Van Zoeren's link between canonical status and the positing and excavation of value makes it possible to offer the following three working criteria for canonical status.

First, the canonized work (either the individual piece or the entire body of works of a given origin or author) is one deemed especially *expressive* of a value or set of values held by the culture that produced it, such that those in a position of power assert (in curricular and curatorial acts, as well as in the arena of criticism and theory) its *necessity* to the education of present and future generations. This criterion includes works that Barbara Herrnstein Smith identifies as embodying part of a countermechanism, that is, recognizably heterodox works whose existence is tolerated as an acknowledgment of the inevitability of divergence.[32]

Second, the work's necessary status must obtain over a certain period of time. The consensus that keeps it in place is no longer a matter of taste, but of cultural identity. This sense of a work's *timelessness* is described by Hans-Georg Gadamer as follows: "What we call classical is something retrieved from the vicissitudes of changing time and its changing taste.... [It] is a consciousness of something enduring, of significance that cannot be lost and is independent of all the circumstances of time, in which we call something "classical"—a kind of timeless present that is contemporaneous with every other age."[33]

Third, while the canonized work is recognized as a timeless source of valuable knowledge, it is also, in its essence, unique and *unrepeatable*.

The canonized work, then, functions as a nexus where the present generation enjoins its debt to the past and meets its obligation to the future, embodying a unifying image of past, present, and future in a recognizable and constant set of moral and (especially in the case of the arts) aesthetic values. There is something of the mythic in a canonical work's unifying power and transcendent scope. Indeed, in China, practical expression of the mythical status of canonized authors can be observed everywhere.[34] Shrines to poets and authors, for example, can be found wherever they were even suspected of having set foot, and supernatural stories involving them abound. Traveling the areas in Anhui and Zhejiang where Li Bo spent the last years of his life, one can find the stains of recent libations to Li Bo's spirit (even if offered with a wry smile) still sticky on steles throughout the countryside. Guardians of his tomb—and the villagers from the area—are more than happy to regale visitors with stories of "firsthand" encounters between their ancestors and Li Bo's spirit. And if shrines and steles erected to Li Bo seem more numerous than those dedicated to other poets, it is not only because of his notoriously peripatetic life. Of all the poets, he is the one whose mythical pedigree—a pedigree that, in some accounts, borders on the mystical, making him a prime candidate for eventual entry into the canon—circulated even before his death.

Stories about Li Bo's provenance (some of which he propagated himself) spark the imagination and, as in the case of Chinese creation myths, several versions coexist peacefully. Sired by a footprint, fathered by a star, descended from the Tang imperial line, born on the borderlands (or beyond), of mixed ethnicity, Li Bo was untraceable in ways that extended well beyond the literary. Today, Sichuan may well be the most frequently cited of his possible birthplaces; but this near-consensus notwithstanding, the sequential erasures and redrawings of traces real and imagined have significantly contributed to the construction of his negative identity of "banishment." This identity provides a suggestive substitute for the requisite knowledge of a writer's birthplace. Like his literary dwelling in negative space, Li Bo's multiple unconfirmed birthplaces broadly sketch the everywhere he is not from. This pedigree of untraceability not only helped preserve Li's liminality, but also supported his later canonical status, his transcendence of geographical belonging and temporal specificity.

How does one pinpoint the moment of canonization? There is really no single moment, but rather a gradual process by which a work is fully integrated into the body of a culture's foundational knowledge, and a growing consensus that it is not possible for later aspirants to contribute to that body of knowledge without first having absorbed it themselves. In my opinion, Li Bo's entry into the canon might best be defined as occurring during the extended moment when critics begin expressing less interest in ascertaining the extent, depth, and content of his knowledge, and more interest in taking his work (whose inimitability is more appreciated than ever) as an object to be integrated as a constituent of their own knowledge. The beginning of this shift coincides with the late Ming (16 c.) attainment of bipolar equilibrium, a moment characterized both by the Archaists' elevation of High Tang poetry to a level of ancientness on a par with the *Shijing,* and the Gong'an school's increasingly positive evaluation of individual expression, unfoundedness, and unlearnability.

The first two chapters of this book are roughly divided around this canonical "moment": when the Banished Immortal was metamorphosing from unlearnable model to a supreme model of unlearnability. In examining how the shifting balance of the various bipolar concepts (comprising the overall impression of his "ancientness") interacted with his real-time and literary recession into the ranks of the ancients, I have identified five overlapping but distinct stages:

1. *Recognition and codification of greatness.* Li Bo's designation as a great poet, and the establishment of the terminological foundation upon which his greatness was to be maintained. At this stage, which I roughly situate from the mid-eighth century (Li Bo's lifetime) through the end of the Tang dynasty (618–907), both negative ("unattainable") and numinous ("immortal") qualifiers begin to appear. This coincides with the earliest manifestations of his pairing with Du Fu, setting the stage for the bipolar critical discourse that later sketched a horizon of poetic possibility and plenitude rather than one of mere sufficiency.

2. *Rhetoric of ranking.* The stage when the Li-Du binary discourse becomes adversarial, when ranking them in relation to

one another became so common that the practice earned its own title, "Li-Du praise-and-denigration." Already incipient during the late Tang, literary debates centering on the content and expression of "knowledge" grew in intensity during the *guwen* debates of the Song, finding acute expression in the relative evaluation of the two poets. In the course of these debates, the terms of the various pertinent bipolar concepts were driven to extremes of polarization and mutual exclusivity. In the writings of some critics, the most notable of whom was the Northern Song critic and reformer Wang Anshi (1021–1086), not only was Li Bo ranked below Du Fu, he was placed at the lowest end of a spectrum of values associated with knowledge.

3. *Reassertion of interdependent pairs over the absolute supremacy of either of two terms.* Reactions against the divisive force of ranking were already observable in the Northern Song when anti-Li rhetoric reached its height. In what seems to be a corrective to the potential rupture of the Li-Du pair (and a move to recover the threatened plenitude it embodied), bipolar terms start to be reformulated so that the boundary between them is more permeable, and the semantic field of each element of the pair is broadened to include some part of the other. Yan Yu's (early- to mid-13 c.) characterological literary criticism, his promotion of the inherently ineffable quality of poetry (and of its highest attainment during the Tang), encouraged the development of a more relativistic discourse, which would gain in popularity during the Ming dynasty.

By the time of the Ming–Qing transition (16–17 c.) bipolar tension had diminished, resulting in a relatively stable blend of *xu* and *shi* within any one value (or poet). In the process, Li's negative and numinous characteristics became imbued with enough positive color to enhance his independence vis-à-vis Du's delineating role.

4. *Canonization.* The moment when displaying and possessing "proper" knowledge of Li's work (and the appended critical tradition) becomes more important than ascertaining Li's own possession of knowledge. As the newly blended binary terms

and the resulting reconceived descriptions of Li and Du gradually neutralized some of the criteria that had been used to distinguish them, complementary bipolarity was recaptured in the interpretation and criticism of opposing bodies of criticism. Almost as though the Li-Du critical tradition had enshrouded Li Bo and Du Fu in a protective shell of ancientness, critics from the seventeenth century onward upheld each poet's expressions of individual nature and experience, but tended to approach the poems indirectly, arguing for or against preexisting currents of interpretation, vying with each other for recognition as the worthiest readers. Li's poetry and persona retreat into the canon of the ancients, where they can endure untainted by the contingencies of history and opinion. With this retreat, he reemerges as a standard against which readers test and compare their own competency.

5. *The test of the modern.* A work's timelessness depends upon its capacity to absorb new meanings as readers change and as the self-projections of a culture evolve. In this adaptation of Harold Bloom's theory of poetic misprision, it is possible to say that evolution of the canon relies on creative misreadings, and that the misread works are thereby forever transformed.[35] Such was the case when reformers of the late Qing attempted to integrate modern, Western literary categories in their reshaping of the poetic canon. The question here is one of how Li Bo's precious unqualifiability and negative role fared in making the transition to a literary discourse bent on becoming highly empirical, scientific, and positivistic. In short, how did his modern, positive, and earthbound "Romantic" *(langman)* persona continue and transform the elusive, liminal, and infinitely resonant persona of the Banished Immortal?

LI BO AND THE PRACTICE OF ANCIENTNESS

Li Bo's poetic persona is not the pure invention of his readers, nor is it merely the impressionistic vestige of his unusual life. If readers came to his poetry with preoccupations about literary ancientness—the bipolar concept pairing textual knowledge with individual authenticity—his poetry answered them. Li Bo's poetry actively engages the binary constructs of "unfoundedness" and "substantiveness," "talent" and "learning"; and, by looking at how it does, it becomes more possible to determine what it was that resonated so strongly with the questions that were regularly being asked (and answered in ever different ways). What exactly made his work worthy of integration into the permanent body of cultural knowledge, where it was codified in the particular terms found in the criticism?

My view, arrived at through the close analysis of individual poems, is that Li Bo's work pointedly subverts the expected implementations of textual learning in ways that renew (if only for the duration of the individual work) the usefulness of ancient texts as expressions of the self. Through a variety of defamiliarizing means, Li Bo draws attention to the constructedness of a variety of "ancient" poetic practices, not to invalidate their usefulness for latter-day poets like himself, but to assert the authenticity of deliberate, constructed poetry. Appearing to rebel against tradition, seeming to throw off the fetters of conventional practice, Li's ironic stance recovers—if only in the short term—the "ancient" ideal of authentic poetic expression. For Li Bo, immediacy is no longer feasible, but authentic self-expression is.

Stephen Owen, and then Joseph Allen, also acknowledged Li Bo's overt manipulations of the past when they proclaimed Li Bo's poetry a new "poetry of the self." Owen, in fact, specifically locates this poetics of the self in Li's deliberate revelation of himself as an active, decisive poet: "Much of Li Bo's poetry is devoted to forming and projecting an image of the self, and that self is partially defined as the creative poet. This occurs both in personae and in disjunctive techniques that reveal the creative, manipulating poet behind the poem."[36] But Owen characterizes this aspect of Li Bo's poetry as constituting an attitude of "laughing at convention." Convention, he says, provides this defiant poet with "something to defy."[37] Li, according to this view, did not partake in traditional views of poetry as a means of authentic expression, and was even less interested in the ancients to whom he dedicated scores of "ancient airs." His was a poetry of self-dramatization and performance, one that found expression in the breaking of rules.

It is impossible to know Li Bo's intentions in writing as he did. But it is possible to take into consideration the respect accorded him by a tradition that set great store both on expressive immediacy and on the ancients. Only Li Bo's detractors accused him of pure performance, and they did not prevail in the debate over his status. Although my work owes much to Owen's readings, and I share many of his perspectives, I am attempting to reconsider Li Bo's poetry in light of his success within the tradition as the poet whose greatness was considered by traditional critics to be worth protecting and promoting. If he did love playing to the crowd (and there is ample evidence that he did), he was also mindful of a crowd that expected more than a play. His particular incarnation of "unfoundedness"—including his ironic performance of certain literary traditions—satisfied the need for a new poetic mode that renews allegiance to the past while avoiding the pitfalls of imitation, a mode that validates the unlearnable, unfounded aspects of personal expression as being congruent with ancientness. Perhaps Li Bo shared his contemporaries' yearning for a renewal of past purity, and in ostentatiously expressing his identity as the self-conscious latecomer, perhaps he quenched that yearning in his readers.

It is not without a certain sense of apprehension that I engage in the continuing tradition of Li Bo criticism. This uneasiness arises in large part from an acute awareness of the same paradox that has both stimulated and challenged previous critics: that of venturing to qualify and analyze the very thing that Li Bo's readers would like to safeguard from qualification and analysis. Confronting the same paradox, I initially follow their lead, seeking out poetic features that lend themselves most readily to being read as manifestations of substantive "learning": genre-consciousness, old-style prosodic and imagistic features, allusion, and so on. However, unlike those traditional critics, my goal is not to determine whether (or to what degree) Li Bo's work is the product of craft or inspiration, or even whether it grows out of a Confucian perspective or a Daoist one.

Instead, I attempt to utilize these (relatively) concrete marks of the past as a highly useful tool provided by the tradition of bipolar discourse. These substantive or positive elements make it possible to delineate the negative spaces—to see heaven by framing it between two mountains.

I do not pretend that this focus provides a comprehensive view of Li Bo's accomplishments as a poet. But concentrating on his uses of the past, I believe, benefits from a certain consistency with traditional interest in situating Li Bo's ancientness and may shed some light on what readers were likely to have noticed when they attempted to judge him in these terms. At the same time, this type of analysis also lends itself to formal readings informed by some of the literary theory recently developed in Europe and the United States by scholars working in other literatures. (Among those I have found useful are Bloom, Genette, and Borges, all of whom have contributed a great deal to our understanding of the intertextual relationship of texts and their predecessors.) In undertaking the second, "practical" part of the book, I have identified three poetic territories in Li Bo's work that bear explicit marks of affiliation with the past: the *Gufeng,* or "Ancient Airs," the *yuefu* (glossed below), and, finally, the uses of allusion.

The Gufeng

The fifty-nine poems known as the *Gufeng,* which have traditionally been cited as Li Bo's (more or less convincing) personal demonstration of his allegiance to the basic tenets of *guwen* thought, arguably provide the most overtly self-conscious and concerted effort by the poet to identify himself with ancientness. Besides his direct statement to this effect, found in poem #1, the more positively inclined traditional readers cite other evidence of these poems' ancient worthiness: Li Bo's liberal use of poetic devices associated with the *Shijing* (most importantly his use of *bi* [comparison]), his invocation of well-known ancient historical figures and stories, overall adherence to a spare stylistic simplicity, and direct and indirect signs of his subscription to a range of admirable Confucian moral principles.

But not all readers were convinced, as attested by diverse reactions to Li's clear propensity even in these poems for celestial flights and encounters with immortals. Reactions ranged from the defensive to the bemused, and, in the most extreme cases, to outright rejection of Li's assertion of his ancient affinity. The view espoused by those who defended Li's "immortality poems" are of particular interest because their discussions constitute an attempt to navigate one of *guwen*'s most disturbing bipolarities: that between the unfoundedness of the authentically stirred imagination and the substantiveness of shared experience in the real world. The suppleness of the *xu/shi* concept, the power of syncretic thinking, and the importance of "unfoundedness" in evolving views of ancientness in particular—and poetic plenitude in general—are obvious in comments both critical and defensive.

This being said, the focus here is not on criticism of the *Gufeng,* but on the *Gufeng* themselves, in which Li's challenge to the ancients goes beyond the simple use of hyperbole and invention. Like the self-consciously ancient poems of Ruan Ji (210–263) and Chen Zi'ang (661–702), both of which provided direct inspiration for Li Bo's *Gufeng,* these poems are hardly lacking in ancient signposts. But in manipulations more radical and provocative than those of either of these poets, Li Bo everywhere switches signs, constantly confounding categories whose understanding had long been agreed upon—categories upon which recognizable ancientness depends. Under his brush, allusion becomes illusion, textual precedent emerges as nearly indistinguishable from direct visual perception, and the ancient devices of comparison and stimulus (*bi* and *xing*)—themselves recognized earmarks of both authenticity and ancient textuality—are ostentatiously lifted and inserted in uncustomary contexts. The resulting performance of ancientness is one that satisfies expectations of authenticity by recognizing the irrecoverable pastness of the past. Li Bo effectively combines ancient naturalness with deliberately quoted bits of ancientness so that each of these qualities supports, rather than contravenes, the other. Read in this way, the *Gufeng* (and related poems whose titles insist on their ancient affiliation) stand as a wonderful example of a poetics of unfoundedness, framed solidly by the recognizable building blocks of ancient times: a poetics of immortality grounded more in the transmission (and transformation) of written words than in the imbibing of any elixir.

The Yuefu

If Li Bo's *Gufeng* have been upheld by his admirers as proof positive of his loyalty to the elite and morally correct ranks of the ancients, his *yuefu* poems have been consistently cited as the truest and most vivid expression of his unfettered nature, the nature of a man whose imbibing of a jug of wine could produce a score of poems, and whose only consideration when in the full élan of composition was the urging of his inner spirit. The equation between unbridled expressiveness and the *yuefu* is of particular interest because of the decidedly fettered character of the genre itself. A genre with a complex history and taxonomy that has not yet been completely unraveled, the *yuefu,* as composed in the period from the end of the Han dynasty through the Tang dynasty, roughly designates poems bearing titles that originated as names of old folk songs. Scholars agree that, by Li Bo's time, the music had long been lost, and that the compositions had already left their folk origins behind, bearing all the markings of self-conscious literary poetics. But the tie with ancientness is a firm one, not only in the retained features of dramatic dialogue and folk themes, but in the strong tendency for poets composing to a specific title to continue the theme with which that title was first associated.[38]

The composition and reading of *yuefu* in the Tang was an exercise in intertextuality. As Joseph Allen has convincingly demonstrated, *yuefu* is unique in the explicitness of its ties to its own past, encouraging a method of composition based on a solid knowledge of specific poetic precedents, and the ability to utilize that knowledge in the creation of new poems that believably express one's own inner feelings.[39] At the same time, from behind these self-conscious literary *yuefu* shines the folk origin from which they sprang—an origin that, in an admittedly abstract way, imbues these poems with those same expectations of natural or authentic expression so valued among the ancients. This combination of text-based tradition and folkloric authenticity make this genre a natural for the poet working within the *guwen* bipolarity, and Li Bo does seem to have been just such a poet.

Li Bo's approach to *yuefu* has much in common with that reflected in his *Gufeng:* the recognition that an authentic attitude toward the past must be built upon an acknowledgment of its pastness. At the same time, in practice, his composition of *yuefu* differs in ways that reflect the particularities of the genre. To the extent that *yuefu* are composed of identifiable images, narratives, and turns of phrase appearing in previous poems bearing the same or a related title, these provide substantive elements of learning that can be easily identified. Li Bo's selection and disposition of these elements often produce a powerful effect of defamiliarization, not only in response to the well-worn quoted parts of those familiar predecessors, but to the practice of borrowing per se. They offer a compelling formal justification, besides that of his role-playing and hyperbolic landscape description, for Li's touted special affinity for the genre. It seems to be in honor of this practice that critics broadened the semantic field of "unfetteredness" from its implications of blissful flouting of poetic convention to include the idea of deliberate, knowledgeable domination of convention.

In the poems I have selected, where Li Bo objectifies convention without invalidating it, "knowledge" takes on a whole new meaning: loss of creative innocence and the abdication of the right even to pretend it still exists. Although this attitude, so described, sounds grim and academic, the poetry is not. The reader scanning through Li's *yuefu* collection is transported from strange, terrifying vistas (as in the mysterious *"Dulu* Composition") to the age-old laments of separated lovers in "Parted Far Away." One chuckles at the knowing wink of a no longer innocent mulberry girl and wonders about the true meaning of suggestive allusions to a certain Han dynasty imperial consort. Whether ironically restoring a longstanding narrative line, defamiliarizing diction, word order, and prosodic practices, or elegizing specific conventionalized features, Li Bo expresses, and provokes, feeling, while offering a last chance at rejuvenating ancientness.

Allusion

Like the ideal of ancientness inscribed in the *Gufeng*, and like the intertextual continuity associated with the *yuefu*, allusion bespeaks knowledge of past writings, and so constitutes an appropriate choice for the poet looking for a substantive link with the ancients. But as early as the writing of Zhong Rong's (469–518) *Shipin*, critical evaluation of allusion's place in the writing of poetry was less than enthusiastic. Unlike the thematic and formal traditions of the *gufeng* and *yuefu*, allusion was not associated with the ideal of natural, immediate expression. Quite to the contrary, Six Dynasties partisans of the expressionist view of poetry like Zhong Rong held that the use of allusion (and its implicit requirement of readerly erudition) actually compromises the ideal of poetry as an unmediated outpouring of emotion.[40] The implications for its reception as a substantive sign of ancientness, then, are clear. Allusion contains the strongest potential for driving a wedge between the two poles of ancientness—continuity and authentic expression—that Li Bo so skillfully integrated in his other poems.

Nevertheless, and quite significantly, Li Bo treats allusion in much the same way we have seen him treat other, more explicit, formal expressions of textual knowledge: in the frank display of its allusiveness and, consequently, of his active editorial and compositional role as a "late" poet. I believe that, despite allusion's problematic status (at least where issues of immediacy are concerned), Li Bo employed it as a mark of immediacy consistent with his attempts to achieve ancient authenticity. The discussion proceeds in three stages, moving from the smallest (and most easily recognizable) form of allusion—that is, textual allusion—to the somewhat broader realm of topical allusion, and finally to consider the gestural and performative allusion of the pouring and drinking of wine.[41]

THE "ANCIENT" ambitions of the "Ancient Airs," the intertextuality of *yuefu*, and the deliberateness of allusion may not add up to a satisfying sum of Li Bo's parts. But they do allow a glimpse into the invisible workings of unfetteredness, and remind us that it is only in revealing what was hidden that poetic expression recovers its naturalness. Like the modernist painter who confronts his viewer with the reality of a textured and bounded canvas, like the filmmaker who willfully steps before the camera at the moment when the audience is most enchanted, Li Bo's immortal poet playfully and irrepressibly leaves traces on the way to his celestial abode. Perhaps he was confident that nobody would try to follow them too closely.

AT JINXIANG, SENDING OFF WEI THE EIGHTH TO THE WESTERN CAPITAL	金鄉送韋八之 西京
A traveler arrived from Chang'an,	客自長安來
And then returned to Chang'an.	還歸長安去
Crazed winds blow at my heart,	狂風吹我心
Then westward catch in the trees of Xianyang.	西挂咸陽樹
There's no saying how this feels,	此情不可道
Or if we'll ever meet again.	此別何時遇
I look hard at the distance but see you not,	望望不見君
Mist rises from linked mountains.[42]	連山起煙霧

PART I

Reading
the
Critics

CHAPTER 1

Finding Substance in Emptiness

Tracking the Immortal, Mid-Tang through Ming

LU JI (261–303) was an exuberant and prolific poet, writing—and reading—at the dawn of the Six Dynasties, a period when lyrical, expressive, and descriptive poetry began replacing the public, didactic mode; a time, too, when practitioners began writing down their reflections on the writing of poetry and the standards for judging it. The first Chinese poet to attempt to describe the poetic process, Lu Ji chose the poetic form as his medium, seeking to cast his impressions in a language both near enough to its object to establish the credibility of homology, and distant enough to afford some perspective. Admitting at the start that he was both hampered and aided by the fact that "in carving an axe-handle, the model is not far," he produced the "Rhapsody on Literature" ("Wenfu"), a free-flowing piece that blends metaphor and declarative assertion, uninhibited fantasy and objective observation. Thus he took his anxiety about translating feeling into acceptable poetry, and transformed it into the object of a poem.[1]

Chinese poetic discourse has since continued through the development of a multitude of rhetorical strategies (many mirroring or derived from philosophical writings) intended to straddle the seemingly mutually exclusive realms of poetic language and "objective" description and analysis. A survey of the vocabulary of this discourse reveals that it embraces rather than shrinks from the realization that, when it comes to discussion of literature, the referent is included within—and therefore exists in eternal retreat from—the sign. The resulting inventory of overlapping terms may be a source of frustration to translators, and scholars both in and outside of China have deplored the lack of a consistent, empirical critical vocabulary. But it would be a mistake to regard the permeability of the line between poetry and the discourse that talks about it as an indication of epistemological deficiency. Rather, as most recently observed by Cai Zongqi, early Chinese poetic discourse reflects an epistemological stance that prefers the holistic to the particularizing, and that aims to join the corporeal, moral, and psychological experiences rather than distinguish them.[2]

Yet even within the supple and imagistic world of traditional criticism, one poet is consistently and explicitly depicted as being particularly resistant to study or analytic description. Fatefully dubbed the "Banished Immortal" by an influential admirer at the Tang court, Li Bo was—even during his lifetime—the subject of anecdotes and poems portraying a personage whose very being defied the bounds of convention and the strictures of historically sanctioned categories. An active participant in the making of his own mythology and in the creation of a poetic category to defy all categories, he trod the fine line between exemplar and iconoclast, early assuming the mantle, alongside Du Fu, of one of China's two greatest poets.[3] And even today, as scholars such as Ge Jingchun, Stephen Owen, Joseph Allen, or Japan's foremost Li Bo specialist, Matsuura Tomohisa, offer thematic and generic analyses of his poetry, it is still common for close readings and attempts at technical analysis to be greeted with reminders, like one offered by a colleague at a recent conference on Chinese comparative literature, that Li Bo's poetry cannot be analyzed.[4]

Admonitions such as this one, specifying what one cannot do to (or with) Li Bo's poetry, are not new, but have their origins in the earliest appearance of Li Bo criticism, which is a criticism characterized by a broad-based negation, not in the sense of denigrating or denying, but in its preference for descriptions of what his poetry *is not*. Negativity, as characterized by Sanford Budick and Wolfgang Iser, embraces a variety of "means of eschewing indicative terminology," so as to "allow the unsayable to speak."[5] And so, when Su Dongpo (1026–1101) declared that "those who would like to learn [how to write Li Bo's] poetry cannot,"[6] he both identified the essence of Li Bo's poetry as unsayable, and staked out a place for its unique voice. It is not possible, Su seems to say, to articulate the element of Li Bo's poetry that makes it both his and wonderful, whether for the purpose of reproducing or of understanding it. Nor was Su Dongpo the first to make this observation. That distinction lies with Li's own contemporary, He Zhizhang, credited with having conferred on Li the sobriquet "Banished Immortal" *(zhexian)*. He reportedly declared that Li Bo's poems were "unattainable," a statement quickly taken up by critics of the mid-Tang period and beyond.

During Li Bo's lifetime, and through the end of the Tang dynasty, statements concerning Li Bo's unattainability were almost always combined with, or implied in, metaphors of divinity and immortality, and these metaphors, to a certain extent, derived from the poetry itself. Over time, as negated descriptives multiplied in the Li Bo critical lexicon, negative qualifiers and numinous metaphors would gradually appear independently of one another. But in the Tang, Li's acknowledged incomparability and unattainability were most often articulated in terms describing his belonging to a different realm from that of mortal men—terms that intriguingly straddle the boundary between metaphor and myth. No bit of criticism more effectively (or more enduringly) blended negative and numinous rhetorical practices than did He's coining of the term "Banished Immortal." Du Fu himself significantly contributed to this practice when he admiringly developed the theme of Li Bo's immortality (and banishment) in the many poems he composed in his honor.[7]

Du Fu's poems to Li Bo constitute one of the primary sources for our understanding of how Li Bo was perceived by contemporaries. But "Old Du" (who was junior to the eternally youthful Li) contributed to the negative rhetoric of Li Bo criticism in yet another way, quite beyond his intentions or his control. According to Yuan Zhen, the names Li Bo and Du Fu had already begun to circulate as a pair during the poets' lifetimes.[8] Yuan Zhen himself is generally credited with entering that pair into the critical lexicon, often but not exclusively presenting Du Fu as the embodiment of qualities against which Li Bo was negatively compared, or depicting Li Bo as the poet who did not possess the qualities of Du Fu. Within this frequently polemical structure, Li Bo was cast as the foil for Du Fu and Du Fu the foil for Li Bo, and the style of the one was understood in terms of the other. On the surface, this rhetorical practice appears to be little more than the natural and inconsequential outgrowth of the dialectical argumentation rooted deep in the earliest examples of philosophical writing. In contrast with other well-known paired poets who dot the pages of literary history, however, this pair—as a pair—came to embody fundamental debates or, more accurately, the bipolar values in which are inscribed some of the most enduring issues of Chinese poetic discourse.

No wonder, then, that soon after the Li-Du pair became part of the critical imagination, that same imagination began attempting to position one above the other. But a measure of their importance as a pair is that, almost as soon as assertions of the superiority of one poet over the other became common, critics began protesting against them. By the sixteenth century, the backlash against ranking was in full swing, and it continues to this day. During the Ming dynasty, the poet, editor, and critic Wang Zhideng (1535–1612) composed a preface to a joint anthology of the poetry of Li and Du, recording the horror he felt at the thought of being asked to rank one above the other.[9] Later, Wang Qi (1696–1774), the Qing dynasty editor of Li's collected works, pleads passionately in his preface against this practice.[10] In more recent times, Guo Moruo, in his 1972 monograph *Li Bo yu Du Fu* (Li Bo and Du Fu), has attempted to reverse some of the more black-and-white distinctions (attributing, among other things, the flaw of drunkenness—usually associated with Li Bo—to Du Fu).[11] In 1975, the Taiwanese scholar Zhou Shaoxian published *Lun Li Du shi* (On the poetry of Li and Du), joining the ranks of those who aspire to put an end to the pernicious habit of choosing either Du Fu or Li Bo as the better poet.

So prolific and vociferous are the protesters that at times they seem both more emphatic and more numerous than the writers against whom they remonstrate. (In reading Zhou Shaoxian's discussion, for example, one is suddenly aware that he seems to be fighting in a battle that, at least in print, has all but ceased to exist.) The history as a whole shows that, whatever the degree of distance posited between them, the integrity of Li-and-Du reasserts itself with a force and a regularity suggesting that the pair, as such, provided something necessary to critical discussions about poetry. At some point, perhaps, there may have arisen a generalized apprehension that too radical a ranking would sunder the pair and invalidate it as a joint avatar of poetic possibility. Certainly by the time of the Ming dynasty, at least one critic was able explicitly to articulate a sense of the duo's primordial status. Hu Yinglin (1551–1602) all but spelled out the belief that Li-Du pairing was fundamental to preserving the promise of aesthetic plenitude: "In [their] pairing lies the capacity for unifying [the many] into one, for realizing the ultimate vision of the universe. It is just that I fear that even Creation's production of matter may not be as bountiful [as that of Li-and-Du]."[12]

Du Fu played an essential role as a constitutive tool in the description and criticism of Li Bo's work. From the late eighth century, immediately following their deaths, through the sixteenth, when the poets' bipolar configuration approached a unifying plenitude (and when that very proximity to plenitude presented a new threat to the fruitful play of their bipolarity), Du Fu gave a distinct, describable shape to a negative critical space that framed, but refrained from defining, Li Bo's poetics. Li Bo, for his part, played a complementary role, not so much by filling any particular lacunae in Du Fu's contribution, but by existing as a salutary corrective to Du Fu's completeness.

The nuances of the Li-Du pair as modeled and preserved by critics over the centuries provide a clear view of the importance not just of Li Bo's poetry, but of his poetry's reputed resistance to cognitive analysis. Li's poetry held forth the promise of the truly ineffable, and for some readers (beginning with Yan Yu [1195–1264]), the truly poetic. Not only did it express a world beyond the reach of words, it lay beyond the grasp of critical language as well. As vividly sketched by Hu Yinglin, "Of the men of the Tang, the one whose genius transcended the entire age is Li; the one whose formal style assimilated the entire age is Du. Li is like the suspension of the stars and the rising of the sun, illuminating the Great Void; Du is like the weight-bearing solidity of the earth and the capaciousness of the oceans, embracing and setting forth the ten thousand varieties."[13]

RECOGNIZING GREATNESS: SETTING THE TERMS

The legend of how Li Bo's greatness came to the attention of the emperor (and, by implication, to that of the world) offers a good starting point for understanding where his greatness was perceived to lie. As one version of the story goes, He Zhizhang, while serving as minister at court, went to meet the already famous Li Bo and read his long *yuefu*, "Shudao nan" (The road to Shu is hard). Whether or not it was this poem in particular that thrilled the minister is a matter of conjecture, but all concur that it was He who proclaimed Li to be a "Banished Immortal" and introduced him into service in the Hanlin academy at court.[14] The celestial epithet stuck, and a range of associated metaphors soon worked their way into the critical lexicon. As for Du Fu, recognition of his talent spread quickly after his death. The modern scholar Wu Guoping notes the existence of a pair of poems exchanged between two friends perhaps as early as the late eighth century, lamenting the passing of Li and Du, guardians of poetry worthy of the ancients.[15]

Barely two generations later, three well-placed and influential literati actively began to compare and rank Li and Du. Reacting against what they saw as the corrosive influence of the more decorative form of writing inherited from the Six Dynasties, these writers—Yuan Zhen, Bo Juyi, and Han Yu—all came to be associated with the *guwen* movement. They found common ground in their desire to revive the writings of the ancients, promoting a socially conscious poetics that both reflected traditional Confucian ethics and exhibited a more plainspoken, transparent style of expression. At the same time, each had his own preoccupations, reflected in their respective critiques. Yuan Zhen, for example, was especially attentive to technical considerations, Bo Juyi to more social and ethical issues, and Han Yu to the need for a more complex and subtle vision of how true ancientness might manifest itself.

It is generally taken for granted that these three, and especially Yuan Zhen, bear the bulk of responsibility for the ranking debates that soon ensued. Although it is true that Yuan Zhen and Bo Juyi tended to favor Du Fu, their critique of Li Bo is hardly as damning as is so often assumed. The more significant and enduring contribution of their evaluations of the two poets lies rather in the terms in which they framed the comparison, in particular their shared adoption of negative and numinous rhetoric in qualifying Li Bo. Such rhetoric establishes his fundamental and distinctive importance even as it opens the door, if only temporarily, for more denigrating descriptions later on.

Critics often cite Yuan Zhen's remark that, when it comes to narrative skill and technical prowess, Li Bo does not come close to Du Fu. But in the memorial inscription in which this comment appears, before arriving at this conclusion, Yuan describes Li Bo in some decidedly untechnical terms, validating the impressions earlier expressed by both He Zhizhang and Du Fu.

> At that time, Li Bo of Shandong was also gaining renown through his extraordinary writings, [and so] contemporaries referred to them as "Li and Du." I have observed [Li's] virile élan and untrammeled abandon, his casting off of restraints, his mimetic rendering of the appearance of things. But when it comes to *yuefu*, songs, and poems, he really is not quite on a par with Zimei [Du Fu]. If [we consider] the setting forth of [an event] from beginning to end, the orchestration of tones and rhyme, the greatest contain one thousand words and the next greatest several hundred. [In all of these] the vitality of [Du's] lyrics is grand and far-ranging, while their musicality is limpid and profound. His couplets are parallel and [his adherence to] regulation precise, and he steers clear of the common and facile. In

this, Li still cannot even set foot in [Du Fu's] courtyard, let alone his main hall![16]

Yuan Zhen clearly prefers Du Fu's discipline and careful craft over Li's apparent rejection of both. (One modern critic, campaigning against the practice of Li-Du ranking, has cited Yuan's preference for Du Fu's *yuefu* as incontrovertible proof of his profound prejudice against Li Bo.)[17] But the more enduring contribution of this comment is to be found in his presentation of certain juxtapositions: his broad qualification of Li's style (encompassed within three brief remarks) against his detailed enumeration of Du's qualities; Li's disregard for rules against Du's mastery of them; and, more subtly but equally significantly (particularly in light of their binary association), Du's position at the center, clearly oriented within the presumably enviable confines of courtyard and hall, against Li's relegation to the outside, surrounded by nothing more than unlimited, undefined space.

Bo Juyi, like his friend Yuan Zhen, adopts a stance somewhat critical of Li Bo, but couches his critique of Li and Du in more moralistic terms. In a letter he wrote to Yuan, this outspoken proponent of the development and practice of the socially critical, morality-driven "new *yuefu*," deplored Li Bo's apparent lack of reference to and, by implication, reverence for the venerable tradition of the *Shijing* (Book of odes): "[When naming] the luminaries of poetry, people cite Li and Du. Li's works are genial and unexpected, [works that] others cannot achieve; but if you look for [evidence of] 'Airs' and 'Elegantiae,' of *bi* and *xing*, in ten [poems] you will not find a one."[18]

Bo Juyi then continues to praise Du Fu in terms not unlike those chosen by Yuan, citing Du Fu's poetry as one that seamlessly blends ancient ethos and modern technique. Preceding this description of Du's perfect comprehension—in the dual sense of inclusiveness and understanding—of past and present, is the reference to Li's poetry that "others cannot achieve" (*ren budai,* more literally, "others cannot reach"). Bo Juyi thus seconds, and somewhat alters, Yuan's implicit pairing of Du's squareness with Li's roundness, Du's comprehensiveness with Li's transcendence. Substituting an image of analyzability versus unpredictability for Yuan's centrality versus liminality, Bo amplifies the typically *guwen* concern with the bipolar value of quantifiable, qualifiable knowledge as measured against elusive, ineffable genius. Although Bo, like Yuan, prefers Du's exhaustive mastery of a repertoire of poetic skills and references over Li's transcendence and infinite capacity to surprise, his pairing them in these terms suggests their joint necessity to any full depiction of poetry. He is perfectly capable of placing them on a par with one another if the occasion so demands, as in his didactic poem, "After Having Read and Inscribed the *Collected Poems of Li and Du*":

[Li] Hanlin's days in Jiangzuo;	翰林江左日
[Du] Yuanwai's time in Jiannan.	員外劍南時
Never obtaining high position,	不得高官職
Always accosted by bitterness and upheaval.	仍逢苦亂離
In his evening years—resentments of the wanderer;	暮年逋客恨
In a floating world, the Banished Immortal grieved.	浮世謫仙悲
But their singing will linger for thousands of years,	吟詠流千古
Their renown shall stir the barbarians of the four quadrants of the world.	聲名動四夷
Upon the field of literature, they've set forth their fine phrases;	文場供秀句
Now yuefu await new lyrics.	樂府待新詞
When Heaven wills it, the Gentleman must be ready;	天意君須會
The World of Man requires good poetry.[19]	人間要好詩

This poem is intended not as an evaluation of Li and Du in relation to one another, but rather as a plea for the importance of good poetry in a just society, and a lament for what is lost when rulers turn a blind eye to talent. But read within the history of Li-Du criticism, it also stands as a reminder not to overstate the importance or the degree of the poets' ranking. Even if Bo Juyi preferred Du Fu to Li Bo, he agreed to write the dedication for the joint edition of their works, and to write it in such a way as to suggest both their equality and their inseparability. If his preference for Du is at all evident, it is in his recasting of Li Bo in Du Fu's ethical mold (a rhetorical mechanism that appears more frequently and is used more consciously as time goes on), so that suddenly the Banished Immortal's impulsive peregrinations reemerge as the travails of an unrecognized worthy.

Yuan Zhen and Bo Juyi, in implicitly qualifying Li and Du in terms of genius versus knowledge, provided the rationale for the perception of both their inextricability and their importance to the most fundamental issues of literary debate, but it was Han Yu who most consistently expressed their contribution in terms of absolute supremacy, and it is no coincidence that such declarations almost always apply to them as a pair. One critic has anachronistically interpreted Han Yu's linked treatment of them as motivated by his desire to counter the practice of ranking them: "Throughout his life, Han Yu focused most intensively on Li and Du, promoting the equal valuation of Li and Du, and opposing their relative ranking."[20] But this practice was not a trend so early on, and I suggest instead that Han's consistent upholding of their joint status directly reflects his grasp of the *guwen* paradox: the tension between adherence to the wisdom of the ancients and reliance on one's own capacity to reason, reflect, innovate.

Han Yu appreciated Li Bo and, as critics like to remind us, allowed himself to be influenced by him. But even absent the comparison with Du Fu, Li Bo presented a particular challenge to Han Yu's criteria for good *wen*, sitting somewhat precariously on the fault line between Han's own emphasis on individuality and his promotion of the *wen* of the sages. Han Yu promoted *guwen* as a form of writing that "necessitated thinking for oneself," and asserted that "only the unusual is remembered and cherished."[21] Li Bo's aesthetic of virile abandon and apparent disregard for the niceties of conventional poetic technique resonated with these ideals and inspired specific aspects of his practice. Furthermore, Li Bo's overt assertions of sympathy for the efforts of the early Tang poet Chen Zi'ang to "return to antiquity" and his revulsion for all that smacked of imitation most likely endeared Li Bo to Han Yu in ways that Du Fu's subtler expression of compatible views could not.

Still, Han Yu's appreciation for originality was tempered by the conviction that, for such originality to be acceptable, it must emerge naturally from an individual writer's internalization, synthesis, and application of the *wen* of antiquity,[22] preferably a *wen* that was characterized by a concern for social action and that excluded any hint of Buddhist and Daoist conceptions of the Dao. The fact that so much of Li Bo's work and the persona that emerged from it drew upon imaginary spirit voyages could not but be anathema to Han Yu's poetic vision.

It seems reasonable, then, to attribute Han Yu's repetitive pairing and equal treatment of the two poets to, in one scholar's expression, his "search for unity"[23]—his inquiry into the paradox of valuing both an erudite knowledge of the past and the autonomy of individual intelligence. This is suggested not only by his consistent pairing of the two poets, but also by his willingness to assign them a level of greatness approaching myth. Li and Du jointly represent poetic and ethical possibility beyond the ken of most people, and beyond the reach of even Han Yu's own abilities as a writer of *wen*. Several poems in Han Yu's collection express this view, the most frequently cited being his panegyric, "Mourning Zhang Ji," of which I offer a partial translation:

Li and Du's writings endure,	李杜文章在
Their incandescent rays thousands of meters long.	光焰萬丈長
I don't understand people's folly,	不知群兒愚
Why did they have to deliberately slander them?	那用故謗傷
Black ants trying to shake a great tree—	蚍蜉撼大樹
How laughable their lack of perspective!	可笑不自量
Now, I was born after them,	伊我生其後
I crane my neck to gaze at them in the distance.	舉頸遙相望
At night, in dreams, I often see them,	夜夢多見之
In the morning I yearn as they return to oblivion.[24]	晝思反微茫

In this portrait of the paired poets, Han Yu offers us a seamless blend of Du Fu as misunderstood, unemployed worthy and Li Bo as unattainable, lofty deity. If Han ever expressed a preference for

Li Bo, it would seem he did so here. As the poem continues, the celestial figure of Li Bo dominates, mostly in subtle references to the *Zhuangzi* that gradually develop into hyperbole and images of spirit voyage.[25] But another important legacy of this poem lies in the sense of grandness, of infinity, that such images convey. Han Yu's choice of Daoist imagery enacts a dramatic inflation of scale, providing him with the rhetorical means to blend the values of knowledge and genius into one complex image, and to project that image onto the vast and venerable screen of the timeless cosmos.[26]

While it is certainly possible to locate the seeds for Li-Du partisanship and ranking in the writings of these Middle Tang literati, it is far from certain that any of them would have condoned definitive expressions of rigid partisanship. Nor are strict allegiances evident among the writings of the Late Tang. Even Pi Rixiu (ca. 834–ca. 883), whose didactic and socially conscious poetics ought to guarantee an easily alliance with Du Fu supporters, pairs Du with Li Bo in naming the two the most worthy inheritors of the revered Jian'an poetic tradition.[27] Late Tang writings consolidated the tendency to regard Li and Du as a complementary pair. Most references to them appear in the parallel, contrastive couplets of poetry, so the binary structuring of the presentation of the two poets becomes further ingrained in poetic discourse.

In the following couplets written by poets normally thought of as being on opposite ends of the poetic spectrum, Du Mu (803–852), who in theory, if not so much in practice, upheld a poetics of Confucian didacticism in line with Han Yu's, and Li Shangyin (813–858), who is hardly known for excessive emphasis on moral content in poetry, Li Bo and Du Fu emerge as two parts of a whole. As such they are projected onto a cosmological plane; opposite and interdependent, they are as different and as united as heaven and earth. In one poem, Du Mu declares:

Ordered to carry on the command of the Odes *and* Sao,	命代風騷將
Who dares to mount the altar of Li and Du?	誰登李杜壇
Before [Du] Shaoling's whale, the sea bestirs;	少陵鯨海動
For [Li] Hanyuan's crane, the sky is chill.[28]	翰苑鶴天寒

Li Shangyin's poem, "Five Pieces on Mancheng: #2," is even more cryptic, but no less evenhanded:

Li and Du—their competence on a par;　　　　　　李杜操持事略齊
Ensconced in the Three Elements and the　　　　三才萬象共端倪
　　Myriad Things, together they comprise the　　集仙殿與金鑾殿
　　Two Poles.　　　　　　　　　　　　　　　　　可是蒼蠅惑暑雞
The [Heavenly] Palace of the Assembled
　　Immortals, the [Earthly] Palace of Golden
　　Bells,
The one could be a common ant, the other a
　　summer pheasant.[29]

Han Yu was the first to borrow Li Bo's use of spirit voyages and divine imagery to project Li and Du's joint greatness onto a mythical level, but Du Mu and Li Shangyin did not hesitate to exploit the poetic possibilities that such a precedent provided. Li above, Du below: this vertical configuration, inherited from Li Bo's use of divine imagery, He Zhizhang's epithet, and Han Yu's elegiac tribute, would remain an important element in Li-Du criticism for several centuries. Not only does it inscribe upon the map of literary history their parity as great poets, it also fixes their inextricable link at a level as fundamental as the bipolar makeup of the universe itself, rooted in the plenitude of the "Three Elements" and the infinite promise of the "Myriad Things." As the "Two Poles," they are necessary both to each other and to the poetic universe. Should either be removed from his position, the poetic universe would be perceptibly diminished.

THE RHETORIC OF RANKING: HONING THE TERMS

If the participants in the *guwen* debates did not yet show clear signs of having adopted an exclusive preference for either Li or Du, the continued development of a binary critical lexicon certainly set the stage for just such a turn of events. As pointed out by the modern scholar Wu Guoping, the Song reassertion of the link between morality and good *wen*, and the importance of classical

erudition in exercising both, inevitably led to a systematic prefer-
ence for the earthbound over the ethereal, the socially responsible
over the fanciful. Building upon the opposition that had been
established in the decades since Li's and Du's deaths, and given
the nature of their own reformative aspirations, Song literati were
bound to favor Du Fu's intricate allusiveness and political lamen-
tations over Li Bo's free-wheeling, expressionistic verse.[30]

But while there are many examples of eleventh- and twelfth-
century poets and scholars who expressed a strong preference for
Du Fu at Li Bo's expense, here, as in all periods of intellectual
and political ferment, the most thoughtful and influential literary
figures were also the least dogmatic and most circumspect in pro-
moting Du and denigrating Li. Ouyang Xiu (1007–1072), credited
both as the initiator of the Song *guwen* movement[31] and as the
first Song writer to discuss Du Fu's work extensively, exhibited an
unabashed appreciation for Li Bo's poetry—much to the confusion
and chagrin of some of his own admirers.[32] Indeed, as Liu Ban
(1022–1088), author of the *Zhongshan shihua,* pithily comments,
"Ou[yang] esteems Han [Yu], but doesn't like [Du] Zimei—a thing
impossible to comprehend. As for Li Bo, he likes him very much,
and is moved by [Li's] celestial flights."[33] Liu Ban's disapproval
aside, he is not off the mark in noticing Ouyang's interest in Li
Bo's work. Ouyang Xiu did write, for example, the long poem
"Upon Reading Li's Collected Works, I Imitate His Form" pieced
together of direct allusions, exhilarating flights above the moun-
tains, and snippets of biographical lore associated with the Ban-
ished Immortal.[34]

Still, Liu Ban's presumption that one cannot like both Li and
Du situates him among those whose infatuation with Du Fu ren-
ders them all but blind to nuanced argument. A quick glance at
Ouyang's essay "On the Elevation and Denigration of Li and Du"
reveals that Ouyang is far from not liking Du Fu. Rather, very
much in line with Han Yu's reading, he appreciates different things
about each poet. As he puts it, "Du Fu can take a small section
from a Li [poem] and surpass it in concision and power; but when
it comes to the liberation of one's own heaven-endowed genius, this
is something that [Du] Fu cannot attain."[35] Here there is a deep-

ening of the now familiar contrast between control and freedom—
and, even more tellingly, the repetition of qualification by nega-
tion in Ouyang's declaration of the unattainability of Li Bo's
achievement.

It bears pointing out, however, that even if Ouyang had really
been unappreciative of Du Fu's work, that position would have
been quite tenable within the parameters of the *guwen* movement.
Modern scholars who see the *guwen* movement as primarily con-
cerned with stylistic issues conclude that such reformers as Ouyang
Xiu had no choice but to take the side of Li Bo, as the foremost
practitioner of a poetics that largely eschewed the niceties of
strict parallelism and tonal regulation.[36] Furthermore, Li Bo's work
exhibits other, less concrete attributes that are of particular interest
to Ouyang. Ouyang Xiu's view of poetry, and of *wen* in general,
dictated that the poet's apprehension of classical writings must be
achieved and manifested not in blind imitation of past writings, but
in an ability to grasp their essence and apply it appropriately to
contemporary life through the exercise of personal talent. While
Li Bo's flair for "old-style" writing is certainly in harmony with
the aesthetic preferences of the *guwen* movement, it is its expres-
sion of his individuality—its unstudied naturalness and unbounded
imagery—that seems to have earned Ouyang's admiration even
more than it did Han Yu's.

Oversimplified renditions of Li-Du critical history not only
obfuscate the two poets' accomplishments, but also gloss over the
passion and nuance informing readers' perceptions of those accom-
plishments. This is not to deny Song readers' nearly unanimous
adoration of Du Fu, a fact that is evident from the sheer number of
shihua commentaries dedicated to discussion of his poetry.[37] Nor
can we be blind to the fact that the Song poet's penchant for
minutely observed everyday details, along with the moral concerns
of *guwen* thought in particular, tended to incline readers toward
Du Fu and away from Li Bo. Huang Tingjian's (1045–1105) own
affinity for densely conveyed detail, along with his active promotion
of Du Fu, are one example.[38] But too much emphasis on these
factors diverts attention from the subtle and insistent (though
sometimes indirect) Song dynasty arguments for continued com-

plementary assessment of Li and Du. Much must have been at stake in maintaining their complementarity, because objections to ranking the two poets were expressed, not by denying the undesirable traits that his supposed detractors had attributed to Li Bo, but by judiciously amplifying them.

One event of the polemical eleventh century, Wang Anshi's edition of selected poems by the four poets Du Fu, Han Yu, Ouyang Xiu, and Li Bo, was particularly provocative, inciting a long-running debate that both contributed greatly to the formation of the vocabulary applied to his work and shed light on the problematic status of Li Bo's poetry. Wang, the controversial reformer and outspoken proponent of the social function of literature, seems not to have appended any particular critique of the four poets, but the order of his selection elicited strong reactions. Why, his readers wondered, did he break all semblance of chronological order and place Li Bo not only after Du Fu, but even after the works of Wang's older contemporary, Ouyang Xiu? At least one modern critic has noted that there is some question as to whether this was the original order as arranged by Wang Anshi.[39] Such doubt is supported by the fact that, while Wang frequently asserts his adoration for Du Fu, there is little evidence that he held Li Bo in low esteem. But the willingness of nearly contemporary readers to accept that these were indeed Wang's intentions suggests that a conflict so readily sparked may well have been smoldering for some time. The debate provided, above all, a forum in which to grapple with the increasing difficulty of legitimizing the elevated status of Li Bo's borderline, unqualifiable poetics in face of the continuing desire to do just that.

We know from Ma Duanlin that, by the Yuan dynasty, Wang's edition was interpreted by many (though not all) as a critical act. According to Ma, "In Wang Anshi's selection of the poems of Du, Han, Ou[yang] and Li, he placed Li at the end and shifted Ou[yang] backward, before him. There are some who say that this was a means of elevating the one and deprecating the other."[40] But much earlier, Hui Hong (1071–1138), the Daoist priest and poet who composed the *Lengzhai yehua,* was among those who took it upon themselves to interpret Wang's decision, apparently joining an already lively discussion: "Shuwang [Wang Anshi] edited the works of Li Taibai, Du Shaoling, Han Tuizhi, and Ouyang Yongshu into [a volume titled] 'Poetic Works of Four Poets.' But he placed Master Ouyang before Taibai, and no one understands what his intentions were. Shuwang has said: 'Taibai's lyrics [flow] in swift succession and there are no lapses. But his knowledge [shi] is of the lowliest sort. Of every ten verses of poetry, nine speak merely of women and wine.'"[41]

These, it would seem, are fighting words, and Chen Shan (12 c.), the author of the *Menshi xinhua* and an impassioned opponent of all attempts at the ranking of poets, was quick to protest what he viewed as a mean, literalist reading of Li Bo's work, and one that clearly denies Li Bo's influence on the much admired Ouyang Xiu. Having repeated verbatim Hui Hong's quotation of Wang, he argues:

> I say that poetry is simply the place where subtle reflection and unhampered thoughts reside. When Taibai's spirit gambols through the territory of the myriad things, he is only positing his impressions in poems. Why would [someone like him] destroy his [poetic] aspirations with women and wine? If that were the case, must we also ascribe "lowly knowledge" to [Tao] Yuanming, whose every piece mentions wine, and to Xie Anshi,[42] who found it necessary to bring along a singing girl every time he traveled in the mountains? Master Ouyang's writings harbor a *xing* both lofty and far-reaching, and he often delights in the language of the leisurely enjoyment of the wind and the moon. In doing this, he probably modeled himself after Taibai, which is why [Su] Dongpo, in his preface to the collected works of Master Ouyang, writes that his poems are composed in the manner of Li Bo. These [poets] can never have been discussed in terms of relative superiority and inferiority.[43]

His annoyance at Wang Anshi's would-be literalism aside, Chen Shan is clearly offended by the moralistic connotations of Wang's alleged judgment of Li Bo—connotations that others were expressing more openly and directly.[44] While he succeeds in countering the moralistic aspect of the accusation on the grounds of natural expression and poetic precedent (and influence), he leaves unanswered the more damning accusation of Li's "lowly knowledge" *(shi bu gao)*, that is, lack of knowledge of and demonstrated regard for the venerable classical and poetic tradition to which he is heir. This charge, only indirectly expressed by Yuan Zhen, had been clearly articulated by Bo Juyi when he deplored Li's lack of reference to the methods and images appearing in the *Shijing*. And although Wang's passage does not directly refer to issues of classical learning, preferring the more general term *"shi"* to *"xue,"* his fellow *guwen* writers quickly picked up on the cue.

One poet who directly accused Li Bo of a lack of classical learning was Lu You. Himself bearing the distinctly un-Confucian epithet "The Old Man Who Does as He Pleases," Lu was a poet of divided allegiance. His philosophy owed much to Wang Anshi's classicism, while his poetry was replete with Daoist imagery strongly reminiscent of Li Bo. In his lengthy response to Wang Anshi's position, Lu limits his dissent to objections to Wang's purported justifying statement, which he declares to be both inauthentic ("I fear that these are not Jinggong's words") and exaggerated ("Outside of his *yuefu*, poems by Li Bo that touch upon women are few"). But he expresses sympathy for the ranking itself, couching his agreement in terms that, already familiar, would enter the basic critical lexicon of both Li's detractors and supporters:

> The "Four Poets" edition did not have to [be organized] in this order; if [Wang] truly didn't like [Li] Bo, he must have had his reasons. Generally speaking, it might be [because Li's] *knowledge was extremely superficial (shi du shen qian)*. When you read verses such as ..., they are as vulgar as the ditties of any commissioned court poet. His collected works contain many examples of this type of language. Most people are moved only by the *virile, strident (haojun)* quality of his lyrics, and so just don't consider [his work] closely. And this [type of writing] is just like his gaining the admiration of the entire Hanlin academy while yet clothed in commoner's garb; is this ["accomplishment"] even worth mentioning? Later he would say, "Those who had previously laughed at me for being lowly and vulgar came nevertheless to visit and exchange pleasantries"; it is fitting that he spent his entire life in dire straits.[45]

Lu You has now trained his sights on the problem of Li Bo's knowledge, divesting his argument of the casual generalizations that could have left him open to charges of superficial reading, charges implicit in both Chen Shan's and his own objections to Wang's alleged statement. Instead, he forestalls any such attack by charging Li Bo with superficiality (rather than lowliness), substantiating the accusation with a selection of couplets whose dominant technique is hyperbole, and whose primary imagery centers on celestial court scenes. The effectiveness of this argument depends on the cumulative impression of fanciful lines (taken out of context) that lack both classical references and any basis in real experience (an important criterion in the work of Lu You, as well as in that of other Song poets). Li Bo's purported superficiality is that of one engaged neither in critiquing the social and political problems of his times nor in practicing the classical wisdom of the sages. As Lu would have it, Li's charm is the charm of surface, the slick seductiveness of élan, cunningly applied. Evident, too, is Lu's implicit contrast between Li Bo's poetry and the eminently respectable precedent of the *Songs of Chu*. The stark contrast between Li Bo's questionable morality and Qu Yuan's lofty stature as misunderstood statesman all but precludes the possibility of elevating Li Bo's imaginings by applying the type of allegorical interpretation unquestioningly applied to Qu Yuan's flights of fancy.

The moral implications of this particular brand of "superficiality," especially when imputed to Li Bo by writers with *guwen* concerns, are potentially very damaging, bringing under suspicion both Li's supposed possession of sagely wisdom and the qualities of naturalness and freedom routinely summoned in his defense. Lu sees a disjuncture between representation and the poet's inner reality, a contravention of the most fundamental rule of poetic composition. Even more provocative is that Lu's accusation goes well beyond casting aspersions on Li Bo to sully his readers as well. These benighted admirers, having failed to discern the difference between sincere, worthy poetic expression and the unrestrained ravings of a self-serving raconteur, are advised to look more closely at those poems and, in recognizing them for what they are, reclaim their own place as worthies.

Given the seriousness of these criticisms and the stature of those who made them, it is natural to wonder why Li Bo's poetic reputation endured and, indeed, thrived. One reason might be the rapid emergence of the well-founded suspicion that the whole debate was inspired by a false assumption. At least one account gives us reason to doubt whether Wang Anshi ever uttered the words first attributed to him by Hui Hong—and even to doubt whether the ordering of the four poets was intended as a critical statement of relative poetic worth. Hu Zi's (1148–1167) *Tiaoxi yuyin conghua*[46] records (unfortunately, without comment) two contradictory accounts of reported conversations with Wang Anshi about the origins and intent of his compilation. The first denies that Wang Anshi ever had any intention to rank Li Bo below Du Fu or anyone else, claiming instead that it was a matter of pure chance:

> Wang Dingguo in the *Wenjianlu* [Record of things heard and seen][47] wrote: Huang Luzhi [Huang Tingjian] asked of Wang Jinggong, "It is said that your *Four Poets* ranks Han and Ou above Li Taibai!" Jinggong replied, "This is not so. Chen Heshu [Chen Yi, fl. 1064] had asked about the four [greatest] poets. I took advantage of the occasion to charge Heshu [with the task of compilation]. At the time, the clerk just happened to bring Du's collected works first; Heshu proceeded to edit following the order in which the works were presented. At the beginning, therefore, there was no question of establishing rank. Li and Du have shared equal status since times of old—how could I have [taken it upon myself to] lower [that of Li Bo]?" Luzhi went back and asked Heshu about it, and [Heshu] concurred with Jinggong's report. *Today, however, the ranking of Taibai beneath Han and Ou is incontrovertible.*

This account is probably apocryphal. Hu Zi himself detracts from its reliability when he juxtaposes it with a second account in which Wang Anshi is portrayed as taking full responsibility for the ranking, justifying it in the greatest possible detail, and even taking his inspiration from Yuan Zhen's criticism rendered four hundred years earlier.

> The *Dunzhai xianlan* says: Someone once asked Wang Jinggong, "When you edited the *Four Poets*, placing Du Fu first and Li Bo fourth, could you have possibly meant that [Li] Bo's talent and literary accomplishments are not on a par with Du Fu's?!" The Master replied, "[Li] Bo's poems and songs are unbridled and sublime (*hao-*

fang piaoyi); others certainly cannot reach him in this. But his poetic mode only extends this far; he does not know how to transform [tradition]. When it comes to [Du] Fu, however, there you find sadness and joy, want and plenty; a letting out and a gathering in, a sinking and a swelling; urgency and leisure, the vertical and the horizontal—there is no mode that he cannot implement.... It is probably that the thread of his poetry is densely woven and his thoughts profound. Readers simply cannot fathom the recondite recesses [of his work]. It is not easy to perceive exactly where his subtlety lies, so how could those who are shallow and myopic discern it? This is why Du Fu can illuminate and extend [the work of] his predecessors, while he himself has no successors. Yuan Zhen took this [ability] as being able to 'encompass what others excel in exclusively *(jian ren suo du zhuan).*' These words are just."[48]

Hu Zi's juxtaposition of these two passages neatly illustrates the truth of Wang Dingguo's closing comment; once Li Bo is so plainly positioned below Han Yu and Ouyang Xiu, no matter what the reason, the judgment presumed to be behind that decision is as good as carved in stone. Even arguments against it seem to ground it only more firmly in the literary landscape, and those that support it, like the second one offered here, take advantage of the debate to expand on previous descriptions of both Li and Du, so that they further entrench them in opposing positions. Indeed, both the form and the content of the *Dunzhai xianlan* account contribute to this polarization. Li Bo is relegated to a relatively brief description, amounting to a nearly verbatim repetition of previously employed negative qualifiers, while the section devoted to Du Fu is characterized by extensive enumeration (of which I offer only an excerpt here) of his qualities, with the intent of demonstrating his all-inclusive perfection, his poetry's status as the culmination of everything that has been done and every emotion that has been felt.

The point of the *Dunzhai xianlan* passage is clearly to free Du Fu once and for all from the limiting association of enforced parity with Li Bo. Although the passage is purportedly inspired by Wang Anshi's anthology, no mention here is made of Ouyang Xiu or Han Yu, who were also placed above Li Bo. At best, Li Bo appears as little more than a rhetorical springboard from which to launch into detailed praise of Du Fu, and one might expect Li Bo to disappear from the scene after outliving his usefulness in this regard. But Hu Zi, himself a virtually unconditional fan of Du Fu, took care to include the Wang Dingguo story, inserting it before the *Dunzhai* account. Li Bo, it would seem, is not so easily removed from the scene.

The description of Li Bo in the *Dunzhai* story situates him once again in that part of the literary landscape that cannot be "attained by others." This phrase, which characterizes Li Bo exclusively in terms of what he is not, preserves his integrity, not in competition with Du Fu (who likewise "has no successors"), but as existing beyond the articulated terrain of aesthetic accomplishment. Even critics who do not think particularly highly of Li Bo's poetry end up invoking him to protect, deliberately or not, the most valued aim of the poetic enterprise: the capacity of words to convey "meaning beyond the words."

This delicate position—unimpeachable in its very precariousness—is preserved in part through Li Bo's repeated pairing with Du Fu, a strategy that is especially effective in periods when Du Fu's popularity is at its height. It is noteworthy that participants in this debate do not bother to compare Li Bo with Ouyang Xiu or Han Yu, even though the dispute was first occasioned by Wang Anshi's ranking of Li Bo below Ouyang in particular. Instead, the disputants persist in comparing Li to Du, devoting lengthy passages to descriptions of Du Fu's work (Li Bo's contribution is understood). He is disposed of quickly, almost in shorthand, with the aid of the sparest and most evocative of code words: unbridled, sublime—unattainable by others. Wang Anshi's contemporary, Li Gang (1083–1140), not coincidentally the author of an essay titled "Preface Written upon Reading *The Selected Poems of the Four Poets*," invokes a similar set of qualifiers, with more emphasis on the numinous aspects of Li Bo's poetry:

> When Jiefu [Wang Anshi] selected the poems of the four poets, he ranked their [implementation of] substance (*zhi*) and *wen* in order to establish the order of their presentation.

I would say that Zimei's poems are broad and deep, classically beautiful, combining the greatest accomplishments of the literary masters [of old]; most of Yongshu's poems are lush and splendid, exhibiting the bearing of exalted officials; Tuizhi's poems are virile and generous, elegant and hearty, their dignity unimpeachable; Taibai's poems are magnanimous and sweeping *(haomai)*, pure and sublime *(qingyi)*, displaying unhampered the will to ride the clouds. All are luminaries of poetry. Their sequence [in this volume] is most certainly a natural expression of their [qualitative] rank.

Those who declaim their poems can imagine that they are seeing how they behaved as men. For we know that the outpourings of the heart's sound, in speaking one's intent and singing one's feelings, are obtained from nature and cannot be arrived at through effort.[49]

Li Gang's justification of the ordering of the four poets is subtler than those we have addressed so far, as he insists on the venerable status of all four. His argument unfurls in three stages: (1) good poetry is a matter of appropriate levels of substance/plainness *(zhi)* and pattern/ornament *(wen)*;[50] (2) these levels are manifest in the individual style of each poet; and (3) there is perfect correspondence between the individual and his poetic expression, so that neither the composition of substance and form, nor the signature style, can be modified, forced, or otherwise tampered with. It is not just Li Bo who cannot be imitated. The essence of all good poetry lies in its inimitability, for it is inextricably bound to the unique qualities of the individual who produces it. All four poets qualify for inclusion because they have attained to naturalness, have given reign to the "heart's sound."

The point of this passage, however, is less to highlight the four poets' joint merits than it is to pinpoint their relative ones. If each has attained the summit of his potential, their achievements are still limited, precisely by the parameters of that potential. The crux of this argument is implicit in the logical transitions linking each point to the next: specifically, in understanding (1) the "ideal" ratio of *wen* and *zhi*, and the implied correspondence between specific instances of that ratio and the stylistic signature Li Gang ascribes to each poet; and (2) what kind of man, morally speaking, is presumed to be behind each of these signatures. Why is the "classical beauty" of Du Fu more valuable than the splendor of Ouyang Xiu? Why is Han Yu's dignity more admirable than Li Bo's purity and freedom? Fortunately, Li Gang provides a clue elsewhere in his writings: "Zimei's poems are never devoid of [literary] patterning (*wen*), but their substance surpasses their patterning. Yongshu's poems are never devoid of substance, but their patterning surpasses substance. Tuizhi's poems are pure substance without patterning. Taibai's poems are pure patterning without substance. When Jiefu edited the Four Poets and placed them according to rank, the order was in accord with this."[51]

Li Gang is a man of his times, ascribing greater importance to substance and the "facts" than to the patterning of their expression, but valuing a combination of the two over the lone possession of either one. In historical terms, the spectrum of values he proposes imitates the typical *guwen* characterization of literary decline from the virtues of the classics to the shortcomings of the Southern Dynasties. By applying this formula to the earlier passage (without imposing a too literal and mechanical equivalency), it is possible to deduce something of Li Gang's view, or at least of his interpretation of Wang Anshi's view, of Li Bo's position. In this view, Du Fu and Li Bo are not complementary opposites, but the two ends of a continuum, with Du Fu incarnating the ideal and Li Bo most removed from it. Specifically, Du Fu's poetry is seen as exemplifying the unforced manifestation of something real. Furthermore, his particular adherence to the substantive is valuable not merely as an accurate reflection of Du Fu's experience in the world, but also as the natural product of a finely honed sensitivity to that world, seamlessly blended with the prior internalization and synthesis of the very best of past writings. Du Fu's personal combination of erudition and receptivity is, in turn, inseparable from his identity as a supremely moral being, as understood by the *guwen* literati of the time.[52] In a passage that overtly links good poetry to personal honor, Li Gang says, "During the Han and Tang [dynasties], many were those who used poetry as a means to express [their discontent]. Only Du Zimei took over the *bi* and *xing* [modes of] expression from the Poets; even when in dire straits, he never forgot his prince. This is why his composition loftily displayed the great integrity of the firm and benevolent gentleman, never contenting itself with mere rendering of images or description of perceptual beauty."[53] For Li Gang, Du's poetry stands as the personal expression of his knowledge in the broadest sense. The depth and breadth of his remarkable knowledge extend to the process of its own exteriorization, so that *wen* is naturally present, never becoming an end in itself.

Li Bo's poems, viewed in contrast, are the external manifestation of no substance at all. His exhilarating urge to ride the clouds is not anchored in the transmitted experience of the sages, but verges on the untenable: a mere expression of the lightness of his own, isolated being. Yet he is included in this pantheon, perhaps for this very reason. His presence just on the edge of (morally) acceptable poetic practice marks out a territory where desire and imagination overtake experience, and where the personal, fleeting whim subsumes the accumulated wisdom of the ages.

But if Song readers are to preserve Li Bo's marginal but essential presence within the bounds of poetic practice, they cannot fully acquiesce in the perception that his knowledge is inadequate and his expression arbitrary and whimsical. Su Dongpo was among the first to insist upon Li Bo's mastery of the past. In the following passage from his essay on calligraphy, "Upon Inscribing *The Collected Poems of Huang Zisi*," Su offers a brief disquisition comparing the short-lived renown of calligraphers who contributed particular innovations to the evolution of their art with the eternal fame of those who integrated previous innovations into a lasting whole. By way of illustration, he describes a similar phenomenon in the history of poetry, in which he neatly places Li Bo side by side with Du Fu in that most enviable of places: belonging to the tradition, but hovering just above it, able to make a selective synthesis that ensures the longevity of all that is worth preserving: "Su [Wu] and Li [Ling]'s natural accomplishment,[54] Cao [Zhi] and Liu [Zhen]'s innate insight,[55] Tao [Qian] and Xie [Lingyun]'s transcendence[56]—all attained the highest level [in their generation]. But Li Taibai and Du Zimei, implementing forms whose exquisite refinement surpassed all others, rode astride one hundred generations."[57]

The designation of Li Bo as a skillful master of his tradition, a title previously all but reserved for Du Fu and often cited in pointed contrast to Li, appears in the writings of several Southern Song critics. Hu Zi lists Li Bo as one of three poets, along with Du Fu and Han Yu, who "studied" or "modeled his writing on" the works of the Jian'an poets;[58] Ge Lifang (d. 1164), a strong partisan of Du Fu,[59] nevertheless exclaims that reading Li Bo's *Gufeng* and Du Fu's *Outi* reveals that their origins extend back into the distant past;[60] and He Jing (1223–1275), a critic who had very much inherited Li Gang's notions of the relative weight of form and substance, credits both Li and Du as having "assembled [the works of] the Wei and the Jin in order to pursue [the poetic] of the Airs, venerating language as a means to express one's nature and feelings, and thus bringing poetry to the apex of this latter period."[61]

But perhaps the most remarkable example of crediting Li Bo with a deep knowledge of past literature has been passed down to us by Zhu Xi (1130–1200), recognized as the father of *daoxue,* or Neo-Confucianism, whose revival of the Confucian classics stands as eloquent testimony to his reverence for those texts and the knowledge *(shi)* they contain. "Li Taibai from beginning to end [never stopped] studying the poems of the *Wenxuan,* and that is why he is good. Du Zimei's best poetry, too, largely imitates *(xiao)* the poems of the *Wenxuan.* Later, [Du Fu] gradually let go [of this model], and so the poetry of his Kuizhou [period] is not the same."[62]

For all his respect for classical erudition, Zhu does not relegate Li to second place; if anything, he seems to be giving Li Bo credit for greater consistency than Du Fu in his use of his knowledge of the past. And it is precisely their poetry's integration and continuation of what came before that makes them, in turn, worthy objects of study, classics in their own right. Consider the advice Zhu offered to aspiring poets: "When composing poems, first read Li and Du, much as scholars master the fundamental classics. Only when the foundation is established can one read Su, Huang, and other secondary poets."[63]

Zhu Xi's words, which shift attention from Li Bo's knowledge of the classics to Li's own standing as an object of required knowledge, are among the first to legitimize, in what might still be considered orthodox terms, Li's eventual entry into the canon. Such a statement coming from a man who passionately believed that a well-defined program of reading was the primary path to moral self-cultivation cannot be taken lightly.[64] But Zhu Xi's effort seems premature; at this point, even he could not completely transform Li Bo into as learned and responsible an heir to the past as Du Fu. Throughout the Southern Song and on into the Yuan dynasty, writers continued to build on the long-upheld contrast between Du Fu's knowledge and Li Bo's relative disregard for knowledge. Only Yan Yu, a proponent of the view that "poetry involves a distinct material that has nothing to do with books,"[65] was prepared to assert that "Taibai has one or two wondrous [phrases] that Zimei could not have uttered, and Zimei has one or two wondrous [pieces] that Taibai could not have composed."[66] In the hands of those both less enamored of Li Bo's work and guided by a narrower view of knowledge, Li's supposed superficiality was parlayed into moral judgments not unlike Wang Anshi's debated condemnation, as well as critics' elaborations of that condemnation. Critics typically resorted to simple juxtapositions that only increased the rigid polarization of the Li-Du pair, as demonstrated in this comment by Zhao Cigong in his *Du Gongbu Caotang ji* (published ca. 1201–1204): "Li and Du are [both] said to be heroes among poets. But [Li] Bo's poems dwell mostly on the wind, moon, plants, and trees, and on unfounded (*xuwu*) tales about spirits and immortals. What can they contribute to a moral education! Only Old Bumpkin Du possesses a talent [worthy of] advisers to princes, and has his attention focused on the world in which he finds himself; but with his lofty, uncompromising spirit, he found himself isolated, without a like-minded cohort. [Du Fu] inscribes everything that brews in his heart into poetry."[67]

Zhao's comment does not touch upon Li Bo's knowledge as such, but on an issue whose link with knowledge had already been well established: the striking disjuncture between his "unfounded" writing and the shared world others know with certitude, whether through experience or through study of the classics. Zhao's final sentence is the most telling, as it asserts his own allegiance to an indissoluble connection between poetic immediacy, moral authenticity, and political worthiness. In this view, Li Bo's passion for intangibles, his "unfoundedness" or "emptiness" (xuwu), disqualifies him from the ultimately one-man club of poet-heroes. Writing approximately fifty years later, Luo Dajing (fl. 1226) concurs, taking specific aim at what by this time was read as Han Yu's bid for Li-Du equality and expressing gratitude to the Song critics who awakened readers to Du Fu's clear superiority:

> When the imperial house was in difficulty, and all the world in a state of collapse and confusion, the poems Li Taibai wrote were nothing more than the effusions of a knight-errant, crazy drunk [in a landscape of] flowers and moonlight. The fate of the people and the country did not engage his mind or heart. If one looks at Du Shaoling's deep concern for his country and people, how can one speak of [Li and Du] as having lived in the same era? People of the Tang always spoke of them as equals; Han Tuizhi was of a vast and lofty vision, yet even he said, "Li and Du's writings endure, their incandescent rays thousands of meters long," refusing to rank them. But with the arrival of the Song, [readers] start understanding how to raise the level of esteem for Shaoling.[68]

Here again, Li Bo's unschooled and incorrigible fascination with the ephemera of "flowers and moonlight" suffers in comparison with Du Fu's "deep concern for his country and people." No trace here of an appreciation for Li Bo's natural heeding of his "heart's sounds," not to mention a glimmer of recognition that there is some historic precedent for his particular brand of poetry. Posited as little more than a foil upon which to build Du Fu's unassailable reputation, Li Bo is characterized primarily in terms of what he did not achieve.

Another expression of this polarization manifests itself in the critique of Li Bo's fascination with the creation of strange or extraordinary expressions, the implication being that his was a poetics of effect, divorced from emotions born of learning, humanity, and worldly engagement. While the link between "lowly knowledge" and a fondness for unusual phrases was implicit in Lu You's earlier discussion of the proper proportions of pattern (wen) and substance (zhi), the Yuan dynasty critic Zhu Yao is much more direct: "Wang Jinggong has said that Taibai's genius (cai) is lofty but his knowledge (*shi*) poor. Shangu [Huang Tingjian] also said: 'In the fondness for making extraordinary phrases (*qiyu*) lie the seeds for flaws in writing.' Ever since the Jian'an period, [poets] have been fond of making extraordinary phrases, which is why [poetry's] imagistic force (*qixiang*) is on the decline. I say that these two gentlemen's discussions of Li Bo's flaws are to be found precisely herein."[69]

Zhu Yao does not explain why inadequate knowledge might reveal itself in extraordinary phrases and images. His assumption seems to echo Zhu Xi's well-known distaste for artful phraseology, even though Zhu Xi apparently did not consider Li Bo guilty. The word "extraordinary" (*qi*) in this context is tinged with the color of the strange. For Zhu Yao, such strangeness in poetry expresses dubious experiences, those confirmed neither by the commonality of everyday experience nor by their codification in canonical texts. They are in their essence "unfounded," and in departing from this normative notion of knowledge, "extraordinary" writing confronts readers with realms of experience beyond their ken and the reality of a poetic self that is distinctly separate from the reader, and ultimately unattainable.[70] Zhu Yao is among those who read this separateness, this willful occupation of negative space, as explicable only through the poet's deliberate artfulness, a sure sign that the poem is lacking the necessary element of expressive immediacy.

COUNTERING LI-DU RANKING: CONSOLIDATING PLENITUDE

As polarization of the two poets reaches this extreme, what arguments can justify Li Bo's continued presence in relationship to Du Fu, and as an essential figure in the model of poetic possibility? The answer seems to lie in finding new applications for old terms—terms like "extraordinary" and "unfounded"—so that they could continue to be used as markers of Li Bo's liminality without endangering his status as great. At the end of the Song dynasty, the ambiguity latent in the verdict of extraordinariness begins to be exploited in Li-Du criticism in ways that, sometimes inadvertently, serve to consolidate their unity.

Of course, even during the Song, polarization was not unanimous, and precedent for treatment of Li and Du as a canonical pair was evident not only in Zhu Xi's comments, but in those of Yan Yu as well. Yan Yu's Chan-influenced reinterpretation of literary knowledge in terms of spiritual enlightenment, and his egalitarian treatment of Li and Du as the standard of all poetry, had already enabled him to characterize the pair's poetic influence in strong, militaristic terms: "controlling the Son of Heaven in order to command the nobles."[71] Perhaps it is in this spirit—where true understanding and its poetic expression derive as much from a particular, undefinable innate genius as from the absorption of previous literature—that the term "strange" begins to be used as a retort to itself. When applied to Li's poetry in comparison with Du's, the positive connotations of the extraordinary or surprising are invoked as a response to its previous derogatory use to signify Li's unnatural and insincere poetics. When Zhu Yao, for example, aligned himself with those who perceived in Li Bo's "strangeness" a love of pure performance eclipsing his allegiance to the dictates of tradition, Chen Yiceng (fl. 1329) chimes in, in perfect counterpoint. He, too, takes note of Li Bo's "strangeness," but only to weave it back into the poetic ideals of authenticity and continuity—coloring it with the irrefutable value of "knowledge": "Li Bo's poetry takes as its ancestors the *Odes* and the '[Li] Sao' [Encountering sorrow], as its guides [the poetry of] the Han and Wei. As for the latter-day [poets], Bao Zhao, Xu [Ling], and Yu [Xin], he occasionally uses [their works]. He excels at wielding [all of] them to produce *strange (qiguai)* [poetry]. When his heart and eyes are surprised and bestirred, [poems] are suddenly cast off, and wondrously enter [the realm of] soundlessness. He is indeed an immortal among poets! Although [Li Bo's] stylistic character is stronger than Du's, his innovation does not measure up."[72]

Chen, then, does not take Li Bo's strange phrases as proof of his departure from tradition, but as hard evidence of his mastery of that tradition. Echoing Yan Yu's metaphoric use of the terms of Chan enlightenment, Chen suggests that internalization of the writings of those who came before is precisely what allows for the convergence of will and spontaneity, knowledge and talent, that enables the production of poetry that is fresh and surprising—without slipping into gratuitous eccentricity. In this context, where critics are seeking ways to wed erudition and genius, the qualifier "strange" acts as a useful pivot around which discussions of Li Bo's poetry could, and sometimes did, turn, providing readers with a rhetorical ground for both semantic consensus and subtly argued disagreements.

Examining Li's poetry for manifestations of knowledge, Zhu Yao and Chen Yiceng traced the external trappings of "strangeness" back to its roots in the creative process; as inheritors of the *guwen* ideal that aspires to a combination of individual talent and learned wisdom, they were bound to examine that process for signs of consistency with that ideal. But where Zhu perceived a break between intention and poetry, Chen saw them linked in an uninterrupted continuum. The tenor of the argument is perhaps as polarized as ever, but use of the same term promotes a certain unity, legitimizing the continued pairing of Li and Du and helping to maintain Li Bo's place and the necessary poetic values he represents in the figure of poetic plenitude.

Ironically, however, Chen's syncretic description of Li Bo's creative process also subtly threatens the fundamental bipolar complementarity holding the Li-Du pair together. In enumerating the steps of the creative process as beginning with learning and concluding with an unbidden, natural outpouring of fresh poetry, Chen attributes to Li Bo a level of erudition usually reserved for Du Fu. But, pulling back from suggesting that Li and Du are interchangeable, he abruptly adds an assertion that speaks volumes, not only about Li's value in the tradition, but about the nature of true innovation: "Although [Li Bo's] stylistic character is stronger than Du's, his innovation does not measure up." Li Bo may achieve surprising phrases, and they may even emerge from a natural, unforced outpouring of highly cultivated emotion; but strangeness—even when rooted in knowledge—must not be confused with innovation, for only innovation both grows out of and becomes the basis for knowledge.

While it would be a mistake to overinterpret this very slight reversal in Chen's argument, I would suggest that the reassertion of their difference (i.e., Du Fu's superiority) at this point bespeaks a desire to save the pair's bipolarity. Chen had compromised that bipolarity, perhaps responding to the need to restore equilibrium; he had balanced, without contradicting, Li's persistent embodiment of the negative by consolidating his position as heir to the tradition. By the same token, he seems to recognize that Du Fu's reputed meticulousness cries out for attributions of creativity, if only to keep him from slipping into the category of stodginess. His comment, written in an attempt to defend Li Bo, provides a glimpse at how some critics found themselves treading that very fine line between portraying Li and Du as so different that they threaten each other's legitimacy, and depicting them as so alike that their usefulness as a pair is neutralized.

Chen's strategy is representative of those who would err on the side of Li and Du's similarity. Elsewhere in his writings, he goes so far as to locate "strangeness" in the literary tradition itself, identifying it as something that can be learned and continued, crediting Du and Li with equal abilities in this regard.[73] In writings that manifest a similar approach, other positively inclined critics legitimize Li's position by finding ancient precedents for his unattainable qualities. This approach has the advantage of rooting Li Bo in the tradition without making exaggerated claims for his erudition; at the same time, however, it potentially brings to the foreground the paradox inherent in trying to legitimize Li's essential negativity by dressing it in the garb of familiar, orthodox poetics.

Unconcerned with the danger of legitimizing the negative attributes on which Li Bo's position depends, such critics as Fan Peng (Fan Deji, 1272–1330) and Gao Bing (1350–1423) seized upon specific, signature aspects of his work and—tracing them back to a morally laudable "ancient" predecessor—began converting ineffable strangeness into classic knowledge. Echoes of Zhu Xi's earlier admonition that those who want to write poetry must first study Li and Du could be heard as critics insisted ever more strongly upon establishing the Banished Immortal's pedigree of ancientness. Historical legitimization proved especially effective when applied to qualities that had long served as foils for Du Fu's learned, meticulous poetics: hyperbole, fantastic imagery, and apparently unreflective and spontaneous composition.

In this context Qu Yuan emerges as Li Bo's most consistently cited ancestor. Critics had already recognized in the shamanistic imagery of the "Li Sao" a precedent for Li Bo's unfounded imagery,[74] and the names "Feng" (for the *Odes*) and "Sao" had become fixed expressions used in critical praise of many a fine poet, but Fan Peng identified a specific stylistic point—Li Bo's apparently illogical and discontinuous lyrical structure—as the site of his continuation of the *Songs of the South:*

> [Of all his pieces,] "Yuan bieli" (Parted far away) is most redolent of the air of Chu. What is valuable in Chu [poetic] language is that, [although it is] broken again and again, thrown into disorder again and again, the significance of the lyrics insinuates itself repeatedly throughout, [so that the poem] is actually never broken or in disorder. This [quality] makes one sigh three times every time one sings [this piece], and even then are lingering notes. And when it comes to suppressing one's tears and chanting, it even inspires [renewed] reverence for the Three Relations and Five Moral Virtues. How can this [be deemed] "vain emptiness" *(xu)!* Rather, it is precisely in this that Li Bo is beyond the reach [of other poets].[75]

In this way Fan, one of Li Bo's more ardent admirers, directly responds to the charge of Li's perceived strangeness, along with its presumed source, "vain emptiness." His defense is a powerful one, for it avoids the pitfall of sacrificing Li Bo's unique qualities for the sake of appeasing his detractors; Li is still implicitly unlearnable, still "beyond the reach" of others. In a break with previous attempts to impart legitimacy through a reconstruction of an idealized and unknowable poetic process, Fan preserves Li Bo's unattainability and his identification by negative rhetoric by emphasizing the specific qualities of the poem as a finished product, and of its effect upon the reader. Citing classical precedent on the one hand and emotional affect on the other, Fan builds to his conclusion that Li Bo's echoing of the *Songs of the South* inspires such a respect for classical moral values that not even Du Fu can compare.

This attempt to legitimize Li Bo in the fullness of his difference relied not on the establishment of a new, positivistic vocabulary to define his contributions, but on a loosening and broadening of the semantic field of key, preestablished critical terms. The reformulation of existing critical terminology in order to evaluate Li Bo's particularities in positive terms, already evident in the writings of the thirteenth and fourteenth centuries, became standard practice by the end of the Ming dynasty.

One critic to initiate this shift in Li Bo criticism was Gao Bing, author of the highly analytical *Tangshi pinhui*, a work that picks up where Yan Yu left off, dividing the Tang dynasty into the four periods still invoked in today's critical texts: early, high, mid-, and late, designating the High Tang as the model period. Although he conceived this historical scheme in chronological terms, roughly modeled on rise-and-fall dynastic historiography, he employed it primarily as an evaluative tool. This he indicated in his own preface, drawing attention to the fact that he did not hesitate to disturb the chronological framework when he felt it appropriate—as when he places Chen Zi'ang and Li Bo together in the High Tang, in the top category of *zhengzong* (authoritative exemplars).[76] In an even more blatant departure from both historical considerations and traditional criticism, Gao separated Du Fu from Li Bo, and demoted Du Fu one rung down the evaluative ladder to the second-highest category, *dajia* (great masters).

Gao's system of evaluation, which emphasizes adherence to the aesthetic requirements of specific formal genres, reveals his nostalgic, *fugu* stance, and frees him to apply a broader range of criteria in his reading of specific poems, opening the category of excellence to a similarly broader range of poets. In evaluating Li Bo, he can and does employ the familiar code words that had long been part of the critical discourse. But even as those words retain their familiar patina of numinosity and negativity, their appearance in the more exacting context of systematic generic criticism minimizes their problematic associations of unfoundedness. In the introduction to his section on five-character old-style poetry, Gao recites almost all the categories of praise, negative and numinous, that had been applied to Li Bo from the beginning:

> When poetry arrived at the Kaiyuan and Tianbao reign periods [the High Tang], the divine elegance of tonal regulation attained its glorious perfection. Li Hanlin's heaven-endowed genius *(tiancai)* wan-

dered with carefree abandon *(zongyi)*, ranging freely through the crowd [of poets]. Of those in the distant past, he grazed the realm of Cao [Zhi] and Liu [Zhen]; of those in the more recent past, he ascended the heights of Shen [Yue] and Bao [Zhao]. As for his *yuefu* and ancient tunes—if he could trip up Chu Guangxi and Wang Changling and overturn Gao Shi and Cen Shen, how much more so those lesser [poets]! Master Zhu [Xi] has said, "Taibai's poems seem without rules *(fadu)* while perfectly at ease *(congrong)* in the midst of rules; this is wherein he is a sage of poetry."[77]

Zhu Xi's remark, which provides the climax for this passage, was likely the inspiration for Gao's evaluation of Li Bo. Zhu's statement is one of the most frequently repeated descriptions of Li's work, partly because of its content and partly because of its rhetorical flourish. In content it is consistent with Zhu's other remarks, in which he credits Li Bo with the knowledge deemed so essential to the production of worthy poetry (it coheres perfectly, too, with Zhu's ideal of sagehood itself);[78] in its style, it suggests Li Bo's elusiveness without condemning him for empty showmanship. All in all, the assertion succeeds in steadying Li Bo's liminal position at the border between articulated poetic ideals and the no-man's-land of infinite possibility. Gao's passage echoes Zhu's rhetorical strategy, moving between the assertion of the value of rules and Li Bo's flouting of those rules, between the categories established in the course of literary history and Li Bo's refusal to be confined by those categories. Gradually the reader is led to understand that the beauty of Li Bo's work lies in his apparently effortless mastery of the very paradigms he appears to override.

One effect of Gao's approach is to appropriate Li Bo's poetics for the mainstream of literary history. Released from contextualizing comparison with Du Fu and set within a larger, rationalized pattern, the heralded ineffable quality of Li's style seems a comprehensible technique, and his outsider's stance reveals itself as susceptible to inclusion in a list of other admirable writers of poetry. Gao thoroughly incorporates Zhu Xi's earlier elegant summation of Li Bo's essence, but in doing so, he seems to deflate it and bring it—and Li Bo—back within reach of critical qualification. Clearly, Gao intends to stake out Li Bo's place in the tradition by specifying the genres in which Li Bo's talent shines, while still adhering to the use of the open-ended, mystical code words with which Li has been associated: "Taibai's lyrics are those of a heavenly immortal *(tianxian)*. Most of his verses are achieved spontaneously, without effort *(shuairan er cheng)*. That is why his *yuefu* are especially fine."[79] Or, in another passage: "The wondrousness of the High Tang five-character regulated line [is captured in] the virile unfetteredness *(xiongyi)* of Li Hanlin's vitality and imagery *(qixiang)*."[80]

In Gao's relatively complex system of evaluation, the pairing of Li and Du is manifestly not as useful as it is in the comparatively free-form genre of the *shihua;* Li Bo can occasionally assume a supreme position based on a specific trait. Gao avoids a bipolar construct, seeming more inclined to either include both Li and Du in a longer list of ranked poets within a genre,[81] or join them in a virtually indistinguishable unity that is subsumed under the category of a particular genre: "Among the High Tang crafters of seven-character old-style poetry ... [of the poets who] usually [manifested] an expansive, magnanimous energy *(zhanghuang qishi)*, [controlled] rise and fall from beginning to end, combined the essence of [writings] ancient and modern, and imbued their patterned phrases with breadth and force, Li and Du are the most admirable."[82]

In this passage, in which Li's acclaimed "expansive energy" and Du's trademark synthesis of old and new are attributed to both of them equally, Gao has effectively removed the capacity—and the responsibility—for performance from the purview of individual poets and resituated it within the preexisting formal genre. Unabashed in his account of Li Bo's technical achievements, Gao opened the way for the acceptance of Li Bo's poetry as fully part of the revered past of high achievement in poetic craft.

Other writers of the early Ming period, especially those considered forerunners of the Archaist movement of the mid-Ming, tended to share Gao's appreciation for the technical achievements of the Tang dynasty, which they considered the apex of Chinese poetry. Keenly aware of the importance of prosodic and generic criteria in the writing of good poetry, they nevertheless profess a profound distaste for all that smacks of self-conscious technique, placing a premium on natural, spontaneous composition. This apparently paradoxical attitude is perhaps best represented by Li Dongyang (1447–1516), author of the *Huailutang shihua:* "Men of the Tang did not discuss poetic technique; [discussions of] poetic technique emerged mostly during the Song. Men of the Song, however, achieved nothing in [the composition of] poetry. What they meant by technique is nothing more than a character here and a phrase there—the meticulous crafting of parallel couplets. 'Heaven-endowed truthfulness and the full manifestation of *xing*,' however, cannot be discussed."[83]

Li Dongyang, in taking the position that one cannot qualify or teach the essential aspects of poetry, focuses instead on citing examples that he perceives as bearing the marks of an unmediated, authentic act of creation that succeeds unintentionally in achieving a particular aesthetic ideal. (Not surprisingly, Li Bo fares well in this inventory of good poets.)[84] Li Dongyang normalized the unutterable poetic quality that supporting critics had used to grant Li Bo both the freedom and the precariousness of his negative position. One result of this move is the new recognition that Li's ineffability no longer needed Du Fu's "partnership" to be understood, a realization made more palatable thanks to earlier assertions that Li Bo's knowledge was not, in reality, inferior to—or even qualitatively different from—Du Fu's.

Younger critics coming up through the ranks under Li Dongyang's tutelage freely explored Li Bo's unique combination of erudition and unfettered expression, drawing inspiration from Yan Yu's Chan-inspired poetics to parlay both qualities into the overarching concept of *shen*—"spirit" or, as it is often translated, "inspiration." Yang Shen (1488–1559), himself a poet and scholar who spent much of his life in exile, pairs Li Bo with the earliest narrator of the "spirit voyage," Zhuangzi: "Zhuang Zhou and Li Bo are inspired *(shen)* in their writings, which is not something that those who [apply] craft *(gong)* in writing can attain. Writing that is not perfect in its craftsmanship cannot be inspired, but inspiration is not something that can be reached through craft."[85]

Yang's comment upholds the tradition of defining Li's poetics by evoking its unattainability. But following the precedents set by Yan Yu, and thoroughly embraced by Gao Bing and Li Dongyang, Yang first shifts Li Bo's unattainable position from the periphery to the center, and then goes even further: he defines Li Bo's poetic process by giving it a name. What had previously been cast off as mere "talent" is here couched in spatially evocative descriptions of Li's sweeping, unfettered style to become *shen,* a term with mystical overtones and a strong base in the literary-critical tradition.[86] As *shen* embraces both talent (or genius) *and* Yan Yu's enlightenment-style knowledge, it can no longer be so breezily set against learning or knowledge as such. Instead, it is paired opposite a more technical type of knowledge (which seems to have been left outside the bounds of *shen's* now vast semantic range), manifest in poetry as *gong* (craft).

This newly revived respect for the faculty of inspiration is typically associated with the shift in Neo-Confucian thought from Cheng-Chu to Lu-Wang Neo-Confucianism: that is, the repositioning of "principle" *(li)* from the objective world to the mind. But circumspection is certainly in order when considering this transformation, whether in the world of literary aesthetics or in that of broader philosophical inquiry.[87] This embracing of the ineffable stirrings of the individual's inner nature as the prime source for what is best in poetry did not, in fact, result in the definitive demotion of Du Fu, Gao Bing's reclassification notwithstanding. Belief in Du Fu's excellence never depended on the denigration of Li Bo, and no amount of terminological redefinition could ever have relegated Old Du to the category of craftsman. Du's standing as the poet's poet was founded upon the perception that his work encompassed all that was poetically possible, skillfully bringing every technique into play while keeping them in balance. His integrative identity remains strong throughout the Ming, but is now perceived as valuable, not because it represents some absolute poetic good, but because it flows forth unimpeded from Du Fu's true nature. When Yang does mention Du Fu's inheritance of previous styles, he often suggests that his implementation of those styles owes as much to his individual nature as to any conscious desire for continuity:

Yang Chengzhai [Yang Wanli (1127–1206)] said: "Li Bo's poetry is as Liezi's riding of the wind; Shaoling's poetry is as Lingjun's [Qu Yuan's] boarding the cassia boat or driving the jade chariot. Isn't the one who is without something solid to rely on the divine spirit of poetry? Isn't the one who has something solid to rely on—without ever having [really] had it—the sage of poetry? In the Song, [Su] Dongpo resembled Taibai; [Huang] Shangu resembled Shaoling."

Xu Zhongche [Xu Ji (1028–1103)] said: "Taibai's poetry is a divine hawk spying the riverbank; Shaoling's poetry is the fine steed coursing beyond the worldly dust."

The evaluations by these two gentlemen are identical in meaning and similar in language. I say: Taibai's poetry is the language of the immortal elder and the errant swordsman; Shaoling's poetry is the lyric of the elegant man of letters and the writer of the "Sao." If I were to compare [their poetry] to prose writing, then Taibai's is the *Shiji* and Shaoling's is the *Hanshu*.[88]

This beautiful stretch of writing both affirms and subverts the usual practice of lineage-building in the establishment of each poet's place in the tradition. Through the cited comment of Yang Wanli, Li Bo and Du Fu are each linked to a predecessor and a successor. Through Yang Shen's own remark, they are also connected across genres. In Yang Shen's writing, he, Yang Wanli, and Xu Ji all appear to maintain the respective identities of Li and Du. Li's divine spirit, divine hawk, and immortal elder still hover in the firmament above Du Fu's earthbound sage, fine steed, and elegant man of letters. Li still spouts poetry on the run, while Du continues to reflect the concerns of past poets.

But beneath the neat parallelism, this passage subtly undermines their traditional opposition. Whereas Du Fu's desirable attributes of learnedness or unfair exile had previously been attributed to Li Bo, now it is Du who dons the cloak usually worn by Li. Like the Song critics we discussed earlier, this Ming critic also tries his hand at upsetting, without dissolving, the traditional Li-Du opposition. This time, however, it is not to redefine and broaden the concept of knowledge as a poetic value, but to affirm the importance of giving free rein to one's wandering spirit. Suddenly it is Du Fu who is boarding conveyances drawn from Daoist lore, speeding beyond the confines of worldly dust, and composing in the voice of Qu Yuan. The impression conveyed is one of Du's own naturalness and spontaneity. If (and where) the product differs from Li's, it is simply because of each poet's adherence to his own nature. For the time being, Li and Du's parity—and the picture of poetic plenitude the pair portrayed—was maintained, even as the bipolar dynamic that held it together was softened.

The Primacy of Inner Nature: Substance in Emptiness

The centralization of such individual attributes as "spirit" and "genius" provided grounds for a relaxation of Li-Du polarization and debate not only by providing an unequivocally laudatory semantic field that partisans of both poets could share, but also by opening the way to a profoundly characterological approach to poetic criticism in general, and Li-Du criticism in particular. Because poetry is the product of the individual's spirit's encounter with the world, that poet's stylistic signature, and his preference for one genre over another, is read as the natural expression of the poet's inner nature.[89] On the face of things, this attitude promotes an equal regard for the two poets not despite their differences, but because of them, and a studied evenhandedness is one of the hallmarks of much of Ming Li-Du criticism. Under the smooth surface, however, the rhetorical push-and-pull necessary to keep the two poets functioning as a pair while upholding the supposed superiority of a given attribute (which only one of them is thought to possess) is every bit as evident as it was in the preceding dynasties.

Examples of equitable treatment abound. Sixteenth-century writers like Fang Hongjing not only assign Li and Du respective genres and styles,[90] but also investigate the nuances of their transformations of those styles as being in keeping with their perceived inner natures. Yang Shen, thinking along the same lines, makes a point of his own evenhandedness: "If you [want to] speak about poetry and essays that are refined and orthodox, then [speak of Du] Shaoling and [Han] Changli. If [you talk about] composing a thousand words in the time it takes to lean against a horse (*yima qian-*

yan),[91] untethering one's language and pursuing the ancients, then Du and Han are probably not as good as Taibai and Zihou [Liu Zongyuan (773–819)]."[92]

The ideas Yang espouses here are hardly new, echoing a view of the two poets that goes back as far as Yuan Zhen. Yang, certainly aware of the historical tendency to rank the two on the basis of these views, couches his comparison in words that discourage any preferential interpretation. Although such careful impartiality should be integral to the characterological analysis gaining currency around this time, not all critics manage to distinguish themselves from their Song counterparts so successfully. Rather, the period's growing emphasis on naturalness skews the very language of poetic criticism in Li Bo's favor, much as the Song dynasty appreciation of knowledge favored Du Fu.

One critic of the period whom one might expect to be unbiased is Yang's contemporary, Li Lian (fl. 1514), who contributed a preface to a joint anthology, the *Li Du shiji* (Collected poems of Li and Du).[93] But even he reveals a corrective preference for Li Bo. After a rather long list enumerating the greatest poets of the Tang, Li declares, "Their talent was not the equal of [Li] Bo; one could hardly place them side by side. Only [Du] Gongbu was of equal renown, and so people referred to them as 'Li and Du.'"[94] As in the passage by Yang Shen, Li Bo here, too, is the standard to which Du Fu must compare. Li Lian then explicitly brings up the matter of the history of their comparison, naming Gao Bing as the first to place Li in a superior position to Du, then commenting, "[Gao's] subtle intention bears overall examination." After that timid endorsement of Gao, Li Lian reverts to his perfectly symmetrical presentation of the two poets. In a passage almost identical to that written eight centuries earlier by Yuan Zhen, Li Bo's negativity and numinous persona are placed opposite Du Fu's solid qualities of perfect knowledge and absolute control—and both poets are presented as the rightful heirs to the *Book of Odes*: "Overall, [Li] Bo's poems are transformations of the 'Airs' (*bianfeng*); [Du] Fu's are transformations of the 'Elegantiae' (*bianya*).[95] Bo's heaven-endowed talent runs free (*tiancai zongyi*), and the natural grace of his spirit is difficult to follow. Fu's erudition (*xueli*) is broad and deep, his meticulous control is everywhere present. This is the difference between Li and Du."[96]

Just as Yuan Zhen's juxtaposition of the two poets was framed in the context of a set of writings that favor erudition over a free-wheeling natural spirit, so Li Lian is more sympathetic to the elusive grace of Li Bo. Indeed, he concludes this particular passage with the unequivocal statement, "[Li] Bo is chief among poets of the Kaiyuan and Tianbao reign periods."[97]

A younger contemporary of Yang Shen and Li Lian was much more daring and straightforward in pinpointing and elevating the critically problematic ineffability of Li Bo's style. Xie Zhen (1495–1575), in numerous comments that sometimes link Li and Du and sometimes deal with them separately, borrows from the familiar lexicon of Li Bo criticism to develop a distinct discourse to account for his style within the tradition. Noted among the Archaists for his interest in leavening their strict emulation of the Tang poets with traces of individual spiritual insight (a stance that eventually cost him his influence in that group), Xie granted particular value to the most intransigently indescribable of Li Bo's attributes: his "unfoundedness" *(xu)*. In a brief reference to his unfoundedness below, Xie applies the Chan Buddhist nuances of the term *"xu"* to transform it from the damning critique it had been in the writings of Zhao Cigong into a potent source of Li Bo's magic: "Guanxiu[98] wrote: 'The courtyard blossoms foggy-foggy, the water chill-chill; / The little boy sniffles searching for the swallow in the trees.' Here, the scene is substantive, but has no charm. Taibai wrote: 'The snowflakes of Mount Yan are big as mats; / Sheet after sheet blown down upon Xuanyuan Terrace.' Here, the scene is *unfounded (xu)* and has *savor (wei)*."[99]

In this vindication of Li Bo's use of hyperbole, Xie has changed the lexical meaning of *"xu"* not one iota. As a strictly literary term, it still refers to images that are not founded in the poet's perceptual experience. But in a move reminiscent of Fan Peng more than two hundred years earlier, Xie dilutes *xu*'s moral implications by shifting the focus away from the link between poem and world, eliminating the question of authenticity or sincerity, and toward that

between poem and reader. Xie's interest is not in the mimetic re-
liability of the scene, but in its savor *(wei)*: its ability to evoke in the
reader that experience that can be felt but never described, and
that lingers long after the encounter with the poem has passed.[100]

Li Bo's penchant for the impossible scene, for the vision that
glories in its independence from empirical experience and, to a
lesser extent, from the shared imagistic realm of received texts,
lends itself nicely to the construction of the open-ended, indefin-
able quality of "savoriness." Although Xie does not explicitly inves-
tigate the link he has drawn between *xu* and *wei* (indeed, the con-
junction that links them in the original, *er,* could also mean "but"),
the implied connection seems to lie in the long-standing ideal of
reaching for "meaning beyond the words."

The two couplets Xie cites differ primarily in the distance each
posits between the words of the poem and the world those words
evoke. The substantiveness of Guanxiu's scene reflects proximity,
if not coincidence, between word and world; the impression of
unfoundedness in Li Bo's lyrics derives from the sense of a greater
distance between what (readers presume) he really saw and what
he describes. Dissolving the bounds of common experience, Li's
hyperbolic flourishes and fabricated images oblige readers—if they
are to join the poet in the production of meaning—to map out a
new territory linking Li Bo's words to the reader's known world. In
executing this process readers' encounters with the elusive area of
xu provokes in them the unutterable experience of *wei*. In Xie's
response to Li Bo's poetry, he has joined the generations of readers
who have accepted the challenge of mapping out a poetics whose
very essence requires the erasing, rather than the tracing, of the
poet's creative itinerary.

At the heart of Xie's appreciation of Li Bo's poetry is his belief
in the spontaneity of its creation. His unqualified veneration of this
particular quality distinguishes his views from those of certain Song
dynasty critics: "Men of the Song said that, in the making of a
poem, [one should] value the prior establishment of [the poet's]
intent *(yi)*. [But in considering] Li Bo's 'bushel of wine, one hun-
dred poems,' is it really that he first established so many intents

and only then selected his lyrics? It is more likely that his intents were born following his brush, and did not undergo any [prior] arrangement."[101]

But Xie is quick to point out that spontaneity does not mean a lack of awareness of technique. On the contrary, the successful poet must apprehend the effect of specific forms and the responsibility that the choice of form entails: "In long pieces, pent-up waters burst forth; in short pieces, burgeoning growth is restrained; Li and Du apprehended this. When long pieces are constrained into shorter ones, [meaning is] latent and [the poem] has *savoriness* (*wei*). When short pieces metamorphose into long pieces, [meaning is] fully disclosed and [the poem's] 'bones' are exposed."[102]

Here, as in the earlier passage, savoriness is a matter of perceived disjuncture between the means of representation and the world that is being represented. In this case, however, readers' recognition of the disjuncture depends less on their experience of the empirical world than on their sensitivity to language. They must be alert to the difference between the density of meaning and the meagerness or simplicity of the words used to convey that meaning. It is useful here to recall Zhu Xi's comment that Li Bo's poems seem to be unbounded by rules while "being at ease in the midst of rules." Zhu was intent upon securing Li Bo's position as master of the poetic tradition, and so guided readers' attention toward the tacit presence of the rules in counterpoint to which his poems constructed their meaning. Xie, too, is careful to situate Li Bo squarely in the midst of rules—but his overall discussion of Li Bo places more emphasis on his natural, instinctive capacity for grasping and playing with these parameters.

Xie's delicacy in preserving the indescribability of Li Bo's technique even while attempting to describe it is especially apparent in discussions detailing Li's use of past writings—what Song critics had proudly pointed to as evidence of his knowledge. Usually, in keeping with common practice in casual poetry-talk writing, Xie simply cites examples of earlier poems, followed by examples of Li Bo's verse that they seem to have inspired, leaving detailed comparisons to the reader. But in the following comment he bursts into a little flurry of metaphorical language as he tries to pinpoint, without pinning down, that magical something that takes place between Li's selection of a past text and his incorporation of it into his own work: "Jiang Yan's [444–505] [works] contain an 'Ancient Parting' ("Gu libie"); Emperor Jianwen of Liang and Liu Xiaowei's [496–549] [works] both contained 'The Road to Shu Is Hard' ("Shudao nan"). When Taibai wrote his 'Ancient Parting' and 'The Road to Shu Is Hard,' he satirized the affairs of his own time. Although he utilized ancient themes, his transformation of their formal qualities are like a sudden thunderclap splitting a mountain, like a whirlwind whipping up the ocean. Unless one is the Divine Spirit of Poetry *(shen yu shi zhe)*, one cannot speak of this."[103]

Nowhere is his desire to guard this privileged domain of Li's work more evident than in this comment pairing Li and Du: "The [way in which] the ancients wrote poems can be compared to walking the Great Road to Chang'an. They did not follow the narrow and uneven small paths, but took the official road as [their] principal [route]. Thus they penetrated to the Four Seas, encountering virtually no obstructions. If [we speak of] Taibai and Zimei, both proceeded in large steps, but they differed in their [respective qualities] of unmoored sublimity *(piaoyi)* and ponderous gravity *(chenzhong)*. Zimei can be taken as a normative standard *(fa)*, but Taibai does not easily [lend himself] to being taken as such."[104]

Xie holds to the conviction that Li and Du followed the same path (natural, unforced, bold expression) to arrive at the same destination: the unobstructed communication of their noble feelings to all. It is only their gaits that differed—naturally. Read out of context, Xie's description of these differences seems derivative at best. By now, readers are more than familiar with characterizations of Li's sublimity and Du's gravity; they are also likely to recognize the declaration of Du's learnability and Li's unlearnability. But read within a larger critical schema valuing spirit and unfoundedness, Xie's assertion of Li Bo's unlearnability is no longer problematic. Not that the qualifiable, describable poetics of Du Fu is necessarily a bad thing (at least, not when the man behind the poem is Du Fu); it is just that the elusive experience of the savory seems to emerge most assuredly from the quirky verses of the Banished Immortal.

In the overturning of the values attached to previously familiar evaluative terms—"unfounded," "empty," "substantive," and "full" (and, to a certain extent, "knowledge" and "learning")—lies the cornerstone of Ming dynasty critical discussion of Li Bo. To the extent that Xie Zhen was an early member of the Later Seven Masters, he was still influenced by a belief in a quantifiable poetics and subscribed to more rigid conceptions of poetic technique. Other writers, however, go further and question the very validity of such categories per se, adapting Daoist and Chan Buddhist discourse to a reworking, not so much of the concepts of fullness and emptiness as of the distinction habitually drawn between them.

One of the writers whose own Daoist proclivities translated into a loosening of these categories was Tu Long (1542–1605), a colorful figure who himself sought, not quite successfully, to carry on in Li Bo's spirit. In the following passage from his "Discussing Poetry and Prose with a Friend" ("Yu youren lun shi wen"), he reworks the whole of their bipolar dynamic and overall poetic value in a straightforward reevaluation of Li's unfoundedness and Du's substantiveness:

> Li and Du's styles truly can be distinguished [one from the other.] In looking at poetry, there is emptiness *(xu)* and there is fullness *(shi);* there is emptying emptiness, there is substantiating fullness; there is that which is full in its emptiness, and that which is empty in its fullness. [These two qualities] proceed side by side and emerge interwoven; how can one be extricated from the other? Then why is it that [most people consider] fullness to be on the right [i.e., primary, mainstream] and emptiness to be on the left, and thus posit the relative value of Li and Du in their [respective] qualities of emptiness and fullness? [Consider] Du's poems, for example, the "Autumn Inspiration" ("Qiu xing") series, in which the intent that has been entrusted [to verse] is profound and far-reaching *(tuo yi shen yuan),* and his "Tune on the Painted Horse" ("Hua ma xing") series, in which the divine spirit ranges freely *(shen qing heng yi),* and which toy with the realms of heaven, earth, and man—how could it be that [the quality of these works] lies in that their "myriad scenes are all substantive"? [Consider, too,] Li's dozens of "Ancient Airs," in which he is moved by his times and posits [those feelings] in things; [consider] their sublime gravity. How could it be that [the quality of these works] lies in that their "myriad scenes are all unfounded"?[105]

This passage arrives at the conclusion of a rather long recounting of a discussion between Tu and someone he happened upon in the street one day. As Tu describes it, the unidentified interlocutor had been holding forth on Du Fu's sheer perfection as a poet, waxing eloquent about the attributes that had long been considered the basis for his renown: his boundless versatility, the perfect and natural correspondence between the events he encounters in the world and the emotions thereby provoked, the ease with which he embraces the elegant and the common. Then, somewhat surprisingly, the man brings his description to an impressive crescendo with a remark that seems almost to be lifted from habitual descriptions, not of Du Fu, but of Li Bo: "[Du Fu] abandons himself to [go] where his genius and feelings lead him, as though he had no intention to make a poem." Finally, as if the mention of the qualities of freedom just brought Li Bo to mind, he then briefly brings Li Bo in as a point of comparison. But this is a Li Bo whose writing is born of nothing more than the occasional unexamined whim: "Li Taibai climbs the Void and utters what he will, striving so that every word embodies an easygoing elegance; and none of them cleaves to the feelings [inspired by] the affairs of the world. How can this count as poetry? The myriad scenes in Du's poems are all substantive, and the myriad scenes in Li's poems are all unfounded."[106]

For all his stodgy anti-Li attitude, Tu's anonymous and perhaps apocryphal interlocutor recognizes that in order to continue venerating Du Fu, one must emphasize his spontaneity, visceral feeling, and the natural connection between his creative instinct and his situation in the world. The updated version of the "Great Preface's" dictum that "poetry articulates intent" requires that the poet's response to the ills of his society *appear* (note the telling "*as though* he had no intention") unpremeditated and natural. In casting Du Fu as the avatar of this ideal, the speaker ends up attributing to Du Fu the very quality that had always legitimized Li Bo, indeed, that quality at the heart of Li's critical survival throughout the Tang. Li, robbed of intent—and thus of any claims to spontaneity—is now left with nothing but instinct. His unfoundedness reverts to the denigrating connotations it bore in the Song.

And how does Tu utilize this setup to make his own argument? Tu's initial response is to reassert the deliberate craft evident in Du Fu's poetry. One should not—just to make a point—suddenly discount the degree of reflection and skill behind a poetics as all-encompassing and profound as Du's. Having reminded readers that certain traditional observations about the two poets are, and will remain, valid, Tu arrives at the crux of his thesis. Invoking the ancient theory of the mutual interdependency of opposites, Tu proceeds to abrogate the mutual exclusivity of the terms "empty" and "full"—the operative critical duality that had thus far held the pair together, but that could also, if taken to an extreme in either direction, threaten the critical survival of one of the two.

Tu Long, as a critic, delights not so much in emptying analytical categories of their meaning as in reanimating those categories by applying them in unexpected ways. While, elsewhere, he does clearly and simply identify Li's natural genius as *xu* and Du's as *shi,* he does not intend these categories to be either absolute or discriminatory. He casts both poets as architects of a sort, with Du applying himself to the construction of immense and intricate palaces, and Li building the "five cities and twelve palaces" of the heavenly realm.[107] For Tu, establishing the poetic usefulness of unfoundedness is beside the point, just as it is unnecessary to reinstate Li Bo through the legitimization of *xu* as a technique (intended or otherwise). Li and Du, empty and full, are as heaven and earth—each insignificant except in their relation to the other. And like heaven and earth, they stand beyond the fluctuations of time, untouched or, as Tu puts it, "untainted" *(buran)* by the historical pulls of the literary practices of their times.[108]

Fang Hongjing was another writer of the sixteenth century who sought to reimagine Li and Du's function as a critical pair. Like Xie and Tu, Fang reacts against Song condemnations of Li's relative and absolute unfoundedness, justifying his hyperbolic, fantastic imagery by squarely situating their objective correlatives in the depths of the poet's emotions—by imbuing unfoundedness with substantiveness. His defense of Li Bo is nothing less than a defense of the unlimited metaphoric imagination: "[Concerning] Li's 'White hair, three thousand meters long, / The melancholy of our fate as long as bamboo': the line is strange (qi), but it is not false (wu). This is because of 'the melancholy of our fate'; when melancholy is great, [white hair] can even be as long as three thousand meters!"[109]

Fang is perhaps more prosaic in his declaration than either Xie Zhen or Tu Long, but his point is just as bold; he points to an example of the supposed disjuncture between word and world, and declares that it is no such thing. In characterizing the image, he has abandoned the term xu, "unfounded," for another, just as ambiguous and neutral. Returning to focus on qi, a term that could mean either "strange" or "extraordinary," Fang subtly shifts the critical focus away from world-word coherence toward establishing the substantiveness of subjective impressions. Then, as if in illustration of the parity between external and internal realities, he lifts Li Bo's metaphorical assertion out of its poetic context and inserts it, unchanged, into a discursive one, presenting it as a reasonable, rationally verifiable observation.

But Fang Hongjing does not limit himself to terse, provocative demonstrations of his point. Later in his work, he offers a more extended and theoretical argument for his conviction, implied in the above passage, that a figurative statement is as substantive as an objective utterance:

> Yan Canglang [Yan Yu] said, "Poetry possesses a distinct draw (bie qu) that has no connection with li (principle); poetry possesses a distinct air that has no connection with books." These words seem true, but are false.
>
> [When Du Fu writes]: "In my reading I've worn out ten thousand volumes, / Lowering my brush, [I write] as though possessed of Spirit (shen)," it is unthinkable that Zimei is being deceptive! In his poems, there is not a single word that does not originate in ancient texts. Since commentators cannot elaborate and trace them all, they mistakenly proclaim them as nothing more than "craft" (gong). Where principle is lacking, how can there be "draw" (qu)?[110] What is beautiful in Tao [Qian]'s poetry is that the draw is genuine; and where the draw is genuine, so the principle is genuine.
>
> [When Li Bo writes]: "White hair, three thousand meters long," for an instant one suspects that it does not conform to principle; but

after mulling it over, and because of "the melancholy of our fate . . . ,"
[one understands that] it does not refer to real hair. [As for] "the fly-
ing torrent plummets straight down" and "I wonder if it is the Milky
Way"—is this [image] merely three thousand meters long!? Since
when are these words absent of principle?![111]

But for a change in vocabulary, Fang's argument is very much
in accord with those of Xie and Tu. In the space of a few lines, he
has: (1) countered the danger posed by Yan Yu's famous declara-
tion, reestablishing poetry's place in a real world unified by prin-
ciple; (2) succeeded in distancing his approach from that of his
Song predecessors by attempting to dissolve, once and for all, the
rigidly binary, and ultimately discriminatory, opposition between
instinctual and considered creativity; and (3) placed Li and Du on
unshakably equal footing by suggesting that there is nothing less
genuine in Li's excited exclamations than there is in the most sober
and straightforward declarations of a Tao Qian (or, by extension, of
a Du Fu). Like Xie and Tu, Fang is playing with the meaning of
essential critical terms. Xie imbued emptiness or unfoundedness
with positive connotations, and Tu insisted on the interdependency
existing between emptiness and its supposed opposite, but Fang
has combined these two rhetorical techniques into a single, two-
pronged argument protecting the integrity of bipolar plenitude.

In the first part of his argument, Fang quotes the irreproach-
able Du Fu to remind us that he, too, composed under the influ-
ence of divine, untraceable inspiration—which can be achieved
only after an untiring exploration of the great books, the storehouse
of observed and recorded principle. Parallel to Tu Long's dissolu-
tion of the absolute distinction between the unfounded and the
substantive, Fang reminds us that there is no inspiration without a
thorough acquaintance with principle. But it is worth noting that
here he offers the argument as much to defend Du Fu against
charges of mere craftsmanship as to protect Li Bo against the cri-
tique of emptiness.

The second part of Fang's argument approaches the question
from the opposite side, reminding his readers that principle is uni-
versal and omnipresent, and thus is as present within the inner
realm of human feeling as it is in the external world of "ten thou-

sand books." Repeating his earlier statement about Li's poem, Fang shows himself to be a bona fide disciple of Wang Yangming, refusing to make qualitative judgments concerning the relative validity of shared and subjective reality. We are to understand that Li Bo, just like Du Fu, operates from a firm grounding in principle; it is just a matter of broadening the semantic ground encompassed by that word.

Xie Zhen, Tu Long, and Fang Hongjing, while very much in keeping with the broader intellectual movement of their time, engaged in one of the oldest philosophical and political rhetorical practices there is: the filling of old bottles with new wine, the recycling of venerable terms to demonstrate that they always signified what some would like them to signify now—even if this new signification appears to reverse previous usage.

But some thinkers of this period were not so easily persuaded. One skeptic was Yuan Hongdao (1568–1610), renowned as champion of a spiritual poetics based on one's inner nature. In the following remark, he opts out of the Li-Du debate altogether in order to promote Su Shi, with the express purpose of defying the Archaist poetics that held that only Tang poetry was of real value.[112] But in order to make his point in positing the value of poetic plenitude in the single personage of Su, he first reinstates the polarization of unfoundedness and substantiveness:

> Master Su's poetry contains not a single word that is not beautiful. [Li] Qinglian can [convey] the empty (xu), and [Du] Gongbu can [convey] the full (shi). But Qinglian is exclusively [invested] in emptiness; that is why what [he] unfolds before our eyes often omits some scenes. Gongbu is exclusively invested in fullness, so his poems can be human but cannot be celestial; they can expand and can metamorphose, but cannot be divine (shen). Master Su's poetry enters and exits the world at will, comprises coarse words and fine phrases. [His poems] always make their way back to the most recondite of mysteries, or [even]—just for an instant—become bizarre (guai). But they always reflect the truth of the feeling. It is probable that not only is the force of his genius (cai) strong, but his erudition (xuewen) and experience (shijian) far surpass the two masters. Therefore he rightly stands astride the ancients. As for his intensity's (qiu) not

being on a par with that of Du, and his sublimity's *(yi)* not being on a par with that of Li, this is because the spirit of the age would have it so—it is not a flaw in his genius.[113]

At the other end of the spectrum is the humorous response of Li Zhi (1527–1602), the philosopher closely linked with Yuan and credited with the most radical assertion of the inner heart's predominance in the construction of reality. Even he seems exasperated, however, with the ease with which defenders of Li Bo play fast and loose with reality. So he embarks on a sardonic diatribe regarding one of the most vexing problems in Li Bo studies: the question of his birthplace, place of death, and all his travels in between. After citing arguments for three different birthplaces, Li Zhi is overcome by the irony of a situation in which, during his lifetime, Li Bo was excluded and exiled while, a millennium after his death, he suddenly "belongs" everywhere:

> Alas! One unique Li Bo, who during his lifetime could find no point of entry! Now he has been dead over a thousand years; those who, out of admiration for him, compete to lay claim to [his birthplace] will never desist.
>
> I say, when it comes to Li Bo, no year was not the year of his birth, and no place is not the place of his birth. He is a star in heaven and he is a blossom on the earth. He is at once a man of Baxi, of Longxi, of Shandong, of Kuaiji, of Xunyang, and of Yelang. The place of his death is glorious, the place of his birth is glorious, the place of his wandering is glorious, the place of his imprisonment is glorious. And in those places where he neither wandered, nor was imprisoned, nor was exiled, nor even arrived, to read his books and see his person—how glorious, how glorious! Stop grappling, stop grappling![114]

Li Zhi's main point, of course, is to ridicule how, during his lifetime, Li Bo had been unwanted, whereas now, centuries after his death, the whole country is vying to make a place for him, both figuratively and literally. But even more biting is his attack on those who fix upon a certain kind of truth, blind to the greater truths passed on to us in Li Bo's unfettered imaginings.

By the turn of the seventeenth century, then, a certain subjective relativism, which was being sustained in the various schools of Wang Yangming Neo-Confucian thought, contributed not only to the legitimization (or, more to the point, substantiation) of Li Bo's unfounded brand of knowledge, but also to the salvation of a threatened bipolar figure of poetic plenitude. Xie Zhen, Tu Long, and Fang Hongjing all reconfigured the received wisdom on Li and Du to illustrate their own ideas on poetry, preserving the integrity of the paired poets.

Two important writers of the late Ming who exemplify the way in which this combined discourse of intertwined, softened bipolarity and characterological relativism played itself out in Li-Du criticism were Hu Zhenheng (1569–1644/5), whose anthology of Tang poetry would become one of the major sources for the *Quan Tangshi* (Complete Tang poetry), and Chen Zilong (1608–1647), whose own seven-character regulated poems are often mentioned as fine examples of boldly free yet deeply melancholic responses to the disintegration of the dynasty.[115]

The following comment by Hu, reviving the old debate surrounding Wang Anshi's edition of the *Four Poets*, neatly summarizes the characterological approach of his time, and cautions against going too far in blurring the individual distinctions that make for Li and Du's respective (and, implicitly, combined) greatness:

> The people of the Song, following [the lead of] Jinggong's *Four Poets*, which did not select Taibai [as a great poet], disapproved of [Li's] coveting of riches and excessively vulgar feelings.... Bo is one who took pleasure in poetry and wine, who simply followed his whim all his life; how could he have concerned himself with whether or not his words offended, or have been restrained by moralistic teachings, thus becoming petty and careful? Each poet writes his unique character and feelings, each constitutes a "school" in his own right. One should certainly not take the exuberant brush of "Brocade Robe" [Li Bo] and then constrain it [to fit] the bitter dryness of "Skinny Rainhat" [Du Fu]. [Rather], one must sing [both] their praises with the same flute.[116]

Closely linked to this Ming dynasty discourse about the complementary heaven-endowed nature of each of the two poets is the notion of balance. Balance must be preserved, not only in the relationship within the pair, but also in the reader's approach to each. In this spirit, writers begin to caution that the works of Du Fu and Li Bo must each be consumed and appreciated in their just measure. In keeping with the guiding concept of the mean, or the just measure, readers are cautioned that the very qualities that make each of them superior poets, those particular qualities that naturally reflect their inner natures, can easily become flaws if they fall short of or exceed the ideal mean. Perhaps Wang Shizhen (1526–1590) revealed his preference for Du Fu when he remarked that "before having read ten of [Du Fu's] poems, Shaoling is rather difficult to penetrate, and after reading one hundred of [Li Bo's] poems, Qinglian is rather easy to tire of."[117] But the ideal of maintaining a just balance within the bipolar qualities of density and airiness is equally important here. And later, Chen Zilong would draw a direct link between the characterological nature of poetry and the notion of balance, identifying balance as the inimitable core of a given poet's expression:[118] "As for seven-character old-style poetry, the Four Masters of the Early Tang were extreme in their ornateness; nor is anything after the Yuanhe reign period (806–820) worth reading. What can be taken as models are Shaoling's vigorous dynamic, and Gongfeng's weightless ascensions ... but those who imitate [Du] Fu come close to a clunky heaviness, and those who imitate [Li] Bo come close to cheap vulgarity.... The essential is: in form to combine the "Airs" and the "Elegantiae," in meaning to emphasize the deep sinews. Just this is artistry."[119]

Chen Zilong's comment elegantly summarizes the Li-Du discourse of his age, the Ming-Qing transition.[120] Li and Du are paired, but not strictly opposed. Their differences emerge as innate and natural; each attains excellence by virtue of unpremeditated adherence to the just mean of his own character. Even as this indescribable mean renders their respective particularities worthy of emulation, it also eludes intentional reproduction. Thus, the aspiring student, obliged to follow the external patterns of Li and Du's inner natures, is also most in danger of distorting them. Still, such paradoxes do not diminish the fact that models are and shall remain necessary, for excellent poetry requires not merely pure intuition, but the application of craft, here best understood as the intuitive apprehension and adaptation of the hidden principles expressed in the worthiest of past writings. The poetry of Li and Du stand as such worthy writings but, as natural expressions of unique characters, are essentially inimitable. And so one must reach further back to a poetry that, while bearing the marks of authenticity, is not associated with individual character. That is the poetry of the *Shijing*, the natural expression of humanity at large, and the inspiration of Li and Du.

CHAPTER 2

To Study
the Unlearnable

Li Bo in the Canon, Ming to Early Republic

HE YISUN (fl. 1650), a poet known for his own "unfettered" style,
looked back in nostalgia to the days when poets naturally produced
works that would not merely withstand the wearing effects of time
and ubiquity, but would benefit from them:

> [Concerning] the poetry of Li and Du, the prose of Han [Yu] and Su
> [Shi]: if you chant but one or two pieces, it seems that you could learn
> [their methods] and attain to their achievements. Only when you've
> chanted several dozens more do you perceive their wondrousness. If
> you set out to chant their entire oeuvres, the more you chant, the
> more wondrous [they reveal themselves to be]. If you chant them
> over and over again more than several thousand times, saliva will flow
> out of your mouth and over your chin, and still, their flavor and suc-
> culence will prove inexhaustible; so much so that if you sing them
> unstintingly from youth through old age, as their depicted scenes
> grow more familiar, their flavor will become more prolonged.

[As for] the poems and prose pieces of latter-day writers, if you randomly select a few pieces and chant them, all will gratify the heart and stir the eye; but when you get to chanting entire collections, they gradually make you feel disgusted and unable to go on chanting. This, then, is the difference between the density of the ancients and the flimsiness of the moderns.[1]

The longing to recover past greatness is hardly new. By the fall of the Ming Dynasty, its expression in the idealization of High Tang poetry was a long-standing practice. The political circumstances surrounding this particular wave of nostalgia, too, are familiar, harking back to the Six Dynasties era, when the disintegration of the Han dynasty had left many members of the court looking back nostalgically to a time of political and cultural dominance. But the critics of the Six Dynasties period strike a somewhat different stance, one slightly more resigned, perhaps. Longing for a recovery of past greatness, Six Dynasties writers had been spurred on to aesthetic debates embracing topics from the spiritual to the highly technical, debates that would serve as the basis for all later formulations of the standards of good poetry. And participants in the various archaist movements of the Song and Ming had been bent on identifying and isolating the precise ingredients of great poetry for their own adaptation and implementation, struggling with the relative evaluation of moral import, innate talent, and stylistic achievement.

During the Ming–Qing transition, however, the underlying belief that the "secret" of good poetry could somehow be extracted from past works and applied to new creativity started to fade. On the most salient level, the confidence in standards that had been regularly expressed in lists of ranked poets was overtaken by a Lu-Wang Neo-Confucian reliance on the "innate heart" as the ultimate criterion for judging poetry. As Tang glory receded into a distant and irrecoverable past, and critics lost confidence in their own age's poetic creativity, the tone of Tang-poetry criticism changed. Increasingly impatient with both the didactic and the technical concerns of Song reformers and Ming Archaists, the writers of the age grew more diffident, more eclectic, and—in the most relativistic development of Ming characterological criticism yet—more given to sweeping appreciations of ineffable, inimitable manifestations of unique personal voice. Rather rebellious in their open adoption of a syncretic view of literature, critics like Wang Fuzhi (1619–1692) increased their focus on the interaction and interdependency of "scene" and "feeling," while those like Jin Shengtan (1608–1661) explored the possibilities opened up by the close structural examination of individual poems. All in all, rather than striving to evaluate poetry along the lines of generally sanctioned formal requirements or didactic worthiness, critics repeatedly asserted that what made poetry valuable was its function as a window opening onto the person who composed it.[2]

POETIC WONDROUSNESS AND THE DISSOLUTION OF LI-DU PLENITUDE

Viewed from this elegiac and relativistic perspective, the Li-Du controversy began to seem quite beside the point. This is not to say that "Li and Du" no longer functioned as a pair, nor even that the critics who discussed them ceased having personal preferences; there are still plenty of writings that juxtapose Li's celestial unfetteredness against Du's earthbound meticulousness, Li's extravagance against Du's understatedness, Li's amorality against Du's compassion and loyalty. And, as often as not, when compared in these terms, Li Bo emerges as the less admirable of the two. But the broader critical context tended toward idealizing the Tang as a whole. In this context, the supremacy of the Li-Du pair emerges as less absolute in relation to other pairs, and Li and Du each become less necessary to the proper reading of the other. Those few who still upheld Li and Du's absolute joint superiority almost had to place them on a par with the writings of the *Shijing* and the *Chuci*, but such statements of superiority tend to appear in prefaces to the increasingly common joint Li-Du poetry anthologies, and are probably more rhetorical than in earnest.[3] More representative, perhaps, is the view of Wang Fuzhi, one of the most adamantly anti-"method" critics of the age.

In what is nearly a landmark statement in the evolution of Li-Du criticism, Wang continues to uphold Li and Du as an apex of authentic poetic creativity. But he identifies their superiority neither in terms of their complementarity nor even in terms of their poetic acumen. For him their supremacy derives from each poet's ability to remain, in the simplest of terms, true to himself. Wang is impressed above all by the fact that they did not try to imitate each another: "And then Li and Du took over nurturing and developing [the tradition], and discussed literature over a cup of wine [in friendship], praising one another in perfect harmony. But Li did not imitate Du, and Du did not model himself after Li. Never did they favor what was similar in one another or attack each other's differences; [rather, each] kept assiduously to his own domain."[4]

Now it is the stubborn authenticity of their differences—not their complementarity—that renders them valuable as a pair, for in adhering to their respective natures, they—as a pair—naturally give voice to the vast breadth of expressions of the world through poetry. Elsewhere in Wang's writings, he attributes the enduring greatness of both Li and Du to their poetry's consistent embodiment of their respective *yi*, (ideas)—the concerns inhabiting the poet's spirit at the time of the poem's composition—making it even easier to see how the essential attributes of naturalness and immediacy translate into consistent manifestations of difference.[5] Other poets and critics of this period concur, expressing literary views consistent with larger contemporary trends in Neo-Confucianist thought toward recognizing the importance of the particular manifestations of principle.[6] They further assert that Li and Du are unique among paired poets precisely in their difference from each another: "Contemporary [paired] poets of equal renown inevitably shared the same tone.... Not only did they sustain efforts to become more similar, but even the expression of the spirit of the age was similar without their intending it to be so. Only Li and Du rode the same road side by side, galloped across the land bridle to bridle, their styles as distant [from each another] as could be."[7]

But with difference now identified as a literary value in itself, Li and Du's position at the apex of all poetry becomes more difficult to maintain. Writers beginning with Qian Qianyi (1582–1664) list Li and Du along with many familiar names, attributing to each his individual style, branding each with the stamp of authenticity, and concluding that, because each steadfastly adhered to his own nature, "their words will not be shameful, and will be transmitted onward through the aeons without decaying."[8] Li and Du frequently appear merely as members of longer lists of other paired poets from the Six Dynasties and the Tang, all of whom are valued for their uncensored and unique responses to the objective world.

The increased emphasis on individual expression and personal immediacy did not dissolve the bonds between Li and Du, but it certainly loosened their interdependency as a pair—or, more precisely, diminished Du Fu's importance as a qualifier of Li Bo's poetry (and of Li's exclusive occupation of negative critical space). Du Fu continues to be cited for his profoundly individual and learned reflection of his world, and Wang Fuzhi cites him as peerless in his ability to bend and break rules to convey his meaning. At the same time, as individual authenticity is increasingly associated with inimitability and unlearnability, the elusive, ineffable aspect of Li Bo's poetics emerges as something that can, within reason, be discussed and valued for itself, even if it is still articulated primarily in terms of what it is not. Zhang Dai (1599–1684?), himself a romantic figure whose writings are admired for their fresh air of spontaneity, identifies such elusiveness as the very essence of poetry, citing a line from one of Li Bo's quatrains as a prime example:

"There is painting in his poetry and poetry in his painting"; because Mojie [Wang Wei] combined these two marvels in his single person, they have continued to be discussed in tandem. [But] if you were to paint the painting inscribed in a poem, that painting would not be good; if you were to compose a poem from the poetry implied in a painting, that poem would necessarily be lacking in wondrousness (*miao*). For example, Li Qinglian's "Thoughts on a Quiet Night": "I raise my head and gaze at the gleaming moon,/Lower my head and think of my home village." What in this line can be painted?... Thus, only through recourse to "empty spirit" (*kongling*) can a poem be wondrous. Poems that can be encompassed in a painting can but persist as little shavings of gold and silver before the eye.[9]

Recalling Yan Yu's use of the language of negativity to describe the essence of poetic expression—that unnameable something that has "nothing to do with principle"—Zhang Dai enjoins his readers to think of poetry in negative terms. This is not just a matter of poetry's being not-painting. Zhang locates poetry's distinctiveness in its ability to encompass those things that cannot be copied and that extend beyond the limits of human perception; then, in an attempt to lend cognitive substance to the aesthetic expression of not-being, he calls this type of expression *miao*, or "wondrousness." Another poet of the time, Chen Hongxu (1597–1665), uses the term "wondrousness" in a similar way, to identify the quality lying at the core of what elevates poetry above all other literary forms. Like Zhang Dai, he pinpoints Li Bo's possession of a most subtle form of wondrousness as responsible for Li's supreme unlearnability, which in this context reads as a point of superiority over Du:

> When Zizhan [Su Shi] discussed poetry, he only discussed "content and moral import" *(yiyi)*. Yet what distinguishes poetry from prose is not its content and moral import, but its "voice and veracity of feeling" *(shengqing)*. Zizhan did not understand this. Qinglian's wondrousness *(miao)* is situated in his voice, Shaoling's wondrousness in his veracity of feeling. The ultimate "veracity of feeling" [occurs when] those profound of heart suddenly encounter something and are naturally stirred thereby. On the other hand, the exquisite subtlety of the ultimate "voice" is not something that can be recognized through a hasty encounter. That is why, ever since the Song and Yuan [dynasties], those who discuss poetry inevitably prefer Shaoling over Qinglian; Zizhan was not alone in his error. It is more difficult to recognize voice and veracity of feeling than it is to recognize content and moral import; and the difficulty of recognizing voice is even greater than that of recognizing veracity of feeling.[10]

In Chen's apparently straightforward valuation of poetry over prose, of Li and Du over other poets, and, finally, of Li over Du is inscribed a veritable map of how theoretical shifts in the definition of poetry and the valuation of the poetic ineffable translate into changes in Li's value within the poetic tradition.

Chen begins his argument by setting up a contrast between a

given text's didactic content, an element potentially present in all pieces of writing, and something he calls *"shengqing,"* present in poetry alone. *"Shengqing"* represents one of a series of attempts to unify the aural aspect of a poem and the feelings that produced it, or, in more fundamental terms, the surface and the depth of a poem.[11] When *shengqing* is juxtaposed with content, its original internal opposition between voice and feeling is supplanted by the newly formed opposition between "voice-feeling" and "didactic content." This opposition not only reinforces the surface-depth unity conveyed by *shengqing,* but also strongly suggests its superiority, as a complete, all-encompassing entity, over all other standards by which to judge poetry. By rooting *shengqing* in the uniquely poetic and indescribable quality "wondrousness," Chen can associate voice and feeling with Li and Du, respectively, without regressing into a simplistic affirmation of the old hierarchy. He thus reduces the sense of their opposition, and even suggests Li Bo's unsung superiority, without seeming to contradict long-standing associations of Li with flair and Du with authenticity. As poetic discourse strove to encompass the notion of poetry's unique wondrousness, this type of play between opposed values and between negative and indicative language allowed Li's position to shift toward the center without becoming so clearly circumscribed as to betray the essence of his (apparently necessary) liminality.

This line of argument allows Chen to assert that Li's true value is even more difficult to apprehend than Du's, and, if anyone's poems should be approached slowly and meticulously, it is Li Bo's. Readers, he seems to imply, have been lulled into believing that his poetry's apparently rapid composition calls for rapid reading, and so have missed out on the true wondrousness of his poetry. Perhaps Wang Fuzhi had also been hinting at this same latent potency when he likened Li Bo to an archer whose strength shows not in the act of letting fly his arrow, but in his ability "to hold back and maintain his position."[12]

Reveling in the relative freedom reigning following the personality-based criticism of the late Ming, many poets active during the Ming–Qing transition wrote enthusiastically, and rather defensively, about Li Bo's work. Freed from the necessity of upholding him as the necessary complement to Du Fu, they benefited from the negative contours of wondrousness to qualify and legitimate the unfoundedness characterizing Li's and their own work. His admirers expressed their passion in writings as impressionistic and idiosyncratic in tone and vocabulary as the poetry of their chosen model.

He Yisun, whose nostalgia for the past and whose appreciation of the steadfast differences between Li and Du have been noted above, wrote extensively in praise of Li Bo. Here he chastises readers who are fixated on technical mastery and less sensitive to Li's attributes; there he attacks Li Bo's critics as guilty of a failure of the imagination, inhibited by their own limited talent from being able to take in the panorama of Li Bo's accomplishments.[13] Throughout his writing he intones the wonders of Li's unique and authentic voice, reminding his readers that Li, like other great poets, possesses a coherent, self-contained vision of the world. But perhaps his most moving plea for an open-minded reception and acceptance of the spirit of each poet's world is his heartfelt, if not perfectly persuasive, argument claiming that flaws are a necessary sign of natural genius and, furthermore, that only geniuses possess them:

> Students of poetry cannot study [by imitation] the flawless places in the works of the ancients, and they do not need to study the flawed places. None but a great master can fail to be flawless; none but a great master can fail to have flaws. Even one whose talent is complete and whose erudition is all-encompassing—who, therefore, has perfected every nuance of depth and surface, richness and paleness, the sweeping and the intricate, and the high and the low—will unavoidably manifest some type of imperfection.... Gifted scholars who give free rein to their passions, but who are not willing to seek deeply that place where resides the ancients' spirit, will, upon noticing that Tao [Qian] can occasionally appear sere and insipid, identify sere insipidity with Tao; upon noticing that Du can occasionally appear stultified and oppressed, will identify stultifying oppressiveness with Du; upon noticing that Li can occasionally appear light and insouciant, will identify light insouciance with Li.[14]

For He, as for many late-Ming critics, a flaw (bing) is not necessarily a mistake, but a sign of uniqueness, a natural—and as such desirable—divergence from a preconceived, impersonal standard of poetic performance.[15] He seems to imply that there are two types of flaws: those arising in the works of lesser poets who attempt to override their innate nature in order to adhere to rules, and those that constitute the earmarks of greatness, insofar as greatness resides in remaining true to oneself. Readers who do not apprehend this principle will mistakenly condemn all departures from the model work as polluting a poet's oeuvre, rather than understanding that this type of "flaw" may be nothing less than the poet's highly valuable signature.

He's plea for open-mindedness, for an abiding respect for personal voice (within limits), conforms to one critical perspective that ostensibly bodes well for Li's position. But his focus on the poem as final product, and on the reader's obligation to cultivate a kind of connoisseurship—a keenness in recognizing and appreciating the individual poet's voice—poses a new threat to the appreciation of Li's poetry. This subtle shift of attention away from the poetic process, already present in comments by Chen Hongxu and Wang Fuzhi, effectively removes from critical consideration one of the important qualities that had ensured Li Bo's overall superiority and his important complementary role vis-à-vis Du Fu: his spontaneity.

Li's purported ability to compose rapidly and without reflection had long been offered as proof of his natural genius, his unfetteredness, and, above all, his authenticity. When Chen admonished readers to savor Li's poetry slowly and carefully, he signaled, whether intentionally or not, that compositional method has little bearing on interpretation. Chen's immediate intention was to elevate the value of Li Bo's poetry, but in inadvertently minimizing the importance of what had once been one of Li's signature traits—and doing so in a period when personality had grown so in importance—he contributed to upsetting the balance that was critical in preserving the Li-Du entity and, by extension, Li's position in the dialectical discourse that had thus far protected him. In short, if poetic process no longer mattered as a tool in the evaluation of poetry, there would no longer be any reason to suppose that Li Bo's poems were more immediate and unfettered than Du Fu's.

A further effect of this shift was to weaken the uniqueness of Li Bo's claim to unlearnability. A characteristic that, like spontaneity, had been closely associated with Li Bo's compositional method (touching upon both the idiosyncrasies of his world-word connection and his purported spontaneity), unlearnability gradually came to be seen as inhering more in each (and every) poet's unique voice as revealed in the finished poem. In a critical climate where all great poets are understood, by definition, as being true to their innate nature, where each naturally exhibits his own personal and identifiable flaws, all must ultimately prove unlearnable. Not surprisingly, then, critics became less interested in determining the relative describability of a poet's oeuvre and more interested in ascertaining that same poet's capacity for describing the indescribable—for exploiting poetry's unique capacity to convey a world thought to lie beyond the reach of prose, drama, and painting. All these changes—from the increased emphasis on individual voice to the decreased attention to compositional method— conspired to loosen the Li-Du bond, reduced the likelihood that Du Fu's rise would continue to carry Li Bo in its wake, and diminished Li's role as the primary poetic figure whose existence defined and protected the necessary indescribability of poetry.

And Du Fu's esteem was indeed once again on the rise, as his poetry was consistently cited as unique and exemplary by the most influential critics of the eighteenth century. One of the critics most enamored of Du Fu also happened to be one who placed the highest premium on poetry's unique ability to render the unspeakable. Ye Xie (1627–1703), the most systematic, if not the most immediately influential of poetic theorists since Liu Xie (ca. 465– ca. 522), attempted an all-embracing account of the true nature of poetry—and, at the same time, a sharp critique of literary criticism up to his time—in his treatise *Yuanshi* (The origins of poetry). In *Yuanshi* Ye elaborates the view of poetry as unique among artistic forms in its ability to transmit the inexpressible and categorically rejects all preconceived standards of excellence. In reading the following description by Ye of the unique essence of poetry, one cannot help but notice its consonance with the notion of *"xu"* (unfoundedness), the characteristic that, during the very different climate of the Song dynasty, critics had so ardently condemned: "Only the natural principle *(li)* that cannot be named in words, only those events (shi) that cannot be perceived on display, and only those feelings (qing) that cannot be reached by way of a set path—and, therefore, [only poems] that take the remote and subtle as natural principle, the imaginary as event, and elusive unsettledness as feeling—can qualify as language in which natural principle, events, and feelings are fully expressed."[16]

While this passage appears to contradict the arguments raised against Li Bo by his most outspoken critics, Ye's imagining of the territory beyond words is, in fact, always solidly based in the real, in the poet's unwavering grounding in the world.[17] But for Ye, the unspeakable is no less real than experience that lies within easy reach of descriptive language. It almost seems that the unspeakable ultimately qualifies as more fully expressible, and more meaningful, than experiences that are easily encompassed in words. This view is repeated throughout Ye's essay, where his further elaboration of the three central elements—natural principle (li), event (shi), and feeling (qing)—reveals his dedication to achieving an appreciation of emptiness as founded solidly within the substantial.

Significantly, Ye, for all his appreciation of the role of the insubstantial in poetry, rarely singles out Li Bo for praise, and he rarely pairs him with Du Fu. Instead, he repeatedly identifies Du as alone in his supreme manifestation of the dual ideals of achieving poetic wondrousness and maintaining fidelity to his nature. In the following critique of a poem by Du Fu, it is Du who earns his praise for the ability to capture in words precisely that insubstantial world that had earlier been Li Bo's privileged terrain. Ye Xie even invokes the same adage about poetry and painting that Zhang Dai had cited earlier when praising Li Bo: "Long ago someone said that in Wang Wei's poetry there is painting. According to such people, anyone who writes a poem worthy of being rendered as a painting can be considered a master of poetry; for there is scarcely a painter unable to depict with his brush [even] the most insubstantial (xu) images of a scene, such as wind and clouds or rain and snow. But facing a scene like this one—a scene of the first chill's inside and outside[18]—even a Dong [Yuan] or a Ju [Ran] reborn would, I suspect, fold his hands and lay aside his brush. In all the world, it is only the movement of natural principle and event into the divine realm that absolutely no ordinary person can achieve by mimetic rendering."[19]

On the surface, this passage seems merely to echo the imagery commonly found in earlier qualifications of Li Bo: evocations of some of nature's more insubstantial properties, the inimitability of the poet's achievements, and the poet's standing as separate from "ordinary" people. But Ye insists upon the "real" within the insubstantial, and selects as exemplary a poem that depicts an experience that is, while very subtle, actually quite familiar to all readers living in a temperate climate. In doing so, Ye Xie performs the ultimate synthesis of the complementary values that had created and sustained the Li-Du pair over the centuries. Like Chen's conflation of voice and veracity of feeling in his coining of the word *"shengqing,"* Ye's highly synthetic and holistic understanding of poetry effects, on a larger conceptual scale, a further attenuation of the traditional opposition inhering in binary concepts associated with surface and content, liminality and centrality. Poetic plenitude, it seems, is better served if identified not with a bipolar pair, but with the individual poet.

Consistent with this view, when Ye Xie does give Li Bo his due, he includes him along with Du Fu in a list of several poets.[20] He shies away from engaging in the traditional comparison between Li and Du, and when he does address it, he seeks neither to invalidate it nor to reinforce it. Rather, he simply reiterates certain of their most commonly cited poetic traits, accounting for them at the deep level of their respective inborn qualities: "Li Bo's heaven-endowed genius and naturalness stand out as unique and superior; and so, since ancient times, he has enjoyed a renown equal with Du Fu. Still, there is some difference between them. That is, [Li] Bo has attained this [level of excellence], not through talent *(cai)*, but through vital energy *(qi)*."[21]

Ye does not question the widely held perception that Li possesses "heaven-endowed genius" *(tiancai)* and "naturalness" *(ziran)*, but Du remains the standard-bearer, and Ye invokes Li's qualities primarily as a justification for Li's enjoyment of the same degree of renown. Even though Ye refrains from comparing the value of their respective endowments of "talent" and "vital energy," the reader can readily sense that they are not equal, complementary attributes. Nor, as Ye makes apparent in the passage below, are *cai* and *qi* mutually exclusive. Rather, vital energy functions to compensate and, to some degree, dissimulate deficiencies in other heaven-endowed assets, including talent: "It has always been the case that moral righteousness, worthy accomplishment, and literary refinement are all endowed by heaven and completed by oneself; but how can there be no difference among them! If one's endowment [of any of these attributes] is not one hundred percent, as long as he possesses vital energy by which to stimulate them, it is like the strength of a bow when pulled taut to its maximum degree: then there is nothing so sturdy that it won't break [under its force]."[22]

Ye concludes this section by declaring that when a poet's *qi* is implemented to its fullest, nothing lies beyond his reach. Li is, in this respect, prodigiously gifted: "If one considers all of the poets since antiquity, of those who achieved great renown, who besides [Li] was possessed of such vital energy!"[23] Still, although Ye never says so outright, it is clear that Li Bo's verve—his vital energy—while important, will always remain secondary, a quality that, at best, makes up for what he lacks in the more complete, somehow more civilized gift of *cai*, best understood here as highly refined talent (as opposed to the wilder "heavenly-endowed genius" with which Li is credited).

As critics increasingly emphasized the centrality of the individual voice and expressed a growing preference for the immeasurable and the intangible, their views paradoxically conspired to diminish, if ever so slightly, the exceptional stature of the poet who for centuries had been regarded as the safeguard for those values. Like Wang Fuzhi and Ye Xie, Wang Shizhen (1634–1711) conceived of poetry as the privileged form in which to capture, through images both natural and understated, the otherwise unutterable convergence of the poet's unique spirit and the things of the world. He encapsulated this defining criterion of poetry in a term that originated in Tang dynasty painting criticism: *shenyun* (roughly, "spiritual resonance"),[24] a term drawn from painting criticism, where it referred to the dimension of painting that subsists above the realm of images. Wang was eloquent in his preference for pure, limpid, unobtrusive—and believable—imagery, embedded in poems bearing no trace of the act of composition, but transparently revealing the character of the poet. Cultivating a sensitivity to individual voices, he nevertheless is careful to shun the practice of simply describing specific voices in pat phrases; in one passage, he even lightly mocks the idea of assigning precise spiritual languages to individual poets.[25]

Wang Shizhen is far less interested in establishing a canonical hierarchy of great poets than he is in seeking and finding specific instances where poets attain to—or fall short of—his ideal. Du and Li figure again and again in his search for *shenyun,* most often in longer lists of poets who exemplify the specific quality he is seeking to illustrate at the moment. Li and Du are rarely compared with each other, and neither consistently emerges as superior. Wang recognizes Li Bo's ability to evoke a world beyond words, but hardly suggests that Li is unique in this regard, instead attributing this quality to a long list of his favorite poets. Wang is more likely to quote Li Bo alongside someone like the Tang poet Meng Haoran (689–740) when attempting to illustrate a particular quality, as he does when elucidating the category of poems the Tang critic Sikong Tu (837–908) had described as *hanxu* (implicitness).[26]

"Sing the Person, Understand the Poetry"

Given the high regard that critics manifested for the natural expression of individual voice, and their relatively reserved appreciation of Li Bo's poetry, it may no longer seem all that surprising to discover that a critic credited with reviving orthodox Confucian poetics happens also to have been one of Li's most vociferous supporters—or, more precisely, one of the most ardent revivers of the Li-Du complementary pair. Shen Deqian (1673–1749), Ye Xie's rather rebellious student, has never enjoyed a reputation for innovation, or even of particular openness regarding the evolution and transformation of poetry. His plea for a return to classical aesthetics, the reinstatement of prosodic rules and generic typology, and his emphasis on a creative basis in social morality remain the defining elements of his critical persona. In the preface to his anthology of Ming poetry, *Selections from the Poetry of the Seven Masters* (Qizi shixuan), we find him listing desirable aspects of poetry in order of importance, separating content from form and musicality from voice: "I believe that the ways in which poetry enacts the Dao differ between the ancients and the moderns. But if I were to unify [these ways] into a whole, then I would say: first, consider [the poem's] governing idea *(zongzhi);* next, take the measure of its personal style *(fengge);* finally, discern its *shenyun*."[27]

Reading only this far, it is easy to go along with the usual characterization of Shen as privileging moral content above all other poetic features, of reinstating a hierarchy that reinforces the traditional schism between meaning and form, between the substantial and the insubstantial. A bit further along in the same passage, however, Shen glosses these terms so as to undermine significantly the old-fashioned distinctions, aligning himself quite closely with Wang Shizhen, from whom he borrowed and adapted the term *"shenyun":* "What I call the 'governing idea' is that which originates from one's inner feelings; 'personal style' is rooted in vital breath and bone; and *shenyun* is overflow from the reflective capacity of native genius, as insubstantial as a slithering snake whose tracks cannot be traced."[28]

Clearly, Shen does not intend to allow his analysis to regress into the easy classifications his teachers had been working to subvert; content and style, as well as the inexplicable *shenyun,* all emerge from the depths of the individual poet's spirit, albeit a spirit that has been cultivated in accordance with certain norms. Once these normative values have been integrated into the poet's inner self, the lyrical expression of that self cannot but exhibit certain desirable moral and aesthetic characteristics: "Rightness in the governing idea, loftiness in personal style, and all-encompassing sublimity in *shenyun* can come together naturally without planning."[29]

Shen's ideal poet, then, incarnates a seamless blend of the Confucian gentleman's moral correctness and the untrammeled sublimity reminiscent of Yan Yu's Chan-inspired divine spirit.

Shen's interest in identifying the personal preconditions for poetic excellence inevitably brings him back to the issue of poetic process, if only to revive the conviction, first clearly articulated during the Song, that only long years of study enable the poet to give himself over fully to the inspiration of the moment: "Of the ancients, none did not study *(xue)* [in order to arrive at writing] poetry. Li Taibai is the sublime genius of all time, yet he started out by spending nineteen years studying at Kuangshan. Du Shaoling speaks himself of his achievement, saying: 'Having worn out ten thousand volumes / I lower my brush and write as one divinely inspired.' From this we know that the means by which the ancients invested their work with inspirited light was invariably through disciplined study."[30]

Having thus proven the universal validity of study as a precondition for poetic expression, however, Shen does not dwell on issues of curriculum. Instead, he devotes most of his writings to apprehending and conveying the tantalizingly elusive nuances of each poet's innate nature, for he is in complete agreement with both Ye Xie and Wang Shizhen in holding that the best poems reveal, almost by definition, the unique natures of their individual composers: "innate emotional response and individual character are fully present in every person."[31] Certainly this approach is evident in his discussions of Li Bo, whose learning is apparently less worthy of description than his character.

Despite his proclaimed interest in each poet's innate nature, Shen Deqian's attempts to capture Li Bo's—and, for that matter, Du Fu's—individual character do not go much further than prior attempts to account for the peculiarities of Li Bo's work. The old depictions of a free-spirited Li Bo, often opposed to a socially concerned Du Fu, are repeated again and again.[32] Even Shen's powerful assertion, quoted above, of the universality of individual character is illustrated with this all-too-familiar, if not altogether clichéd portrait: "Reading Taibai's poetry is like seeing him having his shoes removed by the prime minister; reading Shaoling's poetry is like witnessing him grieving for his country and lamenting his times."[33]

What interests Shen is establishing the transparency of poetry, and if he can impress this upon his readers only through the unsubtle evocation of well-rehearsed personae, so be it. For all their technical precision, many of Shen's comments ultimately rely upon invoking the by now mythic persona of the Banished Immortal (and of Du Fu as well) in order to extol the beauty and authenticity of the poems. The conventional nature of his characterizations suggests that readers are urged to fit the poems into the persona they already know rather than attempt to rediscover the person behind the poems—even when the ostensible thrust of the argument encourages deriving the persona from the poetry. In many of his comments, for example, Shen offers detailed discussions of Li's performance in particular genres, then smoothly shifts to more general, and conventional, statements qualifying his familiar poetic persona: "Seven-character quatrains employ phrases close at hand to convey far-off feelings, relying primarily on the techniques of withholding and nondisclosure. Only when scenes right before the eyes and words most commonly on the lips [harbor] musical tones beyond the capacity of strings and savoriness beyond the reach of taste—only then can they send man's spirit to far-off places: Taibai possesses this [ability]."[34]

Even Shen's linking of genre with character bespeaks a return to the critical habits of earlier times. Generations of critics before him had striven to rationalize Li's appeal by focusing upon his apparent affinity for certain forms. The Song dynasty writers Hu Yinglin and Hu Zhenheng were foremost among these. But the very lateness and redundancy of Shen's argument imbues these unsurprising discoveries with a different order of persuasiveness: that derived from the authority of nostalgia. This nostalgia, rather than resurrecting the past in terms that appeal because of their up-to-date rationale, attempts to salvage past greatness by embracing past forms of its appreciation. In the following celebration of Li's seven-character old-style poems, Shen sounds remarkably like Ouyang Xiu. But now he is persuading by confirming what readers—at least sympathetic ones—already understand: "Taibai's seven-character old-style poems seem to descend somewhere beyond the heavens, and his unorthodox, transforming voice arises from his natural tendencies. [His work resembles] a great river upon which waves rise up of their own accord, without the presence of wind; or a white cloud cleaving to the void, and then, trailing the wind, disappearing from sight. This is the result of heaven's gift, and is not something that can be attained through human effort."[35]

Perhaps only Wang Fuzhi could rival Shen in the ability to employ such lyrical language in conveying the essence of Li's contribution. But for all its beauty, the imagery in this passage is more a refrain than a new melody. At the same time, the essential repetitiveness of the imagery is meaningful in itself, not only as a nostalgic tribute, but as a tacit acknowledgment of the fundamental unqualifiability of Li's poetry. Repetition avoids the stultifying danger of an expanding vocabulary, a proliferation of words that might only confine and deaden the very wondrousness that Li Bo has come to incarnate. Better by far to repeat in agreement, vivify those repetitions with the conviction of your own style, and allow the enriched resonance to make its way unimpeded by attempts at precision.

So familiar and evocative is the profile of the Banished Immortal that it emerges in Shen's poetic criticism as a kind of shorthand for particular poetic qualities found in poems written by others in genres where Li Bo excelled. In his criticism of one of his own contemporaries, the poet Xu Zhusu (Xu Tingheng, 1675–1760), Shen draws upon the Immortal's characteristic wanderings as source and metaphor for Xu's creativity. Expanding upon Li's and, by implication, Xu's "descent from somewhere beyond the heavens," he pinpoints a biographical source of their natural affinities: the vast exposure to the physical world resulting from their exhaustive travels through the empire. "Of course, Qinglian's genius was endowed by heaven, but he [also] lodged in Mount Emei, and ventured up into the Min-Han region [the present-day border area between Sichuan and Shaanxi], sought out the renowned spots of Suzhou and Yue, ferreted out the wonders of Jingting [Mountain] and Qiupu. His skiff and chariot traversed half the world, and he especially benefited from the rivers and mountains [he encountered]."[36]

Shen's idea that Li Bo's travels bear a significant responsibility for his poetic success may have been most immediately inspired by the parallel in Xu's experience, but it resonates very strongly with early associations between travel and learning, with poetic values elsewhere espoused by Shen, and with the familiar metaphorical characterizations of Li Bo's poetic persona.

Considering Shen's insistence on education as a prerequisite for poetic excellence, it is easy to see why he might also value extensive travel. To the educated Chinese reader, travel suggests (even if it does not comprise) a classical education, echoing as it does the oft-cited wanderings of both Confucius and the great Han dynasty historian Sima Qian. When practiced by poets, wandering permits the acquisition of a dazzling collection of real scenes to stir the feelings and inspire the imagination. In the quotation above, the connection between the direct, sensuous experience of the natural world and poetic creativity is deepened by the allusion to Liu Xie's chapter in *The Literary Mind Carves Dragons*, entitled "Wu se" (The appearance of things).[37] When the poet becomes a traveler, he situates himself firmly within the classical lineage of great writers who drew their inspiration from real experience. And when applied to Li Bo, the image of the wandering poet resonates nicely with the accumulated portrayals of his banished immortality: his unfetteredness, his celestial yearnings (and, as some stories would have it, celestial origins), his uniqueness among men.

Shen is hardly the first or the only critic to link Li Bo's wanderings with his poetry, but previous writers had almost always viewed his peregrinations in moral terms. In steering clear of moralistic interpretations of Li's wanderings and opting to view them in aesthetic terms instead, Shen contributes to Li Bo's recession into the ancient past—into the safe, hagiographic pantheon of the worthiest poetic models. More specifically, Shen's recitation of Li's (his person and his poetry's) metaphorical provenance from somewhere beyond the heavens, as well as his hyperbolic description of Li's meanderings, blends biography with criticism in such a way as to ensure the inimitability and unqualifiability of the Banished Immortal, a figure not so much derived from Li Bo's poetry as one that is invoked in order to imbue that poetry with canonical—indeed, mythical—potency.

This particular convergence of mythical attributes is repeated and rendered more explicit in the writings of Qiao Yi (1702–1778), a protégé of Shen and a poet well versed in the experiences of the wandering exile. Like Shen, Qiao Yi makes much of Li Bo's travels, transforming them into a central metaphor reinforcing his persona as Banished Immortal. More emphatically than Shen, however, Qiao presents this portrait as part of an argument reasserting the absolute superiority of Li-and-Du as a unified, complementary pair. Qiao begins with the observation that, ever since Yuan Zhen first discussed Li and Du, literati have almost always positioned Du above Li, and have done so primarily in the name of Du's erudition and faithfulness to lived reality, combined with his indisputable technical mastery. But, Qiao continues, "Taibai spirit-journeyed through the Eight Directions and thoroughly studied the Buddhist sutras, [experiences that are] all manifest in his poetry, in the many phrases expressing his instability and unsuitability for being employed in the society [of his times]. Furthermore, genius was freely granted him by Heaven such that, time and again, his brush would fall to paper like thunder splitting a mountain, and its movements would leave no trace. If one were going to codify his method, where would one take hold of it?"[38]

The seamless transposition of earthly into celestial wanderings is in keeping with Li Bo's own descriptions of mountain-expeditions-become-spirit-wanderings. For example, in "Shudao nan" (The road to Shu is hard) and "Meng Tianmu shan" (Dreaming of Tianmu mountain), expeditions through wild terrain smoothly transform, primarily by means of hyperbole, into spirit journeys reminiscent of the shamanistic songs of Chu. At the same time, Qiao's implicit blending of Li's earthly (substantive) experiences and his celestial, spiritual peregrinations finds its critical precedent in Lu Ji's narration of the internal process of poetic composition, which had appeared 1500 years earlier in his "Wenfu," especially as taken up soon after for a more thorough, theoretical discussion in Liu Xie's *Wenxin diaolong*. The final allusion to a brush that leaves no trace—of a poetic work seemingly conceived and brought forth as a piece—leads the reader even further from imagining concrete mountain and river crossings, toward a poetic process whose negativity and numinosity are firmly conveyed in images of Daoist spirit voyage and Chan enlightenment.

Qiao uses the untraceability of Li's physical and spiritual wanderings as a springboard to return to the contrastive figure of Du Fu, reminding readers that student poets desirous of writing like Li inevitably find themselves "taking directions" (both geographically and poetically) from the more gradual and systematic Du. Although this is understandable, says Qiao, it should not lead to the ranking of Du over Li:

> The Five Peaks and the famous mountains are the most magnificent sites of the Nine Provinces; and the mounts Peng, Ying, and Fangzhang [are] the footprints the immortals [left] upon the sea. If one talks about traveling across them, then one person cannot completely cover all of the distant lands. Nevertheless, the world has continuously transmitted the true form of the Five Peaks ... for it has been passed down by men the likes of the eminent monks and exceptional gentlemen who ventured forth alone. As for the Three [Sacred Mountains], the Five Metropolises, and the Twelve Pavilions: the Great Historian [Sima Qian] told of them all, but who has [personally] been to even one?
>
> Therefore, never to have set foot upon Peng, Ying, or Fangzhang, yet to claim that they are higher than the Five Peaks, is wrong. [Merely] to know that the Five Peaks exist, and [on that basis] claim that they are more venerable than Peng, Ying, and Fangzhang, is also wrong. The poetry of Li and Du is just like this; through this [comparison] we understand that Du is to be admired, but Li cannot be taken lightly. In discussing Li and Du, it can hardly be a question of placing one before the other![39]

Despite his heavy use of the well-worn celestial-terrestrial, immortal-sage contrast between Li and Du, Qiao's reasoning differs radically from the Tang critics' original evocations of heaven-earth contrast and interdependency. In an argument that bespeaks a subtler appreciation of the intricacies of the "unfounded-substantive" relationship inscribed in the image of heaven and earth, Qiao founds his opposition to Li-Du ranking upon the observation that, at least as far as the mortal, homebound reader is concerned, one poet's spirit journey is no less "real" than another poet's extensive earthly travels. On the one hand, their readers' life experiences most likely have no more in common with the one than with the other. On the other hand, every reader, by virtue of his own wandering spirit—a spirit nourished by the same writings that nourished the spirits of Li and Du—has equal access to both realms.

Underlying Qiao's arguments for Li-Du parity is the centuries-old Chan-inspired conviction that Li's unfoundedness and Du's substantiality are essentially one. Throughout his writings, Qiao Yi consistently upholds Li and Du's superiority as a pair, while playing the game of simultaneously propagating and undermining traditional images of their complementarity. In nearly verbatim repetitions of earlier complementary descriptions, we see Li as the heir to the *Zhuangzi* and the "Li Sao," and Du the successor to the Classics and the Histories, or elsewhere compared to complementary military strategists or calligraphers.[40] But Qiao is just as likely to toy with traditional characterizations by inverting Li and Du's usual identities, as when he insists on Li's encyclopedic mastery of nearly all preceding literature, of the ancient techniques of comparison and stimulus, or when he characterizes Du in his later years as unlearnable and unfettered.[41]

While neither Shen Deqian nor Qiao Yi can be said to have distanced themselves fully from the conventions of the Li-Du critical tradition, their writings bespeak a certain playfulness in objectifying and handling those conventions. The nearly universal acceptance of supremacy of authenticity in expression, and the equation of individual authenticity with a venerated ancientness, had by now firmly secured Li Bo his place beside Du Fu. Precious few critics seemed interested in maintaining a position that would denigrate Li Bo in any significant way; at least, very few such writings have been handed down. Nevertheless, an active desire (perhaps motivated by a certain anxiousness) to maintain his status is evident, not only in the growing number of editions of his collected poems and the widespread lamentations of the sorry condition of his corpus (especially as compared to that of Du Fu), but also in the remarkably polemical tone of critical writings praising his work.

CRITICIZING THE CRITICS: LI BO'S ACCESSION TO ANCIENTNESS

A reading of the extemporaneous writings about Li Bo from the mid-eighteenth century reveals that the polemics are not so much directed against contemporary denigrators of Li's work, as—directly or indirectly—against earlier readers, often identified as having egregiously misread Li's poetry and misjudged his contribution to the tradition. Set in the larger context of the age, this assertion of independence from (what was presented as) traditional critical schemas may be interpreted as consistent with two important trends that had come to dominate the eighteenth-century intellectual environment: (1) a growing interest in empirical experience and freedom from inherited paradigms, and (2) the expression of that interest in intense activity in the realm of bibliographic and commentarial scholarship—attempts to determine the original and correct (pre-Song dynasty) readings of the classics and of literature in general.[42] It is possible to argue that past derogatory *criticism* of Li Bo actually came to replace the figure of Du Fu as the foil that helped critics render Li Bo's otherwise indefinable contributions in definable terms. As the contrastive nature of the Li-Du pair was overshadowed by repeated assertions of their equal status as authentic, ineffable, natural poets, there arose a need to find another vehicle for conveying, without destroying or dishonoring, Li's purported indescribable poetics. As the Li and Du pair gradually embedded itself in the canon as a nearly untouchable, untainted, and ahistorical entity, critics transformed the old Li-Du debate into a debate between past and present interpretations of Li and Du, conducted almost exclusively as a metacritical enterprise. In general, Li Bo criticism became more purely reflexive—a trend that the elusiveness of the decidedly limited Li Bo critical vocabulary could only have encouraged.

The trend toward reflexive criticism is evident in the writings of Weng Fanggang (1733–1818) and Li Diaoyuan (1734–1802), two rather passionate devotees of Li's poetry, who appear at least as intent upon overturning various assumptions about Li Bo as upon elucidating the poems themselves. Both promoted Li's equivalency to Du Fu by engaging in a critique that assented to and perpetuated the customary Li vocabulary, while imbuing it with virtually antithetical connotations, namely, with values usually associated with Du Fu. In this practice they may have taken their lead from Zhu Xi and Ouyang Xiu, but the detail and the emphasis on empirical argument is distinctly of their time, as is their strategy of inversion.[43]

Weng Fanggang, a renowned poet, philologist, and critic, is best known for his stand against both the narrowly imitative practices of the Ming Archaists and what he perceived to be the too abstract, relativistic vision of the followers of Wang Yangming, especially as expressed in the poet Yuan Mei's (1716–1798) subjective and expressionistic emphasis on *xingling* (native sensibility).[44] Weng's proposed solution, summarized in his "Zhiyan ji xu" (Introduction to the collected "Intended words"), was the application of classical methodology to poetry. The method was founded upon a philosophical belief that *li* (principle) is as present in poetry as in all other things and can be discerned through careful examination of its outward attributes. A strong proponent of formal rules in poetry, Weng was, remarkably, a passionate defender of Li Bo, using a blend of philological and philosophical argument to demonstrate that Li Bo's learning, gravitas, and subtlety are every bit as elegant and refined as Du Fu's. According to Weng, these qualities are just manifest in naturally distinct styles.

In a letter to an unidentified friend, Weng constructs his argument by equating poetic characteristics that had traditionally been cited distinguishing the two poets. On the technical side, he notes their common adherence to, and implied mastery of, thematic conventions; on the expressive, philosophical, and ultimately moralistic side, he—even more surprisingly—underlines their shared tone of solemnity and weightiness. Weng explains his departure from traditional characterizations by depicting Li Bo's solemnity in terms skillfully developed out of Chan binary discourse: the paradoxical unity of solemnity-within-flightiness, and flightiness-within-solemnity. As he put it, "[Li's] difference from Du consists merely in that Li's solemnity and weightiness are completely attained in sublime unfettered flight."[45]

This unexplained imbrication of opposites, although present in Li Bo criticism ever since Zhu Xi's famous statement that Li Bo's unruliness "meandered about in the midst of rules," seems, in Weng's writings, to be inspired less by specific examples of Li Bo's work than by interpretations of it. For example, one of the most frequently repeated terms in his writings on Li Bo is the expression *mili* (vague). *Mili* seems to encompass the qualities previously labeled *xu* (empty), qualities Weng somewhat contentiously identifies as actually being the highest expression (and point of origin) of Li's substantiveness: "The whole of Taibai's 'Yuan bieli' (Parted far away) pushes *mili* to an extreme. This is not only because of the difficulty of articulating the story of Xuan and Su, father and son. It is more importantly because the poet's transforming fantasy brought [the poem] to this point. If he had spoken about [the story] directly, then, contrary to expectations, the poem would have nowhere [in the objective world] to return to; but it is precisely in pushing *mili* to an extreme that it successfully assumes its origins in that point [in the objective world]."[46]

If Weng Fanggang legitimized (and neutralized) Li Bo's indescribability in the conflation of a couple of key antithetical critical terms, Li Diaoyuan reveled in turning the entire critical tradition on its head, with more or less convincing results. A celebrated erudite, Li Diaoyuan was born in the town of Zhangming in modern-day Sichuan, one of the three or four locales celebrated as Li Bo's birthplace. At least partly because of this coincidence, which he heartily defends in a funny and facetious essay investigating the forever unresolved question of Li Bo's origins, Li Diaoyuan strongly identified with Li Bo. He expresses his nearly maniacal passion for Li's poetry in writings that overflow with humor, verve, and not a little sarcasm directed at those who don't quite get it. Author of a preface to the *Chongke Taibai quanji* (Re-edition of the complete works of Taibai), Li Diaoyuan argues that, far from being unlearnable, Li is precisely the poet one ought to study and emulate:

> How ubiquitous are the arguments of past writers promoting Li and Du as the best of the Tang poets! [Upon reading them,] one notices that, because of his [adherence to poetic] regulation, most consider Du a [suitable] teacher; but when it comes to Li, they say that his is an "immortal genius" (xiancai) that cannot be learned: an extreme case of arbitrary distinctions! It's probable that, since Taibai was skilled in [writing] yuefu, reading the extreme beauty of his extraordinary genius flying aloft like Liezi driving the wind dazzled people's vision and shocked their hearts; but if you examine [his poems] closely, [you will see that] none is lacking a discernible organizational principle.... That is why I believe that those who study poetry must begin with Taibai; only then can they extend their [natural] talent and judgment, and develop their heart's capacity for reflection.[47]

As Li Diaoyuan insists elsewhere, it is Li Bo's "immortal genius" (responsible, as we recall, for his supposed unsuitability for rule-bound composition) that allowed him to master all the traditional poetic forms completely. If it weren't for Du Fu, and readers' benighted habit of pairing poets, everyone would have long since recognized that fact.[48] Li Diaoyuan makes little effort to ground his arguments in even a semblance of empirical observation, relying heavily on citation of past "misreadings" to convey the otherwise unutterable quality of Li Bo's work. In another case, charging the reader to fulfill his obligation and look beyond the surface to the "spirit and vital force" of the poem, he takes issue with the popular belief that Du Fu is Tao Yuanming's heir.[49]

Of course, not all critics during this period employed such radical inversions of past rhetoric in objectifying or taking exception to the critical tradition they inherited. The admired eighteenth-century scholar Wang Qi, renowned for his editing of and commentary on the poetry of both Li Bo and Li He (790–816), presented himself as the voice of reason in an increasingly impassioned and polemical debate. In an echo of Song dynasty reactions to Wang Anshi's supposedly lopsided favoritism of Du Fu, Wang Qi entered the fray by reinstating Li-Du complementarity, but pleading for a more objective and independent reading of each poet.

The first to collate the three previous complete annotations of Li Bo's works, Wang Qi took it upon himself to place the Li-Du debate in perspective, noting the relative paucity of critical editions and commentary on Li Bo as compared to those dedicated to Du. In a lengthy and detailed postface to his edition,[50] he astutely criticizes the history of unsubtle applications of "praise and blame" rhetoric[51] to Li's life and, by extension, to his literary contribution. Wang holds this undiscriminating practice responsible for the tendency of critics to exaggerate and to impose double standards. This type of thinking, he says, causes some critics to denigrate Li's powerful vital force as mere bravado incited by too much wine, and the same type of thinking causes other critics to allegorize his dance tunes indiscriminately, distorting them into political critiques that they never were intended to be. Wang invokes a well-worn notion behind the characterological criticism of the late Ming—still being maintained in the theories of his contemporary, Yuan Mei—reminding readers that each poet possesses a distinct nature, and that each nature encompasses particular biases and tendencies that naturally manifest themselves in poetry. He combines this view with a more contemporaneous belief in the importance of the poet's life experience and concludes by reminding his readers that Li Bo, who traveled widely and enjoyed exhilarating adventures, naturally tended toward joy; Du Fu, in contrast, suffered great pain in his life, and naturally tended toward melancholy.

But the most trenchant of Wang's critiques was aimed at critics who, in understandable reaction against the practice of ranking Li below Du, "stand the truth on end" (diandao shishi) to recast Li in Du's mold, minimizing any and all differences. Wang shows himself to be very much a child of his times, engaged in kaozheng xue, which one recent scholar has translated as "evidential research":[52] the careful examination of earlier texts in hope of unearthing their "true" meaning and correcting subsequent misinterpretations. Instead of ferreting out decontextualized and unreliable "proofs" of Li's love of king and country, he admonishes, better to inform oneself of the facts, immerse oneself in both poets' works and the biographical facts that informed them, and cast off the centuries of prejudicial characterizations. His exposure of one of the most important strategies that, as recently as in the writings of Weng Fanggang and Li Diaoyuan, had been used to maintain Li Bo's lofty position at Du Fu's side, although temperate in tone, is every bit as passionate, and certainly more thoroughgoing, than any of the subversive commentaries of his contemporaries.

Although Wang Qi takes a position in some ways diametrically opposed to that of Weng Fanggang and Li Diaoyuan, his evaluation of Li's work is born of the same wave of protest against what scholars perceived as the blind acceptance of traditional thinking. Erudite, rational editors and iconoclastic polemicists alike tended to articulate Li's qualities through the reevaluation and revision of past criticism of his work.

One unintended by-product of this generalized opposition to the past is Li's emergence as a misunderstood poet rather than as an unlearnable one, a poet whose true value reveals itself only to the most discerning, objective, and independent readers. This theme, which had been latent throughout centuries of polemics, appears now as the unifying—if, by and large, unacknowledged—characterization of the Banished Immortal. It is a characterization that happens to converge nicely with earlier comparisons between his poetry and the "Li Sao" by the misunderstood statesman Qu Yuan.

In this atmosphere of critical revisionism, the Qianlong emperor's (1735–1795) essay on Li Bo, included in the *Tang Song shichun*, his compilation of Tang and Song poetry published in 1751, seems at first glance mysteriously anomalous: "The two masters, Li and Du, [exemplify] what is called 'disparate melodies of equal polish' or 'different paths returning to the same place'; if you look at their poems in their entirety, you will apprehend this. Taibai is lofty and sublime (*gaoyi*), and therefore his words are free-ranging and unfettered (*zongzi buji*); soaring on high (*piao-piao*), he is possessed of a will to leave society and stand alone. Zimei is weighty and solemn (*chenyu*), his words profoundly incisive and clearly manifest; it is only when he has gone to the limit of his brush's propensity, and exhausted each twist and turn of the event at hand, that he stops."[53]

The emperor follows this simple and direct recitation of the stock expressions of Li Bo criticism with an equally familiar account of Li's experiences: his entry into the court through recognition of his natural genius rather than through the usual channels of civil service examinations; his dismissal from court because of his willful lack of propriety; his wanderings over the ancient lands of the empire; and the natural expression in his poetry of a combination of his unfettered nature and far-flung, unique experiences. This description, predictably, is immediately balanced with a parallel narrative recounting Du's travails and the resulting somber tone of his poetry. The whole text, especially when compared to the clear, polemical positions taken by other contemporary critics, reads as quaint and anachronistic.

The apparently formulaic quality of his entire essay, the simplicity with which he juxtaposes Li's celestial bon vivant and Du's solitary, earthbound sufferer, seem to bespeak a critic unconcerned with the polemics of the old Li-Du debates or the complexity of the Li-Du configuration that had been evolving over the preceding millennium. I suggest, however, that the polemical, reflexive critical context lends the emperor's words their significance. These are the writings of the era's anointed preserver and propagator of *wen,* and while most critics are intent upon laying claim, explicitly or implicitly, to an empirically based, objective perspective, the emperor invokes the authority of a more venerable, and less easily debated, argumentation. His rhetorical approach, derived from the "praise and blame" method of the *Book of Documents* (and attributed to China's first canon-former, Confucius), inheres almost exclusively in praise by inclusion and criticism by omission. Just as other critics of this period enact their criticism of Li Bo in their reaction to past criticism, the material under consideration for omission or inclusion extends beyond the poet's works to include the critical terminology that had become inseparable from any consideration of his work.

In the implicit spirit of "praise and blame" historiography, the emperor reproduces both Li's poetic oeuvre and its conventional critical vocabulary simply and without comment. This spare skeleton of unelaborated expressions, this mute reassertion of Li-Du complementarity, leaves room only for interpretation, not for debate. The power of the emperor's "argument" can be felt in the convergence of his authority with the act of sheer repetition: the reproduction of something essential, pared down, and ultimately untouchable.

Yet for all its apparent traditionalism, the emperor's critical stance shares an important feature with that of anti-traditionalist critics like Weng Fanggang, Li Diaoyuan, and Wang Qi, a feature as much derived from their shared late historical moment as from individual views. They all (probably inadvertently) treat Li Bo's poetic oeuvre and its accumulated commentary as one piece. At one end of the spectrum, the emperor mutely transmitted much-debated, if hoary, critical terms as though they, like the poetry itself, were beyond qualification and transformation; at the other end, critics like Weng Fanggang, Li Diaoyuan, and Wang Qi all relied on the transformation of familiar critical terms as their primary means of commenting on the poetry. But together they contributed to Li and Du's withdrawal into the elevated realm of the "ancients," a realm in which criticism and myth-making converge, and authoritative acts of transmission are more eloquent than the most meticulous foray into empirical criticism. This is not to say that everyone acquiesced in the transmission of a mythic, untouchable poetic persona. But the growing tendency to conceive of Li and Du as canonized and untouchable, along with the sheer weight of an ever increasing body of critical writings, made it more and more difficult for readers (especially readers who wrote) to respond directly to the poetry itself. In fact, several *shihua* of the period even seem to express a certain frustrated awareness of this situation in their direct and indirect admonitions to rely on one's own skills and perceptions as a reader of poetry.

Another critic who was aware of Li-Du criticism as a historical phenomenon (but who, like the emperor, tended to repeat the findings of that tradition as fundamental, immortal truths) was the historian and poet Zhao Yi (1727–1814), author of the *Oubei shihua*. A contemporary of the Qianlong emperor, Zhao seems to accept as a given the fundamental reliability of Li and Du's traditional personae, and focuses on rallying biographical and poetic evidence in support of those truths. In this way, Zhao Yi's Li-Du criticism bolstered the poets' claims to authenticity by forging a solid link between their specific poems and biographical experience, while amplifying Li's mythical aura, embedding him more deeply into the untainted and unattainable realm of the ancients.

Reading his review of Li and Du's joint critical history, we notice Zhao's display of his critical distance vis-à-vis that history. He attempts, first of all, to set the record straight, showing that Li and Du had first entered the pantheon as paired equals, and that even the (mistaken) Northern Song denigration of Li ultimately failed to expunge his name from its rightful place. The ensuing hiatus in Li's presence at Du's side, Zhao asserts, arose because "readers believed only Du could be studied, and dared not study Li Bo, proclaiming his divine genius unattainable."[54] Today, students of Li's critical history may well take for granted Zhao's observation that Li's fall from favor resulted more from the vicissitudes of intellectual history than from the innate qualities of his poetry. But this statement, like Wang Qi's earlier comment about readerly manipulations of critical terminology, enables Zhao to present himself as belonging to a more objective era, while also subscribing to the permanence of certain truths produced by, but beyond the reach of, history. In his review of another strand of Li's critical history, Zhao smoothly and eloquently lines up the "permanent truths"—canonizing myths—of Li Bo's poetics in the guise of a historical narrative:

Li Qinglian was himself the fallen incarnation of an immortal spirit. Sima Ziwei [Sima Chengzhen, 647–735],[55] upon his first glance, proclaimed that he possessed the "wind" of the immortals and the "bones" of the Dao, and that he could journey with [him] across the expanse of the eight directions; and He Zhizhang, upon his first glance, also exclaimed that [Li] was a "Banished Immortal." ... Those aspects of his poetry that are unattainable [through imitation or study] derive from the exalted and sublime quality of his spiritual understanding: he arrives as though on a gust of wind, then suddenly departs, neither fussing to carve out each passage and phrase, nor laboring to engrave [in the poem] his heart and incise [in it] his bones. He naturally possessed the irrepressible force of a celestial horse running across the sky. If you speak of his gravity, then it does not compare to that of Du, nor is his virility on a par with that of Han [Yu]. But if you compare Du and Han with him, they employ effort, which invariably leaves its trace; whereas he does not employ effort, and all he touches blooms with the vitality of spring. This is the difference between immortal and mortal.[56]

Other than Zhao's lyrical elegance, readers will find no more surprises in this passage than in the essay by the Qianlong emperor. Zhao summons, in swift succession, the entire array of anecdotes and critical qualifiers that had earlier been offered in lieu of positive description, qualifiers whose meaning used to be delineated at least partly through the contrastive example of Du Fu. Here, even more effectively than in the emperor's essay, the sheer repetition of old—indeed, nostalgic—images, begins to suggest not merely a consensus but an eternal truth. Even without the legitimacy lent by imperial voice, and even with the literary flourish that only a poet can provide, this passage rings with the authority of ancient knowledge. Such authority lends fresh meaning to old, deliberately elusive phrases, transforming them from negative contour to positive myth.

When Zhao turns his attention to Li Bo and Du Fu as a pair, he likewise seems to insist upon the pair's timeless unassailability. In the following passage, Zhao does away with sequential history, identifying Li-Du as both a source from which literature springs and an end after which there can be nothing new, in short, "ancient" in the truest sense of the word. "His whole life, Han Changli's [Han Yu's] heart strove only to reach the two masters, Li and Du. Looking at the time preceding Li and Du, there was as yet no Li-and-Du; thus the two masters' talent and vital spirit had free rein, each opening up a new territory, and each thus attaining eternal renown. By the time of Changli's [arrival], Li and Du were already there before [him]. So, even though he applied all of his strength to the transformation [of the tradition], he could not open even one new path."[57]

Even while joining many of his contemporaries in settling Li Bo and Du Fu safely in the protected niche of the ancients,[58] Zhao Yi does effect one interesting transformation of the Li Bo myth. He attributes to Li Bo the quality of magnanimity, a grandeur of spirit, in explaining why he did not succumb to the righteous bitterness typical of history's unemployed talents and unjustified exiles.[59] After citing numerous textual examples from Li's poems that "merely" mention the injustice of accusations leveled against the poet, Zhao Yi offers this final assessment of Li Bo's character: "Qinglian's breast was vast and capacious. He did not fret over petty grudges."[60]

Although generosity of spirit may seem like a minor addition to the traditional list of Li Bo's characteristics, and although this quality does not seem a far cry from the usual assertions of his lofty sublimity, there is a slight shift in its connotations. In early critiques it was common to present the Banished Immortal's remoteness from worldly cares as—for better or worse—the reason for his poetic "insubstantiveness." Here the same carefree attitude is rooted in the more laudable quality of high-mindedness, his refusal to get bogged down in the small injustices of a small world (and, not incidentally, petty attentions to poetic craft). Zhao's belief in the prominence of this quality permeates his writings about Li Bo, so much so that he frequently invokes poetic expressions of magnanimity (or lack thereof) as a basis for making and ascertaining textual attributions.[61]

Li Bo the Learnable

One of the most interesting phenomena to emerge out of the eighteenth-century Li-Du criticism is the galvanization of Li's inviolate and ineffable ancientness. Li Bo became part of the ancient canon, that body of knowledge recognized as essential to the continuation of literary culture, and also a transmitter of ancient literary and moral values—embodied in a plain, straightforward language closely tied to things real. The transformation, although seemingly inevitable, is not without its ironies. Here the unlearnable poet is ensconced among the literary treasures that must be learned, and the master of the "empty" image and the unfettered phrase is upheld as an avatar of substantive, unassailable authenticity.

Given the history of Li Bo's identification with general un-
substantiveness and fanciful forays through the clouds, it comes
as a bit of a surprise that this particular conception of Li's ancient-
ness is upheld even by writers who, at least in theory, relied heavily
on detailed textual and biographical analysis in their scholarship.
Zhang Xuecheng (1738–1802), for example, the renowned historian
who championed complete reliance on empirical evidence, and
who, in contrast to Zhao Yi, was harshly critical of Yuan Mei's
vision of instinct-based poetry, cited Li Bo as exemplary in his
understanding of the need for poetic truthfulness. Zhang borrows
Sikong Tu's use of the term *"qingzhen"* (pure and true) to charac-
terize Li Bo's poetic philosophy: "In the past, when Li Bo dis-
cussed poetry, he placed the highest value on the 'pure and true.'
This is the standard by which poetry has been discussed ever since
ancient times; and thus, it endures today as a criterion. The 'pure
and true' [writer] draws upon the erudition that lies within, then
recounts in poetry and prose what he has seen."[62]

In the spirit of Han Yu, and along with other scholars of the
age,[63] Zhang consistently makes a clear distinction between *guwen*
as a retroactively recognized (as well as eminently imitative and
learnable) genre and the natural, unselfconscious ancient writings
that *guwen* strives to replicate. He concludes one brief passage on
this subject saying, "The *'guwen'* rubric is distinct from the [actual]
utterances of the ancients."[64] This passage includes Li Bo and Han
Yu among the poets most cognizant of that distinction. According
to Zhang, they understood that the disappearance of the ancients,
and of ancient expression, was brought about by the emergence of
concerns with poetic genre, style, and form. Awareness of perfor-
mance, even if the performance strove to be as austere and spare as
possible, could only be to the detriment of the unpolished stuff of
which true poetry is made.[65] If Li and Han did go ahead and taste
of the tree of poetic knowledge, Zhang implies, they at least rec-
ognized they had done so and remembered full well what poetry
had been like before the fall.

Zhang Xuecheng's unquestioning embrace of Li Bo's ancient
purity comes as a bit of a surprise. Gone, it would seem, is the
old familiar tension between Li's treasured unsubstantiveness and

the avid, somewhat anxious assertions of his authenticity. Perhaps, from Zhang's distant perspective, Li Bo's proclamations of his own ancientness, particularly as articulated in the *Gufeng,* suffice as proof of that ancientness. Nowhere does Zhang, the empiricist historian, respond to the plethora of past charges claiming that Li is no ancient, and nowhere does he even attempt to account for Li's empty imagery.

Zhang's easy assimilation of Li's ancientness (in terms of both his canonicity and his authenticity) into his view of poetic history is the legacy of two important streams of critical argument: one that, in the spirit of Yan Yu's *Canglang shihua,* argued that poetic writing uniquely covers a range of expression beyond the reach of everyday language or articulated principle, and a second that, under the influence of Wang Yangming, debated forcefully and consistently for a substantive basis underlying manifestations of the quality of *xu*—for the recognition that the reality of a poet's inner world is on a par with that of the perceptible world. If Li-Du criticism offered a particularly propitious venue for exercising these ideas in the world of poetics, it seems just and natural that Li Bo be the foremost beneficiary of the critical transformation they inspired. When these two streams join, as they seem to in the writings of Zhang Xuecheng, one's understanding of poetic authenticity shifts accordingly. Now more than ever in the past, authenticity is understood as a function of the poet's cleaving to the experience of his specific relationship with specific objects or worlds. The poet's mode of expression is read as naturally reflecting these particular, inimitable, and irreproducible conditions.

Still, not all expressions of authenticity are equal, as suggested by Zhang's contemporary, Guan Shiming (1738–1798). Guan offers critiques of Tang poets from the perspective not of some absolute relationship between self and world, but of one that varies from person to person:

> "One person—one personality": this is something that Wang [Changling], Li [Qi], Gao [Shi], Cen [Shen], and Taibai all could achieve. But, "every poem—a [different] personality": this is something that Wang, Li, Gao, Cen, and Taibai could not accomplish. Du Gongbu's seven-character old-style poetry coheres with things and

renders their form, and organizes [these renderings] according to theme: like a lion in fury, crashing through rock; like the "fragrant elephant fording the river"[66] ... [his poetry's] innumerable humors and myriad manifestations cannot be fully conveyed in a name. Sorrow and joy without end, gazing above and below and so forgetting oneself, sighing as one stops and observes: meaning lies herein![67]

Guan prefers Du Fu's chameleon-like responsiveness to the outside world over Li Bo's responsiveness to his inner nature: evidence both of his admiration for a fellow empirical spirit and belief in Du's traditionally superior degree of substantiveness. At the same time, however, Guan's praise of Du Fu reflects a significant shift in values, a shift that is at least partly recognizable as one of the fruits of past Li-Du debates. Guan here presents Du's volatility and verve, and the ineffable quality of his achievement, as proof of authenticity. But not so long ago, the same poet's consistency and meticulousness, and the learnability of his method, were the touchstones of his authenticity.

This crossing over of terms from one poet to the other, which had long been a rhetorical strategy for maintaining Li Bo's status in a complementary relationship—a strategy openly criticized by Wang Qi—takes on new significance during a time when it is not Li Bo's poetry or his status that is at issue, but the accumulated critical writings that have become attached to his work. At this point in the process of mythification and canonization, as consensus-building becomes more important than selection and ranking, critics attribute desired literary qualities to both poets. The exchange of terms signals the wholesale attempt to invoke Li, Du, as well as Li-and-Du as ancient avatars of contemporary poetic values and embodiments of poetic plenitude. One of the terms that had been the most polarizing in the early Li-Du ranking debates, and whose semantic purview was most noticeably transformed over the course of the successive readjustments of the bipolar dynamic and the concomitant recession of the two poets into the realm of the ancients, is that of "learning."

Learnability was one of the oldest and most reliable pillars in the edifice of both Li-Du ranking and Li-Du bipolar complementarity. Learning's delineating role faltered with the rise of the personality- and instinct-based criticism of the late Ming, as readers determined that poetry, by its very nature, was unlearnable. Now, in what seems to be a direct reversal, the rise of Qing scholars' faith in textual evidence of even the most elusive qualities dictates that all poets are ultimately learnable.

But this reversal is only apparent. Not only has learning continued to be upheld as a unifying rather than a polarizing principle in evaluating the Li-Du pair, but the Ming view of learning demonstrably informs the criticism of the most empirical writers of the Qing. In reading the works of eighteenth- and nineteenth-century critics, one can see that they do not portray the path from textual analysis to true comprehension as direct and objectively accountable. Rather, the reader, having completed the rational analysis necessary in an initial approach to the poem, is then called upon to make an irrational and definitively indescribable leap into the realm beyond the words. True comprehension of any poet, including the unlearnable Li Bo, can be attained through the same two-step process: (1) intense scrutiny of surface form so as finally to divest the poem of its shell and (2) instinctive penetration into the ineffable core of intentions or vital spirit.

Li Zhaoyuan (n.d.), a tireless philologue and critic, provides a good example of the era's growing interest in the investigation of concrete detail, tempered by a profound awareness of and respect for what is fundamentally unutterable. For all his passion for line-by-line analyses of tone and rhythm,[68] for all his meticulousness in assigning specific biohistorical events to any number of poems, Li Zhaoyuan's understanding of ancientness is articulated in terms that expose this type of literary excavation as a necessary but rudimentary stage in the reading process. For Li Zhaoyuan, all manifestations of poetic excellence can be traced back to the *Shijing* and the *Chuci*, but that excellence must be attained through the effortless, natural expression of one's own vital spirit. In a refinement of Zhang Xuecheng's distinction between ancient genres and ancient expression, Li Zhaoyuan reminds his readers that such natural expression is possible only upon having penetrated and internalized the spirit of the ancients. And for Li Zhaoyuan, there is little doubt that Li and Du occupy a privileged place among the ancients whose spirits are to be internalized.

Incorporating Li and Du as primary models in his instructions for reading and writing poetry, Li Zhaoyuan prides himself on his profound understanding not of the ancient *Shijing* and *Chuci,* but of the ancient Li Bo and Du Fu. Like sacred texts, and unlike more pedestrian literary works, the works of Li and Du cannot be approached lightly, but must be arrived at through a long period of preparation, of self-cultivation ("He who would read [their] poems must first put in order his inner nature"). "In studying the poetry of Li and Du, one must first observe wherein lies the guiding intent of their existence *(mingyi);* one must strive to discern how, in each and every word, the poem cleaves to the [poet's] intent, how each word is fixed and appropriate, how one thread penetrates and completes the whole without there being any obstruction. Only then will you have apprehended it."[69]

Li Zhaoyuan's reading process begins at the microscopic level, where the reader first locates the poet's original intent in individual words, then considers how the words cohere in a unified whole. As the reader becomes more familiar with the poem, Li urges an approach not unlike that applied to calligraphy: recognizing the sequence of words as the trace of a gesture, the reader examines the trace to discern its animating and unifying spirit—or, to return to the first expressionistic definition of poetry, the "intent" *(zhi)* taking form in the words. When one has truly grasped the under-lying intent, and the path through which that intent was incarnated in language, one understands the superfluousness, and even the futility, of trying to copy the external trappings of rhythm and word combinations. Clearly, the ultimate goal of studying poetry is to learn how to do it; perhaps this is why his step-by-step articulation of the reading process echoes Lu Ji's third-century description of the act of poetic writing. When the student or the reader arrives at the moment of attempting his own composition, he must turn inward and forget the factual embodiment of all that he has learned: "He must discard everything [he has learned]; not only does he no longer know of the existence of Li and Du, he knows not that there have ever been the Han and Wei [dynasties], nor that there ever were the 'Three Hundred Poems' [the *Shijing*]. . . . Then he must directly express what he harbors in his breast, completing the whole in a single breath. Only then can our generation also lay claim to having real poetry."[70]

As if in demonstration of its own recommendations, Li Zhaoyuan's model for the study and creation of "ancient" poetry is all the more moving and persuasive for its own ancient tone, for its deep resonance with the pattern followed by many such narratives in the past. Readers will sense its harmony with Lu Ji's powerful account of receptivity to the world (and its writings) followed by the spirit voyage through his inner world (a narrative that reappears, in various forms, in the recommendations of many *fugu* writers). Present, too, is the Buddhist-inspired process of long-term intense study, followed by forgetting, and the spontaneous enlightenment espoused by numerous Neo-Confucian thinkers. In Li Zhaoyuan's text, and in the writings of many of his contemporaries, these two archetypal modes of learning converge in the single ideal of poetic authenticity. And, as the most reliable repositories of ancient poetic authenticity are the canonical texts, in this view, Li and Du are as one, ancient in their authenticity, authentic in their ancientness.

As the Li-Du critical tradition moves into the nineteenth century, critics of varying persuasions tend to agree on two major points: first, that study and inspiration are interdependent, and that that interdependency is manifest in both of the similarly interdependent activities of reading and writing poetry; second, that the nexus of this creative web of study, inspiration, reading, and writing resides in the poet's intent, both as the poem's originating and unifying stimulus and as the reader's ultimate objective. While none of this is new, the syncretic spirit of the age and the accumulated years of debate seem to have honed writers' abilities to soften partisan lines without going to the effort of superfluous explanation. This change, detectable and describable primarily as a rhetorical phenomenon, is a reliable sign of a will directed toward conservation rather than elimination.

In this intellectual context, previously incompatible approaches to Li-Du criticism, and to the evaluation of Li Bo in particular, coexist—occasionally in the writings of a single author—and even seem to support one another. On the one hand, critics continue to develop the technical apparatus for articulating and analyzing the various poetic manifestations of intention,[71] and interest in biographical interpretation continues to grow. This is evident in the work of important figures like Fang Dongshu (1772–1851) and Chen Hang (1785–1826), as well as in that of more minor ones like Chen Guangpu (n.d.), Qiao Songnian (n.d.), and Lin Changyi (1803–1876).[72] On the other hand, hyperbolic and lyrical encomia to unlearnability, naturalness, and unfetteredness remain as common as ever, often composed by the same writers who elsewhere apply themselves to philological discourse.[73] Throughout these writings, Li and Du, now recognized exemplars of venerated ancientness and embodiments of the combined virtues of study and inspiration, seem close to merging into a single symbol of poetic greatness.

One of the literary thinkers of the time who attempted an exhaustive, analytical account of the characteristics that inspiration and learning, respectively, contribute to poetry was the writer and poet Yao Ying (1785–1853). For Yao, endurance through the ages constitutes the ultimate test of greatness in a world where all things—including man and his writings—are ephemeral. Li and Du have endured because both equally incarnate perfect blends of study and inspiration:

> In poetry, there is that which can be attained through study (xue), and that which cannot be attained through study; there is that which can be attained through illumination (wu), and that which cannot be attained through illumination. The refinement and depth of prosodic regulation, the force and precision of tonal resonance, the weightiness of the poet's brush, the crafted beauty of style: these can be attained through study. The understated flavor of poetic intention (yiqu), the soaring loftiness of incitative images (xingxiang), the extraordinary innovations [implemented by] the spirit's inner world (shenjing), the distant stretches of emotive resonance (qingyun): these cannot be attained through study. What can be attained through study does not depend on wondrous illumination; what can-

not be attained through study cannot be achieved without illumination.... The two masters Li and Du stand between that which can be attained through illumination, and that which cannot. Both bring to full realization naturalness *(tian)* and learning *(xue)*.[74]

The confidence in language and rationality that inspired this straightforward separation of the learnable and the unlearnable, the describable and the indescribable, is impressive. Equally impressive is the casual way in which this confidence is balanced with an equally profound respect for the reality—the substantiveness— of the unqualifiable, elusive realm of affect. The symmetry of the passage presents as a given the parity of knowledge and inspiration, and by selecting familiar conventional expressions to evoke inspiration, Yao helps inscribe the unqualifiable in the critical lexicon without limiting it within the boundaries of precise, positivistic description. Just as the coexistence of the learnable and the unlearnable is an undisputed necessity in every poem worthy of the name, so Li and Du emerge as a joint example of these joint virtues.

Thanks to this unifying view, it is possible for the witty author of the *Laosheng changtan,* Yan Junshou (ca. 1775–ca. 1826), to conclude a line-by-line study of Li Bo's poem, "On Ending My Voyage and Returning to My Former Abode at Shimen" ("Xiatu gui Shimen jiuju"), with the exclamation, "If you ask for directions from this point, you will realize that the Wuling Immortal Spring is still within the human realm."[75] Yan thus gently observes that it is possible to "ask directions" from Li Bo as well as Du Fu, and to follow untraceable traces into the inaccessible realm of the immortals—without denying their essential untraceability. Li Bo is still the Banished Immortal. But as an *ancient* poet, he has necessarily bequeathed traces of a voyage that become readers' to follow as best they can. As attentive as one must be to the mechanics of a text, Yan cautions, "When reading in this life, you must both bury your head and attack [study the words with intense focus] and open wide your eyes [to the world around you]; only then can you ferret out the [poem's] intention."[76]

Li and Du's inextricable plenitude is not only expressed

implicitly in the crossing over and broadening of critical qualifiers evident in the writings cited above. In at least one instance, their interdependence is explicitly justified in terms that verge on ontological necessity. Qian Shirui (19 c.) wrote extensively about the history of the notion of *cai* (genius) in Chinese letters. One piece, "On the Genius of Li the Banished Immortal," describes at length Li Bo's unique incarnation of "immortal genius," adhering to the customary rhetoric of negative contours by presenting specific contrasting examples to bolster his case. As might be expected, Qian concludes by comparing Du Fu's achievement with Li Bo's:

> Later generations have called [Du Fu] the Prince of Poetry *(shiwang)*, the Sage of Poetry *(shisheng)*, and the Poet Historian *(shishi)*. As a prince, he occupies [a position of] greatness; as a sage, he reaches the ultimate [of poetic possibility]; as a historian, [his works] possess the qualities of implicitness and rational discourse. It is because of these qualities that he alone emerged as foremost [poet] of his age. But prince, sage, or historian, he remains a man of human affairs. An immortal, however, rises above [the realm] of prince, sage, and historian, to follow a different paradigm.
>
> And so it is that, as long as the universe contains Shaoling's poetic renown, it needs the genius of the Banished Immortal to highlight his distinction.[77]

So it goes through much of the nineteenth century, with some critics portraying Li and Du's interdependence as a function of their complementarity, and others depicting it as a result of their equal successes in incarnating, and inciting, the dual values of knowledge and inspiration. By now the terms of the debate have somewhat settled, and there is the incontrovertible sense that Li and Du's existence marks a defining moment in the history of Chinese poetry. Together, they incarnate everything you need to know about poetic excellence, the plenitude—not just of perfection—but of infinite possibility. Even as writers like Lin Changyi plead for an end to the easy generalizations commonly used to qualify the landmarks of literary history,[78] most critics do not hesitate to name these two as supreme.[79] Shi Shan (1835–?), a much appreciated "rationalist" poet of the time, portrays the understandable exasperation that some readers must certainly have felt at this seemingly uncritical acceptance of the status quo, only to uphold Li and Du's canonical standing after all: "Someone asked, 'Were there no poets before Li and Du?' I replied, 'There were also sages before Confucius. In poetry, to venerate Li and Du is the same as when, in learning, one venerates Confucius. Ever since the existence of Li and Du, who has been able to attain greatness without having studied Li and Du?'"[80]

Some years later, Chen Tingzhuo (1853–1892), a well-known writer and theorist of "song-poems" (ci), characterized their historical status as not simply ancient, but as constituting a turning point: "I would say that [the period] from the Odes and '[Li] Sao' through Taibai constitutes poetry's orthodox period, its ancient period; and from Du Fu onward constitutes poetry's [period of] innovation."[81] This brief statement, uttered on the eve of the reformist upheaval of the late nineteenth century, seems a fitting culmination to the centuries during which critics jockeyed to find just the right balance between the dualities that had characterized poetic debate in general and the Li-Du debate in particular: empty and full, unlearnable and learnable, inspiration and knowledge. Yes, Chen seems to say, these two men embody the whole of our literary tradition; and if, in strictly historical terms, one represents an end and the other a beginning, there can be no literary moment that is not inhabited by both.

ROMANCING THE IMMORTAL

In some ways, it would be nice to end the story here: Li Bo standing shoulder to shoulder with Du Fu, classical, compelling, and, above all, venerable. Except for random, local expressions of preference, and correspondingly superfluous protests against Li-Du ranking (protests that continue today, but are always implicitly aimed at the past), it seemed that their joint survival through the rise and fall of various critical schools guaranteed literary immortality for them both. This moment of equilibrium reflects the attainment of a hard-won recognition of the interdependence not only of the two poets, but of both sets of complementary moments making up the poetic process.

But equilibrium proved neither particularly fruitful nor sustainable. On the eve of the twentieth century, the same centuries-long fine-tuning of critical terms that had ensconced Li Bo in the poetic canon seemed to have brought discussion of their poetry to an impasse. Pithy epithets that stuck—Li's "Banished Immortal" and Du's "Sage of Poetry" being the most enduring—had all but hardened into convenient and all too familiar symbols, while such previously evocative descriptive terms as "strange," "knowledge," "innovation," "ancient," and related expressions had been applied to both poets so often that they were of little use in serious discussion. Li Bo's ascent into the loftiest recesses of the canon, and the mythification and resulting crystallization of his persona, seemed to have raised a significant barrier to fresh, direct inquiry into his poetry—and of the poet that poetry was believed to reveal.

It is impossible to know, of course, how this impasse would have been broken if, at the end of the nineteenth century, China's intellectuals had not had to face the challenge the West posed to their own sense of cultural identity. But, confronted with this new culture, the problem of stagnation—in all its forms—emerged as foremost on their minds. As China's intellectuals confronted Western technological and military superiority, and as they absorbed into their cultural lexicon the new bipolar dynamics of China and the West, and tradition and modernity, intellectual complacency was identified as among the habits of thought most regrettably typical of the so-called Chinese national character.[82] The predominant response was to combat that stultifying complacency by scrutinizing Chinese culture through the newly acquired lens of Euro-American ideas, not merely in the realm of the sciences, but in the realm of cultural expression deemed most fundamental: literature and language.

Liang Qichao (1873–1929) was among those who, in the hope of closing the distance between China and her Western adversaries, initiated the trend toward what Lydia Liu describes as "a radical subversion of the classical canon as the legitimate source of meaning for Chinese culture and literature."[83] Reconfiguring traditional literary taxonomy and critical terminology to conform to Western categories, Liang is often credited with promoting the novel as the most modern (and thus desirable) form of literary expression, eclipsing the long-standing predominance of poetry, and Tang poetry in particular. But in fact Liang Qichao's emphasis upon the novel did not prevent him from suggesting new ways to look at traditional poetry. His description of Li Bo's poetry (apparently one of his favorites in his youth),[84] in particular, would prove to be especially influential, introducing a term that came to rival "Banished Immortal" in frequency of utilization, if not necessarily in suggestive resonance. Presumably looking for a modern qualifier with which to represent—and preserve—Li Bo's canonical status, Liang introduced the term *"langman"* into the body of Li Bo criticism, a term that is the very embodiment of border crossings and so defies easy translation.

Although the premodern expression *langman* had never caught on as a qualifying adjective for Li Bo's poetry, it appears during the Song Dynasty referring to precisely the quality of freedom and unfetteredness with which Li is associated.[85] By the time Liang invoked it, it had been reintroduced into China from Japan, whence it had been borrowed by the Japanese to translate (and transliterate) references to the European Romantic movement.[86] The dual origin of this term, whose foreign and traditional connotations not only coexist but overlap, is remarkably suited to this poet, whose own origins are equally suggestive of the foreign and the cosmopolitan. Practically speaking, its composite signification would prove especially efficient in protecting the Banished Immortal through the first phases of his daunting transition into modernity.

Liang's use of *"langman"* as a qualifier for Li Bo's poetic persona confirms that the introduction of modern, foreign conceptual terms did not simply provoke a passive revision of earlier characterizations of either his persona or his work. Rather, it provides an excellent example of what Lydia Liu has described as the active "'confrontations' ... between China, Japan, and the West at the site of translation"[87]—confrontations that reenact adjustments in the bipolar thought that had shaped Li Bo criticism since the beginning. Belying the radical break from the past that late Qing reformers strove to effect, Liang's essay constitutes a virtual anatomy of this mutual and active confrontation, where the ancient, unattainable Li Bo is revealed to be just as instrumental in framing and consecrating the application of *langman* to the classical canon as was the Western idea of Romanticism in the reconfiguration of Li Bo.

Liang begins his essay "Zhongguo yunwen litou suo biaoxian de ganqing" (On the emotions expressed in Chinese lyrical writings) with a normative description of the quality most prized in the reading of *langman* literature, the imagination (*xiangxiangli*), a quality he quickly identifies as Li Bo's particular gift:[88] "It is always the case that, in *Romantic (langmanpai)* literature, the more fertile and bizarre the imagination, the more evident [the work's] brilliance. Indeed, this point was the specialty of the great master of the High Tang, Li Taibai."[89] At first reading, it is difficult to interpret this opening as anything other than a move toward the complete replacement of classical Chinese terminology with an imported system. Everything about this passage seems to urge the wholesale reworking of previous assumptions about literature in general, and about Li Bo in particular.

To begin with, the switch from classical Chinese to the vernacular (difficult to convey in English translation) emphatically draws the ancient, cloud-jumping poet and his works earthward, to a level more accessible to his readers. Not only does this literary act decree Li Bo describable, it asserts that he is describable in the words of daily intercourse. Second, and just as jarring, Liang's insertion of new, foreign terms to qualify Li Bo suggests that this new, concrete way of describing the past will open the door to "learning" Li Bo once and for all.

But Liang moves quickly to defend the validity of this radical reorientation by appealing to the traditional rhetoric of negativity: "Take, for example, his 'Gong wu du he' (Master, don't cross the river), which was entirely elaborated out of the ancient *yuefu*, 'Konghou yin.' The sixteen words of 'Konghou yin' constitute one of the supreme works of all time; how is it possible to imitate it? The first half of Li's poem ... already depicts a Yellow River that seems invested with numinosity (*shenmixing*). The second half recounts the truth in accordance with the legend, and then says, in illusory images even more fantastic and terrifying [second half of poem]. This poem takes the original 'Konghou yin' and then imbues it with a type of *langman* quality, thus transforming it into an [original] creation *(chuangzuo)*."[90]

Li Bo's *langman* quality, then, consists primarily in his usual inimitability and unfoundedness, at least, that is, until the concluding section of this essay, where Liang subsumes those qualities under the newer, Western rubric of imagination: "Taibai's *Collected Works* contain many examples of this type, all of which can serve to demonstrate the greatness of his imagination, and his ability to invent a world *(gouzao jingjie)* that others could not invent."[91]

Liang's flair for continuity-in-change may be as impressive as Li Bo's genius for substance-in-emptiness. In declaring him capable of inventing "a world that others cannot invent," Liang Qichao marks Li Bo's profound differences, not only vis-à-vis the Li Bo critical tradition, but also in regard to the poetic ideals of authenticity espoused by the critical tradition as a whole. The heart of his critique lies in the phrase *gouzao jingjie*, translated here as "inventing a world," which constructs a neologistic, radically nontraditional concept out of two classical Chinese terms. The late classical term *jingjie*, popularized by Liang's contemporary, Wang Guowei (1877–1927), can be glossed as "a composite impression of coherence in the presented world evoked by a particular poem or by a collection of poems."[92] As used by Wang Guowei, the coherent "world" that emerges from poetic writing is the natural, unintended rendition of the otherwise ineffable encounter with the real, perceptible world. But as the direct object of the verb "to construct," Wang Guowei's ineffable, naturalistic "world" slips into the describable, constructed realm of fictional representation. With this, Li Bo's unfounded panoramas are translated, almost perversely, into explicitly invented scenes understood as wholly coterminous with the text: existing exclusively within the bounds of language. This transposition may have saved Li Bo from charges of inauthenticity, but it also deprived him of a significant degree of his treasured elusivenss. In effect, he is transformed from a Banished Immortal to a teller of immortality tales. Liang appears to be sensitive to this loss, for he attempts to recover it by invoking yet another Western-derived category: that of purely aesthetic (in other words, divinely inspired) beauty: "Lyrics such as these, when regarded from an exclusively aesthetic standpoint, are quite valuable. They are not invested with any significance whatsoever, but mean only to express the ethereal *(kongling)* and unadulterated aesthetic sensibility *(meigan)*."[93]

Liang Qichao's defense of beauty for its own sake is surprising enough.[94] But then, as if defending Li Bo, and perhaps even himself, against the Song dynasty charge of emptiness, Liang actually pairs the poet with his most notorious Song critic, Wang Anshi, yoking them together as two poets whose purely imaginative and aesthetic works are solidly rooted in their unique "lofty and capacious" inner natures: "Those in the category of Taibai and Jiefu [Wang Anshi] possess breasts that are lofty and capacious, and that is why they are able to admit this type of literary work. Du Gongbu, for example, even though he is the Sage of Emotion, would never be able to produce such sentences."[95]

Liang Qichao's overall portrayal of Li Bo's *langman* quality grows out of a traditional comprehension of the faculty of imagination he locates at its core, which is an imagination comprising that familiar blend of textual knowledge and personal nature.[96] This "modern" rendition of Li Bo's contribution to Chinese literature not only maintains the traditional knowledge/talent bipolarity, belying any easy application of the term "Romantic,"[97] it also neatly embraces the traditional critical concept of *qi* (strangeness), so as to include its entire semantic range, covering everything from the unique and extraordinary to the outright strange and bizarre. As Liang hyperbolically explains it, by daring to elaborate "one of the supreme works of all time," Li Bo demonstrates his uniqueness among poets. By imbuing the landscape with shades of the numinous and the terrible, he integrates the strange.

Finally, Liang's most obvious point of continuity with traditional discourse is his tacit acceptance—despite his better judgment, one might say—of Li Bo's status as a great poet. If, as is well known, one of Liang Qichao's main criteria for excellence in poetry is poetry's popular base and usefulness as a political tool, his allowance for a special category of poetry bereft of any invested significance and concerned with nothing more than pure aesthetic sensibility is a bit surprising. But Liang Qichao does not reject or even significantly criticize the canonized poet. His reluctance, partly an expression of Liang's own transitional position among modernist reformers, can also be at least partly attributed to the assimilating nature of Li Bo critical discourse. Seen in this way, Liang's use of the term *langman* can be understood as yet another step in the lengthy process by which Li's poetry had been reformulated and reconciled with successive new (and sometimes potentially hostile) poetic movements, eventually creating a kind of protective shell ensuring his canonical status.

All this is not to say, however, that *langman* made no difference in the depiction of Li's persona or poetry. For all its consonance with accepted readings of Li Bo's unfetteredness and unfoundedness, and for all its reliance on the continuation of received tradition, Liang's application of *langman* brought about an important shift in Li Bo criticism, if only through its as yet tacit exclusion of two heretofore essential ingredients: ancientness and immortality. Both of these qualifiers provoked readers with reformist sensibilities: the one because of its implied acceptance of the innate superiority of the distant past, and the other for its suggestive sanction of certain superstitious holdovers from that past. The immortal, divine associations survived (and still do, if almost exclusively in popular lore),[98] even as Li Bo's celestial aura was all but extinguished under the relatively definable, if not strictly scientific, rubric of the imagination. But Li's ancientness was profoundly and permanently transformed.

Looking back at the emergence of ancientness as the most inclusive and least reductive term in the Li Bo critical vocabulary, it is easy to forget—until the eruption of the modern reform movement in which Liang played a leading role—the emphasis that qualifier places upon the past. After all, as almost everyone from Han Yu to Wang Fuzhi (and beyond) had insisted, to be of the ancients is not to write like them, but to be true to one's own experience in the world during one's own time. The invocation of ancientness to legitimize vivid examples of individual (if not individualist) expression had become common practice. No poet's corpus had served as a more persuasive demonstration of this conception of ancientness, or was more responsible for its transformation, than Li Bo's. Perhaps the independent strain of ancientness had succeeded so well that its nomenclature seemed odd, if not downright oxymoronic. Certainly modern readers bent on reform could have seen little advantage in qualifying unfettered, authentic expression as being in any way ancient; better by far to characterize his inimitable ability to invent worlds as being passionately individualistic and undeniably modern. Liang Qichao's introduction of *langman* into discussions of Li Bo's work, despite Liang's own conservatism, utterly removes the past as a legitimizing agent of Li Bo's unfetteredness. It is replaced with a more contemporary figure of foreign origin: the loner at odds with society.

On the surface, the replacement of ancientness and immortality by *langman* and *xiangxiangli* appears to be consistent with previous transformations within Li Bo critical discourse, especially since the period of his mythification. It is just another example of complementary bipolar characteristics—in this case, east and west—being modified to counterbalance one another. Even Liang Qichao's apparently radical characterization preserved the familiar Li Bo, transmitting the unfetteredness, unfoundedness, and "capacious breast" (not to mention the indispensable pairing with Du Fu) that had thus far permitted an increasingly broad and nuanced, if also gradually neutralized, depiction of both his poetry and his persona. But this particular shift in vocabulary, carried in the new critical language of the vernacular, *baihua*, had another profound effect on the Li Bo critical tradition.

By replacing the suggestive plenitude of literary bipolar expression with the positivistic naming characteristic of the spoken language, Liang Qichao initiated a move away from prudent, open-ended characterization, paving the way toward an assured and confining caricature. From the beginning, the appreciation of Li Bo had been transmitted in the language of divine imagery and negative contour, rhetorical means that relied on the nuances and ambiguities of binary language to capture, without destroying, his precious unqualifiability. Now binary discourse was abandoned in favor of straightforward description, both in the choice of terms and in the unambiguous *baihua* in which those terms are couched.[99]

The term *"langman,"* both because of its neologistic savor and its this-worldly embodiment of a superficially translated Western individualism, effectively clears all traces of ancientness from Li Bo's revered independence, and blots out the divine, celestial aura from his banishment and wanderings. Its limitations, however, lie not so much in what *langman* means, but in what it fails to mean. Lacking the layered historical patina of the older, more repetitive vocabulary, *langman* introduced into Li Bo criticism the promise of a positive delineation of characteristics whose value had always inhered in their very elusiveness. What resulted was not so much an elusive master of uncategorizable poetry as what Michelle Yeh has identified as a "tragic hero," an accessible, mundane reincarnation of the ancient "misunderstood worthy," ready to be inserted into a poem or play as a symbol of the modern writer's "pursuit of supreme beauty at the expense of the approval of the mundane world."[100]

PART II

✧

Reading
the
Poems

CHAPTER 3

The Performance of Ancientness in the "Ancient Airs"

How long since the "Elegantiae" were
*   composed—*
And, with my demise, who then shall carry
*   on?*
The airs of the kings: given over to withered
*   creeping vines,*
And the Warring States: overgrown with
*   brambles and thorns.*
. . . .
I am determined to condense and retell,
The brilliance [my writings] emit will
*   illuminate a thousand springtimes.*
Should an aspiring sage establish himself,
I will stop writing when the "unicorn is
*   caught."*

大雅久不作
吾衰竟誰陳
王風委蔓草
戰國多荊榛
…
我志在刪述
垂輝映千春
希聖如有立
絕筆於獲麟

—Li Bo, *Gufeng* #1

ONE OF THE more puzzling questions raised by the current arrangement of Li Bo's collected works concerns the prominent and isolated position accorded the *Gufeng* (Ancient airs), fifty-nine ancient-style poems grouped together to form the second *juan* of the collection. If frequency of translation and selection for anthologies are any indication, today these poems hardly figure among the most beloved of his works. Compared to the ubiquitous and nearly unanimous praise for Li Bo's *yuefu* poems and his regulated quatrains, unabashed admiration for the *Gufeng* is rare. Even *Gufeng* #1, cited above, the most frequently quoted poem in the group, is judged important less for its poetic quality than for its handy summary of what many readers take to be Li Bo's own critical bent. It offers the only instance of extended overt literary criticism in his entire works.[1]

Neither genre nor poem cycle, the *Gufeng* are nevertheless grouped in a single *juan,* separate from, but on a par with, formal genres such as *fu* or *yuefu.*[2] It is not immediately clear why the *Gufeng* are united to the exclusion of other poems written on similar themes and in a similar style, and under so weighty a title. Even as early as the Ming dynasty, scholars wondered at the rationale underlying this particular grouping, and at least one modern scholar has recently argued against the exclusivity of the *Gufeng,* asserting that any serious analysis of Li Bo's work in this mode must be extended to twenty-eight other similar poems scattered throughout his corpus.[3] In addition, in at least one case, a poem included in the *Gufeng* (#36) is all but duplicated later in the corpus, under the title *"Ganxing* #7" (Spontaneous feelings).[4] Nevertheless, having been reprinted and read as a separate—if frequently shifting—group of poems ever since the first appearance of his collected works, *Caotang ji* (Grass hut collection), edited by his uncle, Li Yangbing, the *Gufeng* have acquired meaning as group.[5]

While not all consider the *Gufeng* to be among the most successful of Li Bo's poems,[6] some of the most influential critics not only acquiesce in their editorially imposed centrality, but celebrate these poems as the essence of all of Li Bo's work. Zhao Yi, the Qing dynasty author of the influential *Oubei shihua,* for example, singles out *Gufeng* #1 as "the culmination of a lifetime of artistic genius."[7] And, discussing the group as a whole, the modern scholar (and author of one of the definitive articles on the subject) Qiao Xiangzhong characterizes the *Gufeng* as encompassing Li Bo's "representative works."[8] "Culmination" and "representative": two words that suggest that at least some critics, especially those writing during the late Ming and beyond, perceive in these poems a compendium of Li Bo's salient characteristics, bestowing upon them the status of a kind of poetic signature.

But what exactly renders this signature recognizable throughout a body of poems as seemingly diverse as any random gathering of pieces from Li Bo's oeuvre? Xiao Shibin, Xu Zhenqing, and Hu Zhenheng—all of them editors of and commentators on the earliest extant editions of Li Bo's collected works—consistently qualify these poems as "articulations of his intent": a mix of declarative statement, allusion, and allegory employed by the poet to convey his most urgent and profound feelings. This unifying reading of the *Gufeng*, invoking both the process of natural, unpremeditated poetic creation first encoded in the "Great Preface" to the *Shijing*[9] and the Confucian allegorical exegesis traditionally applied to the ancient canon, effectively identifies the *Gufeng* as the purest embodiment of Li Bo's fidelity to ancient authenticity. This view of the *Gufeng* justifies, in turn, the application of meticulous exegesis, much more than does Li Bo's declaration of allegiance to pre-Jian'an poetry in the first poem.

Assertions of Li Bo's "ancient" poetics proliferated with the rise of characterological criticism during the late Ming, as critics invoked the "Great Preface" to promote poets' ability to remain true to their inner nature. Particularly useful for defending Li Bo's emptiness against denigrating comparisons with Du Fu's conscientious grounding in reality, the supple, unconfining designation "ancientness" allowed critics to embrace the unqualifiable poetics of Li Bo, encapsulating as it did unspecified blends of knowledge and inspiration, rule-boundedness and freedom.

One means of securing the ancient pedigree of the *Gufeng* has been to confirm its place in the company of other "ancient" poems. Partly in response to allusions found within the poems, and partly because of the critical stance Li Bo ostentatiously assumes in the first poem, critics have been able to situate the *Gufeng* within a lineage of earlier poems already recognized as embodying similar manifestations of ancientness. So Wang Yunxi, in his introduction to the *Li Bo ji jiaozhu*, joins a host of Chinese, Japanese, and

American scholars in assigning these poems to the tradition of Ruan Ji's *Yonghuai* (Singing of my feelings) and Chen Zi'ang's *Ganyu* (Moved by what I have encountered).[10] In such criticism, Li Bo's repetition of certain images and apparent imitations of their utilization are frequently cited as signs of generic affinity, then read as Li's desire to assume a role in both literary and moral history identical to that of the poets with whom he chooses to be associated.

This construction of historical and generic continuity, accurate as far as it goes, both draws attention to and bypasses one of the most arresting characteristics of the *Gufeng*. While these readings encourage the recognition that the *Gufeng* openly aspire to the ancient "authenticity" or immediacy exemplified by Ruan Ji and Chen Zi'ang, they tend to gloss over the way the poet uses those familiar signs of ancientness and the attitude toward ancientness that way expresses. I suggest that Li Bo is neither engaging in a simple continuation of their poetics nor parodying it. Rather, the *Gufeng* manifest—and in effect revive—the ideal of ancientness through the representation of the poetic act in all its blatant repetitiveness.

TOWARD A PERFORMANCE OF ANCIENTNESS: TRANSLATIONS OF A TITLE

Although the term *"gufeng"* was already in use as a way to refer to speech or gestures executed in the spirit or style of the ancients, Li Bo appears to have been the first to use it as a title. Taken separately, the words that compose it—*"gu"* and *"feng"*—have precedents in earlier poetry. *"Feng"* can mean "in the style of," but as a poem title, it translates as "airs," recalling the "Airs of the States" (*Guofeng*), the largest of the five sections of the *Shijing*. With Confucius traditionally cited as its editor and compiler, there is no older or more venerable poetry anthology than the *Shijing*. The attribution holds no real currency today, but Confucius continues to be closely associated with the collection, his reverence for it having been recorded at several points in his conversations.[11] The age-old critical connotations of *"feng,"* most handily translated "influence," further enhance the title's ancient resonance, if only because of its origins in the "Great Preface."[12] When *"feng"* appears in the title of a Tang poem, readers can expect to find a worthy successor to the *Shijing*, endowed not only with its spirit of pure, unsullied virtue, but also with the capacity of inspiring moral integrity in others.

Given the strong "ancient" connotations of "airs," the additional use of "ancient" *(gu)* seems at best emphatic, and at worst redundant. The most familiar use of the term during the Tang appears in the expression *"guti shi"* (ancient-style poetry).[13] Understood primarily in terms of their opposition to *jinti shi* (recent-style poetry), *guti shi* eschewed the strict set of tonal and prosodic rules to which recent-style poems adhered. As recent-style poetry reached its peak, poets who appeared to be ignoring its rules were more likely to be transgressing them in the interest of appearing as spontaneous and authentic as the poets of ancient times.

But *gu* does not merely indicate what a poem is not; it also points to its positive affiliation with certain poetic forebears, implying an intention to continue in or return to the ancient tradition. For the Tang reader, the ancient poem worthy of its name aspired to recover the direct, unselfconscious, and unadorned expression that was identified with the tradition of *shi yan zhi* (poetry articulating intent), as first described in the "Great Preface" to the *Shijing*. Literary ideals that place the "substantial, simple, and moral over the refined, brilliantly crafted, and sensuous"[14] were, by Li Bo's time, recognizable traits of the *fugu* (return to antiquity) movement that came into its own during the first half of the eighth century. On rereading the first of Li Bo's *Gufeng*, one could well read this group of poems as a straightforward expression of his allegiance to past poetic principles.

But Li Bo was no joiner. He was hardly one to subscribe to any particular school of thought, about poetry or about anything else. His occasional impassioned declarations notwithstanding, the rich variation in his poetic practice attests to the fact that Li Bo was hardly a single-minded follower of the *fugu* movement.[15] Certainly contemporary readers did not see him in this light, and it was perhaps only in response to the Li-Du debate that later *fugu* practitioners embraced Li Bo as they had Du Fu. Up until the Ming–Qing transition, *fugu* poets like Han Yu and Yuan Zhen, and even Su Shi, were more inclined to present Li Bo as the self-indulgent foil to Du Fu's socially engaged, altruistic sagehood. As for the possibility that the *Gufeng* represent a change of heart after a lifetime of frivolous self-indulgence, the knowledge that they were composed over the course of the poet's entire productive life precludes any such argument for an aesthetic and moral awakening late in life.

If Li Bo's status as champion of ancient poetics is shaky at best, how is one to approach the *Gufeng*? One solution has been to marginalize them in relation to his work as a whole and dismiss them as just an exercise in style. Critics of this turn of mind identify these works as the descendants of a subgenre of poems originating in the Six Dynasties, whose avowed aim was to imitate the ancients, and whose titles said as much. As early as the fourth century, poems bearing titles like "In Imitation of the Ancients" ("Xiaogu") or "Patterned after the Ancients" ("Nigu") began to appear. While sometimes quite beautiful, they were rarely construed as declarations of allegiance to the past.

On the surface, there is good reason to associate the *Gufeng* with this tradition of imitative performance. They draw from the same pool of images and allusions as did the earlier *xiaogu* and *nigu* poems: the *Shijing*, the *Chuci*, the "Nineteen Old Poems," and the entire store of legendary and historical figures found in the earliest histories. Assignment of these poems to this creative category is also convenient. Outright imitation licenses the poet to invoke the ancient aesthetic while freeing him from having to identify with it fully. By openly declaring that the poem is, at least in part, a self-conscious literary exercise, the poet is set free from the reader's assumption of personal authenticity; and by reading it in this light, the critic is spared the difficulty of resolving contradictions in the poet's oeuvre. It is not hard to see why the reading of the *Gufeng* as a tour de force in imitation is particularly attractive to certain Li Bo critics, especially those in the habit of lamenting Li Bo's penchant for quixotic (i.e., inauthentic) role-playing.

Convenient as such a reading may be, however, it has been embraced by few critics, perhaps because there are clear indications that Li Bo wrote these poems in a different spirit. First, if Li Bo is responsible for assigning this title to any of these poems, his replacement of the transitive verbs *"ni"* and *"xiao"* with the more organic *"feng"* may be of some significance. This new title de-emphasizes the intentionality of stylistic imitation, replacing it with the suggestion of the more natural process of influence. Second, in *Gufeng* #35, Li Bo explicitly raises the problem of literary imitation, and so distances himself from that practice:

The homely girl imitated Xi Shi furrowing her brows,	醜女來效矉
Returned home and stunned neighbors all around.	還家驚四鄰
The lad from Shouling lost his natural gait,	壽陵失本步
Convulsing with laughter the folk of Handan.[16]	笑殺邯鄲人

The allusions to the "homely girl" and the "lad from Shouling" are drawn from the *Zhuangzi*. Readers will recognize the "homely girl" who, admiring the furrowed brow of the beautiful but sad Xi Shi, attempted to emulate her, with rather unfortunate results. So ludicrous was the spectacle of this ugly girl's imitation that neighbors encountering her on the street felt compelled to either lock themselves indoors or flee.[17] Lacking both Xi Shi's innate and artless beauty and the true heartsickness behind her frown, this poor girl embodies the imitator who is not only unable to reproduce the desired effect, but incapable even of perceiving its source.

The "lad from Shouling" suffered even graver consequences. Despite his desire to learn to walk like the young men from Handan, "he didn't acquire their regional ability—and even lost his own old way of walking. He had no choice but to crawl home."[18] Here the dangers of imitation go beyond mere failure to self-annihilation. Attempting to be what you are not, or doing what does not come naturally (which amounts to the same thing), is futile, and results in the loss of everything—of all that is natural. Such frauds are not merely failures. They cease to exist.

If Li Bo's adoption of the "ancient" mode is not intended as imitation (at least not of this sort), then did he compose the *Gufeng* as a continuation of the past, in the innocent, not to say naive, spirit of contributing to an uninterrupted and ongoing genre? Assuming some degree of consistency in his views, this would be the natural conclusion. But once again, the new title suggests otherwise. "Ancient Airs," in qualifying as "ancient" the very thing he would pretend to sustain, gives the lie to any pretended innocence. Such an anachronistic gesture requires a level of pretense far more serious than that of either the homely girl or the lad from Shouling. Even if the title is not of Li Bo's choosing, his explicit Confucius-like stance vis-à-vis the past announces a similar mastery and distance.

Neither imitation nor continuation, the *Gufeng* constitute nothing less than Li Bo's solution to the apparently inescapable paradox posed by all *fugu* aspirations. They bring into play both "ancient" naturalness and deliberately evoked "ancientness" in such a way that each of these qualities supports, rather than undermines, the other. Even the naming of the poems' "ancientness"—regardless of who was responsible—reads well as a natural, and thus "ancient," poetic act, for, like the poems it names, the title imitates the past in the one way that eluded both the homely girl and the lad from Shouling: neither subverting naturalness nor compromising the necessary and undeniable difference between model and copy. The *Gufeng* revel in their distinction from ancient models, appropriating the models' aesthetic and ethical properties without attempting to erase the signs of their pastness.

The means by which Li Bo achieves this most delicate of balancing acts is best summed up in the word "quotation"—not so much of the ancient texts, as of imitations of them. My understanding of "quotation" derives from Genette's models of *transtextualité* as set forth in his work *Palimpsestes: la littérature au second degré.*[19] Following his model, I understand quotation as the insertion of one text within another, delimited through the use of quotation marks (here only intonational), in such a way that maintains the integrity of both the *"hypotexte"* (source text) and the *"hypertexte"* (text in which the earlier work is quoted).

For Genette, "quotation" refers to the most discrete manifestation of intertextuality *(transtextualité)* in a hierarchy constructed in order of descending explicitness and ascending importance for the comprehension of the text. Specifically, he identifies three types: quotation *(citation)*, plagiarism *(plagiat)*, and allusion. Despite its implication of printed punctuation—nonexistent in the Chinese texts—the term "quotation" is more useful for the purposes of our discussion than either *"plagiat"* or "allusion." This is not because of its implication of word-for-word fidelity to the originating text (often undemonstrable and in any case irrelevant), but for its suggestion of the continued isolation and objectification of the inserted text. This objectification heightens the reader's awareness that the insertion is an object to be disposed of and manipulated by the author at will, keeping the reader's attention focused simultaneously on both the significance of the insertion and the poet's imparting of that significance. Through varied and subtle use of this technique, Li Bo's *Gufeng* excel in appropriating past texts even while asserting their distinctiveness. He borrows past utterances while drawing attention to the fact that he is in a position to do so.

How, then, does Li Bo's use of quotation in the *Gufeng* achieve this delicate balance? Here, too, Genette proves a useful guide. Developing the work of Riffaterre, he has shown that all transtextual practice, including quotation, begins with the initial identification of an existing, recognizable idiom to be transported into the newer work. Of course, if this were the sole basis of the *Gufeng*'s claim to ancientness, Li Bo could hardly be credited with more than another creative, but hardly unique, use of allusion. The fascination of the *Gufeng* lies not so much in their use of quotation as in the nature of the elements identified as idioms for citation. At his most masterful, Li goes beyond quotation of previously existing, identifiable texts to incorporate complex poetic devices (as opposed to relatively simple images and figures) that lend themselves to an unpacking similar to that required by the quotation that contains them. Among his most common and effective citations are a wide selection of established *bi*, and the layered, richly generative, and tantalizingly ambiguous Qu Yuan—as much a personified version of the device of allusion as it is the literary and historical person known by that name.

QUOTATION OF METAPHORS: BORROWED AUTHENTICITY

One of the defining characteristics of what came to be recognized during the Tang as the "ancient" style is the predominant use of *bi,* translated by Pauline Yu as "comparison."[20] Liu Xie had already glossed *bi* as the practice of writing "of an object and so endowing it with meaning, to formulate an expression such that it cleaves to some affair."[21] In other words, the poet formulating a comparison actively selects an object found in the natural or historical world, then writes of that object so that it indirectly expresses the poet's response to some thing or event that he has encountered.[22] Often defined in contrast with the technique of *xing* (stimulus), the object selected for comparison need not be present at the moment of the poem's inception, but is offered as a projected representation of an already existing feeling. Paradoxically, the recognition that part of the process involves intentional selection does not exempt this technique from the requirement of the appearance of spontaneous expression and natural resonance. The importance of naturalness applies to comparison as well, despite the obvious difficulty of making an invented construct appear somehow unbidden and unplanned.

Liu Xie was perhaps responding to this inherent difficulty when he cautioned against the hardening of comparisons into an inert collection of symbols, warning that there is nothing predetermined or fixed in the selection and formation of particular comparisons: "As a rhetorical technique, comparison adheres to no constant principle when drawing analogies."[23] It seems that for Liu Xie, the natural resonance between the two elements being compared manifests itself in the freshness and uniqueness of the pairing; the effectiveness of a stimulus, in contrast, would seem to depend more on its universal, visceral comprehensibility. Both techniques convey, through means that are almost diametrically opposed, the poet's unmediated response to his world.[24]

By the time of the Tang, however, the function of the comparison had begun to change. As both Wang Yunxi and Pauline Yu have observed, comparison became associated almost exclusively with political allegory.[25] The skillful use of comparison still conveyed immediacy, but not just because comparison exemplified the poet's clear-eyed discernment of a natural correlation between feeling and image. Instead, the use of comparison suggested a particular type of poetic motivation—the motivation to disguise rather than convey meaning.

During Li Bo's time, it was nearly a truism that the politically engaged poet (that is, virtually all literati with official ambitions or position) would inevitably encounter the need to disguise meaning in order to express it. But this tradition dates back to a much earlier time, to the earliest uses and interpretations of the *Shijing*, and also to Qu Yuan's "Li Sao" (Encountering sorrow), where the protracted use of several intertwined comparisons was read as instrumental in the poet's expression of his moral solitude and desperation. Later, in Ruan Ji's *Yonghuai* and Chen Zi'ang's *Ganyu*, mosaics of more or less opaque comparisons were juxtaposed in ways that confounded many a reader. These, too, were unfailingly understood as the expression of politically upright, although unpopular and dangerous, sentiments.[26] This long-standing association between the authenticity of a poet's expression and the encoding of that expression in the suggestive language of comparison persuasively demonstrates the force of the promise inherent in the poetic tradition as a whole and the "ancient" style in particular: the promise that a poem, once truly understood will yield the "truth" about the poet's feelings. Conversely, the very presence of a code could be interpreted as the stamp of a poem's underlying authenticity.

But Li Bo's *Gufeng* do not continue the technique of comparison so much as they quote comparisons that have already appeared in the works of earlier, exemplary poets. What are the implications for the reading of comparisons, and for their supposed roots in urgent sentiment, when they are recycled in the form of quotation?

What exactly is their function when they are baldly revealed to be artistic constructs borrowed from other poets' experiences and expressions? Finally, if the comparisons, whose power originally lay largely in their idiosyncratic opacity, are of a sudden rendered so easily accessible, then what precisely is their function? Liu Xie asserted that the range of possible combinations between poetic sentiment and object, between tenor and vehicle, should be without limit and beyond the fixity of convention. Yet when *fugu* poets of the Tang looked back at the ancient poems they so admired, many comparisons whose opacity and presumed uniqueness signified poetic authenticity at its purest had become familiar and transparent. This situation enabled an alert poet like Li Bo to reuse the comparisons as universally understood and repeatable equations. Rather than closing his eyes to this gradual evolution toward conventionality and engaging in wistful and inauthentic imitation of a bygone poetic practice, Li Bo embraces these transformed figures and integrates them into his work.

Gufeng #40, probably written as a parting poem to his benefactor, He Zhizhang, on the eve of Li Bo's departure from the capital, is a good example of a poem constructed essentially of quoted comparisons. This work is so smoothly put together that it incited at least one (apparently slightly anxious) critic, Emperor Gaozong of the Qing dynasty, to emphatic protestations of the poet's authenticity: "How earnest his sincerity, as it overflows into representation in words!"[27]

When the phoenix is hungry, he'll not peck at grain,	鳳飢不啄栗
But only feed upon pearls of jade.	所食唯琅玕
Unthinkable that he'd join common fowl	焉能與群雞
4 *To battle with sharpened claw for a single meal!*	刺蹙爭一餐
At dawn he calls from a tree on Mount Kunlun;	朝鳴崑丘樹
At twilight sips at the rapids at the foot of Mount Dizhu.[28]	夕飲砥柱湍
To fly home he must follow a long ocean byway,	歸飛海路遠
8 *He is cold, sleeping alone under frosty skies.*	獨宿天霜寒
By chance he meets up with Wangzi Jin,	幸遇王子晉

And they join in friendship at the green clouds'
    edge.

結交青雲端

But before Wang's benevolence can be repaid,

懷恩未得報

12 *Moved by their parting, he sighs deeply, in*
    vain.[29]

感別空長歎

If semantic simplicity alone were the hallmark of "ancient" authenticity, this poem has certainly earned the emperor's comment, not to mention its place in the *Gufeng*. In typical Li Bo style, the language of this poem is crystal clear. There are no oddly "original" expressions, nor are there any particularly rare or specialized characters. The allusions, too, are comfortably familiar, as both the phoenix and Wangzi Jin are easily recognizable figures from early Daoist lore. The "phoenix" (the conventional if misleading translation of the Chinese mythical bird *feng*) brings to mind a bird of divine beauty and power, dwelling, as indicated in this poem, among the immortals. Wangzi Jin is described in the Daoist classic *Liexian zhuan* (Biographies of eminent immortals) as having the unique talent of being able to imitate the cry of the phoenix on his flute *(sheng)*. Eventually this talent attracted the attention of the Daoist adept Fu Qiu Gong, who was so impressed that he welcomed Wang to join him in a life of seclusion and study on Songgao mountain.[30]

On the surface, it seems that Li Bo's poem simply joins two compatible allusions in a predictable narrative: the phoenix experiences the rare joy of encountering a sympathetic and understanding friend, then feels the pain of their separation. Read as the comparison it clearly is, this "new" story indirectly but plainly recounts the joy and pain Li Bo felt at having found and then lost an unusually sympathetic friend. With neither the event nor its recounting appearing to be surprising or even particularly personal, the poem could easily be included in an anthology of occasional parting poems typical of the age. But at least two critics seem to think this poem particularly deserving of praise. Why does Emperor Gaozong so passionately declare this poem to be an unabashedly sincere expression of the poet's emotions? And why does the eminent Qing critic Wang Fuzhi describe it as especially elusive and mysterious? As he puts it, "This piece is like a divine dragon—not that it has no head or tail, but it cannot be apprehended by discerning the shape of its body."[31]

Rereading this poem with Wang Fuzhi's comment in mind, one sees the poem a bit differently. It is true that the piece reads easily from beginning to end, and that the logic of head and tail is manifest; it is equally true that its divinity does not reside in its shape or its sequential narrative. What is beautiful ("personal") in this poem is Li's insertion of familiar allusions, not simply as an integrated shorthand for conventionally understood complexes of meaning, but as quotations. He subtly highlights both their status as objects and his role in bringing them together in very specific and transformative ways.

First, the phoenix. The mythical powers of the phoenix are not spelled out in the tradition; it functions broadly in poetry as a trope for power and beauty. By comparing it with "common fowl," however, Li Bo quotes Ruan Ji's idiosyncratic and influential transformation of an old tradition of great divine birds, most memorably Zhuangzi's *peng*-bird, whose very existence constituted a lesson in the relativity of the things of this world. As narrated in Zhuangzi's "Xiaoyaoyou" (Free and easy wandering), the *peng* is preparing to set off on his journey to the "southern darkness" when a little quail ventures to comprehend its powers:

> The little quail laughs at him, saying, "Where does he think *he's* going? I give a great leap and fly up, but I never get more than ten or twelve yards before I come down fluttering among the weeds and brambles. And that's the best kind of flying anyway! Where does he think he's going?" Such is the difference between big and little.[32]

斥鷃笑之曰： 彼且奚適也。 我騰躍而上， 不過數仞而下。 翱翔蓬蒿之間， 此亦飛之至也。 而彼且奚適也？ 此小大之辯也。

Six hundred years later, Ruan Ji would fill his poetry with birds as transcendent and majestic as Zhuangzi's *peng*. But rather than reveling in the untrammeled joy of boundless travel and lofty perspectives, they are locked in solitude ("How could he play with the quail / Flapping his wings with theirs as they sport in the courtyard together?"),[33] encased in a loneliness tailored to their vast measure, as in *Yonghuai #79:*

There is a rare bird in the forest,	林中有奇鳥
Who calls himself a phoenix.	自言是鳳凰
In the clear morning he drinks from a sweet	清朝飲醴泉
spring	日夕栖山岡
4 *And at the eve of day he nests on the mountain's*	高鳴徹九州
crest.	延頸望八荒
When he sings his high song, his voice reaches to	適逢商風起
the ends of the empire;	羽翼自摧藏
And when he stretches his neck, he can look off	一去崑崙西
to the ends of the earth.	何時復迴翔
But when he meets the autumn wind rising,	但恨處非位
8 *His very wings [seem to show] his inner sorrow.*	愴恨使心傷
Once he has gone off west of the K'un-lun,	
When will he come soaring back again?	
But alas! that he must stay where he does not	
belong!	
12 *The utter sadness of it wrings my heart!*[34]	

Li Bo's and Ruan Ji's characterizations of the phoenix, while similar, manifest an important difference perhaps best understood in the Bloomian terms of Li Bo's "lateness." Ruan's poignant transformation of this glorious bird into the image of his estrangement through the use of comparison reads as a direct representation of his own feelings. The impression of lyric immediacy is only enhanced by readers' assumptions about Ruan Ji's precarious political circumstances.[35] Li Bo, in quoting him, turns Ruan's comparison into an object of his own discourse. Cloaked in the borrowed robes of Ruan's hard-won moral stature, Li Bo can indulge in the pure but nearly forbidden fantasy of draping himself in the garb of the gorgeous and free birds of Daoist myth while aligning himself with the "ancient," admirable, and sad loneliness of the solitary, misunderstood statesman. As an image, the phoenix thus invoked is powerful and renewed; as a quotation, it fortifies the "ancient" idiom on which the *Gufeng* is based while bearing the stamp of Li Bo's intervention as reader and writer. But Li Bo's quotation is not complete until the last four lines, when the poet introduces Wangzi Jin:

By chance she meets up with Wangzi Jin,
And they join in friendship at the green clouds' edge.
But before his benevolence can be repaid,
She is moved by their parting, and sighs deeply, in vain.

Here readers must assimilate an encounter between two allusions, placed in a dialogic relationship that invites a rereading of both. While this is not unheard of, it is less common than the practice of sequencing allusions in a poem or juxtaposing them in analogous positions in parallel lines. Later, Li He and Li Shangyin build their poetics on a foundation of intricately intertwined allusions, keeping centuries of critics busy in the effort to break the code. But Li Bo's approach, while idiomatic, is not nearly so marginal. The vividness of the imagined encounter between Wangzi Jin and the phoenix allows a lyrical poignancy that retains the integrity of the myth, even while its easy verisimilitude points to Li Bo's active intervention. His presence now plainly inscribed in the poem, Li Bo can openly merge with the phoenix in the final line and sigh that futile but irrepressible sigh, de rigueur in so many of the parting poems of the age. Even this open plea for the reader's faith in his poem's "ancient" authenticity is proffered in figurative quotation marks.

In one of the briefer *Gufeng*, #33, Li Bo alludes again to the "Free and Easy Wandering" chapter of the *Zhuangzi*. In this case he does not rely on the joining of two allusions in an imagined narrative encounter; rather, he quotes the past only to insert himself into it—in some sense replicating the entire operation of the *Gufeng* as a whole.

In the northern wilderness is a gigantic fish,	北溟有巨魚
Its body's length—several thousand li.	身長數千里
With a lift of its head, it spouts three	仰噴三山雪
mountainsful of snow,	

4   *Then, reclining, engulfs one hundred riversful of*　　橫吞百川水
　　　water.　　　　　　　　　　　　　　　　　　　　　　　憑陵隨海運
    Leaning against a wave, it follows the ocean's　　　煇赫因風起
　　　tide,　　　　　　　　　　　　　　　　　　　　　　　吾觀摩天飛
    With glittering fins, it rises on the wind.　　　　九萬方未已
    I watch it graze the heavens as it flies,
8   *At 90,000 li, it still did not rest.*[36]

The first couplet is almost directly copied from the *Zhuangzi*, a quotation not unlike those most familiar to Western readers. Like an old song that practically obliges us to join in, this opening engages the reader, along with the poet, in the pleasurable activity of sharing something familiar and well loved. Rather than the joy of discovery that comes with encountering a fresh, new metaphor, Li Bo offers his readers the joy of recognition, then joins them as they look back fondly upon what is irrevocably ancient. As the poem progresses, he builds on the opening hyperbolic image to create his own, careful never to eclipse the pastness of the image. Li's additions of the spouting of immense quantities of snow and the swallowing of untold volumes of water are among the natural activities of such a beast, after all; if the *Zhuangzi* did not exactly describe these activities, it might as well have. It may be that, precisely because such embellishments as this are sure to encounter no resistance on the part of the readers, they allow Li Bo a certain latitude in impressing upon them his presence, not just as a fellow reader, but as a reader who writes.

As his authorial or commentarial presence becomes more obvious, Li Bo sets the stage for the final couplet, where he inserts himself into the narration as an eyewitness of the flight of this divine animal that began life as a piece of quoted text from distant antiquity. It is extremely tempting to read this poem as either ironic or self-aggrandizing, but in many ways it is not that different from *Gufeng* #40: a quotation that is linked to the present through a bit of elaboration that might be a latter-day poet's best chance of returning to antiquity.

Li Bo quotes others—both predecessors and peers—very much like the film editor who, left alone in the archives, emerges with a film uniquely his own. The realm of creativity has shifted from the metaphor-making (or comparison-constructing) activity of linking up tenor and vehicle (a skill that helped earn Du Fu his reputation as the more "creative" poet) to weaving together pre-existing comparisons to forge a signature pattern. The title, *Gufeng*, also becomes clearer with the realization that reading one of these poems requires first recognizing the pastness of its components, then recognizing the vision behind the links forged between them. In this type of creativity, which is, above all, editorial, Li Bo retroactively establishes a worthy, ancient tradition. Then he positions himself as its latter-day and eminently spontaneous and true-hearted heir.

IRONY AND ANCIENTNESS

Not all readers like to interpret Li Bo's playful handling of tradition in the *Gufeng* or in his other poems as a successful intellectual response to the challenge of recovering the values of ancient poetics in a post-ancient period. A more common and enduring interpretation has been to reject all assertions that Li Bo's poetry involved the high degree of craft that I am suggesting, and to insist that the *Gufeng*, along with all of Li Bo's best poetry, are the spontaneous product of something akin to "ten thousand jugs of wine." Meanwhile, on the opposite end of the spectrum, the contemporary American critics Stephen Owen and Joseph Allen have established Li Bo's active participation in the creation of his identity as the "consummate outsider" or "radical conservative," citing ample evidence of his erudition and playful wit in the transformation of received texts.[37]

Quite rightly, both Owen and Allen stop short of asserting that Li Bo's pastiches and recyclings are in the service of parody of the received tradition. Both scholars convincingly show that the desired effect is one of self-dramatization, in part through the establishment of his superior knowledge and perspective. Nevertheless, implicit in their readings is the idea that Li Bo's separation of the speaking self and the portrayed self constitutes an ironic vision, and (especially for Owen) that his penchant for performance is indulged at the expense of the authenticity for which he has been so loved. Once again it is the old debate: inspiration versus craft, talent versus knowledge. How is it possible to reconcile the textual evidence of his passion for donning costumes and playing to his audience with his traditional reputation for unfiltered, free-wheeling expressiveness? Over the centuries, the divide has expressed itself in the evolving formulations of the Li-Du polarity. Today it articulates itself along the lines of East and West. Chinese and Japanese scholarship still tends toward affirmations of Li Bo's unselfconscious but erudite authenticity, of his status as an avatar of poetic immediacy. Discussions of Li Bo's artfulness appear by and large only in relatively recent American writings about his work.

I believe that these differences stem less from disparate emphases on specific aspects of Li Bo's works than from divergent perceptions of what it means to objectify and to quote fragments of received literature. My reading of traditional readers' annotations and remarks on the use of allusion does not indicate that irony was a primary factor in this practice.[38] Studies of transtextuality in Western literature, however, reveal irony as a chief consideration in the practice of both poetry and the novel, although modern readers seem to associate irony primarily with the novel.[39] Mikhail Bakhtin's work on this subject is particularly suggestive. In his essay "From the Prehistory of Novelistic Discourse," Bakhtin pinpoints the primary difference between poetic and novelistic discourse in that poetry uses language directly to express the poet's meaning or feeling, whereas the novel takes these "primary means of representation" and turns them into an "object of representation" or "a representation that is parodied and stylized."[40] Rather than take issue here with his application of this criterion to distinguish between poetic and novelistic discourse, I would just like to point out that the striking pertinence of his formulation of novelistic discourse to Chinese poetic practice, especially the high degree of intertextuality and stylistic self-consciousness that begins roughly in the Wei-Jin period, provides a useful starting point for a provisional comparison between Chinese and Western motives for intertextual practice.

While allowing for a variety of attitudes in novelistic discourse, Bakhtin considers the parodic, ironic laugh as the originating principle and most fertile ground for the gradual elaboration of such discourse from Greek times through the present. Similarly, Genette's detailed model of transtextuality is elaborated exclusively along an axis extending between playful and serious intent. Both theses assume that the purpose of all transtextual practice is to comment upon either the source text or a related topic, and take the potential use of irony as the lodestar in situating the intended meaning of a given work.

Li Bo's use of quotation in the *Gufeng*, however, is not primarily commentarial, and does not sit comfortably anywhere on the map that Genette has so painstakingly drawn. For Li Bo, the patchwork of more or less discrete quotations that is the *Gufeng* (individual works as well as the group as amorphous whole) renders the act of quotation itself the primary signifier. Humor may or may not be present in any given poem, and its presence is notoriously difficult to prove. But it does bear pointing out that there is scant evidence of a chuckling reception in the reams of commentary that have accumulated around Li Bo's *Gufeng*. In these works the use of past texts is presented as a sign in itself: the sign of a literary mind hard at work in the age-old activity of dragon carving, the sign that someone is engaged in using recognizably poetic means to express interiority. Far from divesting source texts of their meaning, far from rendering them risible or defunct, the poet adheres to Liu Xie's injunction about the suppleness and variety of comparisons, not through creating new ones, but through recombining—and defamiliarizing—the old.

The following poem, *Gufeng* #16, engenders just such a process of defamiliarization in its complex weave of several allusions. The structure of quotation is characterized by two levels of ascendancy, as Li Bo quotes the quotations already used by one of his preferred poets, Bao Zhao.[41] Below is Bao's poem, the sixth of a series titled "Zeng guren Ma Ziqiao liu shou" (Presented to my old friend, Ma Ziqiao: Six poems):

Paired swords about to be parted, 雙劍將離別
First cry out from inside their case. 先在匣中鳴
Mist and rain mixing as evening approaches, 煙雨交將夕
4 *From this point on they separate their forms.* 從此忽分形
The female sinks into the depths of the Wu River, 雌沉吳江裡
While the male flies past the Chu city walls. 雄飛入楚城
The Wu River, so deep that it has no bottom, 吳江深無底
8 *The passes at Chu have towering gates.* 楚關有崇扃
Once separated by the distances of heaven and 一為天地別
    earth, 豈直限幽明
Is this merely the split between dark and light? 神物終不隔
In the end, divine objects will not be parted, 千祀倘還并
12 *After a thousand years, again they will be*
    united.[42]

This poem is a beautiful and at first glance classical example of extended comparison, enlisting a legend from the Spring and Autumn Period to obliquely convey feelings about an event in Bao's own life—apparently, his imminent separation from a friend. According to the legend, Prince Helü of Wu requested that Gan Jiang make him a sword. But when the molten steel failed to flow out of the vat, Gan Jiang's wife, Mo Ye, threw herself in, releasing enough molten steel to make two swords. Gan Jiang gave the male sword to the prince and kept the female one. The female sword, left alone inside her case, missed her companion, and her mournful cries could be heard by anyone who came near.[43]

The final lines of the poem contain another allusion: the story of a Jin dynasty official named Zhang Hua. According to his biography, preserved in the *Jinshu* (the historical records of the Jin dynasty), Zhang one day consulted a diviner by the name of Lei Huan who was renowned for his ability to read the stars. Lei noticed a strange aura about one of the constellations, Douniu, and attributed it to the heavenward emanation of a jeweled sword hidden somewhere on earth. Zhang named him county magistrate, upon which Lei gained access to the local prison and dug four meters deep into the earth under one of the cells. There he discovered a stone case radiating an extraordinary light and containing not one, but two swords. Lei sent one of the swords to Zhang and kept one for himself. He knew, however, that their ownership of these treasures could last only a short while. He reminded Zhang that divine objects sooner or later must transform, and cannot stay long in the service of mere humans. Zhang responded in agreement, and reminded Lei of that earlier pair of inseparable divine swords, Mo Ye and Gan Jiang, as proof that things that are naturally meant to be together will eventually reunite. Later, some time after Lei's death, Zhang was walking by the Yanping ford when, suddenly, his sword leapt out of its scabbard and into the water. Glancing down into the river, he saw a pair of dragons. With a sigh, he exclaimed, "Isn't this the realization of my previous master's words about metamorphosis, and my words about reuniting?!"[44]

Bao's poem contains all the elements prized by those who yearn for the return of the ancient style. It relates personal sentiment to past events and so acquires the dignity of a higher moral vision, and its language is straightforward and unadorned, without a trace of the technical ornamentation associated with poems of the Southern Dynasties. While the allusions are used in such a way as to qualify as a primary means of representation, Bao has taken the first step toward transforming them. For one thing, minor as it may seem, Bao reverses the sequence of separation and the weeping female sword, making her weep in anticipation rather than as a result of separation. As one commentator points out, Bao also added the reference to the walls of Chu, which had no place in the original story. But none of these changes interferes with the impression that Bao is straightforwardly aligning himself with the many lonely literati who have been forced to (and ever will be forced to, it would seem) say good-bye to a friend; his agreement with the past is greater than his difference from it. The lyric aspect of the poem remains firmly rooted in Bao's empathy with the separated pair, and the reasonable assumption that readers will empathize with him.

But the element of Bao's poem selected by Li Bo for quotation and elaboration in *Gufeng* #16 is neither the reference to the swords, nor even the sharing of the same two allusions, but Bao's unique dramatization of the separation of the two swords. In Bao's poem the depiction of the swords' swift and inexorable flight in opposite directions, while dramatic, remains within the bounds of the story. Perhaps because of its brevity, the couplet in question does not attract undue attention, reading as a natural shift in emphasis, all the better to convey his own strong emotions. Li Bo was clearly attracted by the sensational image of the swords in flight, and captures and mounts it in a strikingly different setting:

Gem-like swords—a pair of horned dragons,	寶劍雙蛟龍
Snow petals reflecting on hibiscus.	雪花照芙蓉
A distilled light shoots through the earth and sky,	精光射天地
	雷騰不可衝
4 A surge of thunder none can defy.	一去別金匣
Once they go forth, leaving their golden sheath—	飛沉失相從
Soaring, sinking, they lose those who would follow.	風胡歿已久
	所以潛其鋒
Feng Hu is long since departed,	吳水深萬丈
8 So they hide their blades.	楚山邈千重
The waters of Wu, ten thousand fathoms deep,	雌雄終不隔
The mountains of Chu, a thousand layers removed.	神物會當逢
But as male and female in the end will not be parted,	
12 So divine things shall rightly meet.[45]	

This is no mere continuation of Bao's continuation of the Gan Jiang–Mo Ye story. The allusions are the same, the vehicle of the comparison is the same, but the poem is no longer just a poem of separation. Li Bo's poem is also about the solitude of the superior man, the same theme as that of *Gufeng* #40, and reminiscent of many of Ruan Ji's *Yonghuai*. Li Bo does not content himself with recounting the story, but performs the theme of solitude in the skillful, overt intertwining of both quotation and allusion.

Li Bo begins with a reference to the Zhang Hua story and by implication to the tale of Gan Jiang and Mo Ye. The second allusion, occurring midway through the poem in line 7, refers to Feng

Huzi, a subject of the kingdom of Chu and a contemporary of Gan
Jiang. According to the *Yue jueshu,* the king of Chu had heard that
the two greatest swordmakers who had ever lived were Gan Jiang
of Wu and Ou Yezi of Yue. He thus commissioned Feng to offer
Gan and Ou some of the most precious jewels of Chu in exchange
for making swords. The mission was a success, and Feng returned
with three wonderful swords, which greatly pleased the king. Each
sword had been given a name by its maker. When the king asked
for an explanation of the rather enigmatic names, Feng Huzi replied
most eloquently, demonstrating his discernment, a quality most
prized among men of superior moral worth.

It is no mere coincidence that both the Zhang Hua and Feng
Huzi allusions contain textual links to either Gan Jiang or Mo
Ye, or both. Li Bo's poem makes wonderful use of the connection
between the three stories, braiding them through with the dramatic
image first provided by Bao Zhao: the pull of two magnetically
attracted objects sadly, if only temporarily, separated.

The poem opens with a five-character reiteration of the meta-
morphosis recounted in the Zhang Hua story, first eliciting thoughts
of indissoluble unions and second of divine objects. But Li Bo's
artistry in bridging the gap between ancient and modern becomes
evident only in the second line, where the silvery swords turned
dragons again metamorphose, this time into the radiant whiteness
of snowflakes and hibiscus petals: images of moral purity common
to the Confucian and Buddhist traditions. The visual elegance of
this couplet is worthy of Li Bo's most refined recent-style qua-
trains, while the botanical symbols of divine purity could easily
have been borrowed from Qu Yuan's "Encountering Sorrow." As if
the transformation of sword dragons into flower petals (reminiscent
of dragon scales) weren't vivid enough, Li Bo encapsulates their
radiance in the verb *zhao.* Translated here as "reflecting," it also
signifies "shining," and this dual meaning enlivens an otherwise
tranquil image: the whiteness of each is not only caused by, but
is the reason for, the whiteness of the other. Like an electrical
charge whose movement is invisible but whose power intensifies
with each exchange, whiteness, in the next couplet, is meta-
morphosed and released into a searing beam of light so strong that

it can reach the sky—which is where Lei Huan first spied it, back in the Jin dynasty.

Li Bo, having skimmed the surface of that allusion so lightly that one might wonder whether it is there at all, transforms the light in the sky into the thing most closely associated with it, thunder, carefully matching power for power. With these changes the motion depicted by Bao, not the swords, has become the focus of the poem. The third couplet offers an image of the swords in flight: "Once they go forth, leaving their golden sheath—/ Soaring, sinking, they lose those who would follow." In their separate trajectory across the heavens, one in the waters of Wu and the other beyond the mountains of Chu, they fly inexorably toward solitude, in the process invoking Zhuangzi's *peng*-bird—and Li Bo's own phoenix. The abandoned ones, or one, "who would follow" seems to embrace, in its ambiguity, the companion sword (as each member of the pair loses the other) and, more generally, any other inferior entity that would naturally yearn to join it or control it.

This ambiguity opens the way to Li Bo's introduction of Feng Huzi, the man with the rare ability of being able to recognize true quality. The shift is, as recognized by Wang Qi,[46] the key moment of the poem. The swords are no longer just the desolate members of a wrongly separated pair. Each is an extraordinary weapon that has been separated, not merely from the other, but from the only person discerning enough to recognize their quality: Feng Hu. With the insertion of this new reference, Li Bo aligns himself with the ancestor of misunderstood worthies, Qu Yuan, whose long elegy "Encountering Sorrow" tells of a long spirit journey through the heavens in search of a sovereign who would recognize his moral worth. This suggestion of an affiliation between the two men also justifies Bao Zhao's otherwise mysterious addition of Chu to the Gan Jiang story.

The poem closes with an assertion echoing Bao Zhao's final couplet. By virtue of the montage engineered between the two allusions, however, this couplet takes on a whole new meaning. More redolent of prophecy than of the longing and desire expressed at the end of so many of the *Gufeng*, this finale reprises Zhang Hua's prophetic reply to Lei Huan, imbuing the Feng Huzi story with an aura of hopefulness: those who truly understand each other are divinely paired, and therefore cannot live apart indefinitely. Li Bo paints himself as the lone, superior man, both through his comparison with superior beings in the implementation of a traditional comparison or *bi* and through his highlighted presence as the impassioned, lofty editor of received texts. In a piece comparable to but more complex than *Gufeng* #40, he has woven together threads drawn from three texts, idiomizing the dynamism of Bao Zhao's poem and using that dynamism to suggest his own immediacy. Far from violating the ancientness of his sources, he does them honor by making his use of them the very centerpiece of his poetics.

Significant elements set this poem apart from the "ancient" aesthetic. Most obvious is its strong reliance on highly crafted and slightly fantastic visual imagery, more typical of Liang and Qi poetry than of pre-Han models. This may explain why *Gufeng* #16 has not been consistently included in the group.[47] But the marginality of this poem can serve to illuminate the criteria for its eventual inclusion and, by extension, the inclusion of all the poems in the series. What it does share with the other *Gufeng* is the dominant use of quoted comparisons to convey the poet's inner state, and the comparison it favors takes its ultimate paternity from Qu Yuan's "Li Sao."

QU YUAN AS "QU YUAN"

Qu Yuan's presence lends Li Bo's "Ancient Airs" moral legitimacy and authenticity. But Li Bo's reliance on Qu's spirit-journey allegory, a term I use advisedly, also means that the comparisons on which he builds his authenticity are, again, borrowed—and, I would say, quoted. In this case as in others, the quotation draws attention to itself as such, this time through a rather stubborn refusal to acquiesce in the dominant, conveniently simplified view of the revered poet. Rather than engage Qu Yuan and (what David Hawkes has famously termed) his *itineraria* exclusively as the unambiguously wronged, misunderstood-but-loyal minister in search of a discerning sovereign, Li Bo seems to return to the precanonical original: a package of unresolved contradictions between shamanistic imagery and Confucian tropes, between emptiness and fullness, unfoundedness and substantiveness. Rather than choose between Qu Yuan's shamanistic bent (at least in the writing of poetry) and his supposed Confucian rectitude, Li Bo instead seems to proceed in the spirit that has always made of Qu Yuan such an intriguing but problematic poetic forebear: engaging in *fu*-like rhapsodic descriptions without any thought to the requirements of exegetes yet to come.[48]

Qu Yuan's ignorance of the contradictions he posed is honestly come by; latter-day Li Bo can pretend to no such innocence. By embracing rather than eschewing the contradiction between the celestial and the earthbound, the imaginary and the real, Li Bo invites his reader to apply a politicized reading of comparison as evidence of a motivating sense of danger and urgency. Many readers, of course, attempted to do just that, justifying Li Bo's flights of fancy as expressions of his frustration at not being employed in an official capacity. Today as well, Japanese and Chinese scholars cite Li Bo's thwarted Confucian ambitions as his motive for resorting to Daoist and Buddhist practice in his life and in his poetry.[49]

But given the passions of the arguments over the centuries, this formula, which had been available to scholars since the beginning, seems pat and complacent, conforming more closely to the tradition of maintaining Li Bo's supreme status than to the realities of his life or what some critics recognized as the avowedly joyful tenor of his poetry.[50] Li Bo's particular mode of adoption of the Qu Yuan legacy, especially when read in light of his intertextual practices as a whole, is far too subtle and complex to be accounted for as derived from any supposed personal or situational similarities. Nor, in light of the complete silence of traditional commentary on the subject, is it easy to describe his relationship with his forebear (and the exegetical tradition associated with his work) as parodic in anything approaching the Bakhtinian sense of the term. Rather, Qu Yuan, and the broader *Chuci* tradition of which he is a part, provided Li Bo with one of his preferred sources of quotation and served as one of the most important archetypes against which Li established his own brand of ancient authenticity. It might be argued that *Gufeng*

quotations of Qu Yuan's comparisons were inspired by Ruan Ji's
Yonghuai in much the same way that Li was inspired by Bao Zhao's
quotation of *yuefu* themes. But Li Bo's willingness to assume his
own lateness, and his engagement of past texts on a second level of
ascendancy, preserved—by qualitatively transforming—the ancient
aesthetic he is credited for continuing.

This transformation may best be observed in his particular use
of three sets of *Chuci*-related images and tropes in the *Gufeng*:
nature imagery (as in *Gufeng* #16, discussed above), the trope of
"climbing high," and immortality-related imagery. Two of these
share the potential danger of perceived incompatibility with the
"ancient" aesthetic. Excessively detailed treatment of the sensual,
surface characteristics of nature and landscape can run perilously
close to the ornate Six Dynasties style Li Bo pretended to reject
with the writing of some of these poems, and unbridled fantasies of
Daoist immortality could only offend the Confucian sensibilities of
the *fugu* reformers most likely to embrace Li's "ancient" identity.
But both have been identified as signature elements of the *Gufeng*
and of Li Bo's work as a whole. For Li Bo, forcing preconceived
contradictions in nature and immortality imagery was his preferred
way of forging a new "ancient" path.

Nature Imagery

Nature imagery has always held a prominent place in Chinese
poetry, having appeared as subject, setting, comparison, and stim-
ulus ever since the "Airs" of the *Shijing*. In the context of the *fugu*-
inspired consciousness of the Tang, formal variations in its use also
became a determining factor in distinguishing between an ancient-
style and a recent-style poem. Generally speaking, nature images
employed (or interpreted) as comparison or stimulus that indirectly
signified an event in the poet's world would classify a given poem
as ancient-style verse. Used differently, however, nature imagery
signals the very antithesis of *fugu*-sanctioned purity and rectitude.
As is well known, many poems of the *Chuci*, for all their assimila-
tion into the Confucian exegetical tradition, offer some of the most
sensual portrayals of the beauty of nature. Indeed, the influence of

the *Chuci*'s crystalline waters and cloud-topped mountain peaks on the development of the rhapsodic descriptions of Han dynasty *fu*— eventually condemned by one of its most masterful practitioners, Yang Xiong (53 B.C.–A.D. 18), as nothing more than futile "insect-carving"—has long been established.[51]

The uneasy coexistence between the shamanistic sensuality and otherworldliness of the *Chuci* and the upright Confucian persona of Qu Yuan did not escape Li Bo. Quite to the contrary, he seems to have appropriated that internal contradiction. By quoting lush images similar to those used in Qu Yuan's comparisons but depriving them of the context that permits them to be read as comparisons, Li Bo not only draws the line between "ancient" authenticity and recent-style artifice: he allows them to collide. *Gufeng* #52 quotes Qu Yuan in just this way:

Verdant springtime runs with the reckless rapids;	青春流驚湍
Crimson-bright summer swiftly eddies past.	朱明驟回薄
It's unbearable to see the autumn tumbleweeds	不忍看秋蓬
4 *Wheel aimlessly, nowhere to light.*	飄揚竟何託
The illumined breeze of clearing skies destroys the orchid,	光風滅蘭蕙
White dew spatters the tender bean shoots.	白露灑葵藿
The Fair One will not wait for me,	美人不我期
8 *Though grass and tree wither day by day.*[52]	草木日零落

Qu Yuan's—or the *Chuci*'s—presence is almost tangible in Li Bo's selection of nature imagery and in his repetition of the expression, "the Fair One." Almost all the natural images in this poem—rushing water, restless tumbleweed, and orchids—carry associations established in the earliest poems, and Li Bo takes care to enhance the ancient air of these evocations. He does not simply rely on the familiar signal of rushing water to signal time's passage and remind his readers of Qu Yuan's oft-expressed sense of urgency; he builds on it, tersely running through three consecutive seasons in the first three lines: spring, summer, autumn. Rather than settle comfortably upon the familiar trope of the tumbleweed, he sharpens the rootless anguish of the wanderer through an even more detailed description of its ceaseless drifting.

Yet for all its abstraction and well-worn symbolism, the nature depicted in *Gufeng #52* resists being read as simple comparison. It rises before the eyes in a picture of light, color, movement, its sensual immediacy strongly suggesting its provenance in the poet's experience and subverting a reading that would relegate the image to the relative abstraction of comparison. Li Bo injects irresistible life into traditionally symbolic imagery partly by reframing it in the intricate parallel couplets associated with a distinctly "recent-style" aesthetic, and partly through his use of apostrophe: exclamations and lamentations seemingly elicited by the view before him and directed at the reader. But the most effective, and affecting, aspect of this poem derives from his vivid rendering of time's passage, as though it could be seized by the human eye. His readers behold the movement of the seasons in the water, the destruction of the orchid by the dawn breeze, and the spattering of the tender bean shoots by the icy-white dew.

Li Bo has situated himself in the middle of a "natural," persuasively tangible scene constructed entirely of literary expressions. On the one hand, the montage of ancient imagery provides a fitting setting for the righteous latter-day poet who, not understood by his prince, pines for the ancient era of moral and literary purity. On the other, the visual and emotional intensity of this constructed scene is clearly derived not from the *fugu* aesthetic, but from an aesthetic more closely associated with a poetics he purports to be longing to escape. Is Li Bo innocent of the contradiction or guilty of the self-serving pose of which he has been accused by some of his most exasperated critics? Or might he be honestly parodying the *Chuci?* None of these readings seems likely. Poetic naiveté hardly seems in keeping with his demonstrated mastery of both tradition and poetic technique, and it seems unlikely that a purely performative poetics could have been so widely and consistently misread by successive generations of readers. If he is parodying the past in any way, his mocking smile is certainly not directed at the texts he is quoting. Li Bo quotes a Qu Yuan innocent of generic and exegetical classification, and if there is an ironic laugh, it seems rather to be poking fun at the exegetical tradition responsible for sullying the ancient naturalness it purports to lament. By maintaining the ancientness of his ancient sources but couching them in his latter-day poetic sensibility, Li makes a bid for his readers' faith in his own ancient authenticity, subtly nudging them away from repeating the fatal error of incomprehension perpetrated by Qu Yuan's contemporaries.

His audience—or at least some of its members—accepted this bid, and others like it. *Gufeng* #38, another poem that borrows Qu Yuan's nature imagery to deplore (Li Bo's own) unappreciated talent, elicits another commentary from Emperor Gaozong, this one so laudatory of its ancient authenticity that it takes Confucius' comments on the *Odes* and the "Li Sao" as its model: "The preceding piece grieves, but without causing pain; remonstrates, but without slandering. While it approaches the savor of the wrenching sadness of 'Encountering Sorrow,' this piece is [more] gentle and earnest, aspiring to the 'Airs' and 'Elegantiae.'"[53]

Recalling the emperor's role in canonizing Li Bo's poetry, it is easy to understand why he was drawn to this particular *Gufeng*. In this poem, the personification of botanical images seems consistent with "Li Sao" practice, but sports Li Bo's signature as he tantalizingly pushes that practice to another level of sensual immediacy:

	A solitary orchid grows in a secluded garden,	孤蘭生幽園
	As common weeds conspire to submerge it.	眾草共蕪沒
	Though basking in the rays of springtime sun,	雖照陽春暉
4	*It still grieves at the high autumn moon.*	復悲高秋月
	Flying frost early came whispering,	飛霜早淅瀝
	Green luxuriance feared an imminent end.	綠豔恐休歇
	Without the gust of a fresh wind,	若無清風吹
8	*For whom would it put forth such fragrance?*[54]	香氣為誰發

Li Bo's famed hyperbole is clearly at play in this poem. His ability to sustain the trope over the entire length of the poem contributes to that impression, but the sheer duration of the conceit does not fully account for the poet's strong presence. Li Bo's active quotation of ancient authenticity occurs in the second half of the poem where, as in *Gufeng* #52, he recasts the "Li Sao"–like natural image into a scene of particular sensual immediacy rather more typical of recent-style poetics. In lines 5 and 6, when the orchid's dread of the onset of winter reaches its climax, a vivid parallel couplet unites the orchid's view with the speaker's. With this, the thrust of the comparison shifts ever so slightly from a symbol both shared and sanctified to a personal image, idiosyncratic and strange.

This move toward the acceptable boundary between unfounded and substantive transforms what could have been a mechanical, imitative adoption of recognizably ancient tropes into acceptably ancient lyric expression: to echo the emperor, a tone that is gentle and earnest enough to warrant comparison with the most ancient of Chinese poems. Other strong quotations of comparisons from the *Shijing* and the "Nineteen Old Poems" are present in the opening and concluding couplets. The discreteness of these quotations both highlights and legitimizes the peculiarity of Li's extended and per-sonalized personification. He succeeds in making the acceptable strange, signaling his earnest and undeniable presence as weaver of the text.

Sometimes Li Bo introduces nature into his poetry not as a quoted comparison but as a quoted stimulus: as something in nature that had once inspired an ancient poet's emotions. But even in such cases, he transforms it into a comparison, as in *Gufeng* #42:

	Dipping, soaring—a pair of white gulls	搖裔雙白鷗
	Call in flight; the clear river flows.	鳴飛滄江流
	It's fitting to befriend the boy of the seas;	宜與海人狎
4	*How could they consort with the cranes of the clouds?*	豈伊雲鶴儔
	Laying their shadows to rest, they sleep upon moonlit sands,	寄影宿沙月
	Then, gliding upon fragrance, they play on a springtime isle.	沿芳戲春洲
	"I, too, would like to cleanse my heart—	吾亦洗心者
8	*To forget the world and follow you forth."*[55]	忘機從爾遊

Commentators interpret this poem as having been written in Li Bo's youth when, appointed to service in the Hanlin academy, he was smitten with the desire to retreat into the mountains and live as a recluse.[56] This reading seems plausible and is supported by Li Bo's signature use of quoted stimulus and, especially, comparison.

The poem opens with the believable image of two white gulls flying over a river. Their believability, however, does not exempt the gulls from also being creatures of the textual world; for this picture of two birds calling to one another resonates strongly with "Guanju," the first poem of the *Shijing*. For the moment, the apparent coincidence of "real" nature image and allusion remains unobtrusive, and a development of the "Guanju" courtship theme seems predictable. But almost immediately Li Bo thwarts these expectations, weaving together previously unconnected allusions and bringing the poem to a surprise ending. The abrupt imposition of his presence into the montage of quoted natural images inscribes him once again as both poet and subject of the poem, both observer and observed.

After presenting the birds in the first couplet, Li Bo immediately leaves the natural world behind to step resolutely into the world of pure allusion. From the liminal supernatural world of the *Liezi* he gleans the well-known story of the little boy who lived near the sea and had a remarkable complicity with the gulls. His father wanted to enjoy the gulls as well and accompanied his son to the shore, but the gulls refused to land and remained frolicking in the air.[57] Li Bo's transition from subtle evocation of the *Shijing* to unambiguous allusion to the *Liezi* parallels in structure and in content the transition he executed in *Gufeng* #16 from the Gan Jiang allusion to evocations of the *peng*-bird. In both of these poems, what begins as an allusion to the righteous affinity and courtship between a man and a woman quickly becomes an allusion to the unplanned and irreplaceable affinity between two like-minded friends, or *zhiyin* (lit., "he who understands the tune"). Xiao Shibin, typically continuing the exegetical practice long applied to the *Shijing* and "Li Sao," interprets the cranes as well-placed but undiscerning officials at court, and the gulls as men of talent who prefer to follow their inner natures and live lives in harmony with the fluctuations of the universe.

In the third couplet, Li Bo reinserts those allusive gulls into a scene rich with the vivid sensual detail readers could easily accept as evidence of the poet's presence. The image now presented in this semantically, if not tonally, parallel couplet, while following smoothly from staunchly Confucian references to questions of service and retreat, is completely isolated from any such concerns. Nature, depicted in all its patterned intricacy and elegance, reveals the sensibilities of the early Tang court poet and the Six Dynasties nature poet: the ephemeral impressions of the senses captured for an instant in elusive qualities of fragrance and shadow, the eternal unity of the alternation between play and rest, embraced in the self-sufficient moment of a parallel couplet that dissembles the poet's identity—while setting the stage for the revelation of that identity.

Just when the poet's artistry allows him to withdraw behind the clarity of his own vision, at the very moment when reader and poet are united behind eyes that seem to penetrate the mystery of the visible world, Li Bo reemerges in the very scene he was (and we were!) just observing, as he addresses the gulls and declares his desire to join them in their carefree, eternal gambol on springtime isles. If the transition appears sudden, that impression is softened by its generic familiarity. Such open declarative endings were common in regulated poems of his age. Straddling disparate poetic techniques and aesthetic sensibilities, he draws the reader into his vision while maintaining a separate presence, and weaves together supposedly incompatible elements to suggest a return to a time before any such incompatibility could have been perceived. If Proust's life project was to disentangle the web between perception and memory, place and emotion, and to establish thereby his connection with what is most universally human, it would seem that Li Bo wants to weave them together in such a way that the individual strands remain clearly visible, coming together to form a new, idiosyncratic pattern that only he could have created.

And how is this connected to the *Chuci* tradition? Although he does not specifically allude to the "Li Sao" anywhere in this poem, the implicit link between ideally compatible couples (and, more generally, the theme of courtship) and the theme of a worthy man poorly matched with an uncomprehending prince and court is clearly derived from the Qu Yuan hermeneutic tradition. Furthermore, when Li Bo invokes and subverts the distinction between the natural images employed in familiar comparisons and those captured and perceived by the individual poet, he once again assumes the ancient voice of the poet composing at a time that predated those distinctions. The success of this poem resides neither in Li Bo's would-be self-aggrandizing parodying of that tradition nor in his innocent "imitation" of ancient poetic modes. Rather, he asserts his observance of ancient authenticity by demonstrating his undeniable comprehension of the irrecoverable pastness of his sources.

Animating the Symbolic Landscape: Climbing High

If any thematic subgenre lends itself particularly well to preserving the pastness of the past, it is that of "climbing high," the earliest extant example of which is the *fu* by Wang Can (177–217) titled "Deng lou fu" (Climbing the tower).[58] In poems treating this theme, the poet ascends a tower or a mountain and looks out at the vast landscape unfurled before his eyes. Confronted with the evidence of nature's cycles, he reflects upon his own impermanence and the intransigence of the ills of the world. By virtue of the nature of the sentiment being expressed, treatment of the theme could hardly help but grow more poignant as the theme itself receded into the past and poems on the subject proliferated. Later poets would return to the same high places their forebears had visited and confront the truth that those forebears have since gone the way of the flowing waters upon which they themselves had reflected.[59] Redundancy, far from diminishing the power of this brief narrative, stands as persuasive testimony to its validity.

Li Bo is a poet who understands the efficacy of repetition. A *Gufeng* composed in the mode of climbing high potentially heightens the importance of the signifying power of repetition. At the same time, the effectiveness of both the *Gufeng* and the climbing high poem rests on belief in the reality of a here and now: that the poet's feelings were first moved by his direct observation of nature, at a specific moment in a specific place. Climbing high poems relate the effect of landscape upon memory, both actual and anticipated. They trace (and occasionally enact) the movement from viewed landscape to inspired emotion and poetic memory, then back to a landscape that must then be as much remembered symbol as perceived object, and so on, in an inward-turning spiral. In this way, climbing high poems offer an anatomy of the *xing*, or stimulus. Both individually and as a group, they begin with the conceit that poets' emotions were stirred by observed objects in nature. Then, as the individual poem progresses—and as generations of poems accumulate—the difficulty of distinguishing between perceived and remembered landscape becomes ever more acute.

Viewed in light of my observations of Li Bo's practice of combining quoted comparisons with vividly depicted natural imagery, the structural frame provided by the climbing high subgenre is potentially even richer than usual. In *Gufeng #39*, Li Bo explores that potential, quoting its previous transformation by Ruan Ji in his *Yonghuai #15*, which I offer here:

Long ago, when I was fourteen or fifteen,	昔年十四五
My aims were lofty; I loved the Poems and the History.	志尚好書詩
Clad in coarse robes while my breast harbored the purest jade,	被褐懷朱玉
4 I strove to keep up with Yan and Min.	顏閔相與期
I opened the screen, gazed down upon the Four Expanses,	開軒臨四野
Climbed on high and looked outward toward those in my thoughts.	登高望所思
Grave mounds covered the crests of the hills,	丘墓蔽山岡
8 Ten thousand generations—a single moment.	萬代同一時
After a thousand autumns, ten thousand years,	千秋萬歲後
Where are their names and glory to be found?	榮名安所之
Only now do I understand those sons of the grave—	乃悟羨門子
12 I sobbed, sobbed, overcome by self-scorn.[60]	噭噭令自嗤

Putting aside the debate about whether this poem attests to Ruan's conversion to a life of seeking immortality or to his loyalty to Confucian ideals,[61] the almost total absence of perceived landscape is striking. Even at this relatively early date in the evolution of the subgenre, Ruan has internalized the landscape-viewing gesture, not only making short work of the landscape-memory dialogue evident in earlier poems, but reversing it. Instead of being moved by the landscape to reflect upon the disappearance of those gone before, Ruan reverses the process, shifting his gaze from ancient texts to the landscape, where he hopes to glimpse the authors of those texts: "those in my thoughts." Then, instead of the natural stimulus of eternal mountains and flowing rivers demanded by the subgenre, and instead of the sagely authors sought in response to his own desire, Ruan spies their grave mounds. Having thus superimposed memory directly into the landscape, Ruan almost singlehandedly belies the myth of natural stimulus and demonstrates that climbing high was already, first and foremost, a literary act.

Not unlike his reponse to Bao Zhao's poem discussed earlier, Li Bo composes a poem that takes as its starting point Ruan Ji's transformation of the climbing high theme, rather than simply alluding to it through the repetition of his imagery:

I climb high, and gaze upon the four seas;	登高望四海
How vast and endless the earth and sky!	天地何漫漫
Frost cloaks all things autumnal,	霜被群物秋
4 *Winds whip the great wilderness cold.*	風飄大荒寒
Blossoms of glory—waters flowing east;	榮華東流水
Life's events—successions of ocean waves.	萬事皆波瀾
The white sun is obscured by dusk's colored rays,	白日掩徂暉
8 *Floating clouds with no sure end.*	浮雲無定端
Swallows and sparrows now nest in pawlonia trees,	梧桐巢燕雀
While phoenixes must perch among the brambles.	枳棘棲鴛鸞
To "Return Home" once again!	且復歸去來
12 *On my sword I strum, "The Road Is Hard."*[62]	劍歌行路難

Taking up where Ruan Ji left off, Li Bo reaffirms the essential literariness of the act of climbing high, but does so through his characteristic approach of quotation. Unlike Ruan Ji, he begins the poem with the obligatory inciting natural image or stimulus; but the key word here is "obligatory," for it is no longer possible to read those first two lines without thinking of Wang Can and the climbing high subgenre as a whole. Where Ruan projected funereal inscriptions of human memory on the landscape, Li Bo returns to a natural landscape of hoarfrost and wind, imbuing the initial quotation with the credibility of vivid sensory perception.

Or so it seems until line 5. There the waters and waves reveal themselves as being more suggestive of past comparisons than of spontaneous discoveries of natural correspondences, and the reader reenters the *Gufeng* world of quotation. Images of white sun and floating clouds may appeal to the eye, but they derive from memory of the "Nineteen Old Poems"; the swallows and sparrows could be real features of the landscape—but for the fact that they have displaced Zhuangzi's mythical phoenix-like birds from their rightful place in the pawlonia trees. In the last couplet, Li Bo cries out his desire—or his decision—to "return home," the heartfelt sentiment of which is made comprehensible by the fact that it is a quotation of the famous verse by Tao Yuanming, "Gui qui lai ci" (To return home!).[63] And, about to set off, he invites the reader to picture him, in that quoted landscape, quoting the *yuefu* song "The Road Is Hard" ("Xing lu nan"), versions of which he has written—based upon those written by Bao Zhao.

While it is possible to identify some of the source texts that provide the material for this patchwork of quotations, it is difficult to determine how they come together to convey meaning. Xiao Shibin reads the poem as a lucid statesman's considered determination that the times are out of joint, leading to his final decision to go into seclusion. Wang Qi offers an interpretation more specific to Li Bo's personal situation, suggesting that the final decision to retreat to a life of rural isolation was his imminent banishment from the court because of the slanderous machinations of envious peers.[64] These two readings differ in scope but not in kind, for both accept Li Bo's bid for inclusion in the ancient tradition of the unappreciated worthy. There is little reason to question these readings, except for the subtly strange twist at the end of the poem.

In the last line Li Bo joins the passing parade of dead writers whose grave mounds Ruan Ji had spied from his high place. This poetic gesture, simultaneously volatizing all that is perceptible and concrete and concretizing all that is imaginary, makes explicit what had always been understood: not only is there no such landscape—there was probably no climb, either. The authenticity of this poem derives directly from the fact that it is not telling the "truth" but, rather, that its unfounded (empty) reality is constructed on a basis of "real" erudition. As for the message traditionally conveyed by the climbing high theme—the brevity of life and the inevitability of the poet's own demise—perhaps, by citing it as a recognizable quotation within the realm of authenticity delineated by the *Gufeng*, Li Bo objectifies those all-too-human feelings, and lifts himself beyond the dictates of its pathos in yet another bid for the privileges of immortality.

The Biographical Construct of Immortality

Li Bo's bid for immortality begs to be taken seriously, but it is an open question what "seriously" would mean. Historically, his "immortal" identity has operated on three interdependent levels: stylistic, theoretical, and biographical. On the stylistic level, the symbiotic relationship between his sobriquet, "Banished Immortal," and various stylistic elements of his poems (including Daoist imagery, hyperbole, and his objectification of the poetic tradition) offers the most concrete ground on which to both validate and substantiate that identity. The theoretical level, by which I refer to the critical function of his immortal, celestial persona within the larger context of traditional poetics, was discussed in the preceding chapter.

The biographical construct of his "immortality," however, is the most problematic, subtly working at cross purposes with the theoretical. The power of Li Bo's immortal identity depended largely upon its broad suggestiveness as a figurative construct. That elusive and evocative construct permitted readers to embrace the fundamental if disturbing "emptiness" with which his poetry was associated, without destroying it through strict definition. But at the same time, Li Bo himself quoted familiar comparisons and stimuli from past works that had traditionally been interpreted as veiled references to biographical situations. With the rise of the late imperial craze for textual philology and bio-historical explanations came the drive toward configuring "Banished Immortal" in terms of literal or near literal validity, all but destroying its usefulness as the evocative qualifier it was meant to be. Once readers began thinking along these lines, it was only a matter of time before they found themselves debating whether Li Bo was a Daoist adept, a follower of Chan Buddhism, or just a misguided wishful thinker.

The difficulties posed by the coexistence of these three dimensions of Li Bo's immortal persona become particularly acute when interpreting and evaluating the significance of the *Gufeng*. Commentaries appended to these poems reveal the critics' struggle to fit the poems into their vision of Li Bo both as an individual poet and as a great avatar of the poetic tradition as a whole. Their struggle is palpable, as the strong sensual imagery of spirit journeys and celestial encounters collides with the would-be *fugu* spirit of the *Gufeng*. The Ming critic Fang Hongjing, for example, explicitly raises this issue, placing Li Bo's references to immortality in the same questionable category as wine, women, and "lascivious language": "Taibai has only to open his mouth to immediately start talking about immortals. Yet he wants to revive the 'Great Elegantiae'! His works never stray far from wine and women, and are full of lascivious language (*yinci*). It is in these qualities that he remains distant from [Du] Zimei. How can anyone say [in agreement with Yan Yu] that 'poetry does not involve principle.'"?[65]

Some critics, especially partisans of the characterological critical trends of the Ming (Hu Zhenheng and Yuan Hongdao, for example) find their way out of this contradiction by construing his immortality poems as the broad expression of his unfettered, vigorous, and wild spirit. They wisely caution against a too literal interpretation of the *Gufeng*. Other critics, including Ge Lifang, Xiao Shibin, and Chen Hang, find themselves in the almost untenable position of abhorring the immortal stylistics of Li's poetry while upholding the *Gufeng* as his most authentically ancient, and thus most admirable, poetry. Xiao Shibin addresses this incongruity through the blanket (and occasionally forced) application of biographical exegesis, following the tradition of the Han dynasty commentator Wang Yi's influential allegorical interpretation of Qu Yuan's "Li Sao." Chen Hang deals with it by approving only the strictest selection of those *Gufeng* immortality poems that clearly lend themselves to such a reading.

Chen Hang, known for his elucidation of Ruan Ji's *Yonghuai* in strict politico-biographical terms, is among those who are most affronted by Li Bo's penchant for immortal imagery. In his eyes, the crowd-pleasing presence of airborne deities—whether inside or outside the *Gufeng*—is only so much evidence of Li Bo's lack of discipline and seriousness. Chen complains that such poems, while among the most frequently published, actually constitute what is least admirable about Li Bo's poetry. The best of that work, he feels, is in twenty-eight of the fifty-nine underappreciated and seldom-published *Gufeng*:

> Of poems, there are those that must be annotated before they can be understood; such are [Ruan] Sizong's *Yonghuai* and [Chen] Ziang's *Ganyu*. And there are those that must be edited in a collection before beginning to be appreciated; Taibai's *Gufeng* are such poems. So, when genius is put in the service of feeling, then [poetry's] colors will shine forth brilliantly without being frivolous; when vital spirit is led by intention, then [the poetry's] sounds will be free and unencumbered without being dissolute. In not being frivolous, they can move one deeply; in not being dissolute, their appeal can be longlasting.
>
> All the world sings the praises of Li's poetry, but they select only those that are free-wheeling and sublime. [In such poems], his genius shines brightly, but causes his feeling to be sere; his vital breath is fervid, but causes his intention to flow loosely without focus.... He goes so far as to allow the comparison and stimulus [that would convey his] inner nature and feelings to be buried under antiquated phrases about traveling immortals.
>
> [The propagation of these inferior works at the expense of his better pieces] really [results from] a lack of discernment on the part of uninformed scholars, and not only from the mix of sharp and dull armaments in [Li Bo's] arsenal [the uneven quality of his oeuvre]. Of the fifty-nine pieces in the *Gufeng*, we can print half, and those will prove to be endowed with equal parts of elegance and substance such

that, through them, [the people] "can incite, and can observe." Do not the *Odes* say: "Here and there grow the water plants, right and left we gather them"? And [doesn't it] also say: "Other people have their feelings, I shall ascertain them"?[66]

I have quoted this passage at length because here Chen Hang not only nicely elucidates the tension between an ancient aesthetic sensibility (as supposedly embodied in the *Gufeng*) and Li Bo's immortal reveries. He also shows how the *fugu*-minded reader might reconcile them. Poetry, Chen insists, requires that sensory delight be shaped by (presumably honorable) feelings and intentions. Li Bo's "antiquated phrases about traveling immortals" may be pleasing, but they usually mask rather than convey his true feelings; they may be old, but they hardly qualify as "ancient." Most people are content to enjoy the surface beauty of Li's poetry, but those more discerning will know, like the songsters of the *Shijing*, which are worth gathering.

Chen singles out only two of the *Gufeng* immortality poems as being truly worthy of inclusion among these "Ancient Airs":

> In "To the West, I Mounted Lotus Blossom Mountain" [#19] and "The Traveler of Zheng Westward Entered the Passes" [#31], all of the lyrics are about leaving the world and fleeing its chaos, [feelings that have been] entrusted in [images of] wandering immortals. Of the fifty-nine *Gufeng* pieces, those touching upon immortality comprise half; but only these two pieces contain even a bit of the "ancient" sensibility. This is because their lyrics contain implicit meaning [pertaining to his real experience].
>
> Common people don't normally harbor strange imaginings (*qiyi*); if they talk of rising aloft—of cloud encounters and crane riding—it renders them small and insignificant. If even Taibai is like this [vulnerable to being seen this way], how much more so the multitude that meets the eyes![67]

Even without examining *Gufeng* #19 or #31, it is clear that, according to Chen Hang, "strange imaginings" have no place in the company of respectable "Ancient Airs" unless they exhibit some connection with what is real: that is, unless they can be shown to be the spontaneously produced comparisons of a heart in distress. Li

Bo, with his particular gifts, is capable of placing strange imaginings squarely in the service of conveying such pathos. It is just that he does not always choose to do so.

The arguments of Xiao, Chen, and other like-minded critics may have been intended to defend (if only in carefully delineated circumstances) Li Bo's use of immortality imagery. But the long-term effect of this line of interpretation seems inadvertently to have worked to the detriment of the important function of the "Banished Immortal" as a theoretical construct in the larger context of Chinese poetics. Comparison-based interpretation necessarily increases the focus on the concrete, biographical component of Li Bo's immortal identity, compelling the critic to ascertain the poet's motives for having written the poem, for using comparison, and for selecting the vehicle of immortality in particular. In requiring specific associations between life and poem, such readings probably contributed to the eventual crystallization of Li's inimitable, unattainable immortal identity into that of the banal superstitious Daoist adept depicted by Guo Moruo in *Li Bo and Du Fu*. With the emergence of this figure, the blurred edges of immortality are more clearly defined, but immortality's usefulness as a critical concept is virtually neutralized.

There is, paradoxically, a tendency for this interpretive tradition to adhere to the very categories that Li Bo's practice of ancientness seems so apt at undermining. In precisely the places where ancient comparison and stimulus were viewed as inimical to pictorial brilliance and strange imaginings, Li Bo forced their encounter. Now Li takes recognizable textual allusions (in this case largely from Daoist and Buddhist folklore), presents them as comparisons (quoting the exegetical tradition attached to Qu Yuan and resumed, in poetic form, by Ruan Ji and Chen Ziang), and then breathes the life of sensual intensity into them. The effect is, as in the nature poems of the *Gufeng*, to bring about the ultimately fruitful collision of ancient erudition and "ancient" authenticity.

Like Ruan Ji and Chen Zi'ang, Li Bo draws his immortality imagery from a variety of sources, ranging from the *Chuci* to the Han dynasty anthology of fictional biographies, *Liexian zhuan* (Biographies of eminent immortals), various historical biographies in both the *Hanshu* and the *Shiji,* the "traveling immortal" poems from the Jin dynasty, and beyond. Scholars have struggled with the stubborn opacity of both Ruan's and Chen's poems, concocting interpretations that run from the bio-historical precision of Chen Hang to the most sweeping and generalist readings of Shen Deqian. But whatever the degree of precision of the allegoresis applied by outside readers, it seems clear that both Ruan Ji and Chen Zi'ang were aware of, and deliberately subscribed to, the Wang Yi tradition of allegoresis of the *Chuci.* They saw themselves as Qu Yuan's poetic and political heirs.

Wang Yi's reading, which interpreted Qu Yuan's shamanistic spirit voyages as veiled recountings of his Confucian aspirations, has been viewed as a concerted effort to downplay the patently shamanistic and Daoist heritage of Qu Yuan's immortal-like, journeying spirit, and to pass on to future readers a Qu Yuan who was staunchly Confucian.[68] Narrowly interpreted, Wang Yi, and those who perpetuated and elaborated his reading of the "Li Sao," held that the only justifiable spirit voyage was the symbolic one, enlisted purely to portray the wronged Confucian scholar-official's frustration and his natural desire to escape the society that prohibited his contribution. Not all scholars condemn Wang Yi as being so monomaniacal; some simply see his allegorical reading as a reasonable application of the fundamental premises of reality-based Chinese poetic criticism. But judgments aside, Ruan Ji and Chen Zi'ang successfully perpetuated this allegorical exegesis not through its application but through the making of poems that require its implementation. Both the difficult circumstances of their lives and the isolated, allusive use of images that resonate so strongly with the *Chuci* all but ensure the type of allegorical reading Wang Yi so influentially practiced.

But this is precisely where Li Bo's enlistment of that exegetical tradition differs from that of his predecessors. Whereas Ruan and Chen mix and match isolated images in ways that often defy a coherent reading—whether on the superficial discursive level or on the secondary allusive level—Li Bo enjoys embedding those images in a narrative so detailed and vivid as to allow the reader to join him in "witnessing" the events described. Whereas both Ruan

and Chen are known to have suffered for their political views, the
reputedly self-indulgent Li Bo's case is, at best, less easily defensi-
ble. Li Bo recounts meetings with immortals in full knowledge that
such tales will inevitably attract—and ultimately defy—exegetical
practice. Li Bo was no Qu Yuan, but he was heir to him in a
broader and more exclusively literary sense: as the archetypal
outcast portrayed and transmitted in the works of Ruan Ji and
Chen Zi'ang. *Gufeng* #7, an elegant, coherent, and visually exciting
recounting of a quick glimpse of the immortal An Qi, invokes the
Chuci tradition in just this way:

Among wanderers, there is an immortal astride a	客有鶴上仙
crane,	飛飛凌太清
Flying, flying to mount the Supreme Purity.	揚言碧雲裡
He lifts his voice amid the emerald clouds,	自道安期名
4 *And utters his own name: An Qi.*	兩兩白玉童
Two by two, children of white jade	雙吹紫鸞笙
Play on pairs of purple phoenix flutes.	去影忽不見
Their fleeting shadows suddenly gone from view,	回風送天聲
8 *A gust of wind returns their heavenly sound.*	舉首遠望之
I lift my head to gaze at them afar;	飄然若流星
They are as wispy as the shooting stars.	願餐金光草
I want to dine on "golden-light grass,"	壽與天齊傾
12 *My life enduring as long as heaven itself.*[69]	

Li Bo's poem is reminiscent of the "Nine Songs" by way of the
traveling immortal poems they later inspired: just as seductive, and
even more mysterious. Evoking the longing of the shaman as he
gazes at the unattainable deity, *Gufeng* #7 subtly but effectively
plays with the position of the speaker, whose stable point of view
provided a central signifying element in reading its predecessors.
In Li Bo's poem, the position of the speaker shifts twice: first from
that of neutral biographer (lines 1–2) to privileged witness of a rare
event (lines 3–10), and then from witness to desirous aspirant in
the decidedly unprivileged position of regular mortal, as close to
the reader as to any shaman (lines 11–12). Through these shifts Li
Bo invites the reader to rethink the usual allegorizing response and

consider other ways in which he uses the past, as well as other reasons for choosing to do so.

The poem opens with a vigorous assertion of the real existence of the immortal. The first couplet echoes the impersonal rhetoric of textual or oral history, and the second introduces the evidence of an eyewitness. The transformation of the historian into eyewitness occasions the lengthy and exquisite description comprising the bulk of the poem. This part most clearly recalls the shamans of the "Nine Songs," who catch a fleeting glimpse of the divine immortal only to watch helplessly as the deity disappears again in the firmament. But in the closing couplet, the speaker steps out of this role and seems to be directly addressing the reader in an apostrophe similar to those in the other *Gufeng*. Although some of the "Nine Songs" do conclude with passionate exclamations of (disappointed) desire, Li Bo's declaration differs markedly, especially in the explicitness of his goal of immortality, as opposed to a comparison-based desire for the immortal as a love object. Li Bo's directness subtly works against a Wang Yi–style allegorical reading and resonates with the assumed objectivity of the opening couplet, leaving the reader in a bit of a quandary as to where to situate this narrative on the axis between comparison and reality.

Another move to thwart the allegorical impulse, at least insofar as allegory leads to making Li Bo a latter-day Qu Yuan, is his selection of An Qi as the desired immortal. According to the account in the *Liexian zhuan*, An Qi was an immortal who sold magical herbs of immortality on the banks of the Eastern Seas during the time of the Qin. There the First Emperor met with him for three days and nights, after which An Qi invited him to wait a few years and then visit him on Penglai Mountain, where the immortals dwelled. The emissaries the emperor later sent reportedly encountered rough seas and never made it to the famed mountain.[70] Sima Qian's version of the story adds that An Qi appeared only to those with whom he was compatible, and otherwise remained in reclusion.[71] Based on both these accounts, An Qi incarnates an ideal hybrid of Confucian and Daoist sensibilities: one who is willing to serve, as long as doing so is in keeping with his nature. His steadfast refusal to serve the tyrannical and cruel First Emperor can only be to his credit, whether the judge's stance is strongly Confucian or Daoist.

This allusion, reinserted into a "Nine Songs" format, produces interesting results. Of course, it is possible to read the name as of little importance, deciding that Li Bo mentions it as a way of lending substance to the celestial vision, not in order to invoke An Qi's story. There is some textual support for such an argument. An Qi's only occurrence in the *Chuci*, in the seventh of Wang Yi's "Nine Longings," is quite incidental.[72] When Li Bo mentions the name elsewhere, he does not necessarily grant any particular importance to the story, seeming quite content to mention An Qi as just another immortal. Even in *Gufeng* #20, where Li Bo includes a remark about the Qin emperor's fruitless search, he does little to integrate that specific allusion into the overall meaning of the poem.[73]

Gufeng #7, then, is unique in singling out An Qi. Given Li Bo's penchant for blending allusions in unexpected ways, it is not unreasonable to examine his allusion to the immortal more closely. From the outset, it is difficult to ignore the affinity between the An Qi story and the Qu Yuan tradition. Both employ the narrative structure of the futile quest, both raise the dilemma of service and retreat, and, perhaps most important, both recall the ancient theme of natural complicity and like-mindedness, whether between the righteous minister and his prince, between friends, or between lovers.

The similarity of the An Qi story and the Qu Yuan tradition points to the possible presence of allegory. The traditional allegorical reading of the "Nine Songs" draws an analogy between the shaman and the minister on the one hand, and the divinity and the prince on the other. But when the reticent deity is An Qi, and the admiring onlooker is Li Bo, that particular allegorical structure crumbles. If Li Bo is expressing his own disappointment at not being understood by the emperor, why would he choose An Qi as the object of desire, and so place himself in a position analogous to that of the justly rebuffed First Emperor? The closing couplet provides the answer—or, at least, one answer. Li Bo is not seeking to enter into a Confucian relationship with An Qi after all. Rather, as he directly declares, he wants to partake of An Qi's magic herbs in order to attain immortality. This final twist is disturbing, not only because of its forthright Daoist content, but because of its subversion of the conventional allegorical reading, of the entire *Chuci* exegetical tradition, and, by extension, of the authority of comparison-stimulus poetics as a pillar of ancient authenticity.

For all the obviousness of both the An Qi quotation and the "Nine Songs" quotation, it is difficult to bring them together, especially when scrutinizing the poem through the lens of the "ancient" values to which the *Gufeng* purport to respond. Even Xiao Shibin can do no better here than weakly protest: "This is yet another piece written in the 'wandering immortal' form. I suspect it was composed either for presentation to someone or in response to someone else's poem; it was certainly not written on a whim."[74] Xiao's interpretation seeks to ground the poem in a real-life context, even if that context is irrecoverable. His suggestion allows the reader the luxury of believing in the poem's authenticity and the functionality of Li Bo's use of comparison—without having to understand it. When Xiao further specifies that the choice of vehicle was imposed upon Li Bo by someone else, he effectively excuses the poet from having made an otherwise inexcusable compositional choice. In rationalizing what seems a bit too irrational, the critic ties the fanciful to what is most concrete, remaining faithful to Wang Yi's spirit, if not to the letter.

Ge Lifang, whose preference for Du Fu's poetry is well known, also feels compelled to justify in ancient terms this and the other the immortal poems of the *Gufeng*:

> Of the nearly seventy poems comprising the two *juan* of Li Taibai's *Gufeng*, approximately thirteen or fourteen concern his personal desire to become a divine immortal. Either he is trying to pluck hibiscus and tread the Supreme Purity, or wanting to harness a pair of dragons and ride their inverted shadows, or wishing to obtain jade slippers and climb Mount Peng, or hoping to break off a branch of the Ruomu Tree and travel through the Eight Directions, or yearning to join in friendship with Wangzi Jin, or desiring to pay homage to Wei Shuqing, or aspiring to borrow Chi Songzi's white deer, or longing to dine on the golden-light [grasses] of An Qi Sheng. Isn't it

just because He Jizhen [He Zhizhang] saw [Li Bo] as a "banished immortal," that people believe his stories? But isn't it rather [Li Bo]'s despondency over not being employed and not attaining his ambitions that causes him to contemplate such a lofty retreat?[75]

If Ge seems impatient with Li Bo's predilection for cavorting with immortals and straining his readers' credulity, he is even more impatient with readers who, in the interest of preserving their belief in a narrow interpretation of Li Bo's authenticity, take these fanciful scenes at face value. Ge seems to be taken with the imagery, for his list presents an array of pictures as dazzling as it is deriding. Still, he seems to insist, no matter how vivid the details of his spirit journeys, no matter how visually compelling the celestial panorama, all these images may (or perhaps must) be safely subsumed under the rubric of "lofty retreat" from an unsympathetic world. Readers like Xiao and Ge ensure that Li Bo's "Banished Immortal" is at home on the orthodox terrain of Confucian ethics, and that his immortality poetry remains within the bounds of the *Gufeng*. Although they are correct in granting this poem, however reluctantly, ancient-style authenticity, their reasons for doing so lie not in the poem itself, but in their own theoretical and ethical convictions. In my opinion, this poem's ancientness arises once again from its quotation of literary texts in their precritical or "ancient" state, rendered in vivid sensuality, in revelatory defiance of the emergent *fugu* views that inadvertently threatened the ancientness they attempted to uphold. When such critics as Zhu Xi and Yan Yu insisted on Li's book-learning, they may have been closer to the mark than readers like Ge and Xiao. Such quotation and elaboration of textual precedents confronts readers with a freewheeling imagination that not only derives from hard-won erudition, but showcases it.

Compared with a tantalizing and stubbornly recondite poem like *Gufeng* #7, poem #19 comes as a relief to comparison-minded critics. In this poem, Li Bo offers clear "evidence" of his admirably Confucian social consciousness, indicating to critics that they might be justified in pursuing an allegorical reading and freeing them to decode the comparison rather than troubling them with the question of whether the poem actually contains one.

To the west, I mounted Lotus Blossom Mountain,	西上蓮花山
And, away in the distance, spied Shining Star.[76]	迢迢見明星
Her white-silk hand held a hibiscus flower;	素手把芙蓉
4 *Pacing the void, she trod upon the Supreme*	虛步躡太清
Purity.	霓裳曳廣帶
From her cloud-robes trailed a broad sash,	飄拂昇天行
Which wafted behind as she ascended to heaven.	邀我登雲臺
She invited me to climb Cloud Terrace Peak,	高揖衛叔卿
8 *And there pay homage to Wei Shuqing.*	恍恍與之去
In a flash, off with her I went,	駕鴻凌紫冥
Riding a wild swan to mount the purple dark.	俯視洛陽川
Below, I saw the river of Luoyang,	茫茫走胡兵
12 *And hordes of Tartar soldiers swarming across*	流血塗野草
the land.	豺狼盡冠纓
Spilt blood coated the grasses of the field;	
Wolves and jackals, all sporting officials' caps.[77]	

Chen Hang considered this one of the two immortality poems that actually merit the "ancient" classification. In the eyes of most critics, the last four lines of this poem save it from the ignominy of being yet another gratuitous exercise in cloud-hopping, qualifying it instead as a socially responsible reflection entirely worthy of inclusion in the "Ancient Airs." Uncertainty as to the exact import of the poem—whether it is a criticism of the emperor or a reference to the An Lushan rebellion or to internecine struggles within the court—intrigues rather than confuses the critics, who are perhaps relieved at having something concrete to focus on, something more palpable than the enticing but opaque secrets of his encounter with Shining Star and the pair's subsequent flight through the heavens.

But the two clues that invite readers to attempt a *Chuci*-style decoding also prevent a satisfactory resolution of the puzzle: the allusion to Wei Shuqing, and the condensed "Li Sao" narrative, including the well-known, troubling ending. Like the appearance of An Qi in *Gufeng* #7, the details of Wei Shuqing's biography suggest that his role in this poem may go beyond that of a randomly named immortal invoked as a means of adding concreteness to a decidedly fantastic scene. According to the Eastern Jin collection of tales about immortals, the *Shenxian zhuan*, Wei Shuqing was an immortal who visited, unbidden, Emperor Wu of the Han, in the hope of instructing him in the Dao. But rather than according Wei the respect due a person of his station, the emperor greeted the immortal as a subject. At this, Wei took umbrage and left, never to return.[78] Like An Qi, Wei Shuqing is a figure who engages both Confucian and Daoist belief systems. But whereas An Qi embodies a point of convergence between views of service and retreat, Wei's story points up one of their essential disagreements, that between ritualized propriety and personal freedom. To further complicate matters, Wei's story can be interpreted in two ways, lending itself to quotation for two different purposes.

At first glance, Wei appears to be a Zhuangzi-like hero who, while not averse to offering his services to society and guiding others along the path of enlightenment, is utterly incapable of submitting himself to the strictures of empty Confucian ritual and propriety. But a closer look at Wei's story reveals a strange contradiction in his behavior. It would seem that Wei did not so much bridle at the emperor's insistence on observing propriety as at the emperor's neglect of the propriety to be observed between student (in this case, the emperor) and teacher. Is it possible that Li Bo invokes Wei Shuqing mockingly, as a Daoist immortal somehow still finicky about the ritual recognition of his own hierarchical superiority as teacher? Although critics' silence on the possible interpretations of the allusion to Wei Shuqing implies that they granted the specifics of this story little importance, its thematization of ritual behavior resonates strongly with the ostentatiously insouciant aspects of Li Bo's "immortal" persona, and so invites closer consideration. It also seems reasonable to suspect that Li Bo, as an active participant in the construction of that persona, and as a reader demonstrably well versed in the details of immortals' biographies, mentioned Wei for a specific purpose. The question is, to which reading of the story did he adhere: Wei as upright Daoist teacher, or Wei as hypocrite?

In the tradition of the frequently opaque symbolism of Ruan Ji's *Yonghuai* and Chen Zi'ang's *Ganyu,* the poem itself offers no obvious clue. Wei merely provides the destination—never reached in the poem—of a spirit voyage in which Li "paces the void" alongside Shining Star. If Li Bo accepted Wei as an immortal unable to abide by the rituals of Confucian society, then his intended homage to Wei might be taken at face value, offered by an aspiring immortal to an actual one—and, of course, as a friendly wink from one ritual-free spirit to another. This reading coheres quite nicely with Li's typical portrayal of his own famously unhindered spirit, and maintains the poem's thematic affinity with the *Chuci*. If, however, Li Bo had in mind a status-minded Wei Shuqing, his homage would be ironic, with Li Bo putting himself in the superior position of one who has achieved true independence from the Confucian hierarchies expressed in propriety and ritual. Although this second reading might seem out of keeping with the supposedly straight sincerity of the *Gufeng,* it should not be discounted outright. Not only does this more sardonic reading emphasize Li Bo's autonomy of spirit, smoothing the transition to its grand, abrupt ending, but its mere presence as a feasible option sets up yet another intriguing meeting of supposedly irreconcilable values. The beauty of this ambiguous allusion lies in its appearance of contributing to a sustained, comprehensible comparison while leading the reader to confront its ultimate insolubility.

The ambiguous allusion to Wei is couched within the poem's larger structural reference to the "Li Sao," itself the strongest invitation to a decoding of any suggestive comparisons and allusions. *Gufeng* #19 echoes and condenses Qu Yuan's longer, episodic narrative into one brief—and equally unachieved—spirit journey. But perhaps the clearest reference to the "Li Sao" occurs in the abrupt, unexpected insertion of the last four lines, which recall these final moments of the "Li Sao":

My eight dragon steeds flew on with writhing
undulations;
My cloud-embroidered banners flapped on the
wind.
In vain I tried to curb them, to slacken the swift
pace:
4 *The spirits soared high up, far into the distance.*
We played the "Nine Songs" and danced the
Shao Dances,
Borrowing the time to make a holiday.
But when I had ascended the splendor of the
heavens,
8 *I suddenly caught a glimpse below of my old*
home.
My groom's heart was heavy and the horses for
longing
Arched their heads back and refused to go on.[79]

駕八龍之蜿蜿兮
載雲旗之委蛇
抑志而弭節兮
神高馳之邈邈
奏九歌而舞韶兮
聊假日以媮樂
陟陞皇之赫戲兮
忽臨睨夫舊鄉
僕夫悲余馬懷兮
蜷局顧而不行

With that final glance earthward, not only does Qu Yuan's celestial flight come to an abrupt end, but the apparently unrestrained course of his imagination is overtaken and halted by the banality of longing for his earthly home. Li Bo and his readers most likely shared the belief that the end of the "Li Sao" announced the eventual end of Qu Yuan's life, for Qu Yuan is believed to have committed suicide by drowning. But though these final lines (and the famous *luan* [envoi] that immediately follows) may well predict Qu Yuan's plunge into the river, his death hardly signals his mortality. At least some readings interpret his intention to "join Peng Xian in the place where he abides" as a reference to the Shang dynasty shamans Peng and Xian, allowing readers to imagine that Qu Yuan, too, attained immortality, joining at last those deities whose company he so craved.[80] Working in concert with this allusion is the incontrovertible evidence of Qu Yuan's literary immortality. While achieved beyond the bounds of the poem, it owes its existence in no small part to this supposed poetic account of his own death.

Li Bo was no suicide, but he certainly longed for immortality in all its guises, and borrowed to wonderful effect Qu Yuan's earthward gaze, in which life and death merge in an eternally suspended moment. Li Bo, too, ends his poem in a moment suspended between flight and engagement, between purity and pollution. But without the traditional reading that supplied a justifying ending to Qu Yuan's poem and life, Li Bo's ending affords no possibility of resolution, either within the confines of the poem or in its extratextual circumstances. His finale takes place in the sole act of perceiving. The poet remains a suspended observer, choosing, for the moment, life over death. In light of Qu Yuan's hovering presence, this ironically means mortality over immortality. What may ostensibly seem to be an allusion, an act of deliberate self-identification with Qu Yuan, becomes a quotation, and as such is tinged with a particular pathos marking the irredeemable intrinsic and extrinsic differences between the two.

Comparison-minded readers will recognize that in this poem Li Bo quotes Qu Yuan's use of comparison in order to identify with him. But the point of identification is not Qu Yuan's ethos, but his dissonance. Like Qu Yuan's "Li Sao," *Gufeng* #19 has an abrupt and inconclusive ending; unlike its predecessor, however, Li Bo's poem finds no resolution in the unifying myth of its author's later actions. Unable to lay claim to the whole of Qu Yuan's experience, long invoked as the unifying rationale behind such extremes of expression and behavior, Li Bo nevertheless idiomizes and quotes those extremes, removing them from their original context and making them an end in themselves.

NOT ALL of Li Bo's immortality poems in the *Gufeng* rely so directly on the importation of Qu Yuan's poetic and moral contradictions to assert their status of "ancientness." Some of them—much to the dismay and frustration of certain critics—seem to be straightforward expressions of an apparently heartfelt, unadulterated desire to acquire the elixir of immortality, and so manifest a brand of authenticity that is less easily integrated into the ancient ethos. These poems not only depict visually arresting meetings with known Daoists or mythic immortals, but tend to display an internal imagistic and narrative consistency that seems to render allegorical interpretation superfluous. One good example is *Gufeng #5*:

How lush and verdant Taibai Mountain!	太白何蒼蒼
Stars rise and thickly cluster above.	星辰上森列
Separated from heaven by a mere three hundred li—	去天三百里
	邈爾與世絕
4 So remote it is cut off from the world.	中有綠髮翁
In its midst, a raven-haired elder,	披雲臥松雪
Cloaked in clouds, reposing on the snow of pines.	不笑亦不語
He does not laugh, does not speak,	冥棲在巖穴
8 Silently resides in a cliff's cave.	我來逢真人
I come and meet this True Man,	長跪問寶訣
Kneel, my back straight, asking for the precious prescript.	粲然啟玉齒
	授以鍊藥說
With a broad smile, baring jade-white teeth,	銘骨傳其語
12 He bestows upon me the alchemical method.	竦身已電滅
From deep in his bones the words issue forth,	仰望不可及
Then, extending his body, he's already gone like lightning.	蒼然五情熱
	吾將營丹砂
Upward I gaze, but cannot reach him,	永與世人別
16 Suddenly the five passions burn.	
I shall prepare the cinnabar elixir,	
And quit forever the men of this world.[81]	

Still, in encountering just such a sensual, imaginative poem, the importance of its "ancient" designation becomes most apparent, and the impulse toward a Wang Yi–style interpretation becomes most pressing. One of the most explicit declarations of title-generated criticism was passed down by Emperor Gaozong in a comment he appended to Li Bo's "Xiaogu" (#2 of 2): "Works designated as *xiaogu* or *nigu* are never [comprised of] 'empty' words (*kongyan*), but must always harbor some emotion by reason of which they carry meaning. That is why, when plain words (*zhiyan*) cannot capture [that emotion], then one uses covert words (*yuyan*) to express it. When direct words cannot capture it, then one turns the words around in order to make [one's intended] meaning manifest."[82]

If this is true of *xiaogu* and *nigu* poems, how much more so of the *Gufeng*, which have long been cited separately as a centerpiece of Li Bo's oeuvre! And when a particular *Gufeng* like this one offers little in the way of clues, it becomes a blank slate upon which critics inscribe their own understanding of the poet. Partisans of the most literal and biographical rendering of the "Banished Immortal" persona eagerly read this poem, along with #4, as reminiscences of Li's youthful training with the Daoist Sima Chengzhen. Xiao Shibin authenticates the poems in just this way, insisting that, after all, these poems "are not gratuitous works (*fei fanran zhi zuo*)."[83] Xu Zhenqing, while less specific as to the time and occasion of their composition, believes that #4 and #5 "were probably composed because [Li] Bo really desired immortality."[84]

Readers more inclined toward preserving the figurative and literary dimension of Li Bo's immortal persona, however, tend to interpret the *Gufeng* immortality poems and Li Bo's generalized use of immortal and Daoist imagery as fundamental expressions of his spirit, not necessarily closely tied to the specific circumstances of his life. In the course of making their arguments for a broader reading of immortality imagery, these critics contribute significantly to a broadening of the conception of poetic authenticity. Gaozong, for example, while allowing that Li Bo may have written this poem in a period of exile and Daoist study, does not consider this a necessary condition. Rather, he reads the celestial imagery and immortality narrative as the natural product of Li's "sublime genius" and "wind-tossed, supreme heart" encountering some unidentifiable frustration.[85] Hu Zhenheng goes further and, in direct refutation of Xiao's commentary, completely denies any biographical basis, arguing, along with other critics, that Li Bo could not have believed in immortality as a viable pursuit.[86] As proof of Li Bo's critical attitude toward the interminable quest for the impossible elixir, he reminds readers of three *Gufeng* that actively ridicule that practice: "Consultation of the current 60-poem collection of the *Gufeng* [reveals that] twelve of them relate [themes of] immortality. In nine of these, [Li Bo] speaks of himself as a wandering immortal; in the other three, he mocks those who focus on the search for immortality. It seems unlikely that his understanding and his delusion should be so much at odds. When [Li] Bo speaks of himself as capable of attaining immortality, he is surely borrowing this [expression] to convey his boundless longings and imaginings. How could he possibly be saying that there are divine immortals in this world!"[87]

As he pursues his argument, Hu goes on to attempt a resolution of the apparent contradiction posed by the two types of immortality poems in such a way as to ensure their conformity to proper "ancient" sentiment, simultaneously grounding Li Bo's morality in the social concerns of his times and rooting his use of celestial imagery incontrovertibly in his inner being. Hu argues that poems recounting previous rulers' quests for immortality function as indirect critiques of Xuanzong, while those narrating Li Bo's own imagined experience actually express the more general longings of his unfettered spirit.[88] The Qing critic Fang Dongshu sums up this more general interpretation of immortality imagery when he says of *Gufeng* #4, "Here he talks about immortals as a pretext for releasing [the feelings in his] breast and forgetting worldly affairs."[89]

But perhaps no critic is more effective in the ongoing effort to integrate Li Bo's stylistic use of immortality into *Gufeng* expectations than the Ming critic and poet Tu Long, who was a pivotal figure in the Chan-inspired equation of Li Bo's emptiness with ancient standards of poetic authenticity. In a single fascinating passage, Tu extends his legitimation of Li's unfounded poetics specifically to the immortality poems of the *Gufeng*, not only arguing for the authenticity of their expression, but justifying their images of immortality as being no less real than those employed by Qu Yuan and his literary followers. In the following passage, immediately after suggesting that perhaps not all of the images that appear in Du Fu's poetry are exactly "real" and substantive, Tu turns explicitly to Li Bo's *Gufeng*:

> [Likewise], in poems by Li [Bo] such as the several tens of *Gufeng*, he is moved by his times and entrusts [those feelings] in objects, his feelings both expansive and deep; in what way can his myriad scenes

all be deemed empty? As long as his work is of high caliber, and the resonance of his own natural style (*fengyun*) by its own force extends far, how does his adoption of "sky-mounting" language harm the [tradition of the] "Great Elegantiae"? The great master Qu was pained by his times and loved his prince, and made these feelings manifest in every piece of his writing, [depicting] truthful scenes in full sincerity. In poems like "Distant Journey" ("Yuan you"), when he mounts and traverses the void, is this not lofty? When [Sima Xiangru's] "Great Man" ("Daren") ascends upon the clouds, is this not a fine scene? [Guo Pu's] "Traveling Immortal" ("You xian") and "Seeking the Recluse" ("Zhao yin") are also beautiful accounts. Now, when [Li Bo] climbs the [immortal dwelling] Mount Langfeng, or sits atop Tianmu, or nears the sun and moon, or holds on to a flying immortal—since he cannot [really] attain these goals, he articulates them in order to gladden his heart, in the sheer exuberance of his longing. Must everyone cleave to his single inch of land, and remain under his thatched roof ... and then consider [only] "real" scenes (*shijing*) as valuable?[90]

The power of Tu Long's argument lies in his blend of psychological (internal) and historical (external) evidence to achieve a subtle yet matter-of-fact yoking together of unfoundedness and substance. Tu first cites evidence of the inexorable force by which intense feeling translates into acts of real (but not documentary) poetic expression, implicitly invoking the doctrine of immediacy expressed in the "Great Preface" of the *Shijing*. Building on this point, he substantiates the "reality" of these unfounded expressions by presenting the already canonized poetic lineage documenting those acts, from Qu Yuan to Sima Xiangru (ca. 180–117 B.C.) and Guo Pu (276–324). Appealing both to his audience's profound belief in the reality—the undeniable existence—of a poet's inner feelings and to their unexamined love of the many ethereal evocations present throughout the canon, Tu compels his readers to realize that the literary tradition never was a matter of factual notation, and that they themselves would surely not wish it to become so now.

But Tu's argument, compelling as it is, reveals just how common critical objections to such seemingly impenetrable, or stubbornly superficial, poems as *Gufeng* #5 were. If Tu is correct in suggesting that Li Bo's poem is no more objectionable than its predecessors, why did it provoke so much more objection? Understanding the reasons behind this may offer an indication of the poem's intertextual significance and of Li Bo's intentions in writing such a poem. I have been unable to find any explicit justifications in the critical writings themselves. But, as in previous poems, I have detected a transformation that probably exercised critics writing in a post-*fugu* era.

Critics have noted a specific relationship between Li's *Gufeng* #5 and Guo Pu's "Wandering Immortals: #2 of 7," remarking upon the specific and obvious similarity between the sixth couplets of the two poems (lines 11 and 12):

	The qingxi trees, over one thousand ren tall,	青溪千餘仞
	And, in their midst, a Daoist adept.	中有一道士
	Clouds emerge from among the pillars and eaves,	雲生梁棟間
4	*Winds gust out from the windows and doors.*	風出窗戶裡
	I ask who this might be,	借問此何誰
	They say he is Master Valley-Spirit.	云是鬼谷子
	He walks in the footsteps of Xu You,	翹跡企潁陽
8	*At the river's edge, thinks of washing his ears.*	臨河思洗耳
	From the southwest comes the western wind,	閶闔西南來
	Raising ripples like a fish's scales.	潛波渙鱗起
	The river goddess looks at me and smiles,	靈妃顧我笑
12	Radiantly reveals her jade-white teeth.	粲然啟玉齒
	Jianxiu the matchmaker's time is past;	蹇脩時不存
	If I want her, whom should I send?[91]	要之將誰使

Both Li Bo's and Guo Pu's poems share traits recognizable from the "Nine Songs" of the *Chuci*: a quasi-natural landscape, enhanced to suggest the scale and beauty of divine realms; the appearance, in this faerie setting, of a divine being, a tantalizing object of desire, who seems to be offering something; finally, the concluding recognition of the ultimate inaccessibility of that offering. But Li Bo has, predictably, effected an important transformation, specifically in the relationship between the speaking subject and its object of desire. Whereas Guo Pu's shaman/adept/poet and

the flirtatious, tantalizing deity never consummate their relation-
ship, Li Bo's poet and immortal do. More to the point, in Guo Pu's
poem, the relationship between shaman and goddess maintains its
erotic tenor throughout, while Li Bo drains the relationship of any
hint of eroticism.

This shift effectively eliminates any basis for a Wang Yi–style
allegorical reading. In this blocking of the usual avenues of legit-
imation, Li Bo has once again disturbed critics who try to accept
his fanciful narratives. The element of unfulfilled desire, essential
for the reception of the theme of *itineraria* upon which these
poems' ancient authenticity relied, is replaced by partial fulfillment
of a specific, decidedly non-"ancient" goal. The unattainable god-
dess has disappeared. In her place—and boasting the same tanta-
lizing "jade-white teeth"—is an old man. This nameless, eternally
youthful elder, straddling the border between humanity and divin-
ity, is not so much one Li Bo would like to possess, as someone
Li Bo would like to become. This possibility verges on realiza-
tion when, finally, the elder breaks his silence to accommodate
the questing poet, bequeathing to him the means for just such a
transformation:

> *With a broad smile, baring jade-white teeth,*
> *He bestows upon me the alchemical method.*
> *From deep in his bones the words issue forth,*
> 4 *Then, extending his body, he's already gone like lightning.*
> *Suddenly the five passions burn.*
> *I shall prepare the cinnabar elixir,*
> *And quit forever the men of this world.*

Li Bo writes against Guo Pu's "Traveling Immortal" poetry,
achieving a hybrid of the divine and the mortal, the celestial and
the earthly, through the deletion of erotic desire and, more sig-
nificantly, of the clear ontological categories that erotic desire nec-
essarily inscribes. As in the similar collapsing of rhetorical cate-
gories in the *Gufeng* poems discussed earlier, whether through the
visual realization of allusive or imaginary landscapes or the use of
apostrophe to fuse speaker and writer into one persona, this act ren-

ders the poem immune to allegoresis, insofar as allegoresis relies on the poet's imposition of equivalency on separate categories (one of which is usually presumed more "real" than the other). Enacting his own alchemical transformation upon critical distinctions between empty and full, unfounded and substantive, and mischievously embedding those transformations in the shamanistic, sensual, hyperbolic verse of the "Nine Songs," Li Bo beats the proponents of ancientness at their own game. He has demonstrated the inexhaustibility of the expressive possibilities latent in ancient texts, as long as one does not accept the ossified and ultimately falsifying packages in which they are transported through the generations. He is able, again and again, to quote, and not merely imitate or even continue, those past writings in the most passionate expression of the most ancient of all human desires: the desire of rising above the limitations and disappointments of human existence and achieving eternal life.

Critics consider *Gufeng* #4 the companion piece to #5. In it Li Bo's vivid portrayal of immortal visions and celestial journeys is rivaled only by his tangibly painful yearning to realize them:

The phoenix flies 9,000 ren,	鳳飛九千仞
Five colors patterned in a jewellike brocade.	五章備綵珍
Carrying the letter in its beak, returned home—	銜書且虛歸
mission unfulfilled,	空入周與秦
4 *And penetrated, in vain, the kingdoms of Zhou*	橫絕歷四海
and Qin.	所居未得鄰
In one flight, cut across the four seas,	吾營紫河車
In its haven, it's never known a neighbor.	千載落風塵
I concoct the "purple river-chariot"—	藥物祕海嶽
8 *One thousand years plunged in the dust of this*	採鉛青溪濱
world.	時登大樓山
Medicinal herbs encrust the seas and mountains,	舉首望仙真
I gather alchemical lead on the banks of Green	
River.	
And then I climb Hightower Mountain,	
12 *Lift my head to gaze at true immortals.*	

Winged mounts dissolved in fleeting shadows,	羽駕滅去影
Gust-borne chariots lost in an eddying whirl.	飆車絕回輪
Still I fear that the cinnabar nectar is delayed—	尚恐丹液遲
16 *That my heart's desire will not unfold.*	志願不及申
In vain the hair in the mirror turns to frost,	徒霜鏡中髮
I am shamed before the crane-riding one.	羞彼鶴上人
Where do they bloom—the peach and plum?	桃李何處開
20 *Those flowers are not of my springtime!*	此花非我春
I ought simply to go to that princely abode,	惟應清都境
And consort, a long time, with the immortal Han Zhong.[92]	長與韓眾親

The intensity of emotion that Li Bo displays here is on a par with that expressed by Qu Yuan. The mythical surroundings are comparable; the outright declaration of his fear of time's passing, too, is very familiar. But, as in #5, these similarities serve only to highlight the difference between Li Bo's motives and those traditionally attributed to Qu Yuan, as the speed of time's passage is transformed: an impediment between Qu Yuan and his goal, it is the focus of Li Bo's actions. Of course, one might reasonably express an acute desire for a world where one's talents and righteousness are recognized and put to use, and then embark on an allegorical quest, as Qu Yuan did. And one might also feel regret— or even terror—at the prospect of one's own imminent senescence and death, as Du Fu most famously and influentially did. But here, all allegorical signposts have been removed, and critics must face the possibility that Li Bo's desire to consort with immortals is simply an expression of his desire to live forever, to abandon all pretense to the role of unrecognized worthy. In recognizing this convergence of language, poet, and persona, it becomes possible to appreciate the acuity of Yuan Hongdao's summary of Li Bo's relationship with immortality: "Qinglian's [Li Bo's] passion for immortals and Dongpo's [Su Shi's] passion for the Buddha are well known. Everyone believes that the two masters were lyric composers, but never believed that they were true [followers] of immortality and Buddhism. Even the two masters did not believe it themselves.... Nevertheless, to say that Taibai was not an [adept

of] immortality is to misunderstand [adepts of] immortality....
Only in the two masters' inability to believe in their own devout-
ness, and [in their] frantic dashing about here and there, did they
commit an error."[93]

Underlying Yuan Hongdao's reproach to Li Bo and Su Dongpo
for never having fully assumed the depths of their beliefs in
immortality practices and Buddhism, respectively, is a plea for a
more holistic or syncretic view of what such beliefs entail. Li man-
ifested throughout his writings an irresistible affinity for the world
inhabited by immortals, for the promise that their existence held
for him as a mortal and as a poet. This, Yuan seems to say, is part of
the nature that expressed itself in his poetry. To deny it, allegorize
it, or rationalize it is to misunderstand both the nature of the poet
and of the religion (for want of a better word) in question. What-
ever Yuan's intentions in making this argument, it lends itself well
to my inquiry into the complex relationship of Li Bo's purported
"ancientness" (especially as attributed to the *Gufeng* and related
poems) and his "immortality."

The stylistic, theoretical, and biographical dimensions of Li
Bo's immortal persona join in a poetics that conveys personal feel-
ings not so much through the mocking or rejection of poetic con-
vention as through the consistent refusal to acquiesce in its con-
ventionality. This, too, involves a return to the past, if not quite in
the sense that *fugu* proponents intended. Li Bo seems to have rec-
ognized that the return path can be neither direct nor simple. It is
helpful to think of his approach as consisting in the explicit act of
erasing rather than the covert act of retracing. Such actions inevi-
tably draw attention to the self undertaking the task. But whether
that was the primary goal of his undertaking—any more so than
any other act of poetic writing since (and including) Qu Yuan
himself—is another question altogether.

CHAPTER 4

The *Yuefu*

The Anatomy of an Unfettering

LI BO'S poem "A Summer Day in the Mountains," beautifully translated by David Hinton, is not an expression of the joy of being naked in the woods, but of experiencing nakedness through the realization that one had always been clothed:

Flourishing a white-feather fan　　嬾搖白羽扇
lazily, I go naked in green forests.　　裸袒青林中
Soon, I've hung my cap on a cliff,　　脫巾挂石壁
set my hair loose among pine winds.[1]　　露頂灑松風

Only when he hangs up his cap on a cliff do speaker and reader comprehend that, although stripped bare, he had not been truly naked until that moment. More than the refreshing sprinkling of pine winds on an unaccustomed brow, it is discovering the existence—and the superfluity—of this habitual accessory that creates the feeling of true liberation. And what better instrument of nakedness than this "cap" (*jin*)? It is a sign of rank (or lack thereof), a small cloth head covering that, when worn, is invisible to the wearer, but of striking significance in the eyes of the wearer's cohort. When Li Bo ends the poem by removing his cap, he is also removing himself from at least one system of identifying signs. It is perhaps less obvious that "seeing" the cap is a prerequisite for its removal; one must first recognize the overarching system of signs as being just that, as something separate from a person's nature, in order to accede to such a moment of liberation, an opportunity for authenticity like no other.

Li Bo's *yuefu* poetry at its best reenacts this process of recovered nakedness. In poem after poem, Li Bo acknowledges and either removes or sets askew the lyrical equivalent of the cap—the system of precedents and conventions that make a poem readable but, over time, threaten its power to surprise, move, and incite wonder. The result can be exciting and at times perplexing, almost as though Li Bo were single-handedly attempting to solve the aesthetic paradox of wonder. Just as it is impossible to experience nakedness as liberation unless one has been clothed, readers cannot truly experience the wonder of the "unfettered" lyric unless they have read widely in the codified tradition. As though trying to enable his jaded readers (and, no doubt, himself) to see the ordinary for the first time, Li Bo uses the complex but subtle expectations inscribed in the *yuefu* genre to bring his readers back to that moment when they are still youthful, but "far enough along into the familiarity of the ordinary world to be able to see against this background the truly unexpected, the truly beautiful."[2]

Li Bo's *yuefu* poetry stands virtually unchallenged as his best work, and he remains secure in his position of master of the form,[3] even in the eyes of admirers not especially aware of generic distinctions. Even today, at the mention of his name, urban scholars and rural residents alike will recite lines from his *yuefu*, whether or not they think of them as such. Traditional critics explain Li Bo's strength in this area as the natural expression of his untrammeled spirit, never fully addressing the somewhat counterintuitive nature of this commonly repeated assertion. *Yuefu* poetry had never been singled out as a natural forum for unfettered expressiveness, except when being thought of as a subcategory of old-style poetry.[4] To the contrary, as recent scholars have shown, far from being free and fortuitous, the composition of literary *yuefu* required—at the very least—a solid knowledge of specific poetic forebears and an ability to utilize that knowledge overtly in the creation of new poems that believably express one's own feelings.[5]

Perhaps in an effort to justify this reasoning, some recent scholars have looked more closely at the supposedly natural affinity between unfettered expression and the *yuefu* genre, at least in the context of Li Bo's praxis. Stephen Owen, for example, situates the *yuefu*'s aptness for unfetteredness in the genre's potential for overt role-playing, and further points out that the traditional *yuefu* roles mesh nicely with Li's "outsider" voice.[6] Joseph Allen, also persuaded of Li's love of pure performance, observes that "Li seemed to join the praxis of intratextual poetics only so that he would have something to disrupt."[7] This emphasis on the performance element of his best *yuefu* has helped readers isolate what is most innovative in his work: Li seems to direct readers to seek meaning, not in the story being recounted, but in the formal aspects of his recounting of that story. In that sense, he draws attention to his mastery of the tradition and so suggests that he stands outside it.

For all the present-day admiration for the skillful artist, however, the tendency to identify Li Bo's role-playing and disruptions as ends in themselves betrays a monolithic view of the poet not unlike that underlying Northern Song polemical critiques of Li Bo's "emptiness." The portrait of Li Bo as the cleverly ironic, somewhat cynical performer satisfies modern Western requirements for the position of Great Poet, but it seems at odds with the poetic values articulated by readers who loved his work and passed it down through the generations. As appealing as a jaunty, self-promoting "Banished Immortal" may seem, this portrait does little to explain how Li Bo maintained his supreme place in a tradition that consistently values poetry as the privileged mode of authentic expression of the self. The limitations of reading Li's poetry as pure performance become even clearer when specifically applied to the question of the perceived link between unfetteredness and *yuefu*. Such a reading all but overlooks the complex traditional concept of "unfetteredness" and reduces to caricature the critically evocative figure of the "Banished Immortal"—both of which notions secured Li Bo's identity as authentic enough to weather centuries of debate.

Li Bo's *yuefu,* if far more popular and playful than his *Gufeng,* enact a fundamentally identical poetic vision. Relatively free of the weighty expectations borne by that more sententious subgenre, but still tied securely to the literary past, the *yuefu* offer Li Bo another opportunity to rewrite the scripted relationship between craft and inspiration, knowledge and talent, undermining any attempt to read them as distinct or separate, and clearing a new ground for his own latter-day expression of authenticity. As in the *Gufeng,* Li Bo does not often avail himself of allegorical devices to evince authenticity, but favors the use of quotation of past texts—modified to work in concert with the expectations incurred by this particular genre.[8] Examining the *yuefu* as the most salient example of Li Bo's dialogic relationship with the past makes it possible to see, even more clearly than with the *Gufeng,* how he negotiates one of the defining paradoxes of his age, mediating between the continued ideal of unpremeditated, authentic expression and the expectation of a poem's discernible conformity with the ancients.[9]

For the sake of convenience (rather than because of any belief in Li Bo's programmatic composition), I have identified three modes of quotation in Li Bo's *yuefu* that correspond to three features of poetic expression: narrative (and character), language and prosody, and theme-specific imagery:[10]

1. narrative restoration: the apparent restoration of a disappearing narrative line, but in such a way as to reveal the impossibility of recovering that state of ancient innocence;
2. defamiliarization of diction, word order: closely following an earlier text, but executing direct transformations on a small scale to reveal the lyrical limitations imposed by unacknowledged linguistic conventions;
3. elegiac reframing of the tradition: closely imitating an earlier text, but selecting specific conventions from direct precedents and framing them in a way that inspires a renewed appreciation of their past (irrecoverable) beauty.[11]

On "Rendering Strange" and the Awareness of Unfetteredness

The earliest association of Li Bo's unfettered, immortal persona with his talent for producing great *yuefu* dates back to his own lifetime—indeed, to the same event credited with the invention of that persona: the (perhaps apocryphal) story of He Zhizhang's reading of his "Shudao nan" (The road to Shu is hard). As the oft-repeated tale tells it, so moved was He upon reading this *yuefu* poem that he declared Li a "banished immortal," "not a man of this world," and "the essence of the Great White Star,"[12] and recommended him to the emperor for acceptance into the Hanlin academy. It does not appear that He Zhizhang was thinking about genre when (and if) he uttered those words, but such later readers as the Ming dynasty critic Gao Bing apparently did, as he reveals in his descriptive preface about Li Bo in the beginning of the section on seven-character old-style poems:

> Taibai's phrases—[worthy of] a heavenly immortal *(tianxian)*—were mostly completed spontaneously and without effort *(shuairan er cheng)*. That is why his *yuefu* lyrics are especially fine.
>
> Some say that it all began when his "Shudao nan" was read and appreciated by one who understood him *(zhiyin)*, and that [as a result] he was beloved by the perspicacious ruler. But how could this be [a mere case of] a meager talent benefiting from circumstances to thunder to prominence! This most certainly is not so. The richness of [Li] Bo's work does not end here. If you look today at [his other *yuefu*], ... their coursing energy is every bit as exalted as the autumn colors of South Mountain. Even Shaoling would have to cede to him in this, and others cannot begin to compare. How right it is to raise [Li Bo] to the position of "authoritative exemplar" *(zhengzong)*.[13]

Gao Bing, as we have noted, generally tried to evaluate poets in terms of qualifiable, technical achievements and so enters the arena of Li Bo criticism as one of the first critics to attempt a formal description of Li Bo's work. Working in the tradition of Zhu Xi's famous aphorism concerning Li Bo's use of unruly rule-boundedness (or rule-bound unruliness), which he quotes elsewhere, Gao begins by equating Li's immortal persona with his supposed spontaneity, then establishes his spontaneity as responsible for his remarkable abilities in composing *yuefu*. This thesis of causality surprises, because the greatness of "Shudao nan" is not usually attributed to its fulfillment of the typical expectations of *yuefu*. But Gao does not enlighten us further.

Justified or not, critics readily accepted and propagated the perception of a natural association between *yuefu* and creative freedom. Later, another Ming critic, Wang Shizhen (1526–1590), declares Li's *yuefu* a genre unto itself, coterminous with his unique imagination and genius: "recondite and brooding, they range freely with his volatile imagination, extending his natural genius to the limit; that is why they [are recognized as] 'Taibai-yuefu.'"[14] Zhao Yi, too, perceives a natural connection, stating: "Qinglian was skilled in *yuefu*, probably because when his genius and thoughts overflowed, and he had no vehicle for their expression, he would avail himself of this [form] to give free reign to the force of his writing brush."[15] Most recently, the modern critic Wang Yunxi, one of the leading scholars of both Li Bo's poetry and *yuefu* as a genre, repeats this conviction, stating that *yuefu* "gave best expression to his free-ranging spirit and his unrestrained passions."[16]

Yet, for all the simplicity with which these authorities repeat this judgment, careful readers must wonder at the connection. It is true that, because its musical foundations were long gone, *yuefu* had become relatively free of prosodic regulation of any kind, making the genre appropriate for inclusion in the large group of "old-style" poems that developed in counterpoint to regulated, "recent-style" poetry. And the narrative flow and unadorned language of the traditional *yuefu* poem can be viewed as the embodiment of all that is unreflective and flowing. Nevertheless, especially since the analytical arrangement of Guo Maoqian's thirteenth-century *Yuefu shiji*, it is difficult to conceive of this genre as being especially free. Through Guo's organization of the poems into even then irretrievable melodic families and still observable thematic categories, Guo brought into relief the importance of thematic continuity in the writing of virtually all literary *yuefu*, beginning as early as the Han dynasty.[17]

Interestingly, some Ming dynasty readers, perhaps preoccupied with their own *fugu*-inspired dilemmas, tacitly acknowledge the all-too-apparent tension, if not outright contradiction, between the ideal of free, spontaneous, unplanned poetic expression and the relatively unfree nature of the *yuefu* genre. Hu Yinglin and Hu Zhenheng are among those who pinpoint the essence of Li's accomplishment in his nuanced utilization of past texts—hardly the stuff of wine-induced abandon. Yet each of them, to varying degrees, strives to preserve the authenticity of abandon even as they specify the particulars of Li's craft. Hu Yinglin's creativity in this endeavor is evident in the following statement:

> When it comes to *yuefu*, Taibai takes it upon himself to render strange the works of the ancients and moderns *(qi gujin)*. Shaoling walks faithfully in the footsteps of the *Odes*. [Li's] works, such as "The Road to Shu Is Hard" ("Shudao nan") and "Parted Far Away" ("Yuan bieli") "emerge from the realm of the spirits and enter the realm of the gods"; their brooding depths are unfathomable. [In contrast, Du's] "Soldiers' Chariots" ("Bingju xing") and "Newlyweds' Parting" ("Xinhun bie") tell of emotion and recount events with a sincerity [that makes them] seem to appear before one's eyes. Zhang [Ji and Wang [Jian] wanted to surpass [Li] in unrefined naturalness *(zhuo)*, but [the result exemplifies] what is called "mis-aiming by an infinitesimal measure" *(cha zhi hao li)*; Wen [Tingyun] and Li [Shangyin] wanted to surpass them in cleverness *(qiao)*, but [the result exemplifies] what is called "missing the mark by one thousand li" *(liao yi qian li)*.[18]

What makes this passage so intriguing is Hu's use of the word "strange" *(qi)* as a transitive verb. While words with semantic content in classical Chinese assume different functions depending on word order and function particles, it is rare for *"qi,"* conventionally translated in its nominal form as "strange" or "extraordinary," to appear in poetic criticism in its transitive verbal form. When it is used as a transitive verb, as in the *Shiji*, for example, it may be glossed as "to value" or "to esteem" (or, alternately, "to consider strange or unusual").[19] Although "to value" initially seems to work here, a complete reading of the passage suggests that Hu may have been departing slightly from common usage, employing "*qi*" to mean the more active act of "making strange or special" to describe Li Bo's reutilization of past texts in a new, unaccustomed light. I suggest that, in its implications of skillful strategy and surprise, this modified use of "*qi*" subtly reawakens the word's ancient associations with military strategy. In both the *Laozi* and the *Sunzi shijia zhu*, "*qi*" is opposed to "*zheng*" (frontal attack) to describe the necessary supplementary actions taken by an army to surprise its enemy.[20]

Several points in this passage and beyond it point to such a reading. First, the passage as a whole aims to set Li Bo apart from his peers and immediate descendants. The initial juxtaposition of Li Bo and Du Fu should probably be read as a contrastive comparison: Li Bo's act of "*qi*-ing" a broad range of works is clearly different from Du Fu's reverent following of the most orthodox of all poetic corpora. Second, Hu's immediately ensuing mention of "Shudao nan" (long since associated with the quality of "strangeness"),[21] along with his evocation of ghosts and spirits, suggest that Hu may have had strangeness and deviation from the norm on his mind. Finally, and perhaps most persuasively, this reading resonates with *qi*'s connotations of unexpectedness and heterodoxy, both in general and in specific reference to Li Bo's (and occasionally Du Fu's) creativity or transformations of past convention.[22] It does not seem out of place, then, for Hu Yinglin to distinguish Li Bo's unusual use of past poetry with a correspondingly unusual use of this term. In its suggestions of defamiliarization of the familiar, in its implications of the objectification of poetic precedent and its uses, such a usage comes remarkably close to my description of Li's use of quotation. While *qi* never loses its associations with things otherworldly, its connotations of craft and reason add a knowledge-based dimension to the persona of the immortal, whose method can never be fully described nor imitated even by the most perspicacious and determined of poets.

Hu Yinglin was not the only critic to confront the difficulty of connecting Li Bo's wildness with his method of writing *yuefu*. His near contemporary, Hu Zhenheng, too, meets this challenge by drawing a genre-based line between the wildness of the "Banished

Immortal" and the method of his *yuefu*, suggesting that, in writing *yuefu*, Li Bo departed from his usual creative process:

> Taibai's poems take the *Odes* and the "[Li] Sao" as their ancestors; they look askance upon tonal regulation. He needs but open his mouth for a perfect piece of writing to emerge, and he only has to wave his brush for the fog to be dispelled. His are the words of a heavenly immortal.
>
> But his *yuefu* poems link up with [existing] categories and extract their meanings, and are especially rich in their use of remonstrance and stimulus, comprising [a body of works] such as have never existed from ancient times to the present. So today those who speak of poetry promote Bo and Shaoling as the two great masters, saying that Li and Du cannot be ranked.[23]

Hu characterizes Li's "poems" (*shi*) as being in keeping with ancient precedents by virtue of their pure spontaneity, but recognizes that the *yuefu* exhibit positive elements of continuation with earlier *yuefu*. The two genres, though, are clearly linked in their quality of unattainability, which in turn is part and parcel of the unfettered immortal persona. At the same time, Hu Zhenheng's willingness to recognize the distinctiveness of the *yuefu* within Li's work as a whole and his overall emphasis on affinities between particular poets and poetic forms also seem to have given him the license to venture a bit further in articulating Li's poetic craft: "Taibai is at his most profound in his *yuefu*. In enjoining the ancient tune titles he is never remiss; either he utilizes the original intent or he turns it around completely to extract new meaning. Where [old and new] merge, they seem to diverge; and where they diverge, they actually merge. [These] tunes exhaust the subtlety of 'enjoining the past' (*nigu*)."[24]

Hu's argument, by locating the "profundity" of Li Bo's *yuefu* in his ability fully and subtly to exploit the expressive possibilities inherent in "enjoining" or, somewhat misleadingly, "imitating" the past (*nigu*), illustrates the high degree of similarity in readerly expectations of *gufeng* and *yuefu*. Both types of poems succeed or fail on the basis of their correct positioning in relation to the past.

Hu acknowledges that Li Bo's *yuefu* did not merely fulfill that expectation, but inscribed it, as such, in the poems themselves. Li, he suggests, was able to demonstrate his mastery through the overt management of oldness (as in the titles and implied intent) and newness.

In articulating the deliberateness of Li's approach and in inviting the reader to focus on the significance of the creative process, Hu anticipates more recent characterizations of Li Bo's identity as a performer. Yet, for all the acuity of this observation, Hu leaves ample room for Li Bo's unique magic, in which the empty architecture of performance is filled with the elusive substantiveness of his spirit. This is nowhere so evident as in Hu's warning that nothing in Li Bo's poetry is what it seems: "Where [old and new] merge, they seem to diverge; and where they diverge, they actually merge." Circular and impenetrable, the rhetorical strategy of this binary reversal renders subtle homage to the unreachable foundation of individual spirit underlying even the most cold-eyed artistic decision-making.

Hu was among the most perspicacious in his understanding of Li Bo's approach to *yuefu*, but even he never strayed far from traditional "immortal" characterizations of the poet's larger persona, maintaining Li's position in that realm of unqualifiability that remained beyond the reach of Du Fu. Although previous supporters had frequently asserted that knowledge and craft played an important role in Li's poetry, it is really in the sixteenth-century commentaries that detailed analyses of craft fully coexist with Li Bo's unfettered persona—primarily by creating a broader, more generous view of "unfetteredness": one that encompasses a distinctly self-conscious demonstration of intentionality.[25] Just as Li Bo's *Gufeng* revived ancient authenticity through the exposure of authenticity's ancientness, his *yuefu* revived the ideal of spontaneous composition by exposing spontaneity's composition. The resulting performance of unfetteredness, no longer measured in terms of rule-boundedness, is enacted more as rule-domination. And the more daring the domination, the more unfettered the poet who exercises it.

NARRATIVE RESTORATIONS: RETURNING TO THE SOURCE

In one of his more impressive displays of domination over the tradition, Li Bo gives his readers a demonstration of a textual return to the past by restoring to its original expansiveness a *yuefu* story that had been growing more and more condensed over time.[26] But Li Bo's apparent restoration serves only to call attention to the unbridgeable temporal gap separating the ancient folk song from his own overtly reconstructed composition.

First, the original Han dynasty folk song,[27] "Moshang sang" (Mulberries along the path; also known as "Yan'ge Luofu xing")* as recorded in the *Yuefu shiji*:

The sun rises in the southeast,	日出東南隅
Shining upon our house of Qin.	照我秦氏樓
The family had a lovely daughter	秦氏有好女
4　*Who called herself Luofu.*	自名為羅敷
Luofu took pleasure in silkworm and mulberry,	羅敷喜蠶桑
Picking the leaves south of the city wall.	採桑城南隅
Green silk was her basket's weave,	青絲為籠係
8　*Cassia twigs, its loops.*	桂枝為籠鉤
On her head, a thick coil of hair,	頭上倭墮髻
In her ears, "shining moon" pearls.	耳中明月珠
Pale yellow silk was her skirt,	緗綺為下裙
12　*Her tunic—purple silk.*	紫綺為上襦
When passers-by would see Luofu,	行者見羅敷
They'd set down their loads and stroke their beards.	下擔捋髭鬚
And when young men would see Luofu,	少年見羅敷
16　*They'd doff their caps and show their headscarves.*	脫帽著帩頭
Plowhands would forget their plows,	耕者忘其犁
Diggers would forget their spades.	鋤者忘其鋤

---

*Stanza breaks in this and other songs have been inserted only for ease of reading.

In their comings and goings they'd argue and
    fret—

20 But then they'd stop, and simply sit and watch
    Luofu.

    來歸相怒怨
    但坐觀羅敷

A governor[28] came up from the south,
His piebald horse halted and waited.
The governor sent forth his aide,
24 To ask the maiden's family name.
"The Qin have a lovely daughter,
who calls herself Luofu."
—"And Luofu is of what age?"
28 —"Twenty years she's not yet completed,
She's but fifteen and a bit more."
The governor then paid his respects to Luofu,
    and asked:
—"Might you like to ride with me?"
32 Luofu stood forth and declined:
—"How foolish is the governor!
He has a wife of his own,
And Luofu has her husband!

    使君從南來
    五馬立踟躕
    使君遣吏往
    問是誰家姝
    秦氏有好女
    自名為羅敷
    羅敷年幾何
    二十尚不足
    十五頗有餘
    使君謝羅敷
    寧可共載不
    羅敷前置辭
    使君一何愚
    使君有其婦
    羅敷自有夫

36 —"Over one thousand horsemen in the east,
And my husband is at the top.
And how would one recognize my husband?
A white horse following a black.
40 Green silk ties the horse's tail,
Yellow gold bridling his head.
At his waist a lulü sword—
It may be worth millions and more.
44 At fifteen, he was a young clerk in the prefecture;
At twenty, a grandee at court.
At thirty, a minister in attendance,
At forty, the head of the city.
48 His person is of pure white skin,
His whiskers, long and wispy.
Stately, stately his gait through the court,
With measured step as others rush about.

    東方千餘騎
    夫婿居上頭
    何用識夫婿
    白馬從驪駒
    青絲繫馬尾
    黃金絡馬頭
    腰中鹿盧劍
    可直千萬餘
    十五府小吏
    二十朝大夫
    三十侍中郎
    四十專城居
    為人潔白晢
    鬑鬑頗有鬚
    盈盈公府步
    冉冉府中趨

52   *As he sits among thousands of men,*   坐中數千人
       They all proclaim my husband unequaled."[29]   皆顏大婿殊

Guo Maoqian's preface to this song cites two earlier commentaries explaining the story of Luofu, the virtuous and faithful woman featured here. The account recorded in the *Gu jin zhu* by the Jin dynasty scholar Cui Bao merits a complete translation here: "'Moshang sang' originates from a daughter of the Qin clan. Master Qin, of Handan, had a daughter named Luofu who became the wife of a highly ranked local official named Wang Ren. Wang Ren subsequently became an administrative director in the quarters of the prince of Zhao. When Luofu was picking mulberry leaves along the path, the prince of Zhao ascended a pavilion and, upon spying her, found her pleasing. He thereupon set out some wine in order to steal her [away from her husband]. Luofu was skilled at playing the zither, and when she then composed the song 'Moshang sang,' the prince of Zhao desisted."[30]

Whereas only the latter part of Li Bo's poem is in Luofu's own voice, the *Gu jin zhu* presents the poem itself as Luofu's performance of her own story, attributing to her a very high degree of self-consciousness. The story recounted in the *Yuefu jieti,* slightly different and less elaborate, is also quite emphatic in placing importance on Luofu's sophisticated powers of persuasion, albeit more verbal than musical, in fending off her admirer's advances.[31] In her earlier incarnations, then, Luofu was not only beautiful and loyal, but rhetorically and musically able. This quality of persuasiveness rings out clearly in the original folk song and is strongly supported by the markings of oral poetry still present in this, its Han dynasty version. Recognizable from both the ancient *Odes* and the "Nineteen Old Poems" are the *xing* beginning,[32] the incremental repetition of key images or phrases throughout the body of the poem, the loose parallelism, and other oral formulas. Specifically appropriate to the Luofu character is the structure. The narrative is broken up by dialogue and contains a song within a song. This is not just a fine example of how even some of the oldest folk *yuefu* achieve narrative scope while avoiding the tedium of straight third-person description.[33] It is also a compelling illustration of Luofu's character, allowing readers to observe her external beauty—and to be moved, firsthand, as it were, by the direct expression of her inner being. The overall effect is powerful and vivid, embodying the elements so treasured in folk songs, yet scarcely devoid of its own literary embellishments.

Yet the extant songs subsequently written under the same title do not exploit these characteristics (although Fu Xuan [217–278] closely emulates it in his "Yan'ge xing"),[34] rather they manifest what one scholar has described as the shift from the dramatic, situational storytelling that dominates folk *yuefu* and the narrative, contemplative mode typical of literary *yuefu*.[35] Wu Jun (469–520), whose poem is the earliest in the *Yuefu shiji* to take up any hint of the Luofu story under the "Moshang sang" title, does so only obliquely.

Tender, tender, the mulberries on the path,		嫋嫋陌上桑
Shade the path, then drape over the pond.		蔭陌復垂塘
Lengthy limbs luminous with white sun,		長條映白日
4 Delicate leaves enshroud an oriole's yellow.		細葉隱鸝黃
The silkworms hungry, it overtakes my heart again,		蠶飢妾復思
I wipe away tears, pick up the basket.		拭淚且提筐
Beloved, how can you be so?		故人寧如此
8 Regret at our parting burns the breast.[36]		離恨煎人腸

A lone, weeping woman under the mulberry trees: this is the figure that Wu Jun has distilled from the Luofu story told in the earliest "Moshang sang." Anonymous, presented here without either distant admirers or active pursuers, she reemerges as the stoic, abandoned woman descended from the "Nineteen Old Poems," facing the prospect of another solitary winter. The *xing* opening, however, which like those earlier poems prefigures, in the willow-like attributes of the mulberry trees,[37] the long, lonely distances separating the woman from her lover, also imbues her with a sensuousness inherited from the boudoir-bound women of court poetry. In this blend of oral *Shijing* classicism and courtly sensual observation, Wu reveals—perhaps inadvertently—his idea of how best to recapture the purity and authenticity of the original folk song. Liberating the song from the story, Wu Jun opens up its interpretation to include other beautiful, abandoned women, some of whom work the mulberries. One example is the famous, unnamed wife of Qiu Hu, who appears explicitly in later versions, and whose story, unlike that of Luofu, is truly one of abandonment;[38] and there are others who inhabit the earliest five-character poetry and are forever anonymous.

Wu's distillation of the woman-mulberry figure from the Luofu story reads, on one level, as an attempt to recover the universal mode of the *Shijing*, in particular, and the folk song, more generally. But the contribution of his own literary hand enriches the poem not only with the imagery of tender sinuosity indirectly reflected upon the woman by the trees she is tending, but with a subtle transformation of the gaze and voice so starkly rendered in the original. While the first four lines of the poem function as a highly literary transformation of a *Shijing*-style *xing*, they also suggest—precisely because of the delicacy and refinement of its extended description—a specific point of view: that, perhaps, of one of many passers-by peering through the trees at the lovely girl partly hidden within. His desire only partly dissimulated in the rendering of the willowlike (and womanlike) mulberries, the onlooker's searching gaze finally fixes on the oriole, a bright spot of yellow hidden among the leaves. In the second quatrain, however, the voice and perhaps the gaze unexpectedly shift to the first person, quite clearly not of any male admirer, but of the woman herself. With the shift in voice, the reader must rethink the identity of the person who had been gazing longingly through the branches. Suddenly, the injustice of the woman's uncompromising solitude rankles as, in the end, her plaintive question echoes hollowly through the grove. Her overheard voice contrasts painfully with that of the self-assured, expressive, and individual Luofu, whose song—including its title—is preserved "verbatim" in a narrative for all to hear.

Wu Jun's contribution to the "Moshang sang" narrative line

nicely illustrates some of the typical transformations that literati worked upon the folk origins of the genre.[39] Sensual in its description, subtle in the indirect expression of Luofu's inner feelings, Wu's poem broadens the frame of reference, adding depth to the emotional import of the original largely through the distillation of select elements from the original and its reintegration into the multilayered and refined aesthetic of the age.

A similar, if even more radical, distillation occurs in the "Moshang sang" of another Liang dynasty poet, Wang Taiqing (6 c.)

Auspicious moon unfolds a harmony of shadow,	令月開和景
Everywhere stirring springtime hearts.	處處動春心
Suspending the basket she must fill with leaves,	挂筐須葉滿
She rests, exhausted, in the shade of layered branches.[40]	息惓重枝陰

This is as spare as the story becomes. The poet has omitted any direct mention of another person, of any man responsible for her current state of solitude. What remains is simply the woman. To speak—even to herself—has become futile: as futile, and as daunting, as the task before her must seem. Her unobserved and unconscious seductiveness blended into the play of moonlight and shadow, her loneliness stirred by the season, are both subtly enriched by the multiple evocations provided by the mulberries and the title, by the hovering but silent presences of Luofu and Qiu Hu's wife.

Had the "Moshang sang" tradition continued in this way, never again directly alluding to Qin Luofu, it would be tempting to conclude that her story played no role in the versions written by Wu Jun and Wang Taiqing, and that the Luofu story had been completely rechanneled into other song titles in the same group. But the apparent elimination of her story from this tradition is belied by the next poem by Wang Yun (481–549). As if in recognition that the process of distillation could go no further, Wang replenishes the mulberry woman with direct—but abbreviated—evocations of both pertinent stories.

They tell the story: among the mulberries on the
    path,
'Twas not yet dawn, but harboring a bit of light.
Layer upon layer, each shaded or shone on the
    other,
4 Soft, soft, their own perfumes ambrosial.
Qiu Hu was just halting his mount,
Luofu had not yet filled her basket.
With the spring silkworms already hidden at
    dawn,
8 How could they tarry so long?[41]

人傳陌上桑
水曉已含光
重重相蔭映
軟軟自芬芳
秋胡始停馬
羅敷未滿筐
春蠶朝已伏
安得久彷徨

These lyrics provide a gallery of past images, some having
already appeared in the original Han dynasty version of the Luofu
story, others obliquely present in the poems by Wu Jun and Wang
Taiqing. Presented one after another, couplet by couplet, each
image is framed in a moment of imminent change: dawn just at
the point of breaking, Qiu Hu about to dismount his horse at the
grove's edge, about to commit his fateful decision to gaze upon
the girl half-hidden within, and Luofu herself, her basket on the
verge of being filled. Enclosed within the protective embrace of
the mulberry branches, illuminated only selectively by the accu-
mulated words of poets, said and unsaid, Luofu maintains forever
her seductiveness and her purity, momentarily merging with the
lonely wife of Qiu Hu—as Qiu Hu, for an instant, merges just
beyond the grove with the prince of Zhao.

Wang Yun has isolated the element of imminence, always nec-
essary to the flow of narrative time, and made it the primary signi-
fying element of his poem. Through this array of frozen moments it
becomes clear that, in the lyric world of the "Moshang sang" and
related *yuefu* traditions, these otherwise unrelated events are for-
ever joined and always in process. The more or less specific stories
of abandoned women, the cautionary tales of Luofu and Qiu Hu,
all appear simultaneously, each fully contained in the imminence of
a decisive moment, captured in eternity through repetition in song.
Like his contemporaries, but perhaps more deliberately, Wang Yun

unites these disparate imminences in the permanence of a shared, repeated image: the basket yet to be filled.

This incarnation of eternal imminence conveys the essence of the desire defining the archetypal solitary woman, those anonymous yet familiar women who reappear in Wu Jun's and Wang Taiqing's poems. The women of the *Shijing* and the "Nineteen Old Poems" spend their lives in the imminence of their man's imagined return. Wu Jun's hungry silkworms are imminent victims of the woman's failure to overcome her springtime feelings long enough to harvest the leaves necessary for their nourishment. Wang Taiqing's basket remains empty (perilously so, for those who understand the story) while she rests, exhausted by sleepless nights and, one might imagine, discouraged by the futility of her task. Wang Yun "quotes," in a gesture worthy of Li Bo, these potent evocations of imminence and, implicitly, fate, then introduces them into the other two mulberry-related images: dawn, which is particularly fitting, and Qiu Hu's sighting of the unidentified girl.

Finally, dawn breaks; the action must resume. The poet asks a question so rhetorical as to border on irony: "How can [they] hesitate long?" With this line, the poem ends, but time resumes. The multiple stories, conflated in the ambiguous subject of the question (there is no indication whether the person guilty of hesitation is Luofu, Qiu Hu, Qiu Hu's wife, or the prince of Zhao), spin themselves out in the minds of the readers, whose knowledge of the preordained and endlessly repeated endings (whether sweet or bitter) contrasts so poignantly with the sublime moment Wang has just unfurled before them.

Besides isolating the ever present but heretofore unremarked narrative element of imminence, Wang Yun foregrounds another important and closely related trope: that of the blocked gaze. Both are palpable in the repeated, voyeuristic image of the woman's partial hiddenness among the branches and in Qiu Hu's failure to recognize his own wife. Like the eternalized moment of imminence, the blocked gaze bespeaks a state of desire and calls for the reader's completion of the picture. Readers know what is held in abeyance by the frozen moment and "see" what the desirous onlookers cannot. But imagining the completed picture does not put an end to the narrative, nor does it dampen the desire that set the narrative in motion. Quite to the contrary, the centrality of the unfinished picture in all three Liang dynasty versions of "Moshang sang" guarantees their continuity in a way that telling the whole story cannot, for it bestows upon successive generations of readers the role of actively reintegrating the poetic past into the present. The process of paring down, of eliminating details, does not exclude the *yuefu*'s past, but opens it up to the possibility of encompassing its broader origins in shared human experience. For the *yuefu* poet working solidly within the tradition, distillation acknowledges the universality of that tradition, bringing the literary *yuefu* closer to its treasured folk-song values of immediacy and authenticity.

Something similar occurs in a quatrain written under the same title that is identified by Guo as the work of an anonymous author, although previously attributed to Wang Yun:

Sunrise, the house of Qin grows light,	日出秦樓明
Boughs trailing, the dew still heavy.	條垂露尚盈
Silkworms starve and her heart, of course, grows anxious;	蠶飢心自急
She opens her box, but cannot finish her toilette.[42]	開奩妝不成

Like the longer poem, this delicate, elliptical quatrain depicts nothing so much as imminence, here tersely conveyed in the agonizing tension between time's irrevocable passage and the abandoned woman's own paralysis. In this poem, vision is not blocked. In a direct refutation of this element of the "Moshang sang" tradition, the readers' unimpeded view of the woman erases her as an object of anyone's desire, leaving her in the most absolute of solitudes. The Luofu who had resisted with panache the onslaught of other men's desire has finally been overtaken by Qiu Hu's nameless, silent, and forgotten wife. The extant poems reveal what seems to be a gradual process of elimination in which the reader's unilateral and unimpeded gaze replaces the mutual eroticism of hide-and-seek, and the passive and doomed wife of Qiu Hu takes the place of the spunky Luofu. This transformation of the narrative only intensifies the pathos of the woman's predicament. *Yuefu,* more systematically than other genres or subgenres, engages poet and reader in the joint creation of meaning through the realization of an intratextual web. Clearly, the more "open" the intratextual framework—the more ambiguous and pared-down the narrative— the greater the importance of a shared poet-reader perspective.

Wang Yun's elliptical reinsertion of diverse thematic elements into "Moshang sang" resembles Li Bo's idiomatization and quotation of earlier texts. Almost every couplet of Wang's poem contains a direct allusion, beginning with the first, which cites the tune title almost as though it were the title of the "story" that "they tell"; the song within the song (or, here, the story within the story) has become the song-story itself. Then follows what appears to be an enumeration of the elements of the tradition: dawn, layered branches, Qiu Hu, and Luofu, all converging around the image of the mulberry. Like Li Bo's quotations some two hundred years later, Wang's poem acknowledges the agglomerated nature of this particular thematic tradition. In doing so, this poem entrusts at least part of the responsibility for authenticity to its overtness as a composed (in the dual sense of "written" and "assembled") literary piece. He lets readers see him playing with the elements, playing with the strictures of time, and relies on their equally knowing participation in order to make it work.

But there is a difference between Wang's overt artistry and Li Bo's display of mastery. Wang still affords himself—and his readers—the luxury of emotional identification with the silent, waiting woman. He knows that the pathos at the heart of the poem derives from the shared understanding that time will not be stayed forever, and that the woman, the poet, and the reader must let go and allow events to happen, leading to the ending that all know too well for recounting. Both poet and reader share in the sadness of the fate that awaits the woman, and the foreknowledge does not much soften the pain of beholding her innocence. By remaining within the prescribed boundaries of empathy, by maintaining this shared perspective, Wang might be thought of as relatively fettered, while Li Bo is not:

Beautiful girl, east of the Wei River bridge, 　美女渭橋東
With spring's return, she labors at her silkworm 　春還事蠶作
　　task.
His five horses arrive like dragons in flight— 　五馬如飛龍
4 *Green silk lashed to bridles of gold,* 　青絲結金絡
She knows not from whose family he hails, 　不知誰家子
When, teasing and laughing, he comes by to 　調笑來相謔
　　banter.

It is I who am Qin Luofu, 　妾本秦羅敷
8 *Whose face of jade graced this famed city.* 　玉顏豔明都
The green branches shone on my hands silky 　綠條映素手
　　white,
As I picked mulberry leaves near the corner of 　採桑向城隅
　　the city wall.
I paid no mind to the prince's emissary— 　使君且不顧
12 *Much less heeded that old Qiu Hu!* 　況復論秋胡

Wintry cicadas love emerald-green grass, 　寒螿愛碧草
The calling phoenix perches on verdant 　鳴諷棲青梧
　　pawlonia.
Each has his place where the heart rests, content; 　託心自有處
16 *I am only surprised by the foolishness of passers-* 　但怪旁人愚
　　by.
In vain allow the sun to set— 　徒令白日暮
Your high steed lingers here for nought.[43] 　高駕空踟躕

Li Bo's poem executes a return to the past. Qin Luofu is back, singing her song of refusal and independence. He restores the folkloric song within a song, and even peppers his lyrics with bits of verse lifted nearly unchanged from the *Shijing*, the *Chuci*, and the "Nineteen Old Poems." But in this return, he does not repeat—or even imitate—the distant, irrecoverable past. He enters into a dialogue with it, imposing his present perspective on the old stories in an act no less potent than had been the old stories' domination of subsequent retellings. In doing so, he reclaims, as he repeatedly did in the *Gufeng*, the authenticity of his own place in literary time.

In particular aspects of this poem, Li Bo seems to have taken his lead from Wang Yun, and possibly from the anonymous quatrain above. Wang's overt blending of the Luofu and Qiu Hu stories is, perhaps, the most obvious point of continuity between old and new, but Li Bo's most skillful response to this transformation can be found in his reframing of the tropes of imminence and hiddenness. Within the context of the plot, both had contributed significantly to the onlooker's perception of the woman's desire and desirability. At the same time, outside the poem, the poet's suspension of the inevitable and his manipulation of the onlooker's perspective helped to forge a bond of sadness between the woman (in her innocence) and the readers (in their knowingness). Li Bo appears to have taken note of this contract and reveals it as a poet's coy subterfuge, for, when he is done, the mulberry woman is no more innocent than poet or readers. Now she stands before us, fully aware of her beauty, her renown, and the outcome of her story. The woman has, in a sense, become the poet, the poet has become the woman, and neither seems willing to defer to readers in any way. While this reconfiguration of roles would be effective in any narrative poem, it takes on special significance when implemented in the *yuefu* genre, in light of its dramatic origins and the fluid shifting of boundaries between "author," narrator, and actors.[44]

In this particular poem, Li Bo removes the visual veil right at the start, then destroys the aura of imminence at the very end. There are no longer any shadows, intervening branches, or problems of mistaken identity. In the six-line introduction, readers are granted a full view of the woman and of her high-ranking, horse-drawn visitor. The air of antiquity appears "natural"—conforming to the expectations raised by the genre—replete with folksy expressions ("She knows not from whose family he hails") and dashing dragon-steeds. For the duration of this part of the poem, the reader can enjoy his privileged knowledge of the characters' future, while the characters themselves proceed in the presumed innocence of their storybook setting. But the "not knowing" that had been so instrumental in previous versions ends here. Line 7 introduces a change in rhyme. With this shift, unique among the examples cited, whose rhyme schemes are otherwise uniform from beginning to end, comes a change in voice, as Luofu embarks on what appears to be her expected monologue. In one line—in fact, almost in the single word *ben* (originally, after all)—she dispels all possible illusions, not only about who she is (and she is not Qiu Hu's victimized wife!), but about what she knows. Suddenly the song within the song, previously so instrumental in conveying the woman's innocence and the poem's ancient authenticity, is transformed into a parody of its former self.

Ben is a word of origins, of roots, and in this line its every nuance is brought into play. When the clause in which it occurs is interpreted as "I *was originally* Qin Luofu," the reading carries the recognition that she has been transformed, perhaps through the telling and retelling of her story. The reading "I am *the original* Qin Luofu," shows her to be stripping away all the other incarnations of her personage to uncover the essence of her character. Or *ben* might be glossed as an emphatic particle highlighting the already marked "I," an interpretation that yields my own translation, "*It is* I *who* am Qin Luofu." All three renderings have Luofu reveal her own awareness of the Luofu story and, even more astoundingly, of her incarnations in the transtextual complexity of the "Moshang sang" tradition. This Qin Luofu is not merely singing her song to her admirers and aspiring beaux; she is singing it to readers well versed in the *yuefu* tradition from which she emerged.

Having thus stepped out of her own story to address the readers, Luofu proceeds to describe herself in the clichéd figures of speech that have defined her. "I am the Luofu whom all of you know as having these characteristics," she seems to be saying, as she presents us with her list, including gleaming white hands, her refusal of the prince, and, perhaps most amusingly, her rejection of Qiu Hu. In the final six lines (13–18), which I construe as still belonging to Luofu's "song," she moves into a role that approximates that of the poet himself. As she juxtaposes the cicadas and the phoenix, she makes her own poetic allusions, suggesting both her lofty unattainability (in the tradition of the *Zhuangzi* and the poetry of Ruan Ji) and confirming the "Old Poems" conceit that all beings must cleave to their natural habitats and, by implication, their natures. Line 16, "I am only surprised by the foolishness of passers-by," mocks the advances made by those blind to her nature. They see her beauty, but cannot perceive her inner nobility. Here, the feistiness and independence of the "original" Luofu is not only restored; it is also joined by the ancient voices of misunderstood worthies. When, in the last two lines, she advises her interlocutor that there is no point in waiting, she takes control of the moment of suspended imminence of which, in previous versions, she had been the touchingly innocent victim. She breaks the magic of that moment, insisting in quite practical terms that time is continuing onward—and so should her suitors (and her audience).

Traditional critics are remarkably reticent in attempting to interpret this poem. Among modern commentators, Ono Jitsunosuke proposes, but does not attempt to prove, that Li Bo was inspired to retell the Luofu story in 742 when, traveling just outside the capital, he happened to spy a pretty girl picking mulberry leaves.[45] Allen offers it as a prime example of Li Bo's "multifaceted engagement of the Luofu intratext," but does not go into much detail, content with viewing it as an example of Li's love of disrupting the fabric of the intratext. I suspect that this poem, playful as it seems to be, might profitably be read as an example of practical poetic criticism, its gently ironic barb directed at literary dogmatism of every stripe, although especially, perhaps, at the rise of *fugu* dogmatism. Li's anti-imitation brand of ancient authenticity, expressed directly and indirectly in his *Gufeng*, is put into practice here, as he compels readers to consider in retrospect the fundamental "strangeness" of poetry past and present, the artistry required by continuity as well as disruption. By breaking the contract of pretended innocence between poet and readers, he reminds his readers of its existence, leaving them the option of willful ignorance only at their peril. Li Bo, like his Luofu, is committed to a restoration of authenticity, and not merely to a blind and "innocent" continuation of ancientness.

SYNTACTIC STRANGENESS: DEFAMILIARIZING THE CONVENTIONALITY OF LANGUAGE

The *yuefu* narrative building blocks of plot and point of view are not the only objects of Li Bo's defamiliarizing gaze. Taking advantage of the unusually clear-cut set of texts comprising the *yuefu* writer's poetic lexicon, Li Bo occasionally indulged in the quotation and transformation of antecedents at the syntactic level, to dramatic effect. Perhaps none of his poems exemplifies the qualities of "strangeness" and "unfetteredness" more than "*Dulu* Composition," which has confounded commentators almost without exception. Both Wang Qi and Shen Deqian, however, take notice of Li Bo's almost line-by-line transformation of the original, and also observe his focus on the original version's unusual structure, described by Shen as "now-broken-now-continuous" (*huo duan huo xu*).[46] His remark seems justified.

Dulu dulu,	獨漉獨漉
Water deep, mud turbid.	水深泥濁
Turbid mud is still all right;	泥濁尚可
4 *Deep water could kill me.*	水深殺我
Honking, honking, a pair of geese;	雍雍雙雁
Frolic at the field's edge.	遊戲田畔
I would like to shoot a goose;	我欲射雁
8 *But think of you far off, alone.*	念子孤散
Bobbing-bobbing, floating duckweed;	翩翩浮萍
Catching the wind, lightly drifts abroad.	得風遙輕
With what does my heart unite?	我心何合
12 *It weds itself to this.*	與之同并
Empty bed, lowered curtains;	空床低帷
Who knows no one is there?	誰知無人
Nightdress of embroidered brocade;	夜衣錦繡
16 *Who distinguishes between real and fake?*	誰別偽真
The sword hums in its scabbard;	刀鳴削中
Leans idly against the bed.	依床無施
Without avenging the wrong done my father—	父冤不報
20 *How desire to go on living?*	欲活何為
Vicious tiger all covered with stripes;	猛虎班班
Cavorting in the mountains.	遊戲山間
When a tiger wants to maul someone;	虎欲噬人
24 *He flees neither the brave nor the wise.*[47]	不避豪賢

As is often the case, critical commentary provides a useful starting point for discussion of this poem. Wang Qi and Shen Deqian point out the relative autonomy of each of the six sections of the original and state that Li Bo imitated this same characteristic. Modern readers, too, can observe the lack of narrative transition between sections, which is accentuated by corresponding changes in the rhyming syllable. But as Shen's neat epithet also suggests, a dynamic unifying scheme unites these independent blocks of texts: a scheme that is subtly but undeniably incorporated into the very pattern responsible for the impression of each quatrain's static self-sufficiency. Structurally speaking, the poem on which Li's version is so carefully based forms a widening spiral, beginning with short, staccato binary fragments and gradually building to form an increasingly large binary pattern of images, ultimately encompassing the poem as a whole. This structure, while strongly suggesting both its oral origins and the musical pattern on which it was based, beautifully supports the affective import of the poem, carried by the binary themes of solitude and union, aimlessness and determination.

The smallest binary structure of the poem, which is composed entirely of symmetrical four-character lines, appears in the very first line, in the repetition of the mysterious rhyming binome, "*dulu*." The meaning of this term remains a subject of debate, with two interpretations most often supported by commentators. Guo Maoqian's introduction to the poem cites sources suggesting its use in earlier songs as a reduplicative binomial description of muddy water (interpreted as symbolic of moral turpitude), a suggestion that seems to have been preferred by Wang Qi. Ono Jitsunosuke revives an earlier suggestion that it refers to a place: a mountain in modern-day Hebei, identified as the famous mythical site where Emperor Wu of the Han dallied with his celestial lover.[48] If it really is the name of a mystical place called Dulu, the ensuing line still allows for the simultaneous understanding of an opening evocative of a *xing*-like "gruddy-muddy."

The first quatrain already exhibits a progressive loosening and reinforcement of the binary structure. Beginning with the tightest and most opaque rhythmic and imagistic knot of a repeated

rhyming (and, by the time of Li Bo's writing, perhaps already am-
biguous) binome, the second line, which consists of two parallel
subject-verb statements, is split to form the nearly parallel couplet
of lines 3 and 4. Out of this sundered binary structure emerges, in
the very last word, the first person singular—the subject of the
poem. This pattern forms the basis of the two following quatrains,
as the aimless, solitary wandering of this "I" is delineated again
and again either by its contrast with natural pairs (the "honking,
honking" wild geese of line 5), or its tentative, futile pairings with
others.

The binary division is repeated and enlarged in the split
occurring between the third and fourth quatrains, when the redu-
plicative binomial opening is dropped and, in its place, parallelism
is established, not within individual couplets, but between the two
couplets of the quatrain. This expansion of the binary structure
continues, countering its own inherent tendency to separate into
balanced and isolated parts. As the fragmented units gradually
form a unifying pattern, the narrator's inner world changes as
well. This process—shifting from the first four-character line to
the couplet, and then from couplet to quatrain—culminates in
the concluding quatrain, which mirrors the second quatrain both
imagistically and structurally and brackets the whole poem. The
many geese, scattered and vulnerable, who were first spared by the
narrator who identified with them so strongly have been replaced
by the lone tiger, ruthless and formidable. And once the narrator
steels himself to fight this new adversary, he takes on its qualities.

Between these two defining moments—these two mirroring
quatrains—and spanning the enlarging pattern of paired phrases
and images, the narrator asks a series of questions. These are three
purely rhetorical gestures establishing, both in their content and in
the answering silence, the fearful solitude in which he finds him-
self. "With what does my heart unite?" He answers himself, then
confirms that there is no one there even to remark his solitude or
to discern if his nightdress's embroidery is real or fake. But the last
question—about the necessity of avenging his father—precipitates
an answer, propelling him out of his lonely wilderness. His new-
found determination is embodied in the final, unifying image of the

tiger. In rhythm and in image, then, the poem supports the spiral of emotional intensity as the speaker is transformed from a man inwardly scattered, fearful, and alone to a man of determination and clear purpose.

As pointed out by the commentators, Li Bo's poem plays closely on the original version and skillfully posits his own expression in his idiomatization of its intricate and unique pattern of structure and meaning. But there is more to his transformation of the earlier poem than a knowing foregrounding of its most obvious idiosyncracies. He has perceived its underlying dualities and chosen to amplify and develop the one that is most disturbing—the ambiguous distinction between reality and illusion, between the perceived world and the inner world of emotions—as this is specifically manifest in the persona of a frightened man completely alone and disoriented in a strange place. By playing slightly with syntax, by exploiting the shift from a four- to a five-character line, Li Bo exposes and destroys yet another contract of innocence between poet and readers. As he exaggerates the "broken" side of the "now-broken-now-continuous" quality of the original, he excludes the readers, denying them his own absolute access to the inner state of the speaker and turning what was a mere narrative describing fear and solitude into something closer to a performance of those emotions. Readers are left to witness, without quite penetrating, the extreme subjectivity of a person who feels himself to be truly alone:

Mud in the waters of Dulu;	獨漉水中泥
Water so murky you can't see the moon.	水濁不見月
Not seeing the moon is still all right;	不見月尚可
4 *But water's so deep, a traveler could drown.*	水深行人沒
As birds of Yue fly in from the south;	越鳥從南來
Geese of Hu cross, too, to the north.	胡雁亦北度
I want to bend my bow and shoot toward the	我欲彎弓向天射
heavens;	惜其中道失歸路
8 *Pity that, midway through their journey, they'll*	
lose the road home.	

	Falling leaves part from branches;	落葉別樹
	With a dry flutter follow the wind.	飄零隨風
	A traveler with no place to rest;	客無所託
12	*Grieves to be like them.*	悲與此同
	Gauze bed curtain unfurls and furls;	羅帷舒卷
	Seems that someone is opening.	似有人開
	The bright moon comes straight in,	明月直入
16	*Its mind not one to rouse suspicion.*	無心可猜
	Hero's sword hangs on the wall;	雄劍挂壁
	From time to time a dragon hums.	時時龍鳴
	It will not break through rhinoceros ivory;	不斷犀象
20	*Breeding lacy moss and mold.*	繡澀苔生
	The kingdom's shame not yet washed away;	國恥未雪
	How can one make his name?	何由成名
	The divine hawk over the Marsh of Dreams;	神鷹夢澤
24	*Pays no heed to common kites.*	不顧鴟鳶
	One strike for his master;	為君一擊
	The peng-*bird cuts across the Nine Heavens.*[49]	鵬搏九天

Li Bo begins his transformation by rewriting the opening section of the four-character original "*Dulu* Composition" in pentasyllabic mode. Recent discussions of the significance of pentasyllabic poetry in the development of individual lyric expression in the Chinese literary tradition suggest that this merits a closer look. Kao Yu-kung has persuasively argued that the addition of the fifth character, with the caesura usually situated between the second and third characters, favored the development of descriptive and expressive ("lyrical") poetic modes over the narrative mode.[50] Li Bo's transformation of the earlier poem does seem to bring the reader more deeply into the interiority (to borrow Kao's term) of the speaker, and does so in great part through the exploitation of the five-character line.

This poem's five-character section invites direct comparison with the original, particularly in its use of structure to portray the narrator's subjectivity. In place of the widening spiral of repetition and juxtaposition, Li Bo provides a syntactically constructed world of articulated hierarchies (as in "mud *in* the waters"), and perceptual cause and effect ("water so murky [that] you can't see the moon"). While this might seem to favor a rational, narrative representation of subjectivity, however, Li manages to achieve the opposite effect. In a sequence diametrically opposed to that of the old version, Li takes advantage of the five-character line to assert his presence at the outset in the verb of perception "to see"—or, more to the point, in the modal "not seeing." With this, the narrator commences an inward-turning spiral, as blindness starts to overtake his spirit. From that point onward (in sharp contrast to the increasingly clear and patterned verbalizations that, in the old lyrics, eventually provided some sense of place and direction), Li Bo's broken enunciations defy orientation and preclude even the reader's companionship.

The first impression of this brokenness derives from Li Bo's quotation of repetition in the opening quatrain. Whereas the repetition of paired characters and images had worked within the symmetry of quatrains made up of four-character lines to provided one of the unifying forces of the original poem, its imposition upon a pentasyllabic structure is unsettling. Li's repetition in line 3 of the three-character phrase "can't see the moon" *(bujian yue)* shifts the caesura, confirming the air of disequilibrium and obsession already supplied by his repetition of "water" three times in four lines. The feeling of internal, irrational obsession continues in the abrupt transition to the next quatrain, a feature typical of the Han *yuefu* (and present in the original *"Dulu* Composition"), but which counters readerly expectations of a unified narrative flow in the literati versions. After the first impression of abruptness, however, the reader will recognize the familiar couplet from the venerable pentasyllabic "Nineteen Old Poems" as expressing the natural desire of a traveler for his home. At the same time, the birds seem a natural enough transition from the honking geese of the earlier version, which had also established the solitude of the traveling narrator.

But hope of situating an integrated subject in imaginable space disappears in the next couplet, when the narrator expresses his

desire to aim his bow and shoot. He would like to shoot toward
the heavens, the unattainable byway along which the enviable
birds make their way home and the remote, unfeeling agent of
his destiny. But envy is replaced by sympathy for these fellow
travelers, and he stops short of shooting. The first line of this
unique seven-character couplet emphasizes the assertive "I desire"
and, more compellingly, bursts forth with an energy that is im-
mediately squelched by the equally expansive second line. The
impulsive desire to kill gives way to identification with his intended
victim, and the narrator, contrary to the sequence followed by his
predecessor, begins his descent into a dark, directionless, almost
hallucinatory world.

First, in an image considerably more morbid than the earlier
poet's water-grasses undulating (but never uprooting themselves)
at the mercy of the wind, Li Bo's narrator identifies with a dead
leaf, broken off and conveyed by that same wind to who knows
where. Li Bo carries over this image of invisible agency of visible
movement into the fourth quatrain, where he constructs, through
the use of an ambiguous and nearly ungrammatical syntax, an eerie,
spectral image of furling and unfurling bed curtains and intruding
moonlight. By ending both couplets with transitive verbs deprived
of a specific direct object, he plays with the four-character line,
creating an impression of amputation and discontinuity. This de-
stabilization of the original symmetry helps transform what had
been mere loneliness into hallucination. The bed curtain, borrowed
directly from the original poem and paired with an anthropomor-
phic moon, metamorphoses from a cool, subtle indicator of the
narrator's state of mind into the warped, unreal product of that
state of mind. Li sustains this internal monologue, which acknowl-
edges neither rules nor audience, into the ensuing quatrain, where
the familiar allusion of a humming sword turns unfamiliar and
strange in the form of a dragon.

Near the end of the poem, Li Bo's narrator poses a rhetorical
question about upholding the kingdom's honor that resonates
strongly with the earlier poem's final rousing filial sentiments. Li's
concern with "making one's name" hints, too, at a possible parody
of the original question of "how to go on living." The Confucian

system of ethics poses an ideal equivalency between one's name and the moral worth of one's life, but the ideal is always tempered by the awareness of the fleeting emptiness of reputation and fame. Even as he echoes the filial values that had finally collected the earlier narrator's scattered spirit, Li opts for ambiguity, inscribing in his poem the traditional dichotomy between act and word, between reality and illusion, or, as expressed in the old version, between the "real" *(zhen)* and the "fake" *(wei)*. Ambiguity reigns up to the very end, where Li Bo glides from the Confucian concerns so inspiring to his predecessor to the "unfettered" Zhuangzian images of divine hawk and *peng*-bird. Embracing the fundamental unity of reality and illusion, he flies off through the Nine Heavens, leaving the earlier crusader to join his fierce tiger in battle.

Li's solution to the problem of pitting reality (as defined by others in various manifestations ranging from the physical world to cultural and ethical systems) against illusion (the unconfirmed, unshareable experiences of the individual mind) is to subsume the trappings of the external world in the supreme reality of the spirit. In the realm of poetry, Li Bo defines the real as what exists in the spirit before being processed into literature: one's "intent" *(zhi)* prior to its articulation into "poetry" *(shi)*. In setting his *"Dulu Composition"* against the "old lyrics," Li Bo reveals that the ordered, lucid, and irreproachably spontaneous utterances of the folk song could belong only to a narrator aware of his audience. His own poem isolates its predecessor's nicely orchestrated signs of brokenness and presents them as true, unmediated articulations of the spirit, building them into a new poem to correct the first poem's fakery.

As in "Moshang sang," the plotline of Li Bo's *"Dulu Composition"* piece portrays a personage superior to, and misunderstood by, his contemporaries. In both poems the poet shadows the personage's lofty stance as he quotes meticulously from the past and openly works the poem's form, ultimately engaging in a critique of latter-day poetic authenticity. Once again, he confronts the paradox between ancientness and authenticity, and tries to solve it by asserting the naturalness of artistry.

One might object that Li Bo's circumvention of one paradox hardly spares him from setting up another of his own, as his painstaking implementation of poetic devices to create the impression of unmediated emotion only begs the question of spontaneity. But I believe that focusing on this contradiction leads one to miss the essence of his spirit. Such paradoxes are endemic to all types of reflexive inquiry, and they can be found everywhere across cultures and disciplines. The Chinese poet has his axe handle, the Romantic poet his self-directed quest for self-knowledge,[51] the psychoanalyst his subconscious.[52] In each of these endeavors, the end result is a prerequisite of the process, and the inquiring subject becomes the object of its own inquiry, continually retreating before its own transforming gaze. In like manner, Li Bo applies poetry to critique poetic expression, so must fall prey to his own critique. Perhaps he realizes that the game of mirrors is no less necessary for its absurd impossibility, and that, to the contrary, progress toward the goal of spontaneity consists in demonstrating its unattainable and absolute desirability. The unfetteredness manifest in "Moshang sang" and "*Dulu* Composition" consists in their quiet, irrefutable demonstration that nothing that happens in a poem is automatic or inevitable, even—or especially—the profound strangeness of the most well-worn and familiar poetic conceits.

Nostalgic Quotation

Perhaps the most daring denial of the utopian notion of spontaneous poetic expression, the most uninhibited exposure of the poet's rational role in the creation of poetry, is the flamboyant transcendence of diachronic change. This occurs not with a show of masterful transformation, but with a display of equally masterful nontransformation. The nearly perfect reproduction of the voice of a period not one's own, the convincing refusal to acknowledge that time has passed in the world and, more important, in literature, can constitute a powerful accomplishment on the part of the master poet. Li Bo was not one to forgo such a persuasive means of asserting his authenticity, but his *yuefu* poems expressing this refusal elicit the greatest ambivalence among critics. Unfetteredness as a slash-and-burn approach to convention is easy enough to comprehend and identify, but how is one to locate a sublime, inspired, no-holds-barred spontaneity expressed in cleaving to past models?

Li Bo achieves this approach by elegizing a past form or theme, by embracing, wholeheartedly and at face value, the aesthetic sensibilities espoused by his model. Looking at his *yuefu* as a group, the poems that lent themselves most easily to this approach seem to fall into the category of nonnarrative *yuefu*, those lacking the plot and the characters he found so easy to extract, unmold, and remold to his liking—those that presume that narrator and poet are one and the same. Some of these nonnarrative works appear in the category that Guo Maoqian entitles "Lyrics to Miscellaneous Tunes" ("Zaqu geci"). "Chang xiangsi," "Jiu bieli," "Beifeng xing" are among them.[53] Although one is well advised not to adhere too closely to Guo's categories, his preface to the first *juan* of this section does convincingly suggest that readers approached these poems, and writers composed them, guided especially by the spirit of folkloric (i.e., pure) immediacy and sincerity.[54]

In his preface, he quotes from the *Song shu*'s "Notations on Music" ("Yueji"), which describes the emperor's Han dynasty establishment of the *Yuefu* (music bureau) as a means of acquiring access to the true feelings of the people. This customary linking of good government to music and poetry dates back to Confucius' supposed collecting of the *Odes* in order to gauge the moral state of the people of Zhou. Behind this idea lies the moral and didactic conception of the ideal of poetic immediacy, of *shi yan zhi*, which dictates that while moral turpitude on the part of the governing body may produce libertine and depraved music, the sincerity of poetic expression is beyond doubt. Guo avails himself of this quotation to launch into a veritable inventory of all the modes, motives, and themes comprising the poems of this category and, indeed, of lyric poetry as it had been known since the *Odes:* "'Miscellaneous Tunes' have existed throughout the ages. Sometimes they are that which resides within the heart's intentions; sometimes, that which is stirred in one's emotions and longings. They may emerge from the pleasure of banquets and outings, or be inspired by sadness and melancholy, anger and resentment. Some express the grief of parting, some tell of the tribulations of military campaigns and displacement. At times they adhere to [the thought of] Buddha and Laozi, at times they originate from [the barbarian peoples] Yi and Lu."[55]

The series of poems written under the title "Chang xiangsi" (Infinite longing) nicely illustrates this philosophy of selection. Unlike the preceding narrative poems, the intratext uniting this set of poems derives not from an initial folktale or legend, but from a specific phrase: *"chang xiangsi,"* which, according to Guo's prefatory note to the series, first appeared in two of the "Nineteen Old Poems" as well as in poems by the Han dynasty figures Li Ling and Su Wu. In all of these works the phrase quotes or paraphrases the contents of a letter sent by a loved one far away or, as Guo explains: "'*Chang*' is a word expressing 'a long time' and 'distance,' meaning that a traveler has long been away guarding the frontiers, and has written a letter to send to the one he longs for."[56]

Although the title and the theme of these poems can be traced back to a specific set of texts, these texts were valued for their expression of a widely experienced human situation and the emotions that such situations inevitably elicit. The phrase itself, first used as a quotation of a letter at once intimate and universal, continues its career through the *yuefu* tradition as a quotation of previous poems. Of the twenty-odd poems Guo lists under this title, thirteen begin with this phrase. Perhaps its epigrammatic character contributed to its popularity, both conveying the credibility and venerability of ancient textual allusion and satisfying the aesthetic preference for verbal economy. Its resonant conciseness resides not so much in longing as in the simple *chang*, inadequately translated above as "far away." Guo's comment is a reminder of the painful reality that great spatial distances and great temporal distances were, until recently, inseparable. *"Chang"* conflates these two dimensions, blending objective reality and subjective experience into one sad emotion.

Most of the poems under this title develop the joint connotations of this theme. Chen Houzhu is the first among the authors of

the extant poems who clearly integrates time into a picture of
hopeless yearning:

Infinite longing,	長相思
Memories of you for so long,	久相憶
When will these campaigns at the passes come to	關山征戍何時極
an end?	望風雲
4 *I gaze toward windswept clouds,*	絕音息
News of you cut off,	山林書不歸
Through the mountain woods, return letters do	迴文徒自織
not arrive;	羞將別後面
In vain do I stitch my poem-puzzle,[57]	還似初相識
8 *Afraid to see if this face, since we parted,*	
Is still like the one when first we met.[58]	

The "poem-puzzle" of line 7 alludes to the story of Su Hui, the
wife of the early Qin dynasty general Dou Tao. Longing for her
absent husband, Su Hui composed an acrostic poem of more than
800 characters, which she embroidered in a circular pattern on
cloth so that it could be read forward, backward, and across, with
each reading yielding a different poem. Upon receiving it, the
general was so moved that he sent for his wife to join him, putting
an end to her bitter solitude. But in Chen Houzhu's "Chang
xiangsi" (the first of two poems the emperor composed under this
title), the speaker knows that she is not to be so blessed. The end-
less number of ways to read the poem is like the endlessness of her
longing, and the only response her "vain" embroidered phrases will
elicit are those same embroidered phrases read in reverse. Like-
wise, as the closing couplet tells us, the only return gaze her eyes
are bound to encounter is that emanating from her own aged face,
should she give in to the temptation to look in the mirror. The
allusion to Su Hui appears just before the end, adding to the pathos
of a closing couplet that gives voice to the abandoned woman's
fears of the influence of time's passage on her (and perhaps his)
youthful beauty, and on memory itself.

The dense, polysemous pathos of the word *"chang,"* while

already present in the Six Dynasties versions, was perhaps best suited for the sensibility of a fully developed Tang poetics, where the intricate structure of regulated poetry honed the utilization of polysemy to its finest point, profoundly influencing non-regulated forms as well. Li Bo's "Chang xiangsi" brings the age-old grief of separation into this era, elegizing its ancientness, glazing it with the patina of court poetry, and finally ensuring its continuity through the rejuvenating complexity of contemporary poetics:

Infinite longing for you	長相思
In the city of Infinite Peace.	在長安
Autumn cry of crickets at the rail of a gold-hued well,	絡緯秋啼金井闌
	微霜淒淒簟色寒
4 *A light glaze of frost, the mat's color cold.*	孤燈不明思欲絕
By lone lamp that sheds no light, longing's thread about to break,	卷帷望月空長嘆
Draw back the curtains, behold the moon, sigh long and hollow:	美人如花隔雲端
My love like a flower beyond the far edge of clouds.	
8 *And above—the blue dark of heavens high,*[59]	上有青冥之高天
And below—the swells of a clear river.	下有淥水之波瀾
The sky is wide, the road long, my soul flies forth in pain,	天長路遠魂飛苦
Even in dreams the soul can't reach the rigors of the mountain pass.	夢魂不到關山難
12 *Infinite longing,*	長相思
Pressing the heart.[60]	摧心肝

In its essence, nothing in this poem is at odds with the Six Dynasties transformation of the original Han poetics of helpless separation as exemplified in the "Nineteen Old Poems." Wang Qi says as much in his comment on this poem when, after telling us that "Chang xiangsi" had already become a well-known title during the Six Dynasties, he says, "this piece by Taibai is perfectly modeled after this type."[61] Wang Fuzhi pinpoints exactly what conforming to this "type" implies when he passionately praises this poem for its restraint and its "emptiness": "Within [the conventions of] the title, he deliberately avoids being explicit; in the realm 'beyond images' (*xiangwai*), he insists on leaving one with something extra. In the one case, it is a matter of [Li Bo's] personal style; in the other, a matter of his unrestrained expression. Alas! One cannot hope to see anything greater!"[62]

To these observations—Li's perfect grasp and reproduction of the model, his ability to convey meaning without resorting to direct expression, and his genius for imbuing his poem with that indescribable "something extra"—I would add his aptitude for using contemporary poetic practices in order to make the reader truly appreciate and long for the pastness of the genre he here continues. In "Moshang sang" and *"Dulu* Composition," Li Bo played with the identities of folktale personages, exploiting the fluid relationship between the narrator and these characters to demonstrate his own expressive control. The poems in this section presume a unified point of view. Here his role-playing, as it has been called by Owen and others, is at its most subtle and persuasive. He borrows the characteristics of the archetype and polishes them to a high gloss in a technique that might best be likened to the hyperrealist paintings of today.

The elegant opening couplet engages several opposing or complementary constructs. One complex of composite meaning develops from the word *"chang,"* repeated from the title; another, from the ambiguity of the speaking subject. The question of whether the speaking subject is the abandoned woman or the traveling man, and whether that subject is located in Chang'an—"the city of Infinite Peace"—is reminiscent of similar ambiguities in several of the "Nineteen Old Poems." In those poems this ambiguity, whether intentional or not, seems to enhance the reciprocity of longing and helps the reader to visualize the distance between the two lovers. Carried over into a composition under this title, which inscribes that reciprocity in one possible reading of the second character, *"xiang,"*[63] this ambiguity could not be better suited to the conceit of the originating letter, in which the simultaneous picture of the two separated lovers waiting for, receiving (or not), and sending letters can only add to the depth of the longing conveyed. The Six Dynasties poems generally do not take advantage of this option. Lu Qiong's (537–586) poem, for example, like Chen Houzhu's, clearly takes the point of view of the waiting woman who gazes at the words on the page for so long that she wears them out.[64] Only Li Bo's version seems to make the most of the richness inherent in combining the traditions.

The complex of meaning in Li Bo's use of *"chang"* in the opening couplet points to his direct inheritance of the complex of spatial and temporal distance already noted by Guo and utilized to a certain degree by other Six Dynasties poets. Li Bo combines this inherited complex of meaning with ambiguity of subject to form the building blocks of the poem. His decision to insert the capital's name, "Chang'an" (everlasting peace), imbues *"chang"* with a bitterness not yet apparent in earlier poems and inserts a personal, historical perspective. Given the difficulty of maintaining the capital in the same place over an extended period of time, few Tang readers would remain unresponsive to this invocation of the vulnerability of this, the most glorious of capitals, to the vicissitudes of history and fate. The full force of *chang's* significance, however, does not become clear until the end of the poem, with the experience of the painful infinitude, not just of the lovers' longing for one another, but also of the story of separation recounted—once more—in this poem.

The poem moves from this "innocent" ancient beginning, which already contains the seeds of elegy, to a quatrain as sensually vivid as it is familiar, replete with the imagery of the Southern Dynasties court poems—those refined songs of love emanating from the lonely boudoir of the abandoned woman. This woman, so beautifully bound and defined by this constellation of cold and frosty, yet intimate, images among which she moves, emerges as being as much a vision—a visualized object—of her wandering lover as she is a longing subject herself. The sense of her objectification can be attributed to the sheer perfection of her lyrical rendering, itself the fruit of centuries of repeated renderings of identical women. At the same time, it is precisely in this archetypal framing of her otherness that her lover's presumably very specific and personal longing is subtly conveyed. Finally, added to the age-old scene of unsatisfied longing is the latter-day poet's literary eye: the allusive familiarity of the images—from the autumn crickets and golden well-rails to the frosty mat gleaming under the cold and distant moon—are reminders that the woman is being longingly remembered by the poet as a literary figure as much as the lover is ardently desiring her as an object of love.

The two perspectives resist such clinical separation, of course, and the reader engages in both types of longing simultaneously. In the hands of another poet, the weight of this longing could easily overwhelm any immediate sense of the woman as a desiring subject. But if a lyricist's nostalgia and a lover's desire threaten to blot out the subjectivity of this woman (whom they, incidentally, conspired to create), Li Bo counters that threat with a particularly Tang-style flair. For all the courtly familiarity of the man-made and artificial objects with which he surrounds her, he orchestrates their independent sensual properties so that they play off each other and finally blend into one: the embodiment of a woman's loneliness.[65] Li Bo's Luofu could assert her subjectivity in direct speech. This was a crucial feature of the poet's defamiliarization of past poetry, the essence of his unfettered voice. In his nonnarrative *yuefu*, such as "Chang xiangsi," however, the dual perspective of what might be called his "subjective object" is conveyed through his meticulous handling of what later critics identified as the Tang skill at "blending feeling and scene" (*qing jing jiao rong*),[66] here incorporating the feeling viewer of the scene within the scene itself. And so, in line 6, when the woman draws back the curtains to look (and to be seen looking), the object that all eyes behold emerges as the sum of *all* the preceding parts—and, not incidentally, the convergence of space and time into one overarching universe of *chang*.

In line 7, all upturned gazes unite in one inward gaze when here, in the line located in the exact middle of the poem, they converge on the absent, flowerlike loved one, blocked from vision behind a screen of clouds: an image that still carries the space-time significance of *chang*, but that counters all objective notions of both space and time. From this vision that is at once minuscule and vast, ephemeral and eternal, individual and choral, proceeds the final stanza of the poem, which in many ways is quite in keeping with convention.

Images of the boudoir dissolve into the vast expanses leading out to the mountain pass, and the air of the court poem is replaced by that of the frontier poem, enhanced by Li Bo's hyperbolic celestial imagery. This poet's projection of dual imaginings becomes the new incarnation of *xiang*—the reciprocity between the man and the woman—previously embodied in the original letter. For a moment, in lines 8 through 10, the souls of the man and the woman fly desperately across the same distances, albeit in opposite directions. But just as the letters never reach their destined readers, so their souls are kept apart. Her soul, it turns out, cannot get there from here. Reciprocal imaginings regress into unilateral pain, and the poem ends, somewhat ironically now, with that refrain, *"chang xiangsi"*—to be repeated into eternity, as their small, inconsequent hearts are urged to impotent sadness, "pressed" under the weight of time and space.

In composing "Chang xiangsi," Li Bo has respected and reproduced all the features treasured in the accumulated lexicon comprising previous versions: the layered significance of *chang*, the reciprocity of the lovers' feelings, the sensual imagery of Southern Dynasties poetry, and the harsh landscape of the frontier. But in the parallel symmetry of the two stanzas, in his redisposition of the vectors of voice and vision, in the intense visual quality of the depicted scenes, and, above all, in the historicized sense of literary place and time, Li Bo has refashioned the familiar scenes to heightened levels of both emotion and literariness. At the same time, just as he has united the voices of the lovers in a harmony of mutual longing, he has added his voice to theirs to form a chorus. While the two lovers desire each other in an eternal present, his voice reminds the reader of the ancient beauty of their desire and of its ancient expression.

In another *yuefu* under the related title "Qianli si" (Thousand-mile longings), Li Bo comes very close to expressing his literary nostalgia in so many words, as he sings of the fates of two early writers of "Chang xiangsi," both of whom stood as exemplars of stoic homesickness: Li Ling, the Han dynasty general who was captured by the Xiongnu and died twenty years later in foreign lands,[67] and Su Wu, to whom Li Ling wrote a lengthy letter and some poems (collected in the *Wenxuan*),[68] also defeated by the Xiongnu, but who returned home some fifteen years later, his honor intact.[69]

Li Ling, submerged in the Tartar sands,	李陵沒胡沙
Su Wu, returned to his home among the Han.	蘇武還漢家
Unfathomably far, the Wuyuan Passes,	迢迢五原關
4 *And the northwind snow, a flurry of frontier flowers.*	朔雪亂邊花
	一去隔絕域
Once you leave, cut off by the intervening lands,	思歸但長嗟
You may think of returning, but can only sigh long.	鴻雁向西北
The wild goose heads toward the northwest,	飛書報天涯
8 *Its flying missive a response to the edge of Heaven.*[70]	

CREATED SPONTANEITY

Thus far in my discussion of Li Bo's unfetteredness and its interposition into *yuefu* poetry, I have focused primarily on the poet's defamiliarization of poetic precedent. Encouraged in this approach by traditional and modern criticism, as well as by the nature of the *yuefu* genre itself, I have isolated three particular realms in which Li Bo overtly takes advantage of *yuefu*'s well delineated transtextuality to exercise, and occasionally underscore, his *droit de poète*: the realms of narrative (and character), language, and theme-specific imagery. In each of these cases, he finds a way to split the traditional, "innocent" identity of narrator and poet and so restores the sheen to the songs' patina of authentic, if not unmediated, expression. This way of writing *yuefu*, I suggest, translates into unfetteredness partly because it creates the impression of breaking rules. But this unfetteredness would hardly be so cheerfully accepted if his audience suspected him of self-conscious artifice. Thus his admirers' continuous insistence that this mode of expression was itself the natural expression of his inner self—in *yuefu* as in all other forms of poetry.

Proof of naturalness, of course, has always been hard to come by, so stories of spontaneity would have to do. The lore surrounding and supporting the legend of unfetteredness includes many tales recounting Li Bo's rapid compositions, executed on demand, perhaps fueled by the consumption of some good wine. One of Li Bo's most famous *yuefu* compositions, "*Qingping* Melody in Three Parts" ("Qingping diao") is the subject of just such a story.[71] Li is credited with having whipped off the three quatrains in a drunken instant, and the purported result is this much disputed, sensually appealing work, whose exact meaning—hyperbolic appreciation of flowers or veiled political commentary—continues to incite debate.

I.

Clouds recall her robes, blossoms her face,　　　雲想一裳花想容
Spring winds caress the rail, dew-laden petals　　春風拂檻露華濃
　　grow lush.
If you do not see her atop Jade-Cluster　　　　　若非裙玉山頭見
　　Mountain,
4　Then surely you shall meet her at Jasper Terrace　會向瑤臺月下逢
　　beneath the moon.[72]

II.

On a bough of brilliant red, dew's thickening　　一枝紅豔露凝香
　　fragrance,
The clouds and rain upon Mount Wu recklessly　雲雨巫山枉斷腸
　　break men's hearts.[73]
Should you ask, in the Han Palace who can　　　借問漢宮誰得似
　　compare?
8　Fetching Flying-Swallow, at her ease, adorns　　可憐飛燕倚新妝
　　herself anew.[74]

III.

The "Acclaimed Flower" and "Ruination of　　　名花傾國兩相歡
　　Kingdoms"[75] take pleasure in each other,
So lovely that the prince watches with a smile.　長得君王帶笑看
Unconstrained is the spring wind, its sorrows　　解釋春風無限恨
　　without end—
12　North of Sandalwood Pavilion, he leans on the　沉香亭北倚闌干
　　railing.[76]

The story behind the composition of this set of poems re-
sembles the story of Li Bo's "Shudao nan." Both play key roles in
the creation of Li Bo's unfettered persona. In providing readers
with a unifying narrative linking his behavior to his creative pro-
cess, this piece of biographical criticism, however apocryphal,
stands as a useful profile for understanding not only what is meant
by this quality of unfetteredness, but, indirectly, how it might have
been located in a specific *yuefu*. Although details vary and the
kernel of the story has been embellished and altered over the years,
Wang Qi's annotation, quoted directly from the "Unofficial Biog-
raphy of Yang Guifei," provides the essentials.

According to this version, some time in the middle of the
Kaiyuan era, peonies were planted in the imperial garden. When
they were in full bloom, the emperor called for a nighttime flower-
viewing celebration, which he enjoyed in the company of his con-
sort, Yang Guifei. Song and dance were provided by members of
the Liyuan, the imperial theater company, but a song proposed by
one of its members, Li Guinian, disappointed the emperor, who
found it too old-fashioned for the occasion. He thereupon sent for
Li Bo, asking him to compose new lyrics. Li Bo, who happened to
be just waking up (or, in some accounts, was drunk), grabbed his
brush and, without a moment's thought, composed these poems,
which were then set to music and performed by Li Guinian. Both
the consort and the emperor were extremely pleased. As this
account tells it, "From this moment on, the emperor regarded Li
Hanlin as uniquely excellent among all other scholars." But his
favor at court was short-lived, and a related story identifies this
event as one of the causes of Li Bo's later expulsion. As recounted
in Yue Shi's (930–1007) *Taibai yishi,* the powerful eunuch Gao
Lishi, resentful of Li Bo's rise in favor and particularly vexed at
having been obliged to remove Li Bo's boots, told Yang Guifei that
the "Qingping diao" poems were veiled criticisms of her favored
treatment—with predictable results.[77]

At first glance, there is nothing particularly "unfettered" about
this set of three *yuefu*. They contain none of the hyperbolic imag-
ery of "Shudao nan," no "broken-yet-continuous" phrasing, no
defamiliarization of familiar story lines. Furthermore, unlike the
yuefu examined so far, Li Bo was the first to compose under this

title, and so "Qingping diao" lacks a specific intratext within which it can distinguish itself.[78]

But those who commented on "Qingping diao" all suggest that Li Bo was toying with voices and perspectives, though in a different way from in other *yuefu* poems. Most traditional commentators, including the Yuan scholars Yang Qixian and Xiao Shibin, as well as the Qing scholar Ye Xie, locate the manifestation of unfetteredness in the origin and presentation of the poem, rather than in the poem itself. They believe that these *yuefu* were intended for performance, as recounted in the story, and unquestioningly read these poems as satirizing Yang Guifei's dangerously exalted position at court. (This reading also agrees with Gao Lishi's perhaps apocryphal interpretation.) But it is not the satire that inspires the critics' admiration; after all, critiquing the Han dynasty as a way of indirectly criticizing the Tang was hardly novel. For these readers, it is clearly the supposed provenance and presentation of this particular satire that renders it remarkable.

Like the *yuefu* intratext, the appended performance story provides a basis for Li Bo's reframing of the narrator-poet voice and objectifying of someone's conventionalized innocence. Instead of responding to Li Bo's defamiliarization of specific poetic precedents and conventions, readers of "Qingping diao" respond to his imagined objectification of the protocol of imperial performance, and of the implied audience expectations. Here Li does not objectify the conventionalized innocence of past narrators (like the mulberry woman or the wanderer of *"Dulu"*), but that of the emperor and his consort.

While no commentators make this connection explicit, one cannot but be struck by how easily some of their remarks blend with and support the "unfettered-*yuefu*" thesis. For example, "Qingping diao" (both story and song) elicit from Ye Xie an enthusiastic declaration of Li's abundance of "vital force" (*qi*)—the force by which he can be "be true to his nature"—the *qi* that Ye credited for Li's survival alongside Du Fu.[79] Ye Xie's *qi*, as briefly discussed in chapter 2, points to the daring and independence Li Bo expressed in the submission of these poems for performance before the emperor and in the swiftness of their composition and the degree of risk incurred as well. The obvious pleasure that Ye Xie and others take from this reading and its easy affinity with the "Banished Immortal" persona override questions that others see as cause for reasonable doubt. Wang Qi, for example, asks why, if the satire was so cutting, did no one but Gao Lishi notice it? And if it was so subtle that no one else understood it, then what was the point?[80]

Nevertheless, Wang Qi's skepticism does not lead him to regard these poems as simply banal repetitions of one of poetry's oldest conceits—the comparison between women and flowers. On the contrary, for Wang, and for other readers less reliant on extra-textual evidence for their appreciation of these poems, Li Bo has worked his magic again, finding freshness in an overused metaphor: "piercing the heavens to harvest stone, and catching fish in parched soil."[81] According to admirers, in writing this sequence he has defied those who laugh at the use of such a facile, sterile comparison,[82] and has magisterially intertwined the floral and the feminine so as to render the one indistinguishable from the other. So Shen Deqian, for example, declares: "The three pieces unite flower and human in [the same] utterances: elegantly beguiling, and comely beyond compare. Others say that the first piece sings of the consort, the next piece sings of the flowers, and the third piece sings of both together. Such a [tripartite division] verges on being inflexible and literal-minded."[83]

If Shen's reference to the simultaneous coexistence of competing interpretations suggests some awareness that ambiguity plays an important role in comprehending the poem, Wang Qi later explicitly pinpoints the role of the well-framed illusion. He takes his lead from a specific character in the opening couplet: *"xiang,"* translated here as "recall," but meaning more literally "to think" or "to cause one to think." In Wang's words, "Li's double repetition of the word 'xiang' transforms the 'solid' into the 'empty,' and appears strikingly new and fresh."[84] This comment goes right to the heart of everything I have identified with the unfettered poetic persona thus far: his representation of the essential interdependency of the substantive and the empirically unfounded, his overt use of authorial perspective to defamiliarize—and thus renew—the whole array of poetic conventions, and his ability to conjure up familiar images and imbue them with an unexpected sensory immediacy.

Li has taken a commonplace metaphor and an overworn satirical device and transformed them into a poem worthy of its starring role in one of the central stories of Li Bo's creative life. How is this possible? In my view it is because Li Bo's "Qingping Melody" reorganizes familiar images of elusive and ephemeral beauty so that, at its best, the language itself embodies that same elusiveness. The old conceit is reinvigorated, and readers are compelled to re-experience that original sense of wonder in their primary encounter—not with the woman and the flower (which readers can no longer see for the first time)—but with mediating poetic language. "Qingping diao" invites each reader to recognize, if only subliminally, the fundamental createdness of the customary perceptual and readerly parameters. In contrast with literary practices of more recent times, however, this "deconstructive" awareness of the illusive layering of visual perception, far from denying the poem sequence its meaningfulness, only sharpens the apprehension that "at its center, this beauty harbors a thorn"[85]—an observation that is crucial to understanding these poems.

The sequence's overall tripartite structure interacts with the elliptical quatrain *(jueju)* form to play a key role in the elaboration of the mental verb *"xiang"* (to remind), insightfully singled out by Wang Qi. From the opening ambiguity of the object of our gaze to the closing ambiguity of the object of the prince's gaze, every visual image leads to—and bounces off—every other, in a chain of visual reminders. The reader, naturally seeking a unifying point of view or a clear succession of points of view, looks for a pattern across the three quatrains, and a pattern does seem to emerge in the tantalizing solution of a three-step "consort—flower—consort/flower" sequence, mentioned above by Shen Deqian. This pattern, once adopted, comfortably allows us to fill in the ellipses that the individual *jueju* form helps create and sustain. Thus, the "robes" and "face" in the first poem can credibly belong to the goddesslike creature whom tradition reads as a stand-in for Yang Guifei. Similarly, the question in the second quatrain—"in the Han Palace, who can compare?"—can unambiguously take the lovely peonies as

its subject. And finally, the third quatrain's "Acclaimed Flower"
can be understood as precisely that, one of the lovely peonies
among which the palace beauty amuses herself. This reading works
rather well, in fact, and allows the reader to take the next step and
simply make the transfer from the Han dynasty to the Tang, with
little hesitation.

However, a more open reading of the elliptical relationships
within each of the *jueju* can have a devastating effect on this neat,
satisfying tripartite scheme. Returning to the first couplet of the
first poem, the modern reader is struck, as was Wang Qi, by Li Bo's
repetition of *xiang*. Wang does not explain its significance, except
to note that its presence supports the argument that the first word
of the line should indeed be "clouds" and not "leaves," as some
argued. As evidence, Wang counters his opponents' citations of
precedents in Southern Dynasties poems with a decidedly more
venerable example from the *Chuci:* "Green clouds, her robes; and
white mist, her tunic" (*qing yun yi xi bai ni shang*).[86] The crux of
Wang's argument rests on the superior savor of this reference to an
otherworldly goddess, a reference that becomes explicit in the next
couplet. This savor is prefigured in *xiang*, the insertion of the
poet's, prince's, and reader's roles in the transformation of observ-
able reality. If the clouds and flowers remind us of something else,
it must be because they are *not* that something else. But their
ability to "remind"—to "make one think"—of other things, an
ability bestowed on them as much by the poetic canon as by any
one person's perceptions, ensures that they can no longer simply
be "thought" into clouds and flowers.

Li Bo neatly invokes the power of *xiang* to transform both
subject and object in an unending cycle of responses simulta-
neously visceral and literary, until readers are no longer sure what
they are looking at. This eternal deferral of meaning is certainly
better supported by the reading "clouds" than it is by "leaves."
Not only do clouds suggest visual uncertainty and encompass the
ephemeral and elusive beauty of both flowers and women, but their
image avoids the static equivalency that a strictly botanical image
like leaves would impose on the verse. The classic, accommodating
image sets in motion a transformational progression from clouds

to clothing, from clothing to blossoms, and from blossoms to face. While the shared translucency of all those images suggests the simultaneous overlapping of flower petals—now coyly revealing, now dissembling—readers are also "made to think" the clouds from woman, to flower, and back to woman.

This transformational energy is itself transformed in the next line ("Spring winds caress the rail, dew-laden petals grow lush"), where it shifts its source from the onlookers' gaze to the wind. In this shift, any illusion of control is dispelled, as woman, flower, and anonymous observer (prince and reader) alike are made to feel the spring wind's transforming caress, all the more potent for its effect on the object of the observer's gaze, whether it is the womanlike flower petals or the flowerlike woman.

The second couplet capitalizes on one of the expectations of the *jueju* form. In the third line, the poet executes a radical shift in direction, bringing the previous constellation of images into a comprehensible, if unforeseen, whole: "If you do not see her atop Jade-Cluster Mountain, / Then surely you shall meet her at Jasper Terrace beneath the moon." For readers guided primarily by the tripartite structure and the classicism of the woman-flower metaphor, this couplet offers welcome reassurance that the preceding complex of images was really just a nicely executed homage to the beauty of the goddesslike consort. But for those other readers who have apprehended the centrality of Li Bo's play of illusion and transformation, this shift from elusive metaphor to supposedly explanatory discursive language accomplishes something quite different.

"Jade-Cluster Mountain" and "Jasper Terrace" can only refer to the mythical dwelling of the Queen Mother of the West, so naturally incline one to think more of a female being than of a flower. But not quite hidden behind this enticing spectacle is the poet's sustained reference to the quixotic nature of vision itself, enacting its transformations under the influence of a confusing mixture of memory and desire. Li Bo does not need to remind his readers of the fundamental impossibility of "seeing" or "meeting" the woman-like-flower-like-woman in either of these two places. The mere mention of these unreachable realms only confirms that the promised vision will always remain more *xiang* than *jian*—more blindness than insight. Strangely, as the jade palisades and rays of moonlight add their lambent translucency to that of the clouds, petals, silken robes, and female faces, the resulting layered image loses, rather than gains, in clarity. Readers have not definitively found what it is they are looking at, but they have been pricked by the suspected barb hidden among the blossoms: the human susceptibility to seeing "real" objects where there are only projected images, and to impute solidity and immortality precisely to that which is most elusive and ephemeral. The admonition, while appropriate for the emperor's single-minded passion for his consort, holds for readers' innocent faith in poetic practice as well.

The second quatrain of the sequence begins with a couplet that summons in swift succession the essential images of the first piece, again creating the impression of a clear and meaningful pattern. The first line again has the dew-laden blossoms, whose fragrance has been intensified, perhaps, by the ministrations of the spring wind. The second line contains a composite reference to clouds and immortal goddesses. Then, almost as though this entire quatrain had taken on the role of a *jueju*'s pivot, the reconvened images exercise a change of direction, from an assembly of evocative, mutable images to a specific historical allusion, apparently indicative of some hidden meaning. "Should you ask, in the Han Palace who can compare?/Fetching Flying-Swallow, at her ease, adorns herself anew."

Ambiguity still reigns for readers who seek to understand for whom, or what, they are seeking a counterpart in the Han Palace: Yang Guifei, or the peonies? There is no obvious answer, as both the woman and the flower are clearly present in both preceding lines. What is known is only the answer to the flagrantly rhetorical question of who in the Han palace can compare (to whatever that object is). Few readers have hesitated to embrace the obvious conclusion that the villainous beauty held responsible for the decline of the Han dynasty could, indeed, compare with the Tang consort Yang Guifei.

For some, the problem of this interpretation lies in its obviousness. One thinks back to Wang Qi's misgivings; confronted with a reference that obvious (if indeed it was), how did Yang Gui-fei and the emperor not immediately take umbrage? How could Li Bo have taken such a foolhardy risk? Even those who are skeptical about the poem's supposed submission directly to the emperor can't help but feel disappointed that Li Bo would lapse into such facile language after such a promising beginning. Then again, the best camouflage—especially in an imagistic matrix where all is illusion—may be no camouflage at all; the sheer impossibility of such effrontery (combined with the utter unselfconsciousness of its imperial target) might have served, at least temporarily, to blind the emperor and his company to its all too obvious implications, allowing them the luxury of imagining that the comparison was selected only for its positive associations.

In any case, for all its obviousness as a possible political barb, this couplet also engages the play of visual illusion initiated at the beginning of the poem. The absurd question *"shei de si"*—literally, "who is worthy of resembling her (or it)?"—serves only to highlight the fact that the poem has so far presented nothing but "resemblances." In a metaphorical landscape composed of all vehicle and no tenor, in which any single image compels the viewer to think it into another image, the search for likenesses is both definitive and meaningless. Flying-Swallow's name, offered as the answer to the absurd question, joins the list of self-perpetuating analogies. It is fitting that the second quatrain ends with the image of her applying makeup, presumably before a mirror, attempting to create a better resemblance to that elusive and ephemeral woman-flower she innocently hopes to compel her beholders to think of.

The second quatrain, then, concludes with the likeness of a lovely woman-flower perfecting her likeness, and the third and final quatrain of the series begins the same way: "The 'Acclaimed Flower' and 'Ruination of Kingdoms' take pleasure in each other, / So lovely that the prince watches with a smile." At the risk of belaboring the obvious, it is easy to see how this line supports a neat tripartite reading, finally reuniting the heretofore separately treated flower and woman in one picture.[87] But as likeness gazes upon likeness, and as each reflects the pleased and pleasing image of the other, the perpetual problems of identity and illusion remain unresolved. Since "Acclaimed Flower" so strongly evokes a beautiful woman—almost as much as "Ruination of Kingdoms"—is it not possible that the reflected images in question here are not those of flower and woman, but of Yang Guifei and the just mentioned Flying-Swallow? Or, to continue the image of the preceding quatrain, one (or both) of these women applying her makeup while looking in the mirror?

In this world, where identity is in the eye of the beholder, and the beholder's identity is a function of his or her own looking, the only reality seems to be the power of image: visual, of course, but—even more important—literary. Li Bo's interest in recapturing authenticity by exposing the illusion of conventional poetic images is manifest in many of his poems; perhaps, then, his *qi*, as expressed in this poem, is not just a matter of political daring, but of literary daring. With this in mind, it becomes possible to note not only how the prince's appreciative smile mirrors the pleasure of the reflected images he "sees." One can also register, rather bemusedly, the parallel smile of the willingly deceived reader (or imperial audience), who contentedly settles on a system of sanctioned—but illusory and self-propagating—metaphoric equivalencies.

Finally: "Unconstrained is the spring wind, its sorrows without end—/ North of Sandalwood Pavilion, he leans on the railing." As the "spring wind" passes where it will, exerting its influence indiscriminately on viewers and viewed, some might long sadly for the more salubrious winds of a bygone—ancient—era: a wind such as that emanated by the first "Air" (*feng*) of the *Shijing*, which "blew upon (*feng*) all under Heaven, regulating [relations between] man and woman."[88] Yet others will remain in its thrall. The beauty-drunk prince, like the compliant reader/audience, feels the sorrow of longing without quite seizing on its cause. But Li Bo, whose work has been dubbed inimitable and indescribable, has taken the chance of imitating and describing the cause of poetic affect, revealing the original artfulness of metaphors that had been naturalized—and neutralized—by conventionalized use. In taking this risk he succeeds in inspiring, if only for a moment, the wonder of a metaphor newly created, and in conveying the exhilaration of his unfetteredness.

LI BO'S *yuefu* poetry, in all its various guises, offers readers the chance to recover a sense of freedom and wonder, but only if they are willing to endure the discomfort of alienation and loss of innocence. Whether the cap that he "hangs on the cliff" takes the form of a well-worn narrative, an instance of conventional prosody, or a clichéd metaphor, he invites his readers to appreciate it for the conventionalized sign it has become while offering, in return, the promise of seeing it anew. To borrow from Philip Fisher, Li Bo restores the wonder of old equations—between the mulberry woman and her innocence, between the wanderer's fears and their lucid poetic expression, between women and flowers—by deliberately pointing to the created nature of the syntax that binds them.[89]

In this way, Li Bo invites readers to sample the exhilaration of his fabled unfetteredness. The price of admission, however, is not limited to the pain of lost innocence, or even, as might happen in today's world, the mortification of understanding one's own canon in relative terms. The willing reader, and especially the young poet aspiring to follow in Li Bo's footsteps, faces not only the indisputable inimitability of Li Bo's style, but the virtual impossibility of revisiting a site that Li Bo has chosen to defamiliarize. How can one expect to write another "*Dulu* Composition"? If one continues in Li Bo's defamiliarized language, it will only sink back into the morass of the ordinary, losing both the dignity of long tradition and the freshness of the strange. As Joseph Allen has astutely pointed out, "Li Bo was the preeminent *yuefu* poet because he was essentially an adolescent poet, a young poet all his life." Allen has even gone so far as to credit Li Bo with having "by the fullness of his participation in its conventions ... brought the genre to completion and exhaustion at the same time."[90] The history of the *yuefu* genre certainly seems to bear him out, but I would further characterize Li Bo's participation by borrowing a word from some of Li's Ming dynasty admirers: *qi* (rendering strange). Labels can be stultifying, and nothing is more vulnerable to analysis than wonder. But, as centuries of Chinese critics believed, a well-placed, open-ended word can serve as a perfect window through which to direct the gaze.

CHAPTER 5

Alluding to Immediacy

❖

BY NOW it will come as no surprise to find that there is more than
a bit of playfulness in Li Bo's choice of allusion as another one of
his springboards to authentic, immediate expression—even though
allusion hardly seems the material on which to base a revived
poetics of immediacy. After all, allusion, unlike metaphor (which
speaks to the intuition and draws upon little more than the infor-
mation given within the poem itself), invokes an outside textual
source, calling into play a reader's acquired knowledge. Unlike the
intertextuality of the *yuefu* or the *Gufeng*, allusion is not sanc-
tioned by a poem's identification with an established, backward-
gazing genre. Indeed, the prominence of rational reflection in the
implementation of allusion accounts for the fact that some of the
Six Dynasties champions of natural poetic expression regarded it
with a certain ambivalence.[1]

Yet Li Bo embraced allusion as an integral part of his poetics,
neutralizing the implied tension between immediacy and artfulness

by assuming a frank attitude to allusion's obvious "allusiveness." Li Bo redirected the reader's attention away from the meaning of an allusion to the difference (or, in some cases, the studied similarity) between his use of an allusion and its textual referent. This practice enabled Li Bo to recuperate or better yet recreate lost immediacy in two ways: by renewing the past (if only momentarily) and by acknowledging the willed act behind that momentary renewal. By explicitly referring to the pastness and presumed comprehensibility of allusions, Li Bo defamiliarizes them and encourages his readers to reexperience the commonplace as though for the first time. At the same time, even as they encounter the old allusion with a renewed sense of its (presumably original) authenticity, readers will register the poet's deliberate act and the elevated point of view that made it possible. By explicitly referring to allusions as something externally imposed—as part of a received tradition from which he may select some elements and reject others—Li raises his voice above the chorus of the past, deliberately and authentically establishing that he directs their song rather than being directed by it. This capacity befits the "Banished Immortal" more than any outright claim to ancientness, and it is more persuasive of his existence than any depiction of a flight through the heavens. If allusion is the poetic trace of time's passage, Li Bo realized the possibility of taking a few steps off that path.

ALLUSION AS ILLUSION

Few poems express Li Bo's complex view of allusion with more candor than his poem, "In Which I Write My Feelings to be Sent to My Cousin, Administrator Zhao of Binzhou" ("Shu qing ji congdi Binzhou Zhangshi Zhao") a virtual recounting of the paradoxical act of seeking out vehicles of immediate, individual expression. Time and time again, the poetic past—whether in the form of specific allusions or of conventional modes of expression—unavoidably insinuates itself into the mind of the poet, not only threatening to overshadow original expression, but promising to usurp those original feelings that presumably form its basis:

I laugh at myself, on the road for so long,   自笑客行久

When will I settle down from wandering?   我行定幾時

Already willow branches are ready to be   綠楊已可折

    plucked,   攀取最長枝

4 *I reach up to take the longest bough.*   翩翩弄春色

It flutters as I finger its spring colors,   延佇寄相思

Long have I waited to send it to the one I miss.   誰言貴此物

But who declared that we should value this   意願重瓊蕤

    thing?   昨夢見惠連

8 *My yearning, more precious than a jade flower.*   朝吟謝公詩

Yesterday I dreamed I saw Huilian,   東風引碧草

This morning I was chanting the poem of Master   不覺生華池

    Xie.   臨玩忽云夕

The east wind gives rise to emerald grasses,   杜鵑夜鳴悲

12 *And unwittingly yields a flowering pond.*   懷君芳歲歇

I glanced down to play with it—suddenly it is   庭樹落紅滋

    twilight,

The night cry of the cuckoo is mournful.

I miss you as this fragrant season passes,

16 *As trees in the courtyard drop red nectar.*[2]

    As in many of his poems, Li Bo opens this one with the first-person pronoun, the directness of which primes readers for a poem of spontaneous, "immediate" reflection. In the next couplet, he establishes his physical orientation with equal directness: he sees before him a willow. Almost immediately, however, the boundary between direct and literary experience starts to dissolve. Upon seeing a willow in bloom, any Chinese reader or writer of poetry, especially one far away from his loved ones, will recognize it as a traditional sign for desiring to "detain" *(liu)* the departing loved one. This association, rooted in the homophonic relation of *"liu"* (to detain) and *"liu"* (willow), extends beyond the realm of poetry into the widely practiced social gesture of giving a willow branch to someone who is about to go away.

    For a moment, it seems, Li Bo's "I" confounds the natural object before his eyes and the literary sign of acquired knowledge. He does not immediately recognize that the readiness of the willow (line 3) has little to do with the willow itself, but is rather a function of his framing the scene, with himself in it, through the lens of literary precedent. Moved by the sight of the blooming willow, he lifts his hand to pluck a branch—a gesture so familiar that it is seen before being executed. But, just as his fumbling attempt to express his feelings disturbs the delicate new green, he stops short in exasperation: "But who declared that we should value this thing?/My yearning, more precious than a jade flower." He is unable to complete the gesture, annoyed that conventional expression is molding not only his utterances, but his initial reactions to his "immediate" surroundings. Yet even this assertion, an apparent attempt at proclaiming his autonomy and subjectivity, is couched in words borrowed from poem #9 of the "Nineteen Old Poems."[3] Does this borrowing from the past signal a surrender, a recognition that words fail him, or is it a sense that everything worth saying has already been said? Or does he refresh these ancient words by using them as a weapon against banality? Readers can only withhold judgment and move on to the second part of the poem.

In line 9 the poet recounts a dream he had the previous night, retreating one step from the shared external world, where he just saw the willow, into the private realm of dreams. There he meets Xie Huilian, a poet who lived more than three hundred years before him—a figure who (unlike the willow) exists not at all in the realm of personal experience and is known exclusively through the poems he left behind. The lore recounts that Huilian's mere presence was known to inspire his famous uncle Xie Lingyun to produce his most beautiful lines of poetry. Once when Xie Lingyun was having difficulty writing a poem, Huilian's appearance in a dream enabled him to write the well-known line, "The pond bears spring grasses" (chi tang sheng chun cao) for his poem "Climbing the Tower over the Pond" ("Deng chishang lou").

Li Bo's allusion seems at first glance to serve mainly as a means of paying respect to the poem's destined recipient, Li Zhao, by crediting him with Huilian's ability to facilitate "writing his feelings." But if this were the sole intent, a single reference would have sufficed. One property of allusion is, after all, economy of expression. In this case, however, Li Bo chooses to reproduce all the elements of the original story, not modifying it at all to suit his situation. Even more unusual, the result is that he dreams of a figure who does not belong to his experience and wakes up chanting words that do not spring from his own invention, but belong almost verbatim to Xie Lingyun (line 11). Clearly, then, a muse from the past can inspire only writing that is past. As in the case of the willow in bloom, the allusion to Xie Huilian, though recognized and understood by all, seems restrictive and schematic when put to the test of capturing a poet's contemporary, personal reality.

The parallel between the dream and the willow is reinforced in line 13. Just as the poet reaches out to touch this vision of a pond conjured up by Xie Lingyun's words, night falls and the pond disappears. And just as in the earlier event, this vision is replaced, not by immediate reality, but by a sound from the past to which poets of the past had often tuned every lonely wanderer's ears: the night cry of the cuckoo. With the insertion of this well-known sign, the frontier between landscape and literature is again completely obfuscated, but one thing is clear: having now twice discovered that the lexicon of past poetry cannot sufficiently correspond to immediate experience, Li Bo must find a way to conclude the poem simply in terms of what he feels and sees. He does this by stating simply that he misses his friend as he witnesses the falling of the flower petals.

This poem, insofar as it depicts a poet's search for words to express his feelings, speaks in a voice that is indisputably "immediate." By first rejecting, then selecting convention on his own terms—by making manifest his conscious choice—he leaves no doubt as to the appropriateness of otherwise hackneyed images. In this way he revives those images, giving new meaning to the practice of "pouring new wine into old bottles."

IN HIS use of a broad range of allusions, extending from the textual to the topical, Li Bo also exhibits his awareness of conventionality and assumes his authentic "outsider's" stance. Good examples of his use of textual allusion occur in "In Response to 'Tongtang

Tune' by Censor Lu" and "Composed on Jade Maiden Spring in Ying Cheng, Anzhou." As in "Writing My Feelings," Li Bo demonstrates the "allusiveness" of allusion by attempting, and repeatedly failing, to obliterate the boundary between literary and immediate experience. But in these poems, it is place, not literary convention as such, that occasions the merging of past and present, textual and sensual worlds.

IN RESPONSE TO "TONGTANG TUNE" BY CENSOR LU	和盧侍御通塘曲

So you boast that Tongtang is great,	君誇通塘好
That Tongtang is more lovely than Yexi.	通塘勝耶溪
And where is Tongtang?	通塘在何處
4 *Far off, west of Xunyang.*	遠在尋陽西
There the green vines softly twine, hanging from misty trees,	青蘿嫋嫋挂煙樹
And silver pheasants cluster here and there, all along the sandy banks.	白鷳處處聚沙堤

Through a break between stone cliffs emerges a placid lake,	石門中斷平湖出
8 *A golden pool one hundred* zhang, *reflecting cloud and sun.*	百丈金潭照雲日
And where is the old Canglang fisherman?	何處滄浪垂釣翁
Beating his oars, singing his fishing song, many are his pleasures.	鼓棹漁歌趣非一

Should we meet I'd know him not,	相逢不相識
12 *Appearing, disappearing, circling round Tongtang.*	出沒繞通塘
Through clear water at the shore gleam pearl-white feet,	浦邊清水明素足
Here yet another silk-washing maid of Wu.	別有浣沙吳女郎

Go the length of the green pool, the pool grows more secluded,	行盡綠潭潭轉幽
16 *I'd swear this is the emerald flowing of spring in Wuling.*	疑是武陵春碧流

The chickens and dogs of the Qin amid peach blossoms, 秦人雞犬桃花裡
Compared to Tongtang, the place would be put to shame. 將比通塘渠見羞

Tongtang—one cannot bear to leave, 通塘不忍別
20 Leave ten times and, in time, return nine. 十去九遲迴

Come upon this fine scene, my heart's already drunk, 偶逢佳境心已醉
Suddenly a single bird comes from the sky. 忽有一鳥從天來
The moon rises out of green mountains and accompanies this traveler, 月出青山送行子
24 All around from "bitter bamboo" arise the sounds of autumn. 四邊苦竹秋聲起

For a while I chant "White Snow in Spring" and gaze at the River of Stars, 長吟白雪望星河
Dangling together both my feet I kick up frothy waves. 雙垂兩足提素波
Liang Hong and De Yao's days in Kuaiji, 梁鴻德耀會稽日
28 How could even they have known as much happiness as this?[4] 寧知此中樂事多

"Tongtang Tune" begins with an echo. An echo—a disembodied voice—is the past act that lingers on in the telling, ringing in the ears long after the speaker has disappeared. "So you boast that Tongtang is great," repeats Li Bo, supposedly responding to a poem by Censor Lu, no longer extant. This abrupt beginning, almost a challenge, also establishes the poet's narrator as reader, perhaps allied more closely with his own readers of this poem than with the writer whose feelings were first stirred by the landscape. As a reader, he responds to the scene described in Censor Lu's poem as it might be situated in the context of a wealth of other literary landscapes, including the region of Yexi. Although the poet does not seem to be beholding Tongtang, the place is familiar to him. He knows where it is (lines 3–4), and so, with hardly an effort, its distant image comes before his mind's eye.

At first the image is nothing more than that, an image, lyrical and carefully balanced, depicted in the poem's only parallel couplet: "There the green vines softly twine, hanging from misty trees,/And silver pheasants cluster here and there, all along the sandy banks." Picturesque, yet the work of impersonal craft, this couplet constitutes a literary convention he sets up only to surpass. In another poem, its technical perfection and simple beauty might indicate an acceptance of received form. Here, however, it soon becomes clear that it is employed to demonstrate the very inadequacy of that form, freezing the poet's vision in an illustration that is well composed but altogether inadequate to Li Bo's own perception of the past. It is discarded right after being created, as Li Bo impatiently breaks through this barrier of convention and brings to life the picture he has taken.

Now (lines 7–8) readers are peering through a different barrier, sighting, along with the poet, the distant waters of Tongtang through the gap between the heights of two juxtaposed palisades of stone. With this verbal and visual frame, Li Bo offers the same experience he himself had when reading Censor Lu's poem. It is a reader's experience, in which words uttered by someone else reverberate in the mind, mingling with memory to produce a scene so vivid that it seems to lie right before the eyes.

It is only in the next line (line 9) that, layer by layer, Li Bo begins the process of stripping away the external trappings of a shared objective reality. Gazing now upon the body of water that has been conjured up so clearly, the speaker repeats the rhetorical question of the second couplet, this time asking the whereabouts of the legendary Canglang fisherman. Readers will recognize him as the old fisherman in the "Yu fu pian" of the *Chuci*, who contentedly sang these lines:

When the Canglang's waters are clear,
I can wash my hat-strings in them;

When the Canglang's waters are muddy,
I can wash my feet in them.[5]

The question might be read rhetorically, as a way of expressing the secluded beauty of the place, the perfect setting for a paragon of righteousness who goes into seclusion to escape serving in a corrupt government. But in this new realm of subjectivity, nothing can be purely rhetorical. As allusion borders on the edge of illusion, the stock question of *huaigu* poetry—"Where is he now?"— seems, surprisingly, to permit the possibility of an answer. For the moment, however, that answer is not forthcoming. Instead the poet catches himself at the last minute, confessing his inability to recognize the fisherman he seems to know so well.

Shifting his gaze in line 13, Li Bo's narrator again faces the past, as irretrievable as it is indelible. In this vision, tentatively at first, the earlier comparison of Tongtang with Yexi reemerges. Gleaming at the side of the pool are the white feet of Xi Shi of Wu, a legendary woman whose beauty fated her to become the tool of political warfare and, ultimately, to contribute to the downfall of her husband. Xi Shi was often depicted as washing silk in Kuaiji prefecture, where Yexi is located, so her presence there seems hardly surprising. But the vividness of the illusion dissolves into allusion with the simple insertion of one word—*"bie"*: she is "yet another" copy, not the historical woman.

The pattern of geographical border crossing between literary and perceived reality continues without a break in lines 15 and 16. Echoing Tao Yuanming, the poet-reader recognizes this body of water as the irretrievable utopia Peach Blossom Spring, but this, too, turns out to be a misapprehension. As though in reaction to his error, he explicitly reasserts the division between his immediate experience and the ancient literary landscape, drawing a direct comparison between the Tongtang of his imagination and the Peach Blossom Spring of literary history—even concluding, "Compared to Tongtang, the place would be put to shame."

Lines 19 and 20 are nearly clichés. If this were nothing more than a commemoration of a journey to Tongtang, the poem would end here. But just as Li Bo used a parallel couplet in lines 5 and 6—a form that usually produces (economically and effectively) the impression of immediacy and timelessness—in a way that suggested its inadequacy for that purpose, so here he sets up this familiar "ending" only to betray its usual function. Behind this simply appreciative and uncomplicated refrain, it is possible to sense the poet dramatizing an attempted return to the well-defined realm of lyric poetry, where things are assumed to have a basis in reality.

When the poem's final section opens in line 21, it does so with a shake of the head and a readjustment of vision, as though the poet were excusing himself for having been carried away by the beauty of an intoxicating scene. The switch from allusion to concrete images of reality—a bird, the moon over the mountains—combined with the return to a sense of the linear progression of time seem to signal an awakening from reverie, a return to the familiar world. But the familiarity of this scene also derives in no small part from poetic convention; the poet is still primarily a literary traveler (line 23). Finally, as if in surrender to the primacy of ancient words, Li Bo ends the poem chanting long and low, echoing an ancient tune, and accompanying that music with a gesture whose image is no more likely to vanish than the lake itself: "For a while I chant 'White Snow in Spring' and gaze at the River of Stars, / Dangling together both my feet I kick up frothy waves." Joining his feet with those of Xi Shi, he goes beyond being moved by the echoes he hears to become one himself. The metonymy between the Milky Way—the "River of Stars"—and the waters of Tongtang, a relationship highlighted by their corresponding positions in this pair of lines, suggests that the earthly body of water has been left behind for the "frothy waves" of the River of Stars. He dangles his feet, not in real water (which, in Chinese poetry of remembrance, so often appears as the physical embodiment of time) but in a celestial river of stars that does not flow and is eternal. With this gesture, Li Bo removes himself from the flow of time and relinquishes the temporal perspective that prevents him from seeing allusions as inherited images belonging only to the past.

At this point in the poem, allusion and illusion can now successfully blend to create a highly subjective and unquestionably immediate "reality" for the poet. But, as should be expected by now, at the last moment he undermines this transcendence of temporal and spatial limitations, reestablishing in one phrase his place in real time: "Liang Hong and De Yao's days in Kuaiji, / How could even they have known as much happiness as this?" Li Bo's joy at the prospect of escaping the flow of time and with it the tyranny of the literary tradition finds its final expression in an allusion to a past example of great happiness.

Here a question that is familiar from lines 4–8 of the first poem arises once again: given that Li Bo has drawn so much attention to the distinction between convention and personal expression, does his apparent succumbing to the authority of the past signal a sudden and final concession? Or does Li Bo intend this as an inconsistency underlining his conviction that allusion is inadequate (not to say ludicrous) as a means of personal expression?

Perhaps the answer is that Li Bo neither succumbs to the authority of the past nor rejects allusion. Just as in the poem dedicated to Li Zhao, Li Bo plays with the possibility of a distinction between convention and personal expression; but more decisively than in that poem, he concludes by having them coincide. It would seem that by clearly *choosing* to make the comparison with Liang Hong and De Yao, which can be done only after having demonstrated that a choice does indeed exist, he insists upon its appropriateness to his situation. By first establishing his independence from the tradition, he leaves no doubt as to the authenticity of his decision to conclude his poem within its parameters. At the same time, he infuses an old story with renewed significance.

As demonstrated in these first two poems, Li Bo enjoys employing allusion in such a way as to point up its quality of "allusiveness." By revealing that allusion is an element of conventional expression—a foil to his authentic and subjective expression—Li Bo manifests his role as outsider and conscious creator. The direct link between Li Bo's use of allusion and his immediacy lies here: if immediacy is to be understood as the poet's nonrational and authentic lyrical response to the world, Li Bo includes allusion among the things of the world to which he responds freely, poet that he is. By documenting in his poetry the self-conscious deliberation behind the act of creation, he suggests that such deliberation need not be antithetical to immediacy. On the contrary, the recording of the creative process becomes the most essential component of immediacy.

VERBS DEPICTING mental acts or perceptions, as in "Tongtang Tune," serve as simple but potent tools in the transposition of literary allusion into personal imagination. In the following poem, "Composed on Jade Maiden Hot Spring in Ying Cheng, Anzhou," the poet's blend of allusion and illusion is expanded to encompass the poem as a whole, creating an integrated reality that transcends time.

COMPOSED ON JADE MAIDEN SPRING IN YING CITY, ANZHOU[6]   安州應城
玉女湯作

A goddess died in this secluded realm,	神女歿幽境
Where hot springs flow into a great river.	湯池流大川
Yin and Yang congealed in flaming coals,	陰陽結炎炭
4 *Creation cleaved open the enchanted fountains.*	造化開靈泉
Earth's foundation smolders with crimson fire,	地底爛朱火
While by the sands wafts silk-white smoke.	沙旁歊素煙
Roiling pearls leap within a shining moon,	沸珠躍明月
8 *The dazzling mirror encasing empty sky.*	皎鏡涵空天
Vapor floats forth full of orchid's fragrance,	氣浮蘭芳滿
With color that swells in blossoms of burning peach	色漲桃花然
	精覽萬殊入
Scan it all minutely, the myriad variations merging within,	潛行七澤漣
	愈疾功莫尚
12 *Skim along the waters, the Seven Marshes converge.*	變盈道乃全
	濯纓掬清泚
In curing illness, it is surpassed by none,	晞髮弄潺湲
Only when change reaches fullness is the Dao complete.	
For washing cap strings, cupped hands raise its pure limpidity,	
16 *You can dry your hair while playing with the water's flow.*	

It wanders down through the king of Chu's state,	散下楚王國
And splits off to sprinkle the fields of Song Yu.	分猿宋玉田
It could serve as a site of an imperial tour,	可以奉巡幸
20 Pity that is so remote!	余何隔窮偏
Alone it follows in fealty the honored river,	獨隨朝宗水
And casts its tiny ripples into the sea.[7]	赴海輸微涓

Unlike "Tongtang Tune," Li Bo composed this poem on the occasion of actually visiting a specific location. The first two lines remind the reader of the legend associated with the hot springs of Anzhou, but at this point the reference remains allusive and incomplete. By placing the reference to this myth at the beginning of the poem, Li Bo locates the landscape within the literary tradition and suggests that the act of writing about the place continues the tradition. The strange vapors emitted by the spring—clearly the source of inspiration for the myth of the goddess—also lead the poet into another realm of shared literature: the literature of creation. Water, fire, and smoke frequently play a role in the depiction of the process of creation, and lines 3–6 appear to be a natural transition. They seem to fill in a gap by describing not the hot spring itself, but the metaphysical process that created it and continues to sustain it.

The poet accomplishes this transition by invoking, if only indirectly, "The Owl" by Jia Yi ("Heaven and earth are a crucible, Creation is the smith;/Yin and Yang are the charcoal, the myriad things are the bronze")[8]—a *fu* poem whose metaphorical links between flowing water and the Dao are particularly appropriate here. This echo of ancient descriptions of creation is further reinforced by the evocation of an ancient anonymous poem ("Crimson fire burns in its depths,/blue-gray smoke wafts in its midst").[9]

These metaphysical yet highly visual images prepare the reader for a fresh and vivid view of the somewhat common conceit that follows: "Roiling pearls leap within a shining moon,/The dazzling mirror encasing empty sky." With this parallel couplet, Li Bo subtly moves from a recalled (or imagined) description of the hidden forces responsible for the hot spring to its reality as it appears before his eyes. Still, his vision has been shaped by shared lore. Just as in

"Tongtang Tune," knowledge derived from a shared body of literature enables Li Bo to "see" a landscape that is both literary and metaphysical: "Scan it all minutely, the myriad variations merging within, / Skim along the waters, the Seven Marshes converge."

These last lines set forth Li Bo's privileged view in a way that makes it seem as if anyone whose vision has been similarly shaped would be able to see it as well. While the expression "myriad variations" *(wan shu)* returns us to the Daoist canon[10] and thus to a scene that can only be recalled or imagined, the assertions of his vision in the verb "to scan, survey" *(lan)*, reinforced by its position directly after a parallel couplet of pure perception, constitutes Li Bo's first step, in this poem, toward the blending of common references (allusion) and personal subjectivity (illusion). His simple reference to the Seven Marshes then adds a small but effective flourish. Li Bo has even exceeded Sima Xiangru's expansive vision in "Zixu fu" (Rhapsody of Sir Vacuous): "I have heard that Chu has Seven Marshes, but I have seen only one of them, and I have never seen the others."[11]

In offering his vision, Li draws attention to his presence for the first time since the title. Here at the central point of the poem, this privileged witnessing of the confluence of all things—of the conjoining of disparate bodies—excludes the poet from that very confluence and identifies him as observer. His readers, as observers, are present at his side. From that moment, any pretense to objective (observable) reality is lost, along with the particularity of Jade Maiden Hot Spring. The fantastic, colorful imagery now dissolves into a recitation of the various moral and spiritual values of all waters, as gleaned from such ancient texts as the *Shui jing zhu,* the *Yijing,* and the *Chuci.* In an exhaustive cataloguing of qualities reminiscent of the style of Han dynasty *fu* poetry, Li Bo reminds the reader of water that is now the moral purifier of Confucian lore (lines 15–16), now an indifferent unifier serving native and exile alike (lines 17–18).

So water evolves, undergoing a transformation from a concrete object with legendary associations, to something highly imaginary, and finally, at the moment when the poet explicitly takes his place as the observer, to the totally abstract—a symbol of the poet's aspiration to be able to overcome all barriers (namely, the corrupt emperor) and eventually become one with the impartial, unwavering purity of one ocean. In every case the agent of this transformation is the poet's selection of various literary traditions already associated with water. By the end of the second half of the poem, the spring before our eyes has disappeared and been replaced by a familiar sign, not unlike the willow branch of "In Which I Write My Feelings." In the final couplet, the spring is reduced to its most abstract form as purely linguistic signifier in the phrase *"chao zong shui,"* roughly translated as "water that worships [the sea]." This stringing together of past usage has by now drained away all watery imagery, making the expression nearly interchangeable with "loyal servant."

Once again the explicitness with which Li Bo handles allusion serves as his weapon against convention. Where literary precedent functions as a stimulus rather than a response, and where the poet recognizes precedent as an object belonging to the objective world rather than to his inner nature, he manages to assert the particular brand of subjectivity for which he is renowned, thereby signifying his presence as an outside observer. In this case, by filling out allusions in ways that are comprehensible within the traditional lexicon, but which go beyond the usual associations, he turns schemata into triggers for the imagination. In doing so, he steps beyond the bounds of convention in order to master it, making explicit his role as artist and creating the impression of immediacy.

IN PURSUIT OF FORGETFULNESS

Li Bo's assertion of subjectivity may be expressed in the transformation of the literary past into personal vision, but it is also likely to find expression in the pursuit of forgetfulness. Already familiar as one of the inspirations underlying *fugu* poetry, the desire to clear one's literary memory so as to regain the authentic expression of the ancients is also evident in certain themes that are, by their nature, particularly tied to memory. One of these is the Double Nine Festival.[12]

The writing of a poem on this festival requires an extended act of remembrance on several levels. This subgenre, if it may be so called, evokes the past with a complexity rivaling that of *yuefu,* for it mingles the social conventions of the festival with the literary conventions of the poetic theme. Moreover, the writing of these poems is in itself one convention of the festival, and "climbing high"—which is a subgeneric theme with distinct, if overlapping, conventions of its own—is a convention of the Double Nine treatment in poetry, as well as a ritual of the festival. These elements combine to form a unique poetics of remembrance in which a literary tradition is not simply invoked, but remembered. The resulting multiplication of levels of memory and tradition can threaten to eclipse the rememberer's individual expression, but for a poet like Li Bo, who delights in posing as the outsider, there is perhaps no better juncture at which to shape an individual voice and carve out a particular subjectivity.

Discontinuity of elements and systematic denial of readerly expectations are two ways in which a poet might suggest an internal ordering of the universe that is uniquely his. The elements are drawn from a common world, and expectations are shaped by a shared literature. Li Bo's "Ascending the Mountain on Double Nine" is one poem whose discontinuity has led readers to appeal to external information in an effort to find that elusive unifying thread.[13]

ASCENDING THE MOUNTAIN ON DOUBLE NINE	九日登山

	Yuanming, "Returning Home,"	淵明歸去來
	Did not follow the ways of the world.	不與世相逐
	Since he was lacking the stuff of the goblet,	為無杯中物
4	*He befriended a local magistrate.*	遂偶本州牧
	And having hailed the man in white,	因招白衣人
	With a smile they poured out some yellow chrysanthemum wine.	笑酌黃花菊
	I, in coming here, did not fulfill my hopes,	我來不得意
8	*In vain I passed the time this "Double Nine."*	虛過重陽時

How exceptional, he for whom the carriage was designated![14]　　題輿何俊發

So let us keep our engagement south of the city wall![15]　　遂結城南期

Massing earth into a rise that connects with Mount Xiang,　　築土接響山

12　*Looking down upon the banks of the Wan River.*　　俯臨宛水湄

Northland barbarians call upon jaded flutes,　　胡人叫玉笛

Girls of Yue play their "frosted strings."　　越女彈霜絲

To make of oneself the descendant of generals,　　自作英王冑

16　*In pleasures which none can spy.*　　斯樂不可窺

Crimson carp surge up under Qin Gao,[16]　　赤鯉湧琴高

White tortoise leads forth Bing Yi.[17]　　白龜道冰夷

If the immortals are like them,　　靈仙如彷彿

20　*Pour a libation and they will know from afar.*　　奠酹遙相知

All those who've "climbed high" since times of old,　　古來登高人

How many are still there today?　　今復幾人在

If on Cang Isle old promises break,[18]　　滄洲違宿諾

24　*One can still await the days to come.*　　明日猶可待

Chains of mountains look like startled waves,　　連山似驚波

Their folded layers emerge from a darkened sea.　　合沓出溟海

I raise my sleeves and wave at those seated around,　　揚袂揮四座

28　*In drunkenness what do they know?*　　酩酊安所知

Singing songs of Qi, send goblets all around,　　齊歌送清觴

And all rise up in formless dance.　　起舞亂參差

The guests depart with the scattering of leaves,　　賓隨落葉散

32　*A hat flies off with the autumn wind.*[19]　　帽逐秋風吹

After parting I climbed this tower,　　別後登此臺

Wanting to speak of "Longing for You."[20]　　願言長相思

Li Bo's allusions in this poem take the specific form of naming. By directly referring to a tradition by a key word or phrase, he emphasizes the act of mentioning at least as much as, if not more than, what is mentioned. In this poem Li Bo combines naming with close adherence to elements of the tradition, producing the effect of staying within the mainstream while hovering just above it.

The very first line is naming at its most basic: "Yuanming, 'Returning Home,'" as it is composed of the name of an author and his most representative work[21] and stands at the beginning of the poem as a hard, self-enclosed grammatical nugget that stops readers momentarily before the flow of the sentence leads them deeper into the poem. The title of the poem, which is still fresh in the reader's mind, now reemerges as an act of naming as well— nonspecific in place and time, and evocative of nothing so much as a literary tradition in its entirety.

The linking of the "names" (Double Nine Festival and Tao Yuanming) at the beginning of the poem, otherwise connected only by a traditional association that exists independently of this poem,[22] presents itself as the result of spontaneous recall. The isolated first line soon reveals itself as introducing an equally free-floating six-line set piece. Leaving little to the reader's imagination, the words recount a well-known story, and the poet refrains from adding elements of his personal imagination to bridge the obvious structural gaps.

In the first section Li Bo blends together two stories associated with Tao Yuanming: one about his composition of "To Return Home" ("Gui qu lai ci"), and the other establishing his link to the Double Nine Festival. Tersely couching them in a series of well-known phrases, Li reinforces the initial impression that he is uninvolved but reactive in the face of tradition. Lines 1 and 2 contain the simplest possible reference to a story in the *Jinshu* recounting that, rather than accept an invitation by the prefect, Tao resigned from his low-level position as secretary of Pengzhe County and retired home, where he wrote "To Return Home." Lines 3 and 4 comprise the barest essence of the story of Wang Hong, censor of Linzhou, who was determined to meet with Tao. After having been politely but firmly spurned several times, Wang contrived to have a wine stand set up along a road, which, he was told, Tao would take on his way to Lushan. True to Wang's expectations, Tao could not resist this temptation and "forgot" to continue his journey. Wang joined Tao at the wine stand and engaged him in a long and deep conversation. Were it not for Tao's weakness for the "stuff of the goblet," the censor might not have been able to meet with him. Lines 5 and 6 blend this story into the one in which this same Wang Hong, having heard that Tao was without wine on the Double Nine Festival, sent him some by means of a white-robed messenger.[23]

The isolation of lines 1 through 6 is emphasized by the syntactic integrity of the section as a complete narrative, and it sets up a contrast with what follows.

Line 7, opening the second part of the poem, introduces the subject of comparison: the poet himself. Unlike Tao Yuanming, who was given wine by kind and admiring officials so that he might join them in the traditional celebration, Li Bo has no such opportunity to relinquish, even momentarily, his position as "outsider." He is condemned to pass the holiday unfulfilled, unable to partake of the tradition, but also unable to forget its requirements and remain entirely detached.

The second part of the poem has led commentators to believe that Li Bo addresses the poem to a certain official on the building of a tower south of Xuancheng. This would seem to explain lines 9 and 10, in which he implicitly compares this official to Censor Zhou Jing of the Latter Han Dynasty as well as to his appointed *biejia* (administrative aide), Chen Fan (see note 13). Read in this light, this allusion simultaneously praises both the *biejia* of Xuancheng for his lucidity and steadfastness in recognizing and welcoming Li Bo (who had left the capital in disgrace nine years earlier) and those talents that liken him to the famous *biejia* of the Han.

On the basis of this interpretation, it might be tempting to read the second part of this poem, as does Ono Jitsunosuke, as hyperbolic gratitude and praise for the party to which Li Bo was invited. And the first part could be interpreted as saying that, until the official invited him, he *had been* unfulfilled—until the official had acted as his "man in white," and recognized his worth. The odd, dry opening still resonates, however, subtly undermining such flattery. It has already attuned the reader to a poet who is fulfilling his own obligations (the writing of this occasional poem being one), while remaining aware of his role as an outsider, both in the reality of his exile and in the composition of this poem on the festival of remembrance.

The poet's lofty point of view is sustained in the links from one couplet to the next, all the way to line 20, as a hypothetical, gradual ascent: an imaginary extrapolation of "climbing high." Each couplet is gleaned from a different category of the tradition, arranged in graduated increments of height and pleasure, until the second section ends, as abruptly as it began, upon reaching the domain of immortals—the furthest extreme of height and imagination. Significantly, the immortals' existence is tentatively invoked—"If the immortals are like them"—undermining ever so slightly Li Bo's otherwise vehement conviction.

But Li Bo has fulfilled the demands of both the festival and the subgenre, so he can finally reassume the role he had hinted at but concealed since the beginning: the creator of this poem, and an individual freely considering his literary inheritance. In this role he begins the third part of the poem, line 21, with the rhetorical question directed to all readers: "All those who've 'climbed high' since times of old,/How many are still there today?" With this, he steps out from behind the veils of convention, free to speak in his own voice at last. In retrospect one can recognize other signs that had been pointing to a poet who, having executed his bow to the past, now feels free to reveal himself more directly: the straightforward vernacular construction of the opening rhetorical question; the personal rationalization in lines 23 and 24; the frankness concerning the superiority of his knowledge to that of the other guests (lines 27 and 28); the absence of adornment when referring to these "guests" as they take their leave (line 31); and the account of his solitary climb up this actual tower—emphasized in the Chinese by the article "this" (ci).

This expression of immediacy does not preclude the poet's embracing of the past, however; allusion is as present here as it has ever been. But, unlike the allusions—mere namings—that came before, these are true textual allusions. Consider, for example: "Chains of mountains look like startled waves,/Their folded layers emerge from a darkened sea." Directly reversing a simile from the "Rhymeprose on the Sea" ("Hai fu") by Mu Hua (Jin dynasty),[24] this comparison of mountains to waves strikes the reader as both truer to the poet's own vision and more visually intense. Wang Qi may be going a bit far in his characterization of this reversed line as strange,[25] but its vivid transformation does attract the reader's attention and, combined with the other gestures of immediacy present here, opens the possibility that personalization is one of its primary functions. Though half the lines of this final section echo the poetry of previous writers, the poet's presentation of self is as strong as ever. References to wine help justify (in almost conventionally sanctioned terms) a vision that others might find slightly askew (line 28), permitting him to compose an internal, subjective reality out of bits and pieces of a literary reality that has always been shared.

Li Bo begins this poem alone and sober, then becomes a drunken participant in a communal celebration; but he never relinquishes his outsider's stance. So it seems fitting when those "seated around"—his company of real celebrants and the ghostly others who have "'climbed high' since times of old"—finally scatter, leaving our poet alone in both imagination and reality. In the end, no one else is present to witness the flying off of a hat (see note 19), and none will be there to read the poem that goes unwritten. Once again, the poet's reality makes a mockery of traditional gestures—until, alone again (still?) on Double Nine, he allows himself to climb a bit higher and pour out the desire to express his feeling of missing someone. Perhaps despite himself, he entrusts that feeling to a *yuefu* title that happens to "name" a venerable tradition: "Chang xiangsi" (Infinite longing). The tug-of-war between past convention and present immediacy comes to an end. It was his own longing, Li Bo seems to remind us, that made him climb up the tower, and it is that now conventional holiday climb that stirred longing within him.

But in the poet's solitude, the desire to speak—at least in that *yuefu* tradition—goes unfulfilled, just as it did in the non-execution of the poem inspired by the hat blown away by the wind. Is he silenced by the lack of an audience, the knowledge that the poem has already been written (by himself and others), or the certainty that he himself is destined to join the other rememberers who have "climbed high" only to be lost in oblivion? Whatever it was that he was "wanting to say," this poem is the one he wrote instead, ending it as it began: with the poet's doomed effort to forget what he must remember merely in order to write. No matter how lofty and distant his vision, he still begins and ends the poem with the naming of works already executed, then closes with resigned silence.

This time, Li Bo's response to past literature falls short of creating a new avenue of expression. He neither quietly revolts with the assertion of a highly personal, if simple, statement, nor does he embrace convention with the passion of a returned literary exile. The silence at the end of this poem corresponds to that no-man's-land stretching between personal and universal expression—a terrain Li Bo claims to be unable to cross, at least at the moment of the poem. But in that very moment of silence, he adheres to the ideal of authentic expression.

WINE COMBINES easily with a view from on high, blurring the lines separating perception, imagination, and memory. When this blend is placed in the context of the Double Nine Festival, even the solitary act of wine-drinking attains the status of shared convention. Li Bo was sensitive to the possibilities this complex of motifs held for his explorations of the newly authentic voice, as is evident in "On the Ninth":

ON THE NINTH	九日
Today the sky is fine,	今日雲景好
The water green and autumn's mountains gleaming.	水綠秋山明
I take the gourd and pour some "Rose-cloud nectar,"	攜壺酌流霞
4 *Pluck a chrysanthemum and float the cold petals on it.*	搴菊泛寒榮
The land extends far, pine and stone are ancient,	地遠松石古

The wind carries aloft the clarity of string and	風揚絃管清
reed.	窺觴照歡顔
A peek in the goblet reflects a joyful face,	獨笑還自傾
8 *Alone I smile and then drink myself.*	落帽醉山月
A fallen hat, drunk beneath mountain moon,	空歌懷友生
In vain I sing of missing my friend.[26]	

Li Bo's portrayal of immediate emotion, the apparently simple gesture of plucking a chrysanthemum, is colored by the collective memory inscribed in the textual allusion of lines 7 and 8. The specificity of the allusion suggests that the communication of even the most personal stirrings, if they are to be understood by others, ultimately relies on reference to the past. "A peek in the goblet reflects a joyful face, / Alone I smile and then drink myself," recalls these lines by Tao Yuanming:

Although, with one goblet, one can but toast	一觴雖獨進
alone,	杯盡壺自傾
When the cup is finished, I myself pour from the	
gourd.[27]	

Perhaps because they considered it obvious, neither Ono Jitsunosuke nor the editors of *Li Bo ji jiaozhu* saw fit to reproduce Wang Qi's note confirming the origin of Li Bo's couplet, but this information adds significantly to the understanding of the poem. Until this moment, the poet seems to have successfully sustained his subjective and immediate vision; the "naming" title minimizes the conventional demands of the occasional poem, and the plucking of chrysanthemums, even while the action echoes that of Tao Yuanming,[28] remains above all an image of sensuality. Although aware of the tradition associated with the holiday, Li Bo still seems able to experience it afresh.

But these are clearly the words of Tao Yuanming, a poet well known for his Double Nine imagery—and these words lie at the heart of Li Bo's poem. In Tao's poem, the wine both intensifies his solitude, felt more acutely during this festival, and gives him consolation; it is meant to be shared, but he tries valiantly, although forced to "toast alone," to find comfort in the freedom of being able to drink as he pleases.

Li, too, attempts to disavow his sadness. But for him denying sadness is inextricable from denying the weight of the past. The "joyful face" he finds reflected in the wine cup both confirms and mitigates his solitude. This, his wittiest moment, is the moment when the inescapability of the past overcomes him. In "drinking myself" he may even be playing cleverly on Tao's words, stepping carefully out of the line of received expression and affirming his direct, authentically knowing relationship with the festival and its literary conventions. But neither this knowingness nor his subtle wit spares him the pain of the loneliness provoked by the festival.

The ironic melancholy of solitude during a holiday that, in name and custom, demands wholeness and unity had hardly gone unnoticed by the generations of poets before Li Bo. But he noticed their noticing, and his loneliness is only intensified as he self-consciously reenacts originally immediate gestures rendered almost ritualistic by repetition and the passage of time.

Having made his bow to the past, Li Bo allows himself to remain under the spell of shared memory until the end of the poem. He drinks down his reflection and is left truly alone. Intoxicated, he sees himself as replicating the past personage of *yuefu* fame, the "master of the mountains," Shan Gong, familiarly indicated by mentioning his fallen hat (perhaps combined with the "fallen hat" allusion of "Ascending the Mountain on Double Nine").[29] Drunkenness, previously a convenient catalyst of immediacy, now emphasizes the forced quality of Li Bo's denial of sadness and shared memory. Any remaining impressions of the poet's subjective freedom are subsumed in the reflex recall of Shan Gong, a traditional incarnation of total freedom.

Li Bo concludes with a simple summation of all Double Nine poetry: "In vain I sing of missing my friend." Like the title, each word in this line is as nonspecific (almost generic) as possible. He does not say which friend he has in mind, nor does he give the title of his song. The immediate, personal perspective of "Today" (line 1) dissolves, leaving only the featureless silhouette of a Chinese poet adding his voice to the chorus of the past. At the same time, the final line of this and other poems presents the reunification of the personal and universal voice as the ultimate personal validation of a universally understood emotion.

WINE: AN ALLUSION TO IMMEDIACY

One would think that enough has been written about Li Bo's relationship to wine to make it difficult to add anything new. Whether obligingly offered as evidence of his "Romantic" *(langman)* spirit[30] or sardonically applauded as the agent that succeeded in illuminating a poet previously benighted by Daoist superstition,[31] the presence of wine in both Li Bo's poetry and the apocryphal stories of his life has most often been treated as biographical fact. There would be little point in denying that the poet enjoyed drinking; but it would be equally misguided to attempt to gauge his dependence on wine by calculating occurrences of related words in his corpus.

Wine-drinking, as a practice as well as a poetic gesture, is closely related to the values of immediacy and authentic expression, and it is a gesture well entrenched in the Chinese poetic tradition. In the work of Li Bo, who is so adept at marshaling a wide array of traditionally familiar tropes and motifs to establish an authentic latter-day poet's immediacy, the "stuff of the goblet" proves a pliable and expressive medium; in the hands of critics and biographers, it became the stuff of his legend.

Wine and wine-drinking, very much like the Double Nine Festival in which they played a ritual role, lead a double life in the broadly defined world of Chinese poetry. They are both stimulus and subject, context and content. As stimulus and context, wine surrounds the poet, modifying both his perceptual and his expressive faculties. When the now tipsy poet turns to writing, wine plays the role of creative catalyst, eroding the barrier between the internal faculties of memory or imagination and the outwardly directed act of perception. As one type of poetic act, libation to a deity or a historical personage reads as an agent of remembrance, permitting the rememberer to span the generations. In a contrastive (but not contradictory) poetic gesture, the imbibing of wine as an intoxicant provokes—and evokes—if not forgetfulness itself, then the desire for it.[32] The actively forgetting poet expresses a desire for some respite from hard times. In the particular case of the latter-day poet aspiring to ancient authenticity, this desire is also one for free-dom—however momentary—from the weight of poetic convention.

Li Bo treats the convention of wine-drinking in much the same way he treats other allusions, such as that to the lover's gift (from the "Nineteen Old Poems") or to the literary landscape of Yexi. By exposing wine imagery as a received tradition in need of renewal, he adheres to his own notion of immediacy. He candidly and playfully exposes his creative role by alternately revealing and disguising the minute weave of gestural, emotional, and literary associations held taut by the two poles of wine-related motifs. Simultaneously inhabiting the common ground of allusion and the private world of illusion, the wine-drinking poet reveals the pathos of unfulfilled desire. He is just as liable to slip into forgetful intox-ication during a traditional ceremony as he is to mourn the past in the midst of a "carefree" drinking party. And on both counts, he defies the well-meaning reader to join him.

FACING WINE   對酒

   I urge you not to refuse a cup,   勸君莫拒杯
   For the spring wind has come to laugh at us.   春風笑人來
   Peach and plum trees are like old friends,   桃李如久識
4 *Tipping forth their blossoms to open toward me.*   傾花向我開
   Swirling warblers call from emerald trees,   流鶯啼碧樹
   Bright moon peers into the golden wine cup.   明月窺金罍
   The rose-cheeked lad of yesterday,   昨日朱顏子
8 *Today the white hairs grow apace.*   今日白髮催
   Brambles grew beneath Shi Hu's halls,   棘生石虎殿
   Deer wandered on Gu Su Pavilion.   鹿走姑蘇臺
   The dwellings of emperors since times of old,   自古帝王宅
12 *Their walls and gates shut in yellow dust.*   城闕閉黃埃
   If you do not drink the wine,   君若不飲酒
   Then where are the men of yesteryear?[33]   昔人安在哉

From line 1 through line 12, there is little that may be called original in this standard carpe diem poem. The poet moves from the seductiveness of spring (lines 3–6) to the treachery of its inevitable passage (lines 7–8) to the familiar historical allusions of lines 9 and 10, which illustrate the ephemerality of human effort and fit naturally into the poem. These allusions are strictly within the bounds of readerly expectations. In his skillful adherence to a well-worn tradition, Li Bo thus far is uncharacteristically downplaying his presence as creator and renouncing his usual claim to immediacy—even in the announced subjectivity of his drunkenness.

But then, in the posing of one final question—"If you do not drink the wine,/Then where are the men of yesteryear?"—Li Bo once again steps out of the tradition and looks in, pointing up the duality in the nature of wine and giving the lie to all that had preceded. This final, direct appeal returns the reader to the opening couplet. But this time, the urgency of his invitation derives from the recognition that to drink is to fulfill an obligation to past greatness (a category to which he is destined to belong). Even while writing "drunk," Li Bo still can look into his cup and see there a poetic convention with its own allusive aura.

In writing *about* wine as a way of sustaining the past, and in choosing terms that, except for their allusive quality, verge on being non sequiturs, Li Bo expresses both the obligation to the past and its intrinsic absurdity. One drinks and, guided in part by tradition, uses the desire to forget as a pretext; but, actually, one is obliged to drink and, in the very action, to acknowledge the tradition. Just as one climbs the tower and, in doing so, remembers the rememberers, one drinks with the same result (and, implicitly, for the same purpose). Yet, for all his explicit revelation of implicit convention, Li Bo is neither mocking nor cynical. To the contrary: in reminding the reader of his role as the creator of this poem and insisting on his role as an outsider looking in on the tradition, he both reclaims his own immediacy as poet and reawakens the emotional impetus that first gave rise to whatever convention he happens to be pinpointing—and, by extension, the tradition of which it is a part.

The convention of wine-drinking has yet another dimension

that lends itself to the establishment of the poet's immediacy. It functions as a traditional, though not exclusively literary, allusion to a particularly private state of mind. Like textual allusion, the suggestion of drunkenness opens up a path by which readers might gain access to the poet's internal state, partly because it leads back to their own experience or knowledge. Ultimately, however, this path only goes so far. Everyone may know what it is like to be drunk, but with this knowledge comes the recognition that drunkenness can induce an inner state so subjective as to preclude any ground for shared vision. In the ultimate literary paradox, wine-drinking is subjectivity communicated.

In this final example, Li Bo's use of wine both suggests and catalyzes certain processes of immediacy that I have already discussed. It dismantles the boundaries between allusion and illusion, between what is remembered and what is seen, and between what is imagined and what is perceived. In a gesture that is as much a challenge as an invitation, Li Bo enjoins his readers to share in this vision.

DRINKING ALONE   獨酌

The spring grasses seem to have an intention,	春草如有意
Growing into a weave in the shade of the jade pavilion.	羅生玉堂陰
The east wind blows sadness here,	東風吹愁來
4 *And so, white hairs encroach.*	白髮坐相侵
I pour alone, but urge my lonely shadow to join me,	獨酌勸孤影
And idly sing as I face the fragrant woods.	閑歌面芳林
But, you, tall pines, what do you understand,	長松爾何知
8 *For whom do you whistle and hum?*	蕭瑟為誰吟
My hand dances with the moon on the rock,	手舞石上月
Across my knees rests a zither among flowers.	膝橫花間琴
That which lies beyond this wine goblet,	過此一壺酒
12 *Placid and deep, is not my heart.*[34]	悠悠非我心

The title elucidates every line in the poem: Li Bo is alone—and drinking. He alludes to his own subjectivity even while asking

readers to share in it. When the poem opens, wine is not referred
to. It is there, however, intensifying his solitude in relation to
human society, on the one hand, and creating a companion pres-
ence in the personification of the natural world, on the other. Na-
ture personified, at first rather tentatively in the spring grasses,
then desolately in the shadow, and finally—impatiently and even
desperately—in the pines, recalls the wished-for companion that Li
Bo once found reflected in his wine cup: the presence imagined by
the poet in an effort to deny—and therefore to declare—his isola-
tion. With the addition of the carpe diem theme (made explicit only
in line 4), the would-be companion is quickly revealed to be trai-
torous, as the obstinate indifference of nature becomes a personal
affront. As the apparent cause and, more to the point, as a con-
ventionally understood sign of the skewed rapport between the
poet and his surroundings, wine simultaneously increases the poet's
solitude in the context of the poem and enhances the subjectivity of
his vision as its creator.

The poet's exasperation reaches a peak in line 8, when his
pleading question to the tall pines is left unanswered. The implicit
effect of the wine is to act as an allusion to the poet's immediacy,
inviting readers to go along with the poet in this tirade. At the
same time, though, comprehension of the poet's intoxication also
prevents readers from anticipating the conclusion. For a hopeful
moment, Li Bo engages peacefully with nature and time, dissolving
both his solitude and his mortality: "My hand dances with the
moon on the rock." Thanks to the ambiguous syntax of this phrase,
readers also hear the poet say, "My hand dances in the moon(light)
on the rock," as well as, "My hand causes the moon(light) on the
rock to dance." This is the only ambiguous line in the poem, and it
demands particular attention. For an intoxicated moment, bound-
aries are blurred in the mingling of hand and moon.

Only for a moment, however. In the very next line, the poet
shifts his vision, and the mist clears. Solidly lying across his lap is a
zither—and the possibility of responding to the impersonal "whis-
tle and hum" of the pines, of mingling his human voice with that
of the woods, as his human hand mingled with the moonlight.

But, instead of leading back to the blissfully indeterminate world of line 9, the poet (smitten, perhaps, by the sight of new flowers around the zither) plunges abruptly into a declaration that is nothing if not a clarification: "That which lies beyond this wine goblet, / Placid and deep, is not my heart." The runover syntax of this final couplet, echoing that of the opening, is largely responsible for conveying a feeling of spontaneous and unchecked vehemence. The forceful denial conveyed in the modal word *"fei"* (is not) adds the finishing touch. The poet leaves little doubt that he means what he says, that this statement is an unmediated declaration from the heart. At the same time, however, he excludes his readers from his subjective response to the world. The strangeness of the statement at first prevents readers from fully understanding what the poet means. This combined depiction of unbridled emotion and pure subjectivity incarnates the immediacy so closely associated with Li Bo's poetry.

An examination of the couplet in question reveals the source of its strangeness. The object of the binomial descriptive *"you you"* is unclear. Does *"you you"* refer to "that which lies beyond the wine goblet," or simply to the wine goblet (and the poet's heart) itself? Hoping to solve this part of the puzzle, readers may recall this line from "Zi Jin," one of the "Airs of Zheng" in the *Shijing*: "Green, green, the front of your robe; *you you* my heart."[35] If it is an allusion to the *Shijing* poem, line 12 could be read as a direct contradiction of the original: *"you you* is *not* my heart." In that case, the poet's heart is emphatically different from whatever *"you you"* might be. Yet when divided differently, the couplet may also be understood as a reaffirmation of the line in the *Shijing*: "Everything that is not within the bounds of this wine cup—and *you you*—is not my heart."

The exact definition of *"you you"* is, like that of all binomial descriptives in the *Shijing*, problematic and only reinforces ambiguity. Returning to the line from the *Shijing* cited above, the obvious gloss for this term is the one given as the first definition in the *Ciyuan*: "profound longing" *(shensi)*. This is reinforced by its appearance in another *Shijing* poem, "Zhong feng" (Great wind):

The great wind raises the dust,   終風且霾
Will he kindly come calling?   惠然肯來
He doesn't come, he doesn't call,   莫往莫來
You you *is my longing!*[36]   悠悠我思

This seemingly straightforward allusion again supports the reading that *"you you"* refers most appropriately to the poet's heart. However, it occurs in at least two other places in the *Shijing*, where it is glossed once as "distant and limitless" (*"You you* the azure sky, / Where does it end?"")[37] and once as "calm and tranquil" (*"You you* the banners fly").[38] More effectively than any grammatical analysis, these glosses, especially the first, link the expression more closely to the great expanse of all that is not the poet's heart.

Commentators have remained silent on this somewhat humorous puzzle that Li Bo has left behind. It seems quite possible, however, that Li Bo is standing back and smiling at the commonly held understanding that binomial descriptives in the *Shijing* convey the essence of whatever object is being described. The fact that it is impossible to determine what that object is becomes all the funnier when the emphatic nature of this vague declaration is taken into account.

While this line does provide another instance of the use of allusion to underline the individuality of the creative poet, this is not its essence. The immediacy of the line goes beyond a show of wit, for it is encoded as an allusion. Insofar as wine is traditionally both the catalyst for and the sign of pure immediacy, the act of equating the contents of the cup with one's heart is universally comprehensible. The force of the closing line does not primarily lie in the assertion that wine is a refuge. Rather, it lies in the suggestion that wine is universally recognized as having a vast range of properties going far beyond, and even betraying, its apparent placidity. Li Bo refuses to pinpoint which properties he is alluding to; his readers' confusion, however, may just be the product of the poet's orchestrated tribute to the ultimate subjectivity of wine. For Li Bo, wine is a gesture with infinite links to the poetic past, incarnating the very paradox upon which his "immediate" poetry is built, namely, the use of convention to establish individuality, and the application of artifice to clear new ground for immediacy.

"Parted Far Away": The Endurance of Emptiness

Parted far away.	遠別離
Two women, of olden times: Ehuang and Nüying,	古有皇英之二女
Are there, south of Dongting Lake, on the banks of the limpid Xiang River.	乃在洞庭之南消 　湘之浦
4　*Straight down in ocean waters, ten thousand li deep—*	海水直下萬里深
Who would not call this parting cruel?	誰人不言此離苦
Dim and somber is the sun—dark and brooding are the clouds,	日慘慘兮雲冥冥
Gibbons weeping, shrieking—ghosts whistle in the rain.	猩猩啼煙兮鬼嘯 　雨
8　*Even if I say it, what would that change?*	我縱言之將何補
"I fear the heavens reflect not on my loyal sincerity"—	皇穹竊恐不照余 　之忠誠
"Thunder fills the skies"—about to cry out in anger.	雷憑憑兮欲吼怒
Yao and Shun, too, had to cede the throne to Yu.[39]	堯舜當之亦禪禹
12　*True gentlemen lose official positions, dragons transform into fish;*	君失臣兮龍為魚
Power devolves to mere officials, and rats become tigers.	權歸臣兮鼠變虎
Some have said:	或云
Yao was imprisoned in obscurity,	堯幽囚
16　*Shun died in the wild,*	舜野死
The twists and turns of the Nine Doubts River all look the same.	九疑聯綿皆相似

Why did "Double Pupils" Shun end in a solitary
 grave?　　　　　　　　　　　　　　　　重瞳孤墳竟何是

Emperor Yao's daughter wept among emerald
 clouds:　　　　　　　　　　　　　　　　帝子泣兮綠雲間
20 *"Having followed the wind and waves, never will*　隨風波兮去無還
 you return."

Sob mightily, and gaze afar,　　　　　　　　慟哭兮遠望
Look upon the deep mountains of Cangwu.　　見蒼梧之深山

When Cangwu's mountains crumble and the　蒼梧山崩湘水絕
 Xiang waters cease to roll,　　　　　　　　竹上之淚乃可滅
24 *Only then will the tearstains on the bamboo fade*
 away.[40]

 Of all of Li Bo's poems, few are more universally appreciated—
and variously interpreted—than this *yuefu,* "Parted Far Away"
("Yuan bieli"). As mysterious as "Du Lu Composition," as personal
and passionate as "Infinite Longing" ("Chang xiangsi"), as redolent
of unresolved allegorical promise as any of his most abstruse
Gufeng, and as subtly reliant on allusion as anything written by Du
Fu, this poem takes its place in Li Bo's corpus as among those
closest to achieving poetic plenitude. Readers approaching "Parted
Far Away" as the lyrical expression of this particular poet will find
that it harmonizes—smoothly yet distinctly—manifestations of Li
Bo's (disputed) knowledge and (undisputed) talent. Those seeking
to situate it in its particular moment of Chinese literary history will
notice how the poem fulfills the increasingly paradoxical demands
of "ancientness," while leaving the liminal, outsider voice of the
"Banished Immortal" intact. Its comprehensive integration of the
most important features of Li Bo's poetic practice warrants its
inclusion here.

 Faced with the task of communicating and preserving the elu-
sive charm of "Parted Far Away," critics of different persuasions
turn to the critical language of negation and contradiction. In
Chapter 1, I quoted the comment by the Yuan dynasty critic Fan
Peng, who admiringly described this poem's language as "broken
again and again, thrown into disorder again and again [while]

actually never broken or in disorder."[41] And the eighteenth-century critic Weng Fanggang offered this description: "pushing *mili* to [such] an extreme that it successfully assumes its origins in that point [in the objective world]."[42]

Though separated from each other by six hundred years, both Fan Peng and Weng Fanggang acknowledge, if in slightly different terms, Li Bo's ability to imbue apparent "emptiness" with actual "fullness"—or to utilize emptiness knowingly as the compelling vehicle for fullness that it has always been. "Parted Far Away," they tell us, achieves unity by means of chaos, and substance by means of abstruseness. It is easy to agree with this assessment and to appreciate both its astuteness and its economical, evocative expression in the formulations of both critics. But praise like this carries its own paradoxes. If it is to have any meaning at all, it must be backed up with some assurance that the unsubstantiated path along which Li Bo leads takes willing readers to "that point [in the objective world]." This, perhaps, is why these same critics, along with others who have admired this poem's seductive resistance to cognitive understanding, have assiduously pursued, and continue to pursue, a definitive explanation for just what it "really" means.

This quest to establish an exact referent may seem paradoxical and even in some way self-defeating. But I have already discussed two influential rhetorical traditions that operate in a similar fashion: the tradition of *bi* (comparison) and the rhetorical changes inspired by the rise of Neo-Confucianism. *Bi* refers to the figurative and sometimes impenetrable "comparisons" that had long been read as one of the most reliable signs of authenticity of expression. I have also briefly touched on the long-term effects of what the modern scholar Ying-shih Yü has termed the "this-worldly turn" of Chan Buddhism, set in motion when Han Yu brought Chan spirituality and rhetoric into the service of a Confucian revival.[43] These rhetorical practices, well-established in their respective intellectual domains, make it easier for Li Bo's later admirers to read manifestations of emptiness as the ultimate expression of his literary and ethical substance, of his reality-based Confucian core.

What events do critics identify as the "real-world" inspiration for this poem? Which of the regrettable political events of the period is being lamented here? There is no real consensus, except that it had something to do with the An Lu Shan rebellion and its aftermath. Fan Peng reads it as Li Bo's veiled criticism of Xuanzong's abdication of his throne to Suzong after Xuanzong's infamous flight to Shu.[44] Li Bo's Yuan dynasty editor, Xiao Shibin, proposes that the poet is here expressing his anger at having seen imperial and military power fall into the hands of scheming ministers and warlords like Li Linfu, Yang Guozhong, and An Lushan.[45] Later, Chen Hang, the Qing dynasty author of *Shi bi xing jian,* expressed his dissatisfaction with these and other strictly political readings of the poem, complaining that they ignore the important allusions to the mythical women Ehuang and Nüying in the opening and closing lines. For Chen, this poem's convoluted and passionate language stems from Li Bo's deep sympathy and pain at hearing about the murder of Yang Guifei, the emperor's favorite concubine, on the way to Shu.[46] Most recently, Ono Jitsunosuke has unabashedly defended the quite different position that Li Bo's poem displays his profoundly loyal Confucian character and his distress at discovering that his early suspicions about Yang Guifei's dangerous influence over the emperor had proved accurate.[47]

To be sure, there is plenty of textual support for a *bi*-style reading of this poem. Imagistic and verbal references to the *Chuci,* allusions to Yao and Shun, and a direct declaration proclaiming his unrecognized "loyal sincerity" are among the most obvious. In addition, there is another unspoken reason that readers favorable to Li Bo might want to hold this poem up as evidence of his loyalty to the dynasty: to counterbalance the controversy arising from his short-lived and perhaps treasonous alliance with Suzong's ambitious brother, the prince of Yong, soon after the An Lushan rebellion.[48] Each of these explanations can be successfully applied to at least part of the patchwork of this poem, and all of them provide ample justification for its passionate, mournful tone. None, however, has proven satisfying enough to put an end to the seemingly endless speculation.

In light of the accumulated evidence of Li Bo's highly conscious and creative handling of readerly expectations and the conventions of allusion, it seems reasonable to wonder just how much of this interpretive uncertainty is simply an integral and intended part of the poem at hand. Lack of consensus about the exact referents does not completely discredit these critics' efforts to find them, but it does suggest that the hunt has overrun the quarry. As with most of Li Bo's poetry, something other than the poem's "point of origin" accounts for its fascination.

Rereading the comments by Fan Peng and Weng Fanggang awakens the realization that the poem's appeal derives from the very thing that makes the quest appear at once urgent and impossible: a language that, while intense and strident, making ample use of Chu-style hyperbole and direct exclamation, cloaks the poet's intent in a thick cover of ellipses and changes in the speaking voice. Even now, there is an irresistible attraction in the coupling of the seemingly unfettered (and thus private, unpredictable, and "unsubstantiated" [xu]) language of uncontrollable passion, and the discernible seriousness of purpose grounded in the shared, objective shi world (however ultimately unverifiable that purpose might be). That attraction is the attraction of plenitude: the implicit promise, and eternal deferral, of full comprehension.

Li Bo's "Parted Far Away" begins simply and arrestingly with the short, isolated line: "Parted far away."[49] These words, direct and redundant, immediately invite a dual reading: as a personal sigh of resignation or resentment (over man's fate, the speaker's fate, or both) and, at the same time, as a quotation of the yuefu title under which Li Bo has chosen to compose this poem. The personal voice is touching as a reminder of the painful universality of the condition it names. It speaks with an unimpeachable authenticity and implies that more specificity would only detract from its communicative power. Simultaneously, the voice of the conscious poet draws attention to the textual nature of the piece: its generic identity as a yuefu and the presumably ancient thematic tradition with which the title is associated.

First, as readers of yuefu, and especially as readers of Li Bo's poetry, it is important to become acquainted with the lineage of poems bearing the title "Parted Far Away," in hope of finding out more about the opening line. Guo Maoqian's Yuefu shiji indicates that this is a yuefu that, at least by the time of the Ming dynasty, did not have a particularly long or rich lineage. Guo cites no textual evidence or extant examples of this or any related title existing before the Liang dynasty. In other words, it has no identifiable line of "ancient" forebears. This could mean either that it just happens to be a newer *yuefu*, or that all earlier examples were lost. As presented in Guo's anthology, Li Bo's poem is the earliest of the five (two of which he wrote) bearing the specific title "Parted Far Away." These appear as part of a larger group of nineteen poems whose titles contain the expression *"bieli"* or *"libie"* (both meaning "parting" or "parted"). In contrast to most of the titles listed in the *Yuefu shiji,* among those appearing in the "parting" category, Tang poems outnumber pre-Tang ones almost four to one.[50]

Given the relative lateness of these poems, it is perhaps not surprising that they are virtually indistinguishable from *shi* poetry. Most are composed of consistent five- or seven-character lines rather than the uneven lines left over from the genre's musical origins. The original story line, if there ever was one, has been completely overtaken by the most general adherence to the most universal of themes. Textual allusion as such is rare, though not entirely absent, and is the repetition of distinctive images, expressions, or characters. Precious few detectible signs of intratextuality link the poems assigned to this group.

Guo Maoqian grounds these poems in a specific ancient poetic heritage by proposing in his preface to this group that the *"bieli"* thematic subgenre descends from the "Li Sao," the "Nineteen Old Poems," and a poem composed by Li Ling to Su Wu. He substantiates this claim by quoting specific lines containing the expression "parting," and then concludes by stating, "And so those who came later modeled [poems] after these, called 'Ancient Parting' ('Gu bieli'). Emperor Jianwen of the Liang composed 'Parted in Life' ('Sheng bieli'), Wu Maiyuan of the Song has a 'Long Parted' ('Chang bieli'), and Li Bo of the Tang has a 'Parted Far Away' ('Yuan bieli'). These are all of the same category."[51] Guo's identification of the "Nineteen Old Poems" as one early source is more than just a symbolic gesture toward ancient origins. The "Nineteen Old Poems" had long been valued for their limpid and intensely lyrical expression of a universal, human experience, particularly that of separation. Perhaps, then, the linking element in this thematic subgenre is neither a specific title nor a precise narrative line, but something more amorphous: a studied universality in the treatment of a universal theme. In the hands of the best poets, this linking element, by virtue of its universality, becomes a liberating element as well.

The opening line of Li Bo's "Parted Far Away" functions less as a reference to a particular *yuefu* title than to *yuefu* titles as a convention, broadly gesturing toward the ancientness of both the genre and the sentiment, as also to the folk-based authenticity associated with both. "Parted far away," he states simply, quoting a convention only to reach beyond its relatively narrow confines and toward the "ancient" human sentiments that the *yuefu* is ideally supposed (if only by virtue of its folkloric origins) to preserve and transmit. And if the specific title is, as it seems to be, a refurbished one, its subtle newness hardly compromises the authenticity of its borrowed ancientness. On the contrary, the effect of the gesture is only strengthened as the poet reaches back to insert a new lineage—one he would like to have inherited—among those that he did. "Parted Far Away," then, opens with a line that is both literary quotation and lyrical sigh, producing a strangely natural harmony that preserves the distinctiveness of both voices. As the poem progresses, the two voices separate and reunite at rhythmic intervals, with Li Bo introducing and then stepping away from other ancient conventions that his readers thought they had always understood.

This brief and powerful opening is followed by an equally direct and unambiguously allusive statement. In a long discursive line extending over two verses, and in the nonlyrical mode of four- and six-character verse, the poet adopts the voice of the storyteller who knows that his story is not one that needs retelling. The words "olden times" (line 2) encapsulate one of the tradition's most heart-wrenching tales of separation: the mythical story of Ehuang and Nüying, the two daughters of the sage-king Yao, who were the wives of Yao's would-be successor, Shun. When Shun did not return from an official trip to the south (supposedly exiled, or perhaps killed there by the new ruler, Yu), the two women attempted to follow him. Unable to find him, they drowned in the Xiang River, where their spirits are said still to wander the banks in mourning, and where the spotted bamboo of that region is thought to bear, even now, the stains of their tears.

The link between this story and the generally shared age-old pain of parting is obvious, and the tale's prominence in the tradition alone suffices to explain its inclusion. Yet the personal voice, that lyric sigh of the first line, if not completely silenced, seems to be held in abeyance. Is the poet still mourning something that happened so long ago? Because this poet is Li Bo, whose particular ways of linking himself with the *Chuci* tradition are now familiar, readers must be attentive to Ehuang and Nüying's traditional association with the "Nine Songs." The two have long been considered the women who became the "Goddess of the Xiang," the subject of the third and fourth songs of that series.[52] Geographically, too, this is the area associated with Qu Yuan's wanderings, and the emphatic *"nai zai"* ([they] are there) opening of line 3 of this poem draws attention to the place. The following couplet (lines 4–5) picks up on this geographical focus, transporting the reader, as poetic geography so often will, back into the inscape of the intensely lyric poet: "Straight down in ocean waters, ten thousand *li* deep—/Who would not call this parting cruel?"

Here, even as the lyric self reasserts his feeling of personal pain, the voice of the knowledgeable poet maintains control. Taking full advantage of the opportunities for line-length variation offered by the *yuefu,* Li Bo has switched to the seven-character lyric mode, constructing a couplet that develops the two allusions (to the two loyal wives, and to Qu Yuan) within a personal cri de coeur. The lines' subtle echoing of "Nineteen Old Poems #1" ("Parted by almost ten thousand *li,*/Each at an opposite end of the sky")[53] only intensifies the ancient lyricism of this couplet. If this knot of ancient references already cues readers to begin the search for the unifying (presumably real-life) referent, its evocation of a deep passion, and the ensuing rhetorical comment addressed directly to the reader, only add to the urgency of that search. From whom is the poet—or someone else—so painfully separated? Is this borrowed parting lament a guise for a political complaint? If a political complaint, then, which aspects of these allusions are being brought into play: unjust successions, unfair exile, misled governance?

As if in response to these questions, as well as to his own rhetorical one in lines 4 and 5, in lines 6 and 7 the poet reaches back even earlier to adopt the language and imagery of the "Li Sao," complete with reduplicative descriptives (such as *"mingming"* [dark and brooding] from "Mountain Spirit" ["Shan gui"], the ninth of the "Nine Songs") and the ancient *xi* particle (represented by dashes in the translation):

Dim and somber is the sun—dark and brooding are the clouds,
Gibbons weeping, shrieking—ghosts whistle in the rain.

From the sad but distanced observer in the opening lines, to the deeply empathetic observer of lines 4 and 5, to the all but direct words of the suffering ancients themselves, the poet seems to be moving his readers gradually into the past, allowing them to forget its pastness. A less talented—and, more importantly, a less learned—poet might have allowed this ancient voice to dominate the remainder of the poem. But in line 8, Li Bo abruptly closes the invisible quotation marks that introduced this borrowed plea for understanding. Turning now to his audience and addressing them directly, he reminds them of the futility of such complaints, however eloquent: "Even if I say it, what would that change?" (more precisely, "how could that *make amends for* [this wrong or this pain]?"). Clearly speaking would not change it, whatever "it" refers to.

The rest of the poem is devoted to Li Bo's saying it anyway, braiding together past and present, poet and histor in a way that keeps his readers mindful of who is doing the saying and mystified as to exactly what he is saying (and why). From this point on, he shifts back and forth between speaking the language of the ancients (where, as in line 9, the first-person pronoun seems to be uttered by several voices at the same time: those of the mourning women, of Qu Yuan, and of Li Bo himself) and speaking the almost commentarial language of the latter-day histor (as in lines 11–17). For all his facility for borrowing the tongue of his subjects, however, this histor, like his readers, remains plagued by unanswered questions, his vision impeded by an immense block of time. He peers into the past, confounded by the Nine Doubts River (line 16) and hemmed in by the "deep mountains of Cangwu" (line 21), just as his readers, peering into his poem, find themselves puzzling before the semi-opaque grillwork of his allusions. Here, as in so many of his other poems, Li Bo openly asserts his control as a poet to bring his readers to terms with the unapproachable pastness of the past, even as he makes them feel its—and his—emotive force. There may be some bio-historical "it" that he is referring to, some specific event in his life or in his times that motivated the writing of this piece. But it is also possible that this promise of a real-life referent is being dangled before the eyes of his audience, just behind that fence, as a way of getting them to look hard at—and even be moved by—the grillwork itself.

In the last line, focusing attention on the difference between the invisible and the visible remains of the past, Li Bo brings before his readers' eyes the only visible object that has transcended time: the tearstains left by the grief-stricken women on the bamboo growing at the place of their demise. For all his critics' insistence to the contrary, it is not the solid things—historical events, life's encounters, or even moral fiber—that last. Rather, "empty," invisible things, such as human emotion and imagination, are what prove most durable. This seems to be the meaning of this poem, and its critical history has only proven its point. No one has satisfactorily uncovered its "grounding in objective reality," to borrow the words of Weng Fanggang, but everyone concedes its greatness. Like Li Bo's work as a whole, this poem moves emptiness from the periphery to the center, and shows us how to see it through the solid frame of language and literary history in which it is carried and transported.

CHAPTER 6

Epilogue

Li Bo Remembering and Remembered

Plunge a knife in to break the water—
  the water flows but faster.
Raise a cup to quell the pain—the pain
  grows but deeper.

抽刀斷水水更流
舉杯消愁愁更愁

Man's life in this world does not answer
  my wishes,
Tomorrow morning, hair loosed to the
  wind, I shall pilot my little skiff.

人生在世不稱意
明朝散髮弄扁舟

—Li Bo, "At the Xie Tiao Pavilion in Xuanzhou, Taking Leave
of Secretary Shuyun." 宣州謝朓樓餞別校書叔雲

IT USED TO BE common practice in the elementary schools of
China to require children to learn the great poems of the past by
heart. Young students would memorize the words long before
they were prepared to understand them, so that they could recite
them rhythmically and in loud unison upon demand. This practice
tells of a strong sense of responsibility to tradition, to be sure. But,
as one of those children of the olden days—now a man close to
retirement—told me, there was another, less obvious good that
came of this kind of rote learning. Not, he conceded, that every
child would grow up to remember every line of poetry; but in most
children at least some of these poems would take root. Then,
perhaps many years later, a memorized piece would break to the
surface, either whole or in fragments, when that grown-up child
encountered a scene or an event that unexpectedly called up some
seemingly forgotten turn of phrase or image. And, with each such

encounter, both the poem and the person who carried it would be enriched: the poem rekindled by the present and the particular, the person firmly anchored in the past and the communal.

The man who explained this to me, Mr. Zhang, was a local cadre in the "Cultural Bureau" of the city of Xuancheng in Anhui, not far from the place where Li Bo is thought to have himself remembered his predecessor, Xie Tiao, in his poem, "At the Xie Tiao Pavilion." It was the spring of 1985, and our little group of six or seven—local schoolteachers, cadres from the Cultural Bureau and the Office of External Affairs, an officer from the Security Bureau, and our driver—had just trooped up to the top of Jingting Mountain, the site and subject of one of Li Bo's best-loved qua-trains, "Sitting Alone on Jingting Mountain." We found a comfort-able spot overlooking the valley, vibrant with the bright yellow springtime flowers of colba fields and dotted with dark brick farm-houses. It had rained a great deal over the past few days, and there was still something rough-hewn and stark about the swaths of color and darkness that stretched out before us. As we sat down to our picnic lunch, one of the teachers, Mr. Cui, barely concealing his sense of satisfaction, observed that Xuancheng was still relatively untouched by the Four Modernizations. And indeed, it was easy to imagine that (but for a few choice samples of concrete block architecture) the fields, river, and distant hills still looked much as they did when Li Bo came here in the 740s and again in the 750s.

But, as untouched as the landscape appeared, our walk up the well-worn mountain path had occasioned nothing so much as a narrative of final, irreparable loss. I was told as we walked: Here in this weedy clearing, there used to be a great boulder—the "Cloudroot Stone"—from which the mists and clouds that some-times surround the mountain were thought to arise. Over there behind that copse of trees once stood an inscription of Li Bo's famous poem dedicated to this mountain, perhaps dating from the Southern Song. And, if you just step behind that rise you can see the stumps of pillars that, not so long ago, still supported the Taibai Pavilion—we can go look at them if you like.

We did not. Instead, we wordlessly agreed to stay on the path until we reached a suitable spot for our picnic. This was a special occasion—it was not every day that my companions could enjoy a picnic on the mountain. As we ate, the conversation turned from the fate of the all-too-vulnerable material vestiges of the past (carted away or demolished during the Great Leap Forward and the Cultural Revolution) to the somewhat more enduring traces of lore and landscape. There was some vigorous but laughing argument as the men tried to decide which versions of the various local legends were the real ones. Gradually, we finished our meal and then, each of us momentarily alone with our thoughts, sat looking at the valley and river below. Finally, Mr. Cui stood up and faced the valley.

When I had begun planning this trip, one of the things I had hoped to experience was to hear someone "sing" Li Bo's poetry in the traditional style of *yin shi:* a style of poetic vocalization somewhere between chanting and singing, in which the pitch and length of a note is determined by the tone of the word and, as far as anyone could explain, the emotion of the singer. Time and again I was told that this was a dying—if not an already dead—art. At Fudan University, I had been introduced to one of the few professors who would admit to being able to *yin shi,* and I had even had the chance to record him (against the inescapable background noise of midday traffic) in one of the upstairs department offices. Arriving in Xuancheng, I asked the chief of the Cultural Bureau whether there was anyone available who still practiced this art. And so Mr. Cui, a middle school teacher in his sixties, was invited to join us.

He stood with his back toward us, face to the sun. He was a tall, elegant man, short-cropped silver hair, dressed in a neatly pressed Mao jacket. He began to sing, and the voice I expected was not the voice that emerged. Slowly, barely audibly at first, a tremulous tenor carried words from within his memory out into the valley, short bursts alternating with sustained notes; intense, clearly articulated syllables followed by quiet murmured sounds that trailed off into silence. Mr. Cui "sang" the same poem a second time, and through his distinctive Anhui accent I recognized some of the words of Li Bo's "Sitting Alone on Jingting Mountain":

Flocks of birds fly high and disappear,　　　眾鳥高飛盡
A solitary cloud drifts off, alone and idle.　　孤雲獨去閑
Looking at each other, never tiring,　　　　相看兩不厭
There is only Jingting Mountain.[1]　　　　只有敬亭山

I was surprised and moved. This was not the measured, melodious singing I had heard in a professor's office in Shanghai; the sounds that reached my ears seemed strangely at odds with the poem itself. Li Bo's lyrics, so expressive of a timeless moment of solitary wholeness, were being sung with the sharp, almost harsh, intensity one would expect to hear reserved for a poem of dark melancholy or angry protest. The sublime, inarticulate sadness on the faces of my companions reflected the bruised tones of Mr. Cui's voice. He went on to sing other poems by Li Bo, patiently stopping now and then to explain the technical aspects of what he was doing, trying to convey the intricate relation between the parts of his performance that were prescribed by tradition and the parts that expressed his own feelings about the poem. When it was time to leave, we descended the path quietly, passing by the various invisible ruins without comment. In the end, I thought, no matter which of Li Bo's poems Mr. Cui was singing in that day's demonstration of a nearly extinct performing art, we were listening to the sound of the village schoolteacher plunging his own knife, beside that of Li Bo, in the same ceaselessly flowing waters.

LAMENTING WHAT has been—and what will be—irretrievably lost is hardly, of course, the exclusive domain of the modern condition. In the preceding chapters, I have demonstrated how, in Li Bo's moments of embracing the ancients, he energetically envisioned, longed for, and resisted his own imminent accession to ancientness. I have also explored how generations of critics, contemplating his loss, successively shaped the forms his ancientness would acquire over time.

One detects, however, a distinct difference between Li Bo's wistful nostalgia for the past and his readers' mournful nostalgia for him—a distinction that adds a very human, almost poignant, dimension to the critical writings (including my own) I have reviewed and presented here. This difference is not unlike that separating the sadness one feels at the imminent disappearance of the practice of *yinshi* and the grief caused by the destruction and carting off of the stone stelae of Jinting Mountain. The one harbors seeds of hope for recovery (in some form), and the other does not. One can long for, and even work towards, the return of an admittedly modified ideal—or, more likely, idealized—moral, social, or aesthetic state; but one can only helplessly mourn the disappearance of a specific and fundamentally unrepeatable expression of that state. Li Bo, it would seem, belonged to the first category of rememberers and—not coincidentally—to the second category of the remembered. If he is remembered as irreplaceable and unrepeatable, it is in large part the direct result of his particular way of remembering.

LI BO AS REMEMBERER

Li Bo anticipated Han Yu in longing for the continuation (or perhaps more accurately, the revival) of a presumably ancient poetics identified with the unimpeded expression of real encounters with the world. As I have argued here, this longing was neither despairing nor merely theatrical; it manifested itself clearly and consistently in his poetic practice. An important part of the "world" Li Bo "encountered," and the part that moved him, was the world of past literature. Its generic conventions, imagery, and mythological figures are objectified, framed, and otherwise manipulated in much the same way that he and other poets treat the natural world or personal events. This pointed and playful handling of images real and imagined, invented and inherited, directly contributed to his status as an immortal banished from heaven, or, alternatively, as madman. In making free with the ancients, he realized authentic, immediate expression in a way not seen since the times of the ancients.

But this use of past literature involves a degree of distancing that borders on the ironic, for it also testifies to—with no less authenticity—an individual's arriving late enough in the tradition to objectify certain literary practices and recognize their conventionality. It is the dual, imbricated nature of Li Bo's performance—that of unfettered immortal and of erudite, teasing ironist—that both authenticates and works against the desire for continuity, whether that desire is expressed in Li Bo's own *fugu* sentiments or in his successors' attempts to follow in his poetic footsteps. In assuming a distance from the conventions, the shared language, that constitute the tools of his trade, he gives the lie to those very conventions and renders it nearly impossible for later poets to continue using them. Scholars have noted that the centuries-old *yuefu* tradition all but ended with Li Bo. In the same vein, one is compelled to consider whether the hermetic (and even, on occasion, fantastic) imagery of the later poets Li He and Li Shangyin arose, in part, in response to Li Bo's proverbial burning of poetic bridges. Certainly many a traditional critic conceived of Li Bo and Li He as somehow united in their shared affinity for playing with images and phrasing in ways that almost seemed calculated to confound the reading habits of their audiences.[2]

At the same time, Li Bo's forays into ancientness give literary form to the longing for the return of a past ideal of authentic expression. His playing with aspects of his literary inheritance indicates less an attitude of insouciance (as it is so often labeled by his less sympathetic critics) than something quite the opposite: the awareness that, underlying the stylistic trappings of any particular instance of past literary expression, there lies an ever accessible kernel of ancient sensibility. His explorations of so many different modes of imitation seem to reflect the hope that, if approached in the right spirit, that kernel can be retrieved and represented in ways suited to current modes of expression and understanding.

Intriguingly, Li Bo's recognition and attempted recovery of the retrievable, repeatable essence of the past emerge with particular clarity when he writes poems of mourning for the irretrievably lost. It is notable that his works contain very few memorial poems dedicated to individuals. Even his parting poems, where vacated landscapes might easily lend themselves to a more focused, inconsolable melancholy, primarily seem to express a strangely bittersweet exhilaration at the grandeur and timelessness of his own solitude. An example of this is the simple but representative poem, "The Pavilion of Master Xie" ("Xie Gong ting"):

Xie Pavilion, a place of parting—	謝亭離別處
Always, this scene provokes pain.	風景每生愁
Guests disperse beneath a dark sky's moon,	客散青天月
4 *The mountain emptying; green waters flow.*	山空碧水流
Pond blossoms in spring reflect the sun,	池花春映日
The bamboo by the window at night hums with	窗竹夜鳴秋
autumn.	
So times present and ancient meet and follow one	今古一相接
other,	長歌懷舊遊
8 *I sing long and think tenderly back to outings of*	
the past.[3]	

Li Bo has never made a secret of his admiration for Xie Tiao, and one might expect that a poem dedicated to Xie's memory would express Li's regret at his no longer existing. In keeping with such expectations, he does include the requisite evocations of absence, and more-than-dutifully pairs them with images of time's inexorable passing. These conventional attributes notwithstanding, this poem does not mourn the loss of an irreplaceable Xie Tiao so much as it celebrates the beauty inherent in the repeatable act of mourning. Rather than repeat the codified modes of remembering and longing for what is gone, Li Bo burrows beneath the coded surface to uncover the unexamined assumptions that structure the human experience of time, much as he did in his "Ancient Airs," his *yuefu*, and his applications of allusion. What he uncovers here is the habit of successiveness; what he proposes in its place is simultaneity.

In "The Pavilion of Master Xie," Li Bo brings about the meeting of time past with time present in line 7 in the Chinese word "*jie*" (to meet). In the strict terms of his narrative, "meeting" signifies the very essence of successive linear time. The two temporal dimensions "meet" in the elusive moment when present succeeds past. Consistent with this linearity, Li Bo's "present" visit to the site of Xie Pavilion naturally provokes in him reminiscences of the poet who had been there before. The intensity of this all-too-familiar brand of nostalgia—the helpless witnessing of one era ineluctably succeeding the other—is only sharpened by Li Bo's repetition of Xie Tiao's act of gathering there with friends and saying good-bye to them. But this gesture, in its dual character of the ritualistic and the personal, the timeless and the fleeting, mitigates the apparent sequentiality of the story. The last line leaves readers uncertain whether the subject of Li Bo's tender reminiscences—those "outings of the past"—refer to Xie Tiao's, Li Bo's, or both.

The answer remains ambiguous even upon rereading the poem, perhaps because, as is so often the case in the best Tang dynasty regulated poems, temporal ambiguity is at least part of the point. At Xie Tiao's pavilion, in the world of Li Bo's memory, the leave-takings of the distant and the immediate past merge in Li Bo's own meeting and leave-taking—not merely of his current friends, but, more important, of the ancient Xie Tiao. Succession gives way to simultaneity, framed and suspended for posterity, when the poet immortalizes the moment in his own poem. Almost as though refuting Wang Xizhi's fourth-century lament at the Orchid Pavilion, Li Bo refuses to acquiesce in the unending sequentiality of past and present as the dominant mode of temporal experience. He even refutes himself, going further than merely lifting his cup in a futile gesture to quell the pain of time's passage. He recognizes literature's potential, if not to halt time, then at least to frame it—along with his and our place in it—for viewing and contemplation.

Li Bo's acts of remembrance—whether inscribed in his choice of theme, poetic form, or, as in the poem just discussed, the skillful interplay of both—are founded on and inspired by what is and must be repeated: the very human adherence to a certain quality of ancientness that paradoxically each must define for and by himself. In poetic terms, that adherence consists in the ever more difficult task of sustaining the ability to respond to the world and its conventional formulations with personal immediacy and, even more daunting, to convey that response effectively using the literary means available, codified as they already are.

A recent description of Proust's contribution to the literary expression of the experience of memory offers an enlightening perspective on the challenge faced by any latecomer seeking to situate himself in relation to pasts both personal and literary. Susan Stewart, in her article "Proust's Turn from Nostalgia," demonstrates some of the ways in which *A la recherche du temps perdu* (In search of lost time) critiques nostalgia as a form of "volitional memory" that relies on codified forms that "actually undermine the authenticity of nostalgic feeling." As an alternative to this practice of "willed yearning," says Stewart, Proust "offers the mindfulness of artistic making, the reframing of experience through mental activity by opening a world composed of a plethora of sensual detail and finely wrought coincidences."[4]

Li Bo, too, wrote out of the realization that true commemoration of the past—whether that past is conceived in terms of personal experiences in the world (as in separation from friends) or of an inherited body of literature (as in the literary tradition lamenting separation from friends)—requires a type of aesthetic practice that refuses mere repetition. If Proust exercised his personal vision in the distinctly novelistic devices of detail and coincidence, Li Bo chose the poetic language of ambiguity and explicitly framed allusion. Li Bo's poetry reflects his understanding that "willed or voluntary forms of nostalgia ... are [merely] devices of forgetting in the costume of memory."[5] For him, all of memory can but proceed from, and simultaneously encompass, the rememberer. Sometimes poems can approach a level of self-dramatization that strikes some readers as, for want of better terms, narcissistic and self-indulgent, as in those "Ancient Airs" that give prominence to the immortality theme. At other times, poems emerge that are so playful that they border on self-irony, as in his costumed appearance as a courtesan in his recreations of Southern Dynasties *yuefu*.

But most of his poems fall somewhere in between, as he mingles the collective past with his own present in a complex and skillful encounter that allows for the full range of nuance, drama, and humor that his position, frankly accounted for, demands. While many poets prior to and contemporary with Li Bo have been recognized as masterful stylists of earlier genres (such as his revered predecessors Bao Zhao and Xie Tiao) and even more brilliant practitioners of allusion (who more so than Du Fu?), it seems fair to say that no one remembered himself into the past—and so transformed that past—quite the way that Li Bo did. He asserted his uniqueness so convincingly that he finally, ironically, rendered it impossible for those who followed to encompass him in the vision of simultaneity he himself practiced.

Partly in response to this, generations of critics developed a vocabulary that belonged to Li Bo alone, and when that vocabulary had been smelted and reforged so many times that it no longer adequately expressed his uniqueness, Li Bo himself was released into the untouchable realm of the ancients. There he became, at least for some, a model of sorts, eventually codified in the utterly hybrid and ambivalent term "Romantic." For others, there remained only the language of negativity, taking the form of varied assertions of his stubborn refusal to be tied to the expectations of others.

LI BO REMEMBERED

It was a drizzly Tomb-Sweeping Day when we went to visit Li Bo's gravesite in Dangtu. Set off from a nearby cemetery and situated in a complex comprising a temple and two memorial halls, the grave consists of a large grassy mound supported all around by a stone wall. In that wall, a stone stele—streaked and sticky with recently poured libations of wine—bore characters that were barely legible. The place was packed with schoolchildren on a field trip, and we wended our way through blue uniforms and red flags to take turns posing for pictures in front of the grave. Finally, we retreated into a small conference room in a nearby office building. There our rather formal little delegation sipped tea, waiting for the scheduled arrival of "Old Mr. Bi."

Mr. Bi was, in fact, quite old: well over eighty, blind in one eye, and beloved by all as the local authority on Li Bo. He had memorized, I was told, more than 700 of Li Bo's poems and had witnessed all of the transformations of the gravesite during this century. After presenting himself as the son of generations of the "simple farm people" to whom Li Bo was "so dedicated," Mr. Bi stood in the middle of the room and treated us to a somewhat breathless half-hour spectacle in which he freely alternated poetry recitations and storytelling. All of the poems were presented as having been composed in Dangtu by Li Bo, and all the stories were either about him or about the gravesite. He recounted the heroics of local villagers (including, apparently, Bi himself) in their apparently successful efforts to protect the grave during the Japanese occupation, the Great Leap, and the Cultural Revolution. And he also told stories which were, in effect, modern-day "tales of the strange" (*zhiguai*), reporting various local manifestations of Li Bo's spirit. Myth and geography joined in one especially vivid tale about "Stopped-Corpse Bridge," located a few kilometers north of the gravesite.

The story, though simple, took some time to tell, as one or another member of my party chimed in with a correction or an affirmation. As Old Mr. Bi (and company) told it: Many years ago, local villagers had become aware, over a period of months, of a change in the smell of the air. Sometimes it smelled wonderfully sweet, so much so that everyone in the village behaved as though in a state of profound joy. Other times, the village would be overwhelmed by a fetid odor that drove everyone into their homes. One day two men took it upon themselves to trace the scent back to its origins, and were soon led to a bridge, underneath which they found a perfectly preserved corpse. To all appearances the corpse had floated upriver, against the tide, and lodged itself in the niche where the bridge met the shoreline. When the men undertook to carry the corpse back home, it proved to be extraordinarily heavy, and seemed to resist more strongly with every step they took. Finally, buffeted by high winds and pounding rain, they put the corpse down only part of the way back and went to get help. A larger group returned the next day only to find the corpse gone— and a freshly dug grave in its place. They understood that this was the grave of Li Bo, so they disinterred him and moved him to the proper burial site we see today. People commemorate this event, said Mr. Bi, with the following couplet:

Springtime waves go straight downriver, flowing
    on to the east,
Why did the Poet's ghost fight the current to
    return?

春波直下東流去
詩魂何須逆流回

Such stories of resistance, freedom, and the refusal to "follow the rules," dominated the afternoon—whether the protagonist was Li Bo or the men who protected his grave. More surprising, however, especially given his reputation for independence bordering on arrogance, was the insistence that Li Bo loved, and was loved by, the common people. All present agreed that the poems Li Bo wrote in Dangtu during his old age were written out of sympathy for the sufferings of the poor villagers. This was the first and last time I heard this particular belief uttered with such forcefulness. Besides running counter to the usual representations of Li Bo's persona, their depiction of a camaraderie between the great poet and the local people differed from the local pride I had encountered elsewhere. In other villages of Anhui and Zhejiang, that pride usually inspired my hosts to claim an exorbitant number of poems as locally produced, or to honor a not-extremely-old tree as the place where Li Bo composed a particular piece. In contrast, the sense of proprietorship expressed by the people in the various villages of Dangtu County extended beyond pride of place to the creation of a human, almost personal, connection with this famously aloof, celestial being.

Perhaps the still-fresh memories of risks, both real and legendary, taken to protect the tomb of the "Banished Immortal" could find justification and symmetry only in the belief that he had (or would have) taken similar risks for them. But, more likely, these assertions of Li Bo's "love of the 'old-hundred-surnames'" reflected the absorption of recent political ideals into the rhetoric of popular reception, in much the same way as has happened throughout the history of more formal critical writings. Exceptionality, then as now, provides the unifying thread. If the age in which he lived is regarded as "feudal" and oppressive, then it is only fitting that he reemerge as the avatar of progressiveness and freedom. The impulses that had protected the gravesite from the destruction and desecration that had befallen so many of the other artifacts associated with "feudal" China suggested that, even during periods when the ancients became targets of erasure, the sense of his exceptionality rendered him irreplaceable, immune. Even in the twentieth century, he remained the poet worth fighting for.

Folklore and literary criticism have not been the only ways in which readers of Li Bo's poetry have expressed their sense of his irreplaceability. Admirers also wrote poems of commemoration and mourning. A glance at the two compendia of Li Bo's poetry and criticism, Ju Tuiyuan's *Li Bo ji jiaozhu* and Zhan Ying's *Li Bo quanji jiaozhu hui shi jiping*, reveals that Li Bo's own apparent lack of interest in the composition of memorial poems did not prevent him from being mourned in precisely that way. The twenty-five pages included in Ju Tuiyuan's edition alone, a mere sampling, contains pieces composed by poets from the obscure to the prominent, in genres ranging from the quatrain to extended *yuefu* and *fu* poems. For the most part, the poems themselves are not especially memorable. Their limited range of imagery and sentiment displays a consistency and overall superficiality suggesting that remembering Li Bo quickly became something of a de rigueur exercise in demonstrating knowledge of Li Bo basics, rather than a genuine expression of loss.[6] There are some that acknowledge as much in their titles, for example, Li Gang's "On Reading Li Bo's Collected Works, I Jestingly [Compose a Poem] Rhyming with *nu* (slave)."[7]

Nevertheless, remembering-Li poems have their place in the landscape of Li Bo's reception. They may not alter the picture I have drawn in the preceding pages, but, in their relative uniformity and use of Li-style hyperbole, they function as an ongoing summing-up, a constant reaffirmation of his importance to the tradition. Some elegize the classic attributes of his persona: "immortal," "sublime," "strange," and "unfettered"—and, always, "unmatched."[8] Others rehearse fragments of the poems deemed most representative, offering a pastiche of famous lines and images in which they inscribe the Li Bo persona, producing poems destined to tickle any aficionado of his work.

Yee-hsee-hsee, how strange! How extraordinary!	噫嘻欷奇哉
How many millions of years since the splitting of	自開闢以來
earth from sky—	不知幾千萬餘年
Until, in the Kaiyuan period,	至于開元間
4 *Suddenly, he was born: Li, the Immortal of*	忽生李詩仙
Poetry.	是時五星中
From that time, of the stars that number five,	一星不在天
One star is missing from the heavens.[9]	

A similar blend of citation and folklore can be found in the decidedly more lyrical "Seven Longings: First of Seven Poems" by You Tong (1618–1704):

I miss Li Gongfeng,	我思李供奉
Drunk, scribbling poems on gold-specked sheets.	醉草金花箋
From jade flutes, enchanting new sounds,	玉笛媚新聲
4 *Amid heavenly incense, gleaming fresh beauties.*	天香照嬋娟
One morning, he departed for Yelang,	一朝夜郎去
His brocade robes shrouded in barbarian mists.	錦繡埋蠻煙
All that remained was a cup of wine—	惟餘一杯酒
8 *He scratched his head, questioning the blue*	搔首問青天
sky.[10]	

How is it that precisely those lovers of Li Bo's decidedly anti-nostalgic brand of ancientness—poets like You Tong, who considered himself an unfettered descendant of the "Banished Immortal"—chose to honor Li Bo in predictable performances of poetic nostalgia? The practice is not as surprising as it may seem. This willingness to conventionalize the mourning of Li Bo is actually quite consistent with the desire to celebrate and preserve his fundamental unlearnability. Such poetry as this tacitly recognizes that what is unique and unrepeatable cannot, by definition, be appropriated and rewritten into the evolving tradition. It can only be cited, offered as a reminder of what has been lost. Likewise, if a critic is to continue the tradition of Li Bo's unqualifiability, then it seems most appropriate to repeat, rather than replace, the timeworn phrases that have accumulated so much allusive, elusive resonance.

This mini-subgenre reflects other affinities with the Li Bo critical tradition as well. It exploits, for example, a natural interdependence between the perception of his uniqueness and the experience of final, absolute loss. The perception of uniqueness is a precondition for the feeling of absolute loss, and absolute loss, whether imminent or realized, inspires the realization of uniqueness. Li Bo's particularly close identification with uniqueness, then, renders the memorial poem an especially fitting medium in which to represent him. To love him, in short, is to lament his passing, even before it has happened.

Li Bo's sobriquet, "Banished Immortal," expresses this perception of simultaneity quite neatly. After all, from the "Nine Songs" through the Han dynasty "Seeking the Immortal" *fu* poetry, and through the various immortality poems written by Li Bo himself, immortals have always appeared as unattainable objects of desire, objects that inspire longing and regret from the moment they appear. At the same time, the figure of Li Bo's immortality adds an almost ironic twist to these memorial poems, parlaying the inevitability of his disappearance into a mythic recognition of its ultimate impossibility. Even if one recognizes that *"xian"* does not necessarily signify beings that never die (as the conventional English translation certainly implies), its reference to "feathered beings" capable of defying the temporal and spatial restrictions to which human beings are subject identifies *xian* as an alternate state to mortality.

This intriguing imbrication of uniqueness, mourning, and Li Bo's "immortality" was not lost on Du Fu, whose many poems dedicated to missing his friend seem remarkably unconcerned with the difference between longing and mourning, between Li Bo's presence in the world and his ultimate disappearance from it.

In olden days there was a wild traveler,	昔年有狂客
They called him "Banished Immortal."	號爾謫仙人

*The lowering of his brush would startle wind
    and rain,*
*The poem finished, ghosts and spirits would
    weep.*[11]

筆落驚風雨
詩成泣鬼神

At first glance, "Twenty Rhymes, Sent to Li the Twelfth," from which these lines are excerpted, hardly seems worthy of the great Du Fu. Composed almost entirely of borrowed images and the simplest of sentiments, it apparently offers little in the way of personal feeling or the subtle plays of form and language that earned Du Fu his standing as a poet's poet. Perhaps its plain surface offers itself as virtually unassailable proof of the purity of Du Fu's (unrequited) feelings for Li Bo. But what makes this poem special is that it mourns—indeed, mythologizes—someone who is still alive. Du Fu, poet that he was, understood that the exceptional Li Bo could most fittingly be "captured" in the image of treading the earth as one already departed, absent even while present, and therefore ever the fitting subject of mourning.

Li Bo, it has to be admitted, finally did die. After his death, poems dedicated to his memory continued to focus on the persona of the immortal while incorporating as many of the markers associated with Li Bo as possible: wine, moon and stars, banishment, his exploits at court, and the required vocabulary of sublimity and impossibility. One especially complete encomium by Pi Rixiu bears the wordy but aphoristic title, "Li Hanlin: Those Who Assume Their Sublime Nature Must Be Truly Unfettered, and I Consider Li Hanlin among the Truly Unfettered."[12] It begins with a declaration of nothing less than love, echoing one of Du Fu's memorial poems, "On Not Seeing Him":[13] "I love Li Taibai, / His body, the Wine Star's spirit." The fifteen remaining couplets then enumerate virtually every morsel of lore and rumor that could be construed as proof of unfetteredness, from Li Bo's spontaneous outbursts of creativity ("His mouth emits the patterns of heaven, / His footprints are those of a wanderer among men.... In a drunken stupor he scribbled some *yuefu*, / Ten scrolls completed in the brush-stroke of one breath"), to his having been personally served a meal by the emperor ("Summoned to an audience in the imperial halls, / The

Son of Heaven himself served him his meal"), and finally to the story of his exile.

But the final crescendo of Pi Rixiu's poem is what most vividly encapsulates the essence of Li Bo—the part of him that readers, both learned and simple, embrace most fervently. That is the Li Bo who always says no.

The great peng-bird cannot be caged,	大鵬不可籠
Nor can Zhuangzi's undying cedar be cultivated.	大椿不可植
Immortal Isles of Penghu cannot be seen,	蓬壺不可見
4 *Nor can the immortal's Guye Mountain be known.*	姑射不可識
The Five Mountains of Yue: his sharp-toned writings,	五岳為辭鋒
Four Seas work as his surging breast.	四海作胸臆
Alas! In a hundred million years,	惜哉千萬年
8 *His supreme excellence cannot be attained.*	此俊不可得

TRACKING THE BANISHED IMMORTAL

My trip through Anhui and Zhejiang was coming to an end. In each town and village, people who love the poetry of Li Bo had gone to great lengths to share their knowledge and their stories. Each visit occasioned a lavish banquet, which would always end in a crescendo of drinking (in honor of Li Bo's love of wine), boisterous poetry recitals (by heart, of course), and—most disconcerting to me—spontaneous poetry-writing to commemorate the occasion. When it came my turn to write, I protested that I was no poet and that Chinese was not my language, but the disappointment on the faces of my hosts told me that these excuses were not acceptable. Writing a poem, I realized, would be the only way to reciprocate their generosity and kindness, and the only way to convince them that I was as serious about Li Bo as they assumed me to be. And so, before the dawn of our last day in Guichi, an industrialized town on the south shore of the Yangtze, I sat at a desk in the hostel and tried to write a rough approximation of a Tang dynasty poem (which I would only attempt to rhyme in modern Mandarin).

For some reason, I suddenly recalled a moment during my visit several days earlier to the still rural and remote Peach Blossom Pond in Jingxian. Li Bo had famously referred to the "thousand meter" depth of this pond as equal to the generosity of a recluse named Wang Lun, who had hosted him nearby.[14] Everywhere I went in the village, I was followed by a host of ruddy-faced children. They would not come near, but looked at me with wordless curiosity. After lunch on the second floor of the Taibai Pavilion near the pond, I had gone over to the window and seen them down below, looking up at the window and waiting.

LOOKING DOWN AT PEACH BLOSSOM POND FROM THE "ANCIENT STAMPING-SONG SHORE" IN JINGXIAN	在涇縣沓歌古 岸臨桃花潭

Separated by a thousand years from the springtime of Green Lotus Li,	千載相隔青蓮春
A traveler of ten thousand miles in pursuit of Taibai.	萬里遊客尋太白
She looks down at the pond and sees only brilliant bits of pink,	臨潭只見紛紛紅
4 *Cheeks of village children—peach blossoms open.*	村童面頰桃花開
Beneath bare feet, stelae of ancient times,	赤腳之下古石碑
Brilliant eyes look up, an outsider has come.	亮睛望上外人來
You ask where the "Banished Immortal" may be found today?	問余謫仙今安在
8 *On flowing water, hair loosed to the wind—he returns bearing the moon.*	流水散髮載月來

ABBREVIATIONS

The following abbreviations are used in the notes and in the bibliography.

CLEAR	*Chinese Literature Essays Articles Reviews*
CSJC	*Congshu jicheng*
CSJCCB	*Congshu jicheng chubian*
CSJCXB	*Congshu jicheng xinbian*
CSJCXB2	*Congshu jicheng xubian*
HJAS	*Harvard Journal of Asiatic Studies*
LBJJZ	*Li Bo ji jiaozhu*
LBZLHB	*Li Bo ziliao huibian*
LDSH	*Lidai shihua*
LDSHXB	*Lidai shihua xubian*
LTBQJ	*Li Taibai quanji*
QSHXB	*Qing shihua xubian*
QTS	*Quan Tangshi*
SBBY	*Sibu beiyao*
SBCK	*Sibu congkan*
SKQS	*Siku quanshu*
YFSJ	*Yuefu shiji*
ZZJC	*Zhuzi jicheng*

NOTES

Introduction

"Wang Tianmen shan" [Looking toward Heaven's Gate Mountain], in *LBJJZ*, 2:1255. Except where noted, I have based my translations and discussions on the versions of Li Bo's poetry provided in this anthology, both because of its overall reliability (including the meticulous care taken in providing information about textual variants) and its ready availability.

1. One scholar writing in English who has, to my mind, succeeded in beautifully engaging Li Bo's poetry (and, to the extent possible, biography) in its minutest technical details while sustaining—and even enhancing—our appreciation of his work's impression of exhilarating unfetteredness is Elling O. Eide. See his article "On Li Po" in Wright and Twitchett, *Perspectives on the T'ang*.

2. In the dissertation on which this study is based (*Transformation and Imitation: The Poetry of Li Bai*) and in articles I have published in the interim, I have consistently employed the term "immediacy." See especially "Immediacy and Allusion in the Poetry of Li Bo," revised here for inclusion as chapter 5. A detailed account of its meaning in this tradition is also offered by Michael Fuller in his article, "Pursuing the Complete Bamboo in the Breast: Reflections on a Classical Image for Immediacy." See also David Palumbo-Liu's book, *The Poetics of Appropriation: The Literary Theory and Practice of Huang Tingjian*, for a discussion of the "Illusion of Immediacy" in the work of that late Tang poet.

3. For detailed discussions of the tradition of reading the "Great Preface," see Steven Van Zoeren, *Poetry and Personality: Reading, Exegesis, and Hermeneutics in Traditional China;* Stephen Owen, *Traditional Chinese Poetry and Poetics: Omen of the World;* and Pauline Yu, *The Reading of Imagery in the Chinese Tradition*, 44–83. See also Owen's annotated translation in his *Readings in Chinese Literary Thought*, 37–56.

4. For an elucidation of the "expressionist" theory implied in the "Great Preface," see James J. Y. Liu, *Chinese Theories of Literature*, 63–87.

5. E. Shan Chou has written an analogous study of the critical history of Du Fu: *Reconsidering Tu Fu: Literary Greatness and the Cultural Context*. Of particular interest is her concluding chapter, "Sincerity Reconsidered," 197–207.

6. Tradition attributes the coining of this epithet to He Zhizhang (659–

ca. 744), a scholar and poet who held a number of high-ranking positions in the Tang court. According to one legend, as recorded in the "Lofty and Sublime" chapter of the Tang dynasty anthology of remarks on poetry, *Benshishi*, when Li was visiting the capital in 742, Minister He paid him a visit, interested in meeting this already well-known poet. Li showed him his *yuefu* "Shudao Nan" [The road to Shu is hard] and it was upon reading this poem that He Zhizhang supposedly dubbed Li Bo the "Banished Immortal." See Meng Qi's *Benshishi* in *LDSHXB*, 1:14. Other early sources, such as Fan Chuanzheng's tomb inscription for Li Bo (see *LBJJZ*, 2:1781) and Liu Xu's *Jiu Tangshu* 15:190b.5053–5054, concur in attributing the invention to He, but do not associate the event with "The Road to Shu Is Hard," the dating of which is much debated.

7. Culler, 196.

8. Plaks, 44–46.

9. Benjamin I. Schwartz's early observations about the bipolar nature of Confucian values seem especially prescient now. See Schwartz, "Some Polarities in Confucian Thought," 50–62.

10. Yuan Zhen, "Tang gu gongbu yuanwailang Du jun muximing," in *Yuan Changqing ji* 56.277.

11. *Jiu Tang shu*, 15:190b.5054–5057.

12. In Yuan Zhen's words, "He attained the form-and-force *(tishi)* of [poetry] ancient and modern, and brought together the particularities of each individual." See again his funerary inscription for Du Fu, "Tang gu gongbu," 277. For the earliest remark concerning Du Fu's reputation as "poet-historian" *(shishi)*, see Meng Qi's *Benshishi, j.* 1.

13. Plaks, 48.

14. Scarry, 29.

15. Ibid., 47–48. Emphasis mine.

16. Owen, *Readings*, 590. I have here substituted the Pinyin romanization system for Owen's use of Wade-Giles.

17. See ibid., 425.

18. See Cheng, 45–46.

19. The *Shuowen* definition of *"xu"* is "large hill," and, more specifically, a large administrative district. See Xu Shen, *Shuowen jiezi zhu*, 390. The *Hanyu dazidian* further remarks that the practice of constructing dwellings inside of hills may have been the source for the eventual development of its sense of "void" or "empty space."

20. Wu Qiao, *Weilu shihua*, 1.10.

21. As stated by Zhao Cigong (fl. 1201–1204) in his *Du Gongbu Caotang ji* (Notes on Du Fu's "Thatched hut"), 42.10a.

22. Owen, *Great Age*, 120–121.

23. This view is explicit in Wu Guoping, "Li Du shige bijiao pingshu," 101–121.

24. For all of Li Bo's legendary indescribability, the libraries are full of relevant material, ranging from pithy one-liners scattered throughout poetry anthologies to extended essays in the vast body of extemporaneous writings on poetry known as *shihua*. Needing both a guide and some limits in navigating through

these writings, I have been greatly aided by two important sources that have appeared in recent years: the two-volume anthology of his works, *LBJJZ;* and *LBZLHB.* This latter, a collection of criticism, anecdotes, poetry, and commentary relevant to Li Bo, covers the period from the Jin (1115–1234) through the Qing dynasty (1644–1911). While the poetry anthology was particularly useful in identifying reactions to specific poems, and also had the advantage of including prefaces, commentary, and essays written during the Tang and Song dynasties, the *LBZLHB* provided me with a clearer sense of chronological developments during the subsequent late imperial period.

25. By "literary writing," I refer to both poetry and prose, and in doing so follow the precedent set by Peter Bol, as well as Charles Hartman and William Nienhauser. See Bol's justification for this practice in *"This Culture of Ours,"* 24–25. Bol cites both Hartman and Nienhauser's translation of *guwen* as "literature of Antiquity." See Hartman, 14; and Nienhauser et al., *Liu Tsung-yuan,* 19.

26. Bol, 125.

27. Adele Austin Rickett, "The Anthologist as Literary Critic in China"; Pauline Yu, "Poems in Their Place: Collections and Canons in Early Chinese Literature"; Mark E. Francis, "Canon Formation in Traditional Chinese Poetry: Chinese Canons, Sacred and Profane."

28. See also John B. Henderson, *Scripture, Canon, and Commentary: A Comparison of Confucian and Western Exegesis.*

29. Herrnstein Smith, 5–39.

30. Van Zoeren, 6.

31. For a discussion of the motives inspiring Song canonization of Tang poets, see Owen, "Ruined Estates: Literary History and the Poetry of Eden." See also Pauline Yu, 194–195, and Francis, 69.

32. Herrnstein Smith, 8.

33. Gadamer, 255–256.

34. There appears to be an interesting connection between the suasive powers of these mythologized historical figures and Herbert Fingarette's earlier arguments for the sacredness of Confucian texts. See his *Confucius—The Secular as Sacred.*

35. Harold Bloom, *Anxiety of Influence.*

36. Owen, *Great Age,* 137; Allen, especially 165–168.

37. Owen, *Great Age,* 184.

38. I do not intend, however, to minimize the important distinction between folk and literary *yuefu.* For a cogent reassertion of their differences and a useful bibliography of previous discussions of this question, see Cai Zongqi, "Dramatic and Narrative Modes of Presentation in Han Yüeh-fu."

39. See Allen, especially 64–102. See also Frankel, "The Development of the Han and Wei Yueh-fu as a High Literary Genre."

40. Zhong Rong, for example, asks in his introduction to the *Shipin,* "When striving to sing out one's emotive nature, what good are allusions?" In He Wenhuan, *LDSH,* 1:4. For studies of the *Shipin,* see John Timothy Wixted, "The Nature of Evaluation in the *Shih-p'in.*" Note, too, Wixted's point that Zhong Rong was not strict in applying this criterion in his ranking of poets (241). See also Yeh

Chia-ying and Jan Walls, "Theory, Standards, and Practice of Criticizing Poetry in Chung Hung's *Shih p'in.*"

41. For a detailed discussion of the distinction between topical and textual allusion as used in the Chinese poetic tradition, as well as the important function allusion played in T'ang cultural and political life in general, see David Lattimore, "Allusion in T'ang Poetry." See also James Hightower's taxonomy of allusion in Chinese poetry in his article "Allusion in the Poetry of T'ao Ch'ien."

42. "At Jinxiang, Saying Farewell to Wei Ba, Who is Going to the Western Capital," *LBJJZ*, 2:988–989. My translation of the third couplet is borrowed from David Hinton's translation of the same poem. For this and other excellent translations of Li Bo's poetry, see his *Selected Poems of Li Po*.

Chapter 1 Finding Substance in Emptiness

1. Lu Ji, "Wenfu," in *Wenxuan*, 17.1a–10a.

2. Cai Zongqi, "Wenxin diaolong," especially 326–330.

3. Stephen Owen has most famously rendered a portrait of Li Bo as intentionally projecting a varied range of personae in his essay "Li Po: A New Concept of Genius" in *Great Age*, 109–143.

4. In this case, it may be the exception of Yu-kung Kao and Tsu-lin Mei's close analysis of Li Bo's exceptional quatrain "Jade Steps Plaint" (in their jointly authored "Meaning, Metaphor, and Allusion") that proves the rule. After I presented a paper on Li Bo's *Gufeng* at the 1999 annual meeting of the American Association of Chinese and Comparative Literature in Vienna, a scholar from Hong Kong privately commented that it is better not to analyze Li Bo's poetry so closely, for what is best about his work cannot be grasped in this way.

5. See Budick and Iser, xii.

6. See Su Shi's "Shu xue Taibai shi" in *Su Shi wenji*, 67.2098.

7. Most of Du Fu's poems dedicated to Li Bo have been conveniently collected and reprinted in *LBJJZ*, 2:1833–1837.

8. Yuan Zhen, "Tang gu gongbu yuanwailang Du jun muximing," in *Yuan Changqing ji*, 56.277. Yuan's statement, however, has been disputed by later critics. The Ming author Hu Yinglin, for example, suggests that, because Li Bo kept his distance from Du Fu, and Du Fu expressed avid admiration for quite a few other poets of his day, the image of them existing as a pair must have begun after their deaths. See Hu Yinglin, *Shi sou*, "Outer Chapters," 3.180.

9. Wang's insistence that he doesn't have the expertise to judge poetry is accompanied by a thorough account of the comparisons others have made, as well as by quotations from the works of both Li and Du. See his "Heke Li Du shiji xu," in *LBJJZ*, 2:1798–1799.

10. *LTBQJ*, 3:1685–1686.

11. Guo, 306–328.

12. Hu Yinglin, *Shi sou*, "Inner Chapters," 3.50.

13. Ibid., 4.70.

14. For a brief comparison of the different versions of this story, see James J. Y. Liu, *Chinese Theories of Literature*, 63–87.

15. See Wu Guoping, 101.

16. Yuan Zhen, "Tang gu gongbu yuanwailang Du jun muximing," in *Yuan Changqing ji*, 56.277.

17. Luo Zongqiang (7) points out the injustice of claiming that Li Bo's *yuefu* are "almost on a par" with those of Du Fu, and of implying by omission that Li Bo was not even a contender in the composition of regulated poetry.

18. Bo Juyi, "Yu Yuan jiu shu" in *Bo Juyi ji*, 3:961.

19. *Bo Juyi ji*, 1:319.

20. Jiang, 142.

21. Cited and translated in Bol, 125.

22. Han Yu's "Letter in Reply to Li I" is a central document for those who want to understand his ideas about the practical relationship between past works and the act of composition. See Gao Buying, *Tang Song wen juyao*, 1:199–203 or *Han Yu quanji jiao zhu*, 3:1455–1459; also Hartman's translation and discussion in *Han Yü*, 242–246.

23. While Charles Hartman, who coined this term for the title of his study of Han, referred primarily to Han's quest for unifying the practice of literature and the Confucian way, I borrow it here to signify Han's efforts to solve this other, closely related, paradox.

24. *Han Yu quanji jiao zhu*, 2:703–709.

25. The Song Dynasty critic Hong Mai, in his 1197 collection of extemporaneous notes on miscellaneous subjects, the *Rongzhai suibi*, offers the following comment on Han Yu's remarks concerning the Li-Du discussion: "The coda of the 'Biography of Du Fu' in the *New Tang History* says: 'It is reasonable to say that Han Yu is meticulous in his essays.' So when, in his poem, he alone promotes [both poets], proclaiming, 'Li and Du's writings endure,/Their incandescent rays thousands of meters long,' it is truly reliable. When I read Han's poetry, [I notice that] he mentions Li and Du very often."

The author goes on to cite six poems in which Han places the two poets on a par. I suggest that Han is being cited as an authority to counter the entire practice of ranking Li and Du. See Hong Mai, *Rongzhai suibi*, 3.512.

26. Han Yu's willingness to use Daoist imagery here—and, indeed, his positive evaluation of Li Bo—should not be seen as anomalous. This surprising suppleness on the part of the famed critic of Buddhism and Daoism is actually quite congruent with what Ying-shih Yü has described as Han's larger contribution to the early foundations of Song Neo-Confucianism, that is, his creative synthesis of the "negative" criticism of Buddhism and Daoism with the "positive" efforts to revive the Confucian Dao. As Yü puts it, under the growing pressure of the otherworldly orientation offered by Chan Buddhism, "Han Yu clearly showed a way to return to this world without abandoning the other world which had been all along the main attraction of Buddhism to the Chinese."

I would add that the same syncretic nimbleness exhibited by Han Yu— the same creative spirit that set in motion the eventual development of Neo-Confucian thought in the Song and Ming dynasties—enabled the critics I discuss to sustain the bipolar plenitude of Li and Du. See Ying-shih Yü, esp. 163–169.

27. As Pi Rixiu puts it, "The style of [poetic] composition during Xuanzong's reign was greatly influenced by Jian'an [poetic] form; those who discuss this pro-

mote Li Hanlin and Du Gongbu as superior." See his essay "Yingzhou Mengting ji," in *Pizi wen sou*, 70–71.

28. Du Mu, "Xue qing fang Zhao Gu jie xi suo ju san yun" [When the snow cleared I called upon Zhao Gu's dwelling west of the street: Three rhymes], in *QTS*, 521.5960.

29. Li Shangyin, "Five Pieces on Mancheng: No. 2," in *QTS*, 540.6216.

30. Wu, especially 106–114.

31. Echoing Peter Bol, I use the term "movement" here advisedly, in recognition that there was not yet, at the time of Ouyang Xiu's writing, a sense of any coherent, consistent movement.

32. Although much has been made of Ouyang's supposed preference for Li Bo over Du Fu, my own readings suggest that he appreciated each on his own terms. For one view of this question, see Luo, 10. It is interesting to note that, while Luo Zongqiang subscribes to the view that Ouyang preferred Li, the examples he cites suggest a more balanced evaluation. Having recognized this contradiction, he simply—and somewhat evasively—concludes, "But, in fact, Ouyang's relative appreciation of Li's poetry over Du's poetry is nothing more than a question of taste, and in no way represents a deeply considered critique."

33. Liu Ban, *Zhongshan shihua*, 6.

34. *Ouyang Xiu quanji*, 1:1.38.

35. Ibid., 2.5.113.

36. According to Wang Yunxi, for example, the disparity in the evaluations of Li Bo appearing in Liu Xu's *Jiu Tangshu* [Old Tang history] and Ouyang Xiu and Song Shi's revised *Xin Tangshu* [New Tang history] can be explained in precisely these terms. That is, the Five Dynasties contributors to the *Jiu Tangshu*, in their appreciation of parallel prose and formally regulated prose and poetry, were motivated to adopt, however indirectly, Yuan Zhen's relatively deprecatory view of Li Bo, whereas the *fugu* aesthetics of Ouyang and company ensured a more positive reception of Li. See Wang Yunxi, "Liang 'Tangshu' dui Li Bo de bu tong pingjia."

37. According to Craig Fisk, "Far more remarks were devoted to Tu Fu than to any other poet in the poetry criticism of this period, as witnessed by collections such as Hu Tzu's *T'iao-hsi yü-yin ts'ung-hua*, Ts'ai Meng-pi's *Ts'ao-t'ang shih-hua* [Criticism of the poet of the grass cottage], and Chang Chieh's *Sui-han t'ang shih-hua* [Criticism of poetry by a man in a cold season]. Ko Li-fang's *Yün-yü yang-ch'iu* [Annals of verse], dating from the early twelfth century, also gives more space to Tu Fu than to any other poet in what is probably the most extensive collection of criticism by any Sung author." See his essay "Literary Criticism," in Nienhauser, 54.

38. See also Yoshikawa, 122–130. But even Huang Tingjian was openly opposed to ranking the two poets. In a frequently cited evaluation of Li Bo, he states: "In my criticism of Li Bo's poetry, I liken it to the Yellow Emperor playing music in the wilderness of Dongting Lake. [His music] has neither head nor tail, and demonstrates little concern for the usual. This is not something that can be formulated by the plodding pedant. When my friend, Huang Jie, read 'Treatise on the Ranking of Li and Du,' he said, 'In discussing writing, this is precisely what

one should not do.' I take this to be a knowledgeable pronouncement." See his "Ti *Li Bo shi cao hou*," in *Huang Tingjian xuanji*, 429.

39. Luo Zongqiang (11), for example, argues that the first mention of this edition occurs in a comment by Hui Hong (1071–1128) who would have seen it only several decades after its appearance, during which time it might have been altered.

40. Ma Duanlin, *Wenxian tongkao*, 248.1957.

41. Hui Hong, *Lengzhai yehua*, 5.43.

42. Xie Anshi (320–385), also known as Xie An, rose to prominence as a high-ranking Jin dynasty official, but only after having spent much of his life (until the age of forty) in leisurely retirement in the Eastern Mountains (in modern-day Zhejiang province). He is often referred to in literature as exemplary in combining both literary and martial skills, and for his free and unrestrained behavior. This passage refers to his days in the Eastern Mountains, when he was always accompanied by a singing girl. See Liu Yiqing, *Shishuo xinyu*, "Chapter 7: Shijian," §21, 1:223, and Mather's translation in Liu I-ch'ing, *Shih-shuo hsin-yü*, 207.

43. Chen Shan, *Menshi xinhua*, A:3.26.

44. One of the more vehement judges of Li Bo's moral qualities was Su Shi's brother, Su Che (1039–1112), who plainly stated: "Li Bo's poems are in keeping with his person: impetuous and unbridled, all flower and no fruit, enamored of affairs and renown, without any understanding of where to find righteousness or principle." Su goes on to condemn Li's careless behavior at court and his decision to follow the rebel Yongwang, concluding, "Today when I read his poems, I find them to be in keeping with [that behavior]. . . . Du Fu has a good and just heart, which Li Bo does not approach." See his "Five Flaws of Poetry" ["Shibing wushi"], in Su Che, *Luancheng ji*, 3:8.1553.

45. Lu You, *Lao xue an biji*, 6.6.

46. In *Tiaoxi yuyin conghua*, Hu Zi brought together, and usually commented on, notes and commentaries that had been made by other critics in reference to poetic works organized chronologically from the *Shijing* through the Northern Song.

47. I have been unable to identify this particular work. The *SKQS* contains a short work of the same title, but it is written by Yao Xuan (968–1020), not Wang Dingguo.

48. Hu Zi, 6.4b–5a.

49. Li Gang, *Liang Xi xiansheng wen ji*, 9.16a–16b.

50. As glossed by Stephen Owen, *zhi* signifies "'content,' 'substance' in a piece of writing, as opposed to *wen*, 'pattern.' [*Zhi*] is also used to characterize style, in which case it is something that is 'plain,' 'direct,' and treats the heart of the matter with a minimum of elaboration and ornament. [*Zhi*] exists in the world and is usually not 'content' in the sense of authorial intent or concept. . . . [*zhi*] are 'the facts.'" But, as Owen elsewhere points out, the relation between the two, while diachronic, is not purely oppositional. Rather, *wen* is the organic, exterior manifestation of *zhi*. See Owen, *Readings*, 114–115, 585.

51. Li Gang, "Du *Sijia shixuan* hou" [After reading *The selected poems of the Four Poets*] in *Liang Xi xiansheng wen ji*, 162.3a–3b.

52. In a related comment, Huang Che (1124 *jinshi*), a contemporary of Li Gang and Wang Anshi, goes so far as to compare Du Fu to Mencius. He writes, "I would submit that Old Du resembles Mencius, for he follows his [original] heart/mind." See Huang Che, *Gongxi shihua*, 1.6.

53. Li Gang, *Liangxi xiansheng wen ji*, 17.4b.

54. This refers to a group of seven poems, traditionally attributed to the Western Han heroes Su Wu and Li Ling, anthologized in the *Wenxuan*. Although modern scholars now recognize that this attribution is false, these poems were traditionally held to have been exchanged between the two men, and were regarded not only as among the earliest examples of five-character lyric poetry, but also as the embodiment of its aesthetic ideals of simplicity, naturalness, and understated resonance.

55. Cao Zhi (192–232) and Liu Zhen (d. 217) both belonged to the group of poets known as the Seven Masters of the Jian'an Era, celebrated for their practice of a poetics that was unornamented and highly individual. Its language was characterized by a virile directness, and its subject matter reflected the instability of the disintegrating Han dynasty at the turn of the third century.

56. Tao Qian (365–427) and Xie Lingyun (385–443) are often cited as the exemplary pair of the development of nature poetry during the Six Dynasties period. While Tao is thought of as the "poet of field and garden" and Xie is recognized as the "poet of mountain and water," together they represent the practice of using elements of landscape to express their own spiritual concerns.

57. Su Shi, *Su Dongpo ji*, 1:22.

58. Hu Zi, *Tiaoxi yuyin conghua*, A:1.3b–4a.

59. Ge Lifang, in a long passage that cites Du Mu's hyperbolic praise of Du Fu, concludes, "Thus, in the Tang, there was only this one [poet]; how could [Li] Bai even hope to [compete]?" See his *Yunyu yangqiu*, 1.4.

60. Or, in his own words, "After I'd perused Li Bo's *Gufeng* and Du Fu's *Outi*, I realized that the sources of the two masters extend far indeed." Ge Lifang, *Yunyu yangqiu*, 3.2.

61. He Jing, "Yu Qian Yanju lun shi shu" in *He Wenzhong gong ji*, 10.5a.

62. Zhu Xi, *Zhuzi yulei*, 8:140.5342.

63. Ibid., 5354.

64. For a cogent elucidation of Zhu Xi's attitude toward study and its potential influence on moral development and social worth, see Gardner, especially 35–56.

65. Yan Yu, *Canglang shihua jiaoshi*, 5, as translated in Owen, *Readings*, 406.

66. Yan Yu, *Canglang shihua jiaoshi*, 166.

67. See Zhao Cigong, *Du Gongbu Caotang ji*, 42.10a.

68. See Luo Dajing, *Helin yulu*, 6.341.

69. Zhu Yao, *Gufu bianti*, 7.7b.

70. For a brief discussion of the ambiguity of "*qi*" (strange) when applied to experiences in the natural world, see Zeitlin, especially the introduction.

71. Yan Yu, *Canglang shihua jiaoshi*, 168. Interestingly, the editors of this edition find a precedent for this expression in the Tang poet Wang Changling's (ca. 690–ca. 756) statement, "Wang Wei's poetry is the Son of Heaven; Du Fu's poetry is the Prime Minister" (169).

72. Chen Yiceng, as cited in *LBJJZ*, 2:1872.

73. As Chen puts it, "Guo Pu's conceptualizations were stark and bizarre (*xianguai*), his constructed phrases distilled and round. Li and Du's distilled strangeness (*jingqi*) is all derived from him." See *LBJJZ*, 2:1860.

74. The Song dynasty critic Zeng Jili, a contemporary of Zhu Xi and sympathetic to the studied ancientness of Huang Tingjian, was among the first to grant this pedigree exclusively to Li Bo: "Of the poets throughout the ages who possess the 'Li Sao' form, there is only Li Bo; even Old Du does not resemble the [poet of the] 'Sao.'" Then, after quoting both "Yuanbieli" and "Minggao ge," Zeng concludes, "Lines such as these are no different from the 'Sao'" (*Tingzhai shihua*, 25b).

75. Fan Peng, "Li Hanlin shi," *j*. 1, as cited in *LBZLHB*, 64.

76. As Gao Bing puts it, "Among these are one or two accomplished masters whose unique position was at odds with their times, and so I did not place them in chronological order." *Tangshi pinhui* ("Fanli"), 1:14.

77. Ibid., ("Wuyan gushi xumu"), 1:47.

78. Insofar as the sage is one who acquaints himself thoroughly with the classics and takes care to interpret them by his own lights, free from the influences of received tradition. See Gardner, 52–56.

79. Gao Bing, *Tangshi pinhui* (Qiyan gushi xumu), 267.

80. Ibid., (Wuyan lüshi xumu), 2:506.

81. As in Gao's discussion of long five-character old-style poems, where he quotes Yuan Zhen in extolling Du Fu's merits, and repeats Yan Yu's ranking of Du Fu, Li Bo, and Han Yu (*Tangshi pinhui* ["Wuyan gushi xumu: changpian"]), 1:53.

82. Ibid., ("Qiyan gushi xumu"), 268.

83. Li Dongyang, *Huailutang shihua*, 4a–4b.

84. Li's reputation for speedy composition, however, does not impress Li Dongyang as being inherently more "authentic" than Du Fu's more painstaking method. After repeating the lore about Li Bo's ability (especially under the influence of alcohol) to write a perfect poem swiftly, and about Du Fu's correction-filled manuscripts, Li Dongyang declares: "But the two masters are equal in renown and none can rank them. As for those few who differ from this [opinion], Han Yu had a saying: 'The mass of people in this world are fools; how can one rely on them to belittle and demean [others]?' *In any case, why must poetry be discussed in terms of the slowness or rapidity of its composition?*" In *Huailutang shihua*, 34b.

85. Yang Shen, *Zongzuan Sheng'an heji*, 124.11a.

86. Lu Ji's "Wenfu" is not only the first extended account of the poetic process, but also the first to use the spirit journey (*shenyou*) as the primary figure for describing the workings of that process. But it was Liu Xie who, alluding specifically to the *Zhuangzi*, attempts to develop *shen* into a full-fledged literary concept in chapter 26 of his *Wenxin diaolong*, "Shensi" [Spirit thought].

87. We know, for example, that Zhu Xi, for all his advocacy of an "investigation of things" (*gewu*), which presupposed a clear distinction between mind and principle, was hardly unaware of the power of subjectivity. One expression of his recognition that mind directly influenced the results of its investigations is found

in his *Jin si lu* [Reflections on things at hand], where he declares: "When I was twenty, I interpreted the meanings of the Classics in no other way than I do today. But when I come to think of it, I feel that today they mean something quite different from what they meant at the time when I was young." This flexibility finds practical expression in Zhu's positive evaluation of Li Bo. See Zhu Xi, *Jin si lu,* 3.2a. (as translated by Wing-tsit Chan in Zhu Xi, *Reflections on Things at Hand,* III:8.91).

88. Yang Shen, *Zongzuan Sheng'an heji,* 149.9b–10a.

89. For a general discussion of a possible link between the characterological approach to literature and the emergence of Lu-Wang Neo-Confucian thought, see Ching-I Tu's essay, "Neo-Confucianism and Literary Criticism in Ming China." Tu draws an analogy between Wang Yangming's (and his disciple Wang Ji's) formulation of "innate knowledge" *(liangzhi),* and the Ming dynasty development of the literary notion of "original color" *(bense).*

90. Fang Hongjing aligns Du with the "Airs" and "Elegantiae" of the *Shijing,* and Li with the "Li Sao" and the *Wenxuan.* See Fang Hongjing, *Qianyi lu,* 9.20a.

91. The expression *"yima qianyan"* is associated with the Jin dynasty writer Yuan Hong (328–376), most famously author of the *Hou Han shu* [Later Han history]. An entry in the *Shishuo Xinyu* tells of how Yuan, accompanying the grand marshal, Huan Wen, on an expedition, dashed off, on command, a beautiful and brilliant piece of writing, seven pages long, while propped against his horse. See Liu Yiqing, *Shishuo Xinyu,* 4:§96; Mather, 140–141.

92. Yang Shen, *Yang Sheng'an waiji,* as cited in *LBJJZ,* 2:1874.

93. The Ming dynasty saw the production of several anthologies bringing together the poetry of Li and Du. For a description and a history of some of these editions, see Zhan Ying, 8:4601–4603, 4606–4630.

94. Li Lian, "Tang Li Bo shi xu," in *LBZLHB,* 1:303.

95. The expression "changed 'Airs' and changed 'Elegantiae'" *(bianfeng bianya)* derives from the "Preface to the 'Guanju'" in the *Shijing,* and refers to the natural way in which a decline in the moral direction of government makes itself heard in the music and poetry of the people. As explained by Van Zoeren, Zhu Xi took issue with the prefaces, and argued that the changed, or debauched, *Odes* were deliberately included as a negative example. As translated by Van Zoeren, Zhu Xi wrote, "The reason that Confucius included both [normative and debauched Odes] ... is because he wanted to make apparent the good and bad mores [behind the Odes]. The Sage taught people in this way as well" (Van Zoeren, 229; Zhu Xi, *Zhuzi yishu,* 3.32).

96. Li Lian, "Tang Li Bo shi xu," in *LBZLHB,* 1:303.

97. Ibid.

98. Guanxiu (832–913), whose real name was Jiang Deyin, was a monk celebrated for his poetry, calligraphy, and renderings of Buddhist immortals.

99. Xie Zhen, *Siming shihua,* 1.22.

100. Xie Zhen is far from being the first to apply this term to poetry; it appears as early as the writings of Sikong Tu. For a convenient and concise summary of its significance in poetic criticism, see Owen, *Readings,* 351–352,

593–594. François Jullien has written a longer exposition of the closely related term *"fadeur"* (blandness). See his *Eloge de la fadeur.*

101. Xie Zhen, *Siming shihua,* 1.23.

102. Ibid., 2.34.

103. Ibid., 1.26.

104. Ibid., 3.74.

105. Tu Long, *Youquanji,* 23.8a–8b.

106. Ibid., *j.* 23.7b.

107. Tu Long, *Hongbaoji,* 17.18a.

108. Ibid., 11.35b.

109. Fang Hongjing, *Qianyi lu,* 11.27b.

110. In translating the term *"qu,"* a central one in Ming criticism, I have attempted to combine its connotations of interest, pleasure, and distinctive essence. See Jonathan Chaves, "The Panoply of Images," especially 345–347, for a discussion of this term and a comparison of its various translations into English.

111. Fang Hongjing, *Qianyi lu,* 12.16a–16b.

112. For a thorough study of Yuan Hongdao's literary thought and its place in Ming literary history, see Chih-p'ing Chou's *Yuan Hung-tao and the Kung-an School,* especially 27–70. See also Richard Lynn, "Alternate Routes to Self-Realization in Ming Theories of Poetry," for a succinct comparison of the Archaists and anti-Archaists of the Ming.

113. Yuan Hongdao, "Da Mei Kesheng kaifu," in *Yuan Zhonglang quanji,* "Chidu," 37.

114. Li Zhi, *Fenshu, Xu Fenshu,* 5.210–211.

115. See Kang-i Sun Chang, *The Late-Ming Poet Ch'en Tzu-lung,* for a full-length study of Chen Zilong's work as a compelling unity of loyalist political conviction and aesthetic principles.

116. Hu Zhenheng, *Tangyin guiqian,* 25.219.

117. Wang Shizhen, *Yiyuan zhiyan,* 4.3a.

118. Chen Zilong's interest in the balanced expression of all literary values is pithily expressed when he says of poetry in general: "If it is too literary, then it will be weak, but if too casual, it will be vulgar; if it is too straightforward, it will be superficial, but if too sturdy, it will be off the mark; if too conforming, it will be derivative, and if too eccentric, it will be uncouth" (Chen Zilong, "Liuzi shi xu" in *Chen Zhongyu ji,* 5.17a).

119. Ibid.

120. It is particularly remarkable that Chen, a Ming loyalist with a deep belief in the notion that poetry should reflect the widespread suffering of his time, did not promote the more socially minded Du Fu over Li Bo, but rather consistently represented them as being of equal value. Perhaps a key to his appreciation for Li Bo lies in what Kang-i Sun Chang (in her book-length study of the poet) and Florence Chia-ying Yeh (in her article "Ch'en Tzu-lung and the Renascence of the Song Lyric") have shown to be his rare interest and talent in combining political concerns with intense emotional expression in poetry. A brief description of Chen Zilong's pivotal role as a transitional poet-thinker is offered in Zhang and Liu, II:278–282.

Chapter 2 To Study the Unlearnable

1. See He Yisun, *Shifa*, in *QSHXB*, 1:135.

2. Among the writers overtly invoking this notion are Shi Runzhang (1619–1683), a well-known poet of Xuancheng often compared to Mei Yaochen for his social awareness and unpretentious verse, and the playwright You Tong (1618–1704). After quoting Mencius and then enumerating a wide range of emotional states and their corresponding poetic styles, Shi states: "In regarding the collected works of Tao [Qian], Wei [Yingwu], Wang [Wei], Meng [Haoran], Li [Bo], Du [Fu], Han Tuizhi [Han Yu], Meng Dongye [Meng Jiao], and Su Zizhan [Su Shi], one can distinguish their persons." See Shi Runzhang, "Chucun shiji xu" [Preface to *The Chu Village poetry anthology*] in *Shi Yushan ji*, 4.79. You Tong, perhaps truer to his vocation as playwright, divides pairs of Six Dynasties and Tang poets between those whose characters are *dong* (dynamic) and *jing* (quiescent). See "Cao Zixian nancun shi xu" in You Tong, *Xitang zazu*, A.32.

3. One example appears in Ying Shi's preface to his *Li Du shiwei*, as cited in *LBZLHB*, 2:688–690. See also another preface to the same volume by Ding Guyun, cited in *LBZLHB*, 2:700. According to Zhan Ying, the *Li shiwei* and the *Du shiwei* were originally published separately, sometime around 1679, but the only extant edition is a jointly published volume, currently stored in Chengdu. For a detailed description of this edition, see Zhan Ying, 8:4660–4664.

4. Wang Fuzhi, *Jiangzhai shihua*, 2.§29.156.

5. In *Jiangzhai shihua* 2.§2.146, Wang states, "The reason Li Bo and Du Fu are acclaimed as great masters is that such a [governing] concept (i.e., *yi*) is absent in less than ten or twenty percent of their poems." Translated by Owen in *Readings*, 457.

6. This trend has been cogently traced by On-cho Ng in his article, "A Tension in Ch'ing Thought." See especially 567–570 for his discussion of the thought of Wang Fuzhi. For an overall study situating Wang's aesthetic views within the history of Chinese philosophical thought, see François Jullien, *Procès ou création: une introduction à la pensée chinoise: essai de problématique interculturelle*.

7. See He Yisun, *Shifa*, in *QSHXB*, 1:142. Wang Shizhen also takes issue with the claim that most pairings of poets are founded on the principle of contrast, stating, "Of all the writers [He Yisun] mentions, only Li and Du constitute radically different schools; the others are not so distinct one from the other." See his *Daijingtang shihua*, 1.38–39. A similar sentiment is expressed by one of Li's great admirers, Tian Wen (1635–1704), in his *Guhuantang ji, j.* 1, in *QSHXB*, 2:694.

8. See Qian Qianyi, *Muzhai youxue ji*, 17.12a.

9. Zhang here makes reference to Su Shi's well-known statement describing the Tang poet and painter Wang Wei. See Zhang Dai, "Yu Bao Yanjie" [To Bao Yanjie] in *Langhuan wenji*, 152.

10. See Chen Hongxu, *Chen Shiye xiansheng ji/Shizhuang chuji*, 4.46a.

11. One earlier example occurs in the critic Lu Shiyong's (17 c.) discussion of *yun* (harmony) in his *Shijing zonglun*. In a variation of the Confucian dictum that for words to "go far" (*yuan*) they must be "patterned" (*wen*), Lu Shiyong contended that for a poem to inspire its readers, the words had to be harmonious (*yun*), and that harmony had to be a natural reflection of true feelings. As he puts

it, "That by which poetry can inspire people is its veracity of feeling and the harmony of its words. What supplies the smile that makes [the reader] joyful, and the tears that make him sad, is veracity of feeling. What produces [the feeling of] awe upon hearing bells and drums and [the feeling of] mystery upon hearing reeds and flutes is the harmony of sound. That is why, in feeling, [the poet] strives for veracity, and in harmony, he strives for resonance. These two words suffice to completely express the Way of poetry." See Lu Shiyong, *Shijing zonglun*, 9b.

12. Translated by Owen, *Readings*, 470.

13. See He Yisun, *Shifa*, in *QSHXB*, 1:167.

14. Ibid., 178–179.

15. See Chaves, "The Panoply of Images," for a discussion of the relationship between flaws and genuineness or naturalness in Ming literary theory.

16. See Ye Xie, *Yuanshi*, "Inner Chapter, II," 587. For an alternative reading of this passage, and of these terms in particular, see Karl-Heinz Pohl, especially 10–11.

17. For a detailed discussion of this aspect of Ye's thought, see again Pohl's discussion of Ye's "Confucian orientation" (and its Neo-Confucian methodology), in Pohl, especially 28–31; and Owen, *Readings*, especially 528–538.

18. Ye Xie is referring here to Du Fu's poem "Dongri Luochengbei ye xuanyuan huangdi miao" [A visit to the Laozi temple on a winter's day in northern Luoyang], which contains the following couplet: "Green glazed roof tiles beyond the first chill, / Golden pillars beside the One Breath." *Qian zhu Du shi*, 2:276. For an alternative translation and discussion, see Pohl, 25–27.

19. Adapted from Owen's translation in *Readings*, 532.

20. Ye Xie identifies the mark of authenticity—and the sign of greatness—as lying in a poetic oeuvre's ability to reflect its author's *mianmu*—his countenance or person—fully. Li Bo's poetry is recognized as bearing this mark, but so is that of Du Fu, Han Yu, and Su Shi. Ye devotes several sentences of this passage to Du, Han, and Su, but he seems to mention Li only in passing. See *Yuanshi*, "Outer Chapter, I," 596–597.

21. Ibid., "Outer Chapter, II," 603.

22. Ibid.

23. Ibid.

24. For a rich discussion of this term, see Richard Lynn's "Orthodoxy and Enlightenment," especially 247–253. Lynn's analysis breaks this term down into three related ideas, which he sums up this way: "Sometimes it refers only to personal tone, sometimes to intuitive cognition and intuitive control, sometimes to intuitive control and personal tone, and sometimes to all these at once" (253).

25. Wang humorously writes, "I have jestingly discussed the works of Tang poets as follows: Wang Wei [spoke] 'Buddhese,' Meng Haoran—Boddhisatvese ... Li Bo and Chang Jian—'Flying-Immortalese,' Du Fu—'Sage-ese,' etc." See his *Daijingtang shihua*, 1:1.42.

26. *Daijingtang shihua*, 1:3.70. Apparently responding to someone's request to elucidate the opening lines of this section, the eleventh category of Sikong Tu's "Twenty-Four Categories of Poetry," Wang quotes in full one poem by each of the two poets. Sikong Tu's description of this category of implicitness or reserve

has been aptly translated by Owen in *Readings*, 326: "It does not inhere in any single word,/Yet the utmost flair is attained." In *LDSH*, 1:40–41.

27. Shen Deqian, *Qi zi shi xuan*, 1a.

28. Ibid., 1b.

29. Ibid., 2a.

30. See Shen Deqian, "Xu Shuangji Baoshanyin xu," in *Guiyu wenchao*, 13.1a.

31. See Shen Deqian, *Shuo shi zui yu*, A.10a.

32. Shen pairs them as both peerless—and distinct—in provoking readers to "lose themselves" (*Shuo shi zui yu*, A.11b) in their works, but similar in that they follow their natures as far as possible, a practice that makes their work inimitable (ibid., A.14a–b).

33. Ibid., B.11b.

34. Ibid., A.16a.

35. See Shen Deqian, *Tangshi biecai ji*, 6.1.

36. See Shen Deqian, *Guiyu wenchao*, 14.2a.

37. As translated by Owen, the concluding paragraph of this chapter reads: "Mountain forests and the marshy banks of rivers are indeed the secret treasure houses of literary throught.... Yet the reason Ch'ü Yüan was able to fully examine the mood of the *Book of Songs* and *Li Sao* was, I am sure, the assistance of those rivers and mountains" (Owen, *Readings*, 285).

38. See Qiao Yi, "Preface to 'The Poems of Xu Zhusu,'" in *Jianxi shuoshi, j.* 1, in *QSHXB*, 1118–1120.

39. Ibid.

40. Ibid.

41. As he put it, "After his [exile in] Kuizhou, [his poetry] naturally went beyond the rules, and [therefore] cannot be studied. Great Confucians freely traverse the expanse of the heavens; as for poetry, when its depths are attained, it is also like this." *Jianxi shuoshi*, A.1081.

42. For a thorough and concise discussion of the rise of "evidential research" (*kaozhengxue*) and its place in Chinese intellectual history, see Mote, 928–935.

43. It might even be argued that, in their unacknowledged but creative implementation of this element of past discourse (especially evident in the case of Li Diaoyuan), these writers mimic Li Bo's own position vis-à-vis his received tradition: the outsider fully apprised of the conventions he inherits and able to apply them in ways that reveal their conventionality.

44. This translation, borrowed from James J. Y. Liu (85–86), is helpful in understanding the significance of the term *"xingling"* in the context of Chinese literary thought as a whole. But it falls short of a satisfying rendering of its nuances, especially as suggested by the combination of the two words *xing* and *ling*. The modern scholar Guo Shaoyu helpfully analyzes the two components of this term, glossing *xing* as "true feelings" (*shigan*) and *ling* as "imagination" (*xiangxiang*). Essentially, this is a blending of the broader qualities of the substantial and the unfounded, or "full" and "empty." He then goes on to pair each of them with a host of more familiar terms, concluding that Yuan Mei's *xingling* doctrine is one that seeks to join fidelity to one's true feelings with a genius

for effortlessly producing new and vital forms of expression. See Guo Shaoyu, 494–497.

45. See Weng Fanggang, "Yu you lun Taibai shi" [To a friend: Discussing Taibai's poetry] in his *Fuchuzhai wenji*, 11.22a–23a.

46. See Weng Fanggang, *Shizhou shihua, j.* 1, in *QSHXB*, 1372.

47. See Li Diaoyuan, *Yucun shihua, j.* B, in *QSHXB*, 1525.

48. See in particular Li Diaoyuan's "Chongke Taibai quanji xu" [Preface to *Li Bo's complete works: Re-edited*] in his *Tongshan wenji*, 5.58–59.

49. As he puts it, "Li's poetry derives from Tao Yuanming, and Du's poetry derives from Yu Zishan [Yu Xin]; I have often held this theory, but others usually doubt it. [They believe that] it is reasonable [to hold that] Du derives from Yu, but Li and Tao seem not even remotely alike. They do not understand that in reading the writings of the ancients, [the essential lies in] observing that place between [the author's] spirit and vital force, and not in *meticulously conforming to the traces of his appearance*. For example,

> You ask for what reason I lodge in the emerald mountains;
> I smile, not answering, my heart at its ease.

> Peach blossoms, flowing water, darkly depart;
> There is another world, not among men.

How could this not be based on [Tao's] 'Peach Blossom Spring'?" See Li Diaoyuan, *Yucun shihua, j.* B, in *QSHXB*, 1525–1526.

50. See Wang Qi, "Ba wu ze," in *LTBQJ*, 3:1689–1694.

51. "Praise and blame" is a term used to describe the rhetoric used— supposedly by Confucius himself—in his edition of the *Shujing [Book of documents]*. In these writings, the Master's judgments were inscribed indirectly, largely through a pattern of omission and inclusion that was thought to transmit the facts in a way that allowed them to speak for themselves.

52. Mote, 929.

53. *Yuxuan Tang Song shichun*, 1.1a–1b.

54. Zhao Yi, *Oubei shihua*, 2.§7.20.

55. Sima Chengzhen was an important literary and religious figure during the Tang and had an especially close relationship with Emperor Xuanzong. See his brief biography in Nienhauser, 719–720.

56. Zhao Yi, *Oubei shihua*, 1.§1.3.

57. Ibid. 3.§1.28.

58. Similar nostalgic claims for the benchmark status of Li and Du and the impossibility of innovating since their appearance in the literary pantheon can be found scattered throughout the *shihua* of this period. For example, one critic, Guan Shiming (1738–1798), also sympathized with Han Yu's plight, saying, "After the demise of Li and Du, the 'right harmony' went awry. [Han] Changli rose up with vigor and was, at first, outstanding, but then exhibited an air of the 'family man': the awkward, guileless ripples he stirred up were too small to reach [the level of Li and Du]." See Guan Shiming, *Du Xueshanfang Tangshi xuli*, "Qigu fanli," 6b.

59. Or, in his words, "Qinglian was banished from the Hanlin academy and returned to the mountains; certainly he could not be without resentment. Never-

theless, his poetry does not reveal feelings of bitterness or frustration" (Zhao Yi, *Oubei shihua*, 1.§10.8).

60. Ibid. A similar demonstration of Li's breadth of spirit is found in another passage as well, concluding that, despite his exile, "his expansive *qi* was as it had always been" (Zhao Yi, *Oubei shihua*, 1.§12.10). A certain bias in both of Zhao's accounts can be detected in his silence concerning the fact that all the poems he cites were composed either for officials at court or for recluses, both of whom were arguably in a position to help Li during his banishment.

61. In the same passage quoted above, Zhao quotes lines from an attribution entitled "Xuechanshi" [On cleansing oneself of slander], and then comments, "Qinglian's breast was vast and capacious. He did not fret over petty grudges. How could he have gone so far as to complain in this way? I fear this is not the authentic brush [of Taibai]." And in another passage in the same *juan*, Zhao expresses his doubt concerning the authenticity of the poem "Shaonian xing" [Song of youth], asking, "Try reading this in light of Qinglian's other poems; do [any of the others] contain this kind of back-country, small-minded air?" (*Oubei shihua*, 1.§12.10).

62. See Zhang Xuecheng, *Wenshi tongyi bubian*, 5, in *CSJCXB*, 5:609.

63. Fang Dongshu, for example, thinking in similar terms, identifies the *nigu* (modeling-after-the-ancients) genre as useful in distinguishing between true and "fake" (*wei*) poetry: "To model [one's poetry] on the ancients (*nigu*) and posit one's own intentions therein (as the Cao's did when they employed the *yuefu* to convey, themselves, the concerns of their day) constitutes one genre. Acceptable, too, are Taibai's *Gufeng* and Qujiang's [Zhang Jiuling] *Ganyu*, in which, in a manner similar to the 'historical mode,' they pour forth what they harbor in their breast. But [for poets] to model [their poetry] on the ancients without positing their own intentions therein, especially literati who are naturally adept at expanding their abilities [to include many types of writing], can only lead people to make fake poetry." However, Fang does seem more tolerant of self-conscious genre affiliation, as long as the expression of intention is authentic. See his *Zhaomei zhanyan*, 1.§112.37.

64. Zhang Xuecheng, *Wenshi tongyi bubian*, 10, in *CSJCXB*, 5:610.

65. Ibid. In a further development of the same theme, Pan Deyu (1785–1839) offers a detailed discussion of how true ancientness is transmitted in one's adherence to "heaven"—to what is natural. This translates into an acceptance of evolution in literary form: "The fact that the *Odes* and the 'Elegantiae' could not but have given rise to the 'Songs of Chu,' and that the 'Songs of Chu' could not but have given rise to Su and Li, are all [manifestations] of heaven. [To know] whether or not a poem is 'ancient,' just see whether it is [in accordance with] heaven." See Pan Deyu, *Li Du shihua*, 1.8a.

66. This expression, which had first been applied to poetry by Yan Yu in a description of Li and Du's poetry, is drawn from a Buddhist tale. It recounts how three animals—a hare, a horse, and a "fragrant elephant"—crossed a river; only the elephant succeeded in crossing the whole way by walking solidly upon the river's bottom, while the rabbit merely floated the whole way and the horse alternated walking and floating. In theological terms, this parable refers to the ele-

phant as possessing the most profound apprehension of the teachings. Likewise, in poetic criticism, the elephant is understood as the poet who is not content to write about the world in its superficial manifestations, but who dares to see beyond appearances. Guan follows this expression with a long series of allusive and imagistic comparisons in a similar vein. See Yan Yu, *Canglang shihua*, 177.

67. See Guan Shiming, *Du Xueshanpang Tangshi xuli*, "Qigu fanli," 6a–6b.

68. For an extended example of Li Zhaoyuan's discussion of rhythm and tone, as well as biographical analysis of Li Bo's poetry, see especially his *Shi'erbifang zalu*, *j.* 8, as cited in *LBZLHB*, 3:1022–1024.

69. Li says, "This description is uniquely applicable to the best poems; those that are of secondary quality do not have to be read this way; and when it comes to inferior poems, a quick reading will suffice" (ibid., 1026).

70. Ibid.

71. Fang Dongshu (1772–1851), for example, writes at length about the importance of various Tang poets' use of connecting particles or "empty words," concluding with the assertion that Li's achievement, the true rigor of his poetics, is to be found herein. According to Fang, "People do not grasp the arduous depths of his intention, the sheer riskiness of his composition, the subtlety of his technical application; they attend only to his choice of expression, [which, they believe] slips into being glib and facile. This was never Taibai's flaw. It was just that latter-day [readers] were unable to master [his techniques], and so it became necessary to censure him." See his comments in *Zhaomei zhanyan*, 20 (*j.* 1).

72. Chen Hang, a renowned poet in his own right, was best known as the author of the *Shibixing jian* in which, among other things, he was the first to assign detailed allegorical significance to Chen Zi'ang's *Ganyu*. For a convenient compilation of Chen Hang's line-by-line treatments of Li Bo's poems, see *LBZLHB*, 3:1152–1155. For Chen Guangpu, author of the *Shiping*, see ibid., 1260–1263; Qiao Songnian, *Luomoting zhaji*, 4.5b–9b, 5.5a–6a. It is interesting to note that these critics tend to insist on the traditional dichotomy between immortal and sage, with all of its usual implications.

73. Here, too, it is useful to cite Fang Dongshu, who repeatedly lauds Li Bo's "immortal's language" (*xianyu*): "Overall, Taibai's poetry and Zhuangzi's prose are alike in their wondrousness (*miao*): meaning carries through when phrases do not, inspiring thoughts without end, like the white clouds in the sky, furling and unfurling, dissolving and reappearing without having any fixed form." *Zhaomei zhanyan*, 249 (*j.* 12). See also other comments on Li Bo, beginning on 248.

Perhaps one of the most interesting examples of the blend of learnability and ineffable sublimity is to be found in Pan Deyu's *Li Du shihua*. Pan, an extremely conservative Confucian critic, vehemently opposed *xingling* discourse, attempting at every turn to refute all past descriptions associating Li Bo with Chan or Taoist notions, especially those surrounding his "immortal" persona. Everywhere he points to examples that demonstrate Li's mastery of past literature and of poetics, citing Zhu Xi as the reader who perhaps best understood Li Bo. Nevertheless, Pan adheres strongly to Li's characterization as "*haoyi*" (free-ranging sublime)—a term most frequently invoked to support his "immortal" identification. See the entire first *juan* of his *Li Du shihua* in his *Yangyi zhai shihua*.

74. See Yao Ying, *Dongming waiji*, 1.12a–b.

75. See Yan Junshou, *Laosheng changtan*, 24a (*CSJCXB*, 159:180).

76. Ibid., 31a (*CSJCXB*, 159:184).

77. See Qian Shirui, *Chang Xingxing zhai wenji, j.* 6, as cited in *LBZLHB*, 3:1203–1204.

78. See Lin Changyi, *Haitian qinsi lu*, 1.4a–b.

79. Zeng Guofan (1811–1872) is typical when he says, in his "Shengze huaxiang ji," "When I [set out to] copy over the [best] poems of all time, from the Wei-Jin period up to the republic, I accept nineteen poets.... And if, among those nineteen, I restrict myself further to just include four of them, then for the Tang [I choose] Li and Du, and for the Song, Su and Huang." In *Zeng Wenzheng gong wenji*, 3.24a–b.

80. Shi Shan, *Jianglu'an zaji*, 2:6.5b–6a.

81. Chen Tingzhuo, *Baiyuzhai cihua*, 7.4b–5a.

82. Lydia Liu identifies Guang Sheng's 1917 essay, which describes the Chinese national character as being self-defeatingly tolerant, as having "[crystallized] all seminal arguments surrounding the notion of national character prior to the May Fourth movement." See her discussion of this essay and of the thought surrounding issues of national character in her *Translingual Practice*, 45–76.

83. Ibid., 235.

84. Levenson, 16.

85. Su Shi uses the term in the first of his poem series, "Mengzhen tongyou Changzhou sengshe" [Traveling together with Meng Zhen to the monk's abode in Changzhou]: "In recent years I've come to see that this is but a floating life / Once again I take off on an *unfettered (langman)* journey of the Wu Gorges." In *Su Dongpo ji*, 1:37–38.

86. According to Bonnie McDougall, Tian Han (1898–1968), whom she identifies as "one of China's leading romanticists," (88) identified several terms that were then in use to translate "romanticism": *langman zhuyi, luoman zhuyi, chuanqi zhuyi*, and *huangdan zhuyi*. The first, writes McDougall, "came from the Japanese *romanshugi* and is a partly phonetic transcription plus the normal translation of "-ism".... T'ien Han urged that in China *lo-man-chu-i* should be generally adopted. At the time when he was writing, this term was not the most popular, partly because it was thought to have too specific a reference to European literary history, and partly because it was mistakenly thought to mean 'exaggerationism'.... The issue was still being debated in *Short Story Monthly* in 1923 (XIV, 2), with *lo-man-chu-i* and *lang-man-chu-i* still as the main contenders; in the 1923 anthology *Critical Essays on New Literature*, both were used" (96). Lydia Liu also characterizes *langman* as a "round-trip loan replacement," a category the identification of which Liu attributes to Victor Mair, used to describe the category of Sino-Japanese-European neologisms composed of "classical Chinese expressions used by the Japanese to translate Western terms that were then imported back into Chinese with a radical change in meaning" (Lydia Liu, 33).

87. Liu describes her adaptation of Gayatri Spivak's term "confrontation" (as opposed to "transition") in describing China's encounter with Western literature

in *Translingual Practice*, 27–32. See also the introduction to Guha and Spivak, *Selected Subaltern Studies*.

88. Liang is quite consistent in considering the imagination to be a central feature of Romanticism, stating elsewhere: "The defining characteristic of Romantic [literature] is in the application of the imagination to invent a world. Of course, it is best when the imagination is applied to the purified aesthetic sensibility" (*Yinbingshi wenji*, 71.49a).

89. Ibid., 71.47b.

90. Ibid.

91. Ibid., 71.48a.

92. See Owen, *Readings*, 585.

93. *Yinbingshi wenji*, 71.48b.

94. Although, as Levenson points out, if Liang eventually banished culture from his concerns, it was probably, paradoxically, "out of concern for his culture" (193).

95. *Yinbingshi wenji*, 71.48b. Liang repeats this sentiment in another essay when he writes, "But how could every single person be like this? It is because most people [cannot invent worlds through their imagination that] they end up walking the path of the bizarre. 'Summoning the Spirit' of the *Chuci* already opened this [path], and half of Taibai's works are of this type. After the Middle Tang, this type of writing grew more plentiful" (*Yinbingshi wenji, j.* 71.49a).

96. It is interesting to note that in recent times, scholars are returning to the traditional "empty" and "full" terminology as a way of accounting for Li's imaginary scenes (as juxtaposed to the real ones described by Du Fu). For a well-developed recent application of these terms, see Yuan Xingpei, "Li Du shige de fengge yu yixiang."

97. For a related discussion of the inappropriateness of the "Romantic" label when applied to classical Chinese poets, see Chaves, "The Expression of Self in the Kung-an School."

98. During a series of study trips over the course of 1984–1985 to some of the places in modern Anhui and Zhejiang that Li Bo frequented in his later life, interviews with local residents—most of whom had memorized, but could not read, Li Bo's works—revealed the persistence of supernatural stories related to Li Bo. Some stories had been formulated during the unlikely period of the Cultural Revolution.

99. Actually, the term *"langman"* frequently appears juxtaposed against *"xianshi,"* another Sino-Japanese-European loanword, designating something like mimetic realism, and used to qualify—not surprisingly—Du Fu. Interestingly, in the late 1950s and 1960s, *xianshi* appeared alone in such essays as those by Lin Keng ("Li Bo shige de xianshixing"), Wang Yao ("Li Bo shige de yishu chengjiu"), and Fan Ning ("Li Bo shige de xianshixing ji qi chuangzuo tezheng"). All three of these essays have been conveniently anthologized in Yu Pingbo's edited volume *Li Bo shi luncong*. As recently as the 1980s, however, surveys of Chinese literature once again designate Li Bo as *langman* and Du Fu as *xianshi*. See, for example, You Guo'en's essays on each of these poets in his *Zhongguo wenxueshi*.

100. For a complete discussion of Li Bo and Qu Yuan as "tragic heroes," see Michelle Yeh, 30–34.

Chapter 3 The Performance of Ancientness in the "Ancient Airs"

1. Xiao Shibin, editor of the Yuan dynasty edition of Li Bo's works, *Fenlei buzhu Li Taibai wenji*, was one of the first to identify this poem as the definitive summary of Li Bo's poetics. Xiao comments, "The *Benshi shihua* states: 'Li Bo's genius is sublime and his vital breath is lofty; and his name is equal with that of Chen Zi'ang, the former and the latter [poets] sharing in moral integrity.' In his discussion of poetry, [Li] writes that, ever since the Qi and Liang [dynasties], [the practice of] ornateness and superficiality has become extreme. [He suggests that] since Shen Xiuwen [Shen Yue, 441–513] expressed his esteem for tonal regulation, if we want to return to the way of the ancients, 'who besides me [is capable]?' Reading this poem, one can perceive Taibai's intention. This is why he has been named among the masters of the Tang poets!" (*LBJJZ*, 1:92).

2. Critics generally agree that these fifty-nine poems were composed at various times throughout Li's life. Their assembly into a group under this title occurred toward the end of Li Bo's life, or even afterward. The modern scholar Ono Jitsunosuke has placed *Gufeng* #2 at about 724, and #58 just three years before Li's death, in 759. He lists twenty-nine of these poems as undatable. See Ono, 11, 993, 1148–1184. For a recent review of the editorial history of the *Gufeng*, see Yu Xianhao, "Lun Li Bo 'Gufeng' wushijiu shou," as well as Zhan Ying, 1:18.

3. Jia Jinhua quotes Hu Zhenheng (1569–1644) as critiquing the separate inclusion of the *Gufeng* in Li Bo's collected works, saying: "As for [the anthology's] generic classification, I especially do not understand why it places the *Gufeng* first, followed by the *yuefu*, then followed again by *Gufeng*" (Jia, 130). While Stephen Owen does not attempt to justify the precise selection of the *Gufeng*, he helpfully reminds his readers that these poems do belong together as "*ku-feng* in the subgeneric sense we have been using the term: *fu-ku* poetry in the style of the Chien-an, Wei, and Chin" (Owen, *Great Age*, 132).

4. *LBJJZ*, 2:1384.

5. Some scholars consider Li Yangbing's creation of a separate section called *Gufeng* as evidence that Li Bo had envisioned their existence as a separate category. See, for example, Qiao Xiangzhong, "Li Bo *Gufeng* kaoxi"; Jia Jinhua, "Li Bo *Gufeng* xinlun," 132.

6. Lu Shiyong, a disgruntled Ming dynasty critic, for example, found the *Gufeng* derivative and superficial. Comparing them with the *Yonghuai* by Ruan Ji, he claims that Li Bo "tries to convey similar [feelings of] bitterness, [but they] are not as deep, nor does the execution [of the poems] achieve the wondrous subtlety of [the *Yonghuai*'s] sinuousness and solidity" (*LBJJZ*, 1:189).

7. See Zhao Yi, *Oubei shihua*, 3.

8. See Qiao Xiangzhong, 17.

9. For comments on the first *Gufeng*, see Xiao Shibin's quotation above in note 1. Xu Zhenqing is cited in the Ming edition of Li's works as saying specifically in regard to *Gufeng* #1, "In this piece, [Li] Bo articulates his own intent." And Hu Zhenheng is inspired by Li's own allusion to Confucius to read this intent as being especially (and perhaps excessively) weighty: "He discusses as a whole the sources of the ancient poetry that came before; his intent is to edit those poems and

bequeath them to posterity, thereby initiating a [new] beginning. The responsibility he assumes is not slight" (all cited in *LBJJZ*, 1:92).

10. See Wang Yunxi's introduction to *LBJJZ*, 1:17. For a discussion of the history of this association, see Pauline Yu, *Reading of Imagery*, 175.

11. In fact, according to Steven Van Zoeren, only the latest stratum of the *Analects*—that part least likely to have any direct link to the biographical Confucius—talks about the *Odes* as having a proper place in the Confucian curriculum. The most famous reference is probably 17.9, translated here by Van Zoeren: "The Master said, 'Little ones, how is it that you have not studied the Odes? The Odes can be used to stimulate (moral insight), to observe (character), to reaffirm one's commitment to the group, or to express resentment. Close at hand one can serve his father and farther away his lord; and you can increase your acquaintance with the names of birds, beasts, plants, and trees'" (Van Zoeren, *Poetry and Personality*, 44–45).

12. Stephen Owen offers a concise and useful summary of the full semantic range of *"feng"* in his *Readings*, 586–587. See also Donald Gibbs, "Notes on the Wind: The Term 'Feng' in Chinese Literary Criticism."

13. Yu Xianhao (87) has hypothesized that, because Li Bo's poems constitute the apex of the genre of poetry written in the spirit of the ancients, *gufeng* soon became interchangeable with the term *guti shi* to refer to the formal genre of ancient-style poetry.

14. As described by Bol, 23.

15. For all the disdain for Six Dynasties poetics he expresses here, Li Bo (and even the reputed patriarch of the *fugu* movement, Han Yu) has been justly charged with continuing that very tradition of formally refined poetry. The *Zheng tang zha ji* cites this comment by Yan Jiuneng: "The poems of [Li] Taibai and [Han] Changli do emerge from the Six Dynasties; all these assertions are nothing more than the words of would-be heroes deploring [the accomplishments of] others" (Zhou Zhongfu, *Zheng tang zha ji*, 1.3a).

16. *LBJJZ*, 1:156.

17. *Zhuangzi jijie*, "Tianyun pian," in *ZZJC*, 3:91–92.

18. *Zhuangzi jijie*, "Qiushui pian," in *ZZJC*, 3:107.

19. As he puts it, "J'appelle donc hypertexe tout texte dérivé d'un texte antérieur par transformation simple ... ou par transformation indirecte" (see Genette, 16–19).

20. Pauline Yu, *Reading of Imagery*, 57.

21. Liu Xie, "Bixing pian," in *Wenxin diaolong*, 394–395. Cf. Owen, *Readings*, 259; Liu Hsieh, *Literary Mind*, 196.

22. This is to be understood in contrast with the technique of *xing*, usually thought of as the actual stimulus for the emotion expressed. For a detailed account of the evolving conception of *xing*, see Pauline Yu, *Reading of Imagery*, especially 58–67.

23. Liu Xie, 394–395.

24. Xu Fuguan makes the argument that, while *bi* and *xing* differ as modes of expression, they both express the poet's emotions and cannot be separated into rational and irrational approaches to imagery. In practical terms, he asserts, they

cannot be easily distinguished; they are the elements that make poetry poetry. See his 1958 article "Shi shi de bixing   chong xin dianding Zhongguo shi de xinshang jichu," especially 104–108.

25. Pauline Yu, *Reading of Imagery*, 177–182; and Wang Yunxi, "Tan Zhongguo gudai wenlun zhong de bi xing shuo."

26. The Tang commentator Li Shan, for example, calls Ruan's poems "mysterious and remote," and further quotes Li Chongxian as declaring his works "most cryptic and elusive" (cited in Huang Jie's introduction to the *Yonghuai*, in *Ruan Bubing* Yonghuai *shi zhu*, 14). For a description of Ruan Ji's life and its influence on his poetry, see Holzman, *Poetry and Politics*.

27. In *Yu xuan Tang Song shichun*, 1.6b.

28. Dizhu and Kunlun appear in the *Huainanzi* as the mountain dwellings of the transcendents, and as places frequented by the phoenix.

29. *LBJJZ*, 1:163.

30. *LBJJZ*, 1:164.

31. Wang Fuzhi, *Tangshi pingxuan*, 53.

32. Zhuangzi, "Xiaoyaoyou," *Zhuangzi jijie, j.* 1 in *ZZJC*, 3:2–3 (translated by Watson in Zhuangzi, *Chuang Tzu: Basic Writings*, 25).

33. Ruan Ji, *Yonghuai* #79 (translated by Holzman in *Poetry and Politics*, 216–217). For a discussion of Ruan's uses of bird imagery and its associations with the archetypal "Great Man," see Holzman, 212–218.

34. Holzman, *Poetry and Politics*, 216–217.

35. As Holzman remarks more than once, Chinese commentators have long viewed the bulk of Ruan's corpus as consisting of more or less veiled political satires.

36. *LBJJZ*, 1:151.

37. Owen, *Great Age*, 109–143; Allen, 165–206.

38. Hightower, however, does note the possibility of an ironic or parodic use of allusion; but the examples he presents use irony to poke fun at the subject of the poem, rather than at any aspect of poetry itself ("Allusion in the Poetry of T'ao Ch'ien," 17–18).

39. In fact, the playful and serious uses of intertextuality in poetry have been treated in discussions ranging from Aristotle's definition of parody in his *Poetics* to the New Critical equation of ironic structure within poetry itself, as in Robert Penn Warren's essay, "Pure and Impure Poetry."

40. Bakhtin, 44.

41. Joseph Allen has explored in some depth the various uses Li Bo made of Bao Zhao's poetry, "imitating," as he puts it, over half Bao's corpus (Allen, especially 189–206).

42. Bao Zhao, *Bao Shi ji*, 5.282.

43. One version of this is found in the "Helü neizhuan" chapter of the *Wu Yue chunqiu*, 40.

44. *Jinshu*, 36.075–76.

45. *LBJJZ*, 1:123.

46. *LBJJZ*, 1:125.

47. According to Wang Qi, in both the Song dynasty edition of *Li Taibai*

wenji, and the Kangxi, Miu Yueqi edition of Li Bo's works, #16 is not included among the *Gufeng*. See his note in *LBJJZ*, 1:123.

48. One manifestation of critical efforts to fit the "Li Sao" into a Confucian model of remonstrance is the long-standing effort to apply *Shijing* exegetical techniques to Qu Yuan's poem. For a recounting and interpretation of the history of the allegorizing exegesis of the "Li Sao," see Pauline Yu, *Reading of Imagery*, especially 110–117. She locates motivation for linking the two texts on two levels: (1) the exegetes' desire to deflect "attention from the less orthodox aspects of the poem and [situate] the poet with the mainstream of upright official behavior" and (2) the profound belief that the use of natural imagery was not the product of poetic artistry, but grew out of preexisting affinities between the images selected and the concrete situations they are used to depict.

49. This seems to be the accepted version of his life. Ono, Yu Xianhao, and Wang Yunxi are among the most important proponents of this view.

50. Wang Qi was one critic who maintained that Li Bo's poetics emerged from an essentially joyous and exuberant nature. See his introduction to *LTBQJ*, especially 1693–1694.

51. As David Knechtges points out in *Han Rhapsody* (123, n. 15), the earliest instance of categorizing Qu Yuan's poetry as a *fu* is in the *Hanshu* (30.7, 1747). For a recent summary of the rationale for this traditional classification, see Li Yuegang, 88–98.

52. *LBJJZ*, 1:179.

53. *Yu xuan Tang Song shichun*, 1.6a.

54. *LBJJZ*, 1:160.

55. Ibid., 166.

56. Both Xiao Shibin and Xu Zhenqing hold this view. See *LBJJZ*, 1:166–167.

57. "Huangdi pian," *Liezi zhu*, in *ZZJC*, 3:21.

58. *Wenxuan*, 11.1b–3b.

59. This tradition is beautifully recounted by Stephen Owen in *Remembrances*. See especially chapter 1, "Lush Millet and a Stele: The Rememberer Remembered," 16–32.

60. *Quan Han Sanguo Jin nanbeichao shi*, 1:303.

61. For a summary of this debate and an alternative translation, see Holzman, *Poetry and Politics*, 163–165.

62. *LBJJZ*, 1:161.

63. *Tao Yuanming ji jiaojian*, 5.390–401. See the discussion below in chapter 5.

64. *LBJJZ*, 1:162.

65. See Fang Hongjing, *Qianyi lu*, 12.14a.

66. Chen Hang, *Shi bi xing jian*, 3.131.

67. Ibid., 139–140.

68. Discussions of Wang Yi's Confucian allegorization of the "Li Sao" can be found in Schneider, 27–31, and Pauline Yu, *Reading of Imagery*, 89–100.

69. *LBJJZ*, 1:107.

70. As described in the *Liexian zhuan*, 70–72, and in the "Jiyan pian" of Ge Hong, *Baopuzi*, 30.242.

71. Sima Qian, "Fengchan shu," *Shiji*, 28.1385.

72. In "Shangshi" [Distressed by these times], An Qi is but one of many immortals encountered by the speaker. Toward the end of his unsatisfying journey (beginning with line 31), the speaker mentions:

> *I gave my team the reins and whipped them up again,*
> *Leapt like a whirlwind, floated like a cloud,*
> *Treading an airy passage across the sea,*
> *Following An Qi to the Isle of Bliss.*
> *Then ascending heaven's ladder, I mounted the northern sky.*

Translated by Hawkes, *Songs of the South*, 315.

73. His *yuefu* poem "Facing the Wine" opens with the following couplet:

> *Songzi perches on Jinhua Mountain,*
> *An Qi enters the Penglai Sea.*
>
> *These men were immortals of old:*
> *And where, in the end, did these metamorphosed wings go?*

See *LBJJZ*, 1:453–454. At the conclusion of *Gufeng* #20, he alludes to the jade slippers that An Qi gave the emperor before his departure:

> *Finally I leave you the crimson jade slippers,*
> *And eastward mount the road to Penglai.*
>
> *If the emperor of Qin should look for me—*
> *Vast and blue, nothing but mist.* (*LBJJZ*, 1:131)

74. *LBJJZ*, 1:107.

75. Ge Lifang, *Yunyu yangqiu*, 11.133–134.

76. "Shining Star Jade Maiden" was said to have dwelled on Huashan and, having drunk a broth made from white jade, ascended to heaven in broad daylight (*Taiping guangji*, 59.362).

77. *LBJJZ*, 1:129–130.

78. See Ge Hong, *Shenxian zhuan*, 8.240–249.

79. As translated by Hawkes, *Songs of the South*, 78.

80. Whether "Peng Xian" refers to a Shang dynasty minister who drowned himself or to Peng and Xian, two legendary shamans, remains ambiguous (Hawkes, *Songs of the South*, 333).

81. *LBJJZ*, 1:102.

82. *Yu xuan Tang Song shichun*, 8.5a.

83. Xiao Shibin, cited in *LBJJZ*, 1:103.

84. Ibid.

85. Gaozong, cited in ibid.

86. This seems to have been a fairly common observation. Among other readers who cite these satirical *Gufeng* as proof of Li Bo's rational skepticism are the Yuan critic Liu Lu (1317–1379), otherwise very critical of Li Bo's poetry and dubious about his motivations for composing the *Gufeng*, and the Ming critic Zhu Daqi. See Liu's *Fengya yi*, 11.5b, and Zhu's "Li Du shi tong xu," in Huang Zongxi's *Mingwenhai*, 227.7a, 8b. The Ming dynasty critic Fang Hongjing, who assertively and consistently argued for the presence of principle throughout Li's poetry, also believed that it was impossible for someone like Li Bo actually to have

thought seriously about becoming an immortal (Fang Hongjing, *Qianyi lu,* 15.25b–26a).

87. *LBJJZ,* 1:101–102. For the complete text from which this passage is excerpted, see Hu Zhenheng, *Tangyin guiqian,* 6.1a–b.

88. Hu Zhenheng, *Tangyin guiqian,* 6.44.

89. Fang Dongshu, *Zhaomei zhanyan,* 7.205.

90. Tu Long, *Youquanji,* 23.8a–9b.

91. *Wenxuan,* 21.23b–24a.

92. *LBJJZ,* 1:100.

93. Yuan Hongdao, *Yuan Zhonglang quanji,* 2.22b–23a.

Chapter 4 The *Yuefu*

1. *LBJJZ,* 2:1347. Translation by David Hinton in *The Selected Poems of Li Po,* 27.

2. Fisher, 19.

3. See Allen, 165–170, for ample statistical information in support of this observation.

4. The only comment I have found that attempts to locate anything like "unfetteredness" in a particular, genre-specific quality of *yuefu* is written by the author of the *Li shi wei:* "*Yuefu* do not aspire to conform to [examples set by] ancestors, but to recount events. This is why, if [a poet] is slow [to compose], he will miss the mark—which is why Du Fu ['s corpus] contains no *yuefu*" (cited in *LBJJZ,* 2:1876).

5. Allen demonstrates this point throughout his study.

6. Owen, *Great Age,* 135.

7. See Allen, 170.

8. Many traditional readers, believing in the ongoing influence of *yuefu*'s folk origins, have attempted to allegorize specific *yuefu*. The allegorical reading of *yuefu* stems from an emphasis on its folk origins rather than on its development as a self-conscious literary genre. Readers who subscribe to this type of interpretation explain Li's penchant for *yuefu* in terms similar to those used to explain his *Gufeng.* One example is the author of the *Li shi wei,* who writes, "Taibai was frustrated with the smallness of people, and so returned to the mountains where he abandoned himself to wine, roaming freely without aim. How could one view him as a man fulfilled! It is because of [these circumstances] that, in his *yuefu,* he usually [expresses] his purity and resentments" (cited in *LBJJZ,* 2:1876).

9. This paradox exists in intriguing parallel with the well-known paradox of self-consciousness that guided much of the writing of Romantic poetry. See Cyrus Hamlin, *Hermeneutic of Form: Romantic Poetics in Theory and Practice,* especially chapter 4, "The Poetics of Self-Consciousness," for a full exposition of this problem.

10. Because I am primarily interested in Li Bo's exercise of unfetteredness in regard to past poetry, I have not selected for analysis any *yuefu* in which the primary manifestation of "strangeness" or "unfetteredness" resides in visionary flights and hyperbolic landscape imagery. This has been admirably accomplished elsewhere. See Owen, *Great Age,* 123–129.

11. For a full appreciation of the uniqueness of Li Bo's approach to *yuefu*, it is worth comparing his methods of recomposition to the eight methods of composition during the Han, as identified by Yu Guanying in his *Han-Wei Liuchao shi luncong*, 26–38. See also Joseph Allen's diachronic analysis of the transformation of a *yuefu* from its Han origins through Li Bo's contribution in the Tang (Allen, 209–223).

In situating Li Bo's works within specific narrative lineages, I rely on the compilation by Guo Maoqian (fl. 1264–1269), *Yuefu shiji*, which conveniently places all extant *yuefu* under the same or related titles in chronological order. Guo's anthology cannot have included all of the *yuefu* circulating in each period, and it is likely that Li Bo read (and responded to) many that we will never see. Nevertheless, it seems worthwhile to examine his use of those that are accessible to us as broadly indicative of his overall approach to the pastness of *yuefu* precedents.

12. Ji Yougong, *Tangshi jishi jiaojian*, 1:477.

13. Gao Bing, *Tangshi pinhui*, 1:267.

14. Wang Shizhen, *Yiyuan zhiyan*, 4.14.

15. Zhao Yi, *Oubei shihua*, 5.

16. Wang Yunxi, "Han Wei Liuchao yuefu dui Li Bo de yingxiang," 94. Elsewhere, Wang states that Li preferred the "freer forms of old-style poetry and quatrains *(jueju)*, and did not like writing in the regulated mode in which formal restrictions were quite severe" (preface to *LBJJZ*, 1:17).

17. Joseph Allen is inspired by this anthology to define *yuefu* poetry exclusively in terms of their reliance upon these intratextual influences, a definition that he has gone far in proving to be the most useful for understanding the creation and reading of these poems (Allen, especially 64–68).

18. Hu Yinglin, *Shi sou*, "Neipian," 23.

19. The *Zhongguo dacidian* (2:1520), cites, among others, this phrase from the "Biography of Yuan Ang and Chao Cuo" ["Yuan Ang Chao Cuo liezhuan"]: "His writings numbered in the dozens, and although the emperor Xiaowen did not heed them, he *considered his talent to be extraordinary (qi qi cai)*" (Sima Qian, *Shiji*, 101.2746).

20. In Sunzi's words, "There is nothing to military efficacy but *qi* and *zheng*—deviation and directness. The alternation of *qi* and *zheng* is unconquerable." And again, "All warriors employ *zheng* to join forces, and *qi* to overcome." See *Sunzi*, 5.68, 70. My translation of the difficult term *"shi"* as "efficacy" is inspired by François Jullien's study *La propension des choses: pour une histoire de l'efficacité en Chine*.

21. This characterization first appeared during Li Bo's lifetime. Yin Fan, in his *Heyue yingling ji*, published in 753, describes "Shudao nan" as *qi zhi youqi*, or "strangeness upon strangeness," borrowing the expression from Wang Chong (A.D. 27–91), who developed an argument for recognizing that strangeness can be a sign of extraordinariness and superiority. (Gao Bing repeats the phrase verbatim in his comment on "Shudao nan" as well.) For Yin Fan's comment, see *Heyue yingling ji*, 1.5a. For Wang Chong's use of *"qi,"* see his essays "Qi Guai" and "Zhao Qi" in *Lunheng*, as well as Alfred Forke's translation. Cf. my discussion in "Transformation and Imitation," 30–37.

22. One of the earliest examples of *"qi"* used to describe Li Bo's unorthodox approach to poetry is to be found in Bo Juyi's markedly ambivalent comment contained in his famous "Letter to Yuan the Ninth": "[When speaking of] those whose poetry is virile and sweeping, people will name Li Bo. Li's genius for creation is *qi* (unorthodox, startling); others cannot attain it" (*Bo Juyi ji*, 45.961). See also my discussion in chapter 1.

23. See Hu Zhenheng, *Li shi tong* (cited in *LBJJZ*, 2:1873).

24. See Hu Zhenheng, *Tangyin guiqian*, 9.4a–b.

25. Wai-yee Li discusses late Ming reconciliations of spontaneity and the various manifestations of a divided consciousness (including that of adherence to the rules of an aesthetic orderliness) in "The Rhetoric of Spontaneity in Late-Ming Literature."

26. A full account of the *yuefu* permutations of the Luofu theme would include poems written under the titles "Cai Sang," "Yan'ge xing," and "Richu dongnanyu." For a fuller review of the theme, and a brief discussion of Li Bo's poem, see Allen, 209–223.

27. By the "original" version, I refer to the *yuefu* designated by Guo Mao-qian as *"guci"*—"old lyrics"—which he places first in a given chronologically organized tune sequence. The previously assumed Han identity of all Guo's designated *guci* has been roundly questioned, however. For good critical summaries of recent arguments relating to the early development of the genre, see Anne Birrell, *Popular Songs and Ballads of Han China,* and, more recently, Cai Zongqi, "Dramatic and Narrative Modes of Presentation in Han Yüeh-fu." See also Joseph Allen's very useful bibliographic note in Allen, 267–270.

28. According to the *Ciyuan,* the term *"shijun,"* translated here as "governor," is the Han dynasty equivalent of *cishi.* Hucker (558–559) does not have an entry for *shijun,* but gives the translation of the latest usage of *cishi* as "unofficial reference to a Department Magistrate."

29. *YFSJ,* 2:410–411. For an alternative translation, see Allen, 210–211.

30. *YFSJ,* 2:410.

31. Wu Jing, *Yuefu jieti,* 2–3. Beyond this one obvious trait, Luofu's identity has been a matter of debate, as scholars attempt to reconcile her menial labor and her self-avowed aristocratic standing. For a summary of these disparate interpretations, see Cai Zongqi, "Dramatic and Narrative Modes," 117–118, n. 37.

32. *"Xing"* (stimulus) is the term assigned by the Mao commentary to the opening lines of many of the *Odes,* usually containing images from the natural world that bear an unspecified relation to the human events recounted.

33. See Wang Yunxi, "Handai suyue he min'ge," 36.

34. *YFSJ,* 2:417–418. Cf. Allen, 212–213.

35. In "Dramatic and Narrative Modes," Cai effectively demonstrates both the rationale and the usefulness of reestablishing the folk-literati distinction along these lines.

36. *YFSJ,* 2:412. Cf. Allen, 217.

37. Willows have long been used in poetry, and in life, as a symbol of parting. Allen notes the mulberry-willow fusion in his discussion on (217).

38. The biography of the wife of Qiu Hu of Lu, Qiu Jie, is recorded in the *Lienü zhuan jinzhu jinshi*, 190–193. Renowned for her virtue, she remained loyal to her husband when, five days after their wedding, he departed on official duty, not to return for five years. On his way home, he spied a beautiful woman picking mulberries and, not recognizing his own wife, offered her money to come away with him. She refused him. After confronting him upon his return home and accusing him of being both unfaithful and unfilial, she drowned herself in the river.

39. For a concise study of these characteristics, see especially Frankel, "The Development of Han and Wei Yueh-fu as a High Literary Genre."

40. *YFSJ*, 2:413.

41. Ibid.

42. Ibid.

43. Ibid., *LBJJZ*, 1:417.

44. As pointed out by Frankel, the single performer of the post-Han *yuefu* takes on the roles of both narrator and actor, often impersonating more than one character. See "The Relation between Narrator and Characters in *Yuefu* Ballads," 107.

45. Ono, 145–146.

46. As Shen puts it, "The old lyrics of the Jin were originally now-broken-now-continuous; Taibai imitates this form" (*Tangshi biecai ji*, 6.5a–b).

47. *YFSJ*, 3:790.

48. See *YFSJ*, 3:790; *LBJJZ*, 1:282; Ono, 864.

49. *LBJJZ*, 1:283.

50. See Yu-kung Kao, especially 334–345.

51. Cf. Hamlin, chapter 4, "The Poetics of Self-Consciousness."

52. For recent explorations of the effect of the interacting subconscious upon the psychoanalytical process, see Christopher Bollas, *Being a Character,* and Nancy Chodorow, *The Power of Feelings*.

53. *YFSJ*, 3:936.

54. According to Masuda (443), Guo was guided in his arrangement and selection of poems in this category by Tang scholar Wu Jing, who himself was inspired by a description offered by Shen Yue (441–513).

55. *YFSJ*, 3:884.

56. *YFSJ*, 3:991.

57. This line can also read: "In vain I stitch circular patterns," which engages the homophone of *"si"* (silk thread), a pun that evokes the endlessness of longing, used by poets since the Han, and portrays the woman's sense of futility. Here, this alternate reading suggests that the speaking subject could also be the lonely woman, thus sustaining the speaking subject's ambiguity, a trope that seems to have been in use since the "Nineteen Old Poems."

58. *YFSJ*, 3:992.

59. I am indebted for the translation of this line to Stephen Owen, *Great Age*, 127.

60. *YFSJ*, 3:994; *LBJJZ*, 1:244. For a beautiful, if free-form, translation of this poem, see that of David Hinton in *The Selected Poems of Li Po*, 48.

61. *LBJJZ*, 1:244–245.

62. Wang Fuzhi, *Tangshi pingxuan,* 19.

63. The other common reading of *"xiang"* is as the direct object of the verb, which would transform *"xiangsi"* into something like "missing you/him/her."

64. *YFSJ*, 3:993.

65. Li Bo accomplishes something similar in his well-known quatrain "Yujie yuan" (Jade steps lament):

Jade steps seep white dew,	玉階生白露
Night goes on; it penetrates gauze stockings.	夜久侵羅襪
So she lowers the crystalline curtains,	卻下水晶簾
Gazes at the moon through lambent beads.	玲瓏望秋月

LBJJZ, 1:374. For an alternative translation and discussion of the workings of the images in this poem, see Kao and Mei, "Meaning, Metaphor, and Allusion," 317–318.

66. While Wang Fuzhi is most commonly credited with fully formulating the interdependency of the poet's inner world and his depiction of a scene in the natural world, Pauline Yu has identified a much earlier articulation of this principle in the writings of the less well-known critic Zhao Fang (1319–1369), who brings the terms together in a comment on Du Fu's poem "Jiang Han" [Yangtze and Han]. See Yu, *Reading of Imagery,* 196.

67. "Li Ling zhuan," *Shiji,* 9:109.2867–2878.

68. *Wenxuan,* 29.8b–9a; 42.1b–7a.

69. In "Li Guang Su Jian zhuan," *Hanshu,* 8:2459–2470.

70. *YFSJ*, 3:996.

71. There has been some debate concerning the authenticity of these poems, but the consensus seems to be that they are genuine compositions by Li Bo. For a brief, clear summary of the discussion, see Bryant, 107–109.

72. Jade-Cluster Mountain, also known as Jade Mountain, is one of the mythical places where the Queen Mother of the West is said to reside. Jasper Terrace is the name of her palace atop the mythical Mount Kunlun.

73. Mount Wu, located in the modern-day Three Gorges in Sichuan province, is the legendary site of the Prince of Chu's tryst with a goddess, as recounted in Song Yu's "Gaotang fu." According to the legend, the goddess told the prince upon parting from him forever: "At dawn, I am the clouds of morn; at evening the coursing rain." "Clouds and rain" has since become a term referring to sexual encounters; here it also connotes the evanescence of the encounter.

74. Flying-Swallow refers to the much-loved wife of Emperor Cheng of the Han dynasty, so named because of the lightness of her body. She was famous for the favor lavished upon her by the emperor.

75. "Ruination of Kingdoms" is an expression for an extremely beautiful woman taken from a poem written by Han dynasty poet Li Yannian (140–87 B.C.), whose sister was much loved by Emperor Wu.

76. *LBJJZ*, 1:389–393.

77. For all these references, see ibid., 389, 392; *YFSJ*, 4:1133.

78. There is some debate about whether Li Bo composed these lyrics to be sung in accordance with preexisting music, or whether the music was com-

posed for this occasion. See the annotation regarding the title in *LBJJZ*, 1:389–390.

79. Ye Xie, *Yuanshi*, 4.603.

80. *LBJJZ*, 1:392.

81. Attributed to a "Dan Weng" [The old man of pellucid peace] by the Ming critic Zhou Ting in his discussion of seven-character quatrains in *Tangshi xuanmai huitong*, 14a.

82. "Liu Tuntian [Liu Yong, 987–1053] is recorded as saying, 'If I were to use "renowned flowers" as a comparison, others would most likely make fun of me, saying how easy it is.'" Included in Tang Guizhang's *Cihua congbian*, 631.

83. Shen Deqian, *Tangshi biecai ji*, 20.3a.

84. Wang presents this view as part of his refutation of the argument that the line should contain the word "leaves" rather than "clouds," Wang's point being that the heart of the poem lies in its evocation of visual illusion, better enhanced by the ephemeral and allusive clouds than by leaves. *LBJJZ*, 1:391.

85. See Zhou Ting, *Tangshi xuanmai huitong*, 14a.

86. See *LBJJZ*, 1:391.

87. Nor do commentators find anything worth noting here. As Ono Jitsunosuke (227) paraphrases it, "It is feasible that a beautiful flower such as the peony and the supreme beauty of her generation, Yang Guifei, look upon each other."

88. Preface to "Guanju," *Maoshi zhengyi*, 1:37.

89. Fisher, 22–24.

90. Allen, 206, 234.

Chapter 5 Alluding to Immediacy

1. Examples of such critical views on the use of allusion are common in the writings of critics like Zhong Rong, Shen Yue, and even (although less categorically) Liu Xie. The same attitude was exemplified in the Tang dynasty by Wang Changling and Jiaoran. Zhong Rong, for example, is quite explicit in his introduction to the *Shipin* when he writes: "When striving to sing out one's emotive nature, what good are allusions?" Zhong follows this by a list of preferred verses that reflect the expression of immediate perception alone. He concludes the section by saying, "How could [such verses as these] have been drawn from the classics or the *Historical Records*? Looking at the finest writings from ancient times to the present, most have not borrowed [from earlier works], and all are born of direct investigation" (*LDSH*, 1:4–5).

2. *LBJJZ*, 1:868.

3. This poem concludes, "But what in this thing is worth the giving? I am moved only by time's passage since we parted" (*Ci wu he zu gong / dan gan bie jing shi* [*Wenxuan*, 29.5a]).

4. *LBJJZ*, 1:591.

5. As translated by Hawkes, 207. Zhu Xi, *Chuci jizhu*, 5.§7,116–117.

6. Wang Qi cites from the *Yiwen leiju*: "Sheng Hong's 'Notes from Jingzhou' says: 'In Huizhe of Xinyang Country there is a hot spring. During the winter months, before you have come within several miles of it, in the distance you can

see white steam wafting up like smoke, reflecting colors above and below, in a shape like filigree window frames. There is even the form of a pair of cartwheels, so people recount that in ancient times there was a fair [jade-like] maiden who rode a carriage into this spring. Nowadays people see a young girl, glowing and lovely in appearance, whose comings and goings are sudden and brief'" (*Yiwen leiju*, 9.166). Wang Qi also includes a note from the "Yi tong zhi" mentioning that the local people say that Jade Maiden Spring is where the "Jade Maiden" would go to smelt cinnabar to attain immortality (*LTBQJ*, 2:1007).

7. *LBJJZ*, 2:1263.

8. Translation adapted from J. R. Hightower in Birch, *Anthology of Chinese Literature*, 1:138–140.

9. Cited by Wang Qi in *LTBQJ*, 2:1008. See also Dai Qinli, ed., *Xian Qin Han Wei Jin Nanbeichao shi*, 12.334.

10. See for example, the *Huainanzi*, "Ben jing," 8a: "[Yin and Yang] continue the harmony of heaven and earth, give form to the entities of the myriad variations *(wan shu)*." "Crimson flame" is also mentioned in the context of creation in *Han wudi neizhuan*, 8:6086.

11. *Wenxuan*, 7.18a (translated in Knechtges, 2:55).

12. See Davis, "The Double Ninth Festival in Chinese Poetry," for the origins of the festival and an interesting discussion on how the theme was transmitted and transformed from Tao Yuanming through Li Bo and on down. Davis neglects to mention, however, one origin of the tradition, cited in *Yiwen leiju*, which adds some background to the custom of large gatherings on that holiday: "'The Record of Looking upon the Sea' says: 'Forty paces north of the prefecture, there is a lakeside mountain, very flat and even. There is room for several hundreds of people to sit on it. The common people valued it highly. Every "Ninth," on the morning [of the festival of] chrysanthemum wine, the attendants at the banquet on this mountain would number as many as three or four hundred people'" (*Yiwen leiju*, 4:81).

13. Ono Jitsunosuke follows Wang Qi's lead in suggesting that the title is probably incomplete, that this is probably an occasional poem commemorating the construction of a viewing terrace south of Xuancheng by a *biejia* (administrative aide). This may well be the case, but Ono seems to feel that understanding this point illuminates the poem completely. But as in many of Li Bo's poems (such as "Chang xiangsi" and "Du Lu Pian"), the apparent discontinuity characterizing this poem arises from an unexpected reshaping of conventional links. See chapter 4, above.

14. This is a reference to Zhou Jing, a censor of Yuzhou in the Latter Han dynasty, who stood firm in his evaluation of one Chen Fan, naming him to the position of administrative aide *(biejia)*. When Chen did not take up his position, Zhou refused to change his nomination and inscribed Chen's name on the *biejia's* carriage seat anyway. When Chen Fan heard of this, he hurried to accept his appointment (recorded in the *Taiping yulan*, 263.1b). Li Bo uses this allusion to flatter the local *biejia* of Xuanzhou, where he probably composed this poem.

15. This is probably a personal allusion to a previously arranged meeting for the holiday.

16. Qin Gao is a figure from the *Liexian zhuan* [Biographies of eminent immortals] who lived at the end of the Zhou dynasty. Because of his extraordinary talent in playing the zither, he became resident musician at the court of Prince Kang of the Song. One day he told his disciples that he was going to go into the Zhuo River to fetch the dragon's egg, and he fixed the day of his return. When on the appointed day they waited for him at the river's edge, Qin Gao finally emerged on the back of a carp. He remained on shore for a month, then plunged back into the water (*Liexian zhuan*, A.§26, 670).

17. Bing Yi is identified in the *Shanhaijing* as an immortal who has a human face, rides a pair of dragons, and is the only creature who can inhabit the depths of the remotest springs (see Yuan Ke, *Shanhaijing jiaozhu*, 7.316). The white tortoise is an unrelated figure; Wang Qi proposes that it might be a variant of 白龜 from the "He bo" chapter of the *Chuci*.

18. Cang Isle is an island where immortals dwell.

19. Citing "The Biography of Meng Jia" in the *Jinshu*, Wang Qi states: "Meng Jia was Huan Wen's aide-de-camp. He was gentle and upright, and Wen valued him highly. On the Double Ninth, Wen went for an outing on Longshan Mountain and gathered all of his cohorts. At that time, all the attendants were wearing their military uniforms. A wind blew off Jia's hat, but Jia did not realize it. Wen indicated to all of the guests not to say anything, so that he might observe his reaction. Jia went to the privy and was gone for a long time. Wen commanded that the hat be returned to him, and ordered Sun Sheng to compose a piece of writing teasing Jia and put it where Jia had been sitting. When Jia returned, he saw it and [wrote a piece] in response. His composition was very beautiful, and all around sighed [in admiration]" ("Biography of Huan Wen," *Jinshu*, 98.2581).

20. *LBJJZ*, 2:1204.

21. It is not absolutely necessary to read "Returning Home" as an abbreviation of the title of Tao Yuanming's well-known work, "Gui qu lai ci" (*Tao Yuanming ji jiaojian*, 5.390–401), and many punctuated editions are printed without indicating that one should. But few readers would miss the association, even while the two lines still read smoothly as a grammatical sentence.

22. For the story of Tao and the Double Nine Festival, see *Yiwen leiju*, 4.81.

23. For the story of Tao, Wang Hong, and the composition of "Gui qu lai ci," see the "Biography of Tao Qian" in *Jinshu*, 8:94.2461.

24. The original lines (lines 34–35), as translated in Knechtges (1:307) are: "Waves like serried mountains, / Now joined, now scattered." "Rhymeprose of the Sea" in its entirety may be found in the *Wenxuan*, 12.1a–8b.

25. *LTBQJ*, 2:962.

26. *LBJJZ*, 2:1206–1207.

27. From Tao's poem "Drinking Wine, #7." See *Tao Yuanming ji jiaojian*, 3.224.

28. "Pluck chrysanthemums at the eastern hedge, / And behold, in the distance, the southern mountains" (*cai ju dong li xia, / you ran jian nan shan*). See Tao's "Drinking Wine, #5" in *Tao Yuanming ji jiaojian*, 3:219–220.

29. "Shan Gong" refers to Shan Tao of the Jin dynasty, one of the "Seven

Sages of the Bamboo Grove," and perhaps best known for getting drunk beside Gaoyang Lake. He appears in Li Bo's *yuefu* poems "Xiangyang Tune #4" and "Xiangyang Tune #2":

> Whenever Shan Gong gets drunk
> Tipsy and reeling, he goes down to Gaoyang
> On his head a cap of white
> Replaced upside down, and he remounts his horse.

See *LBJJZ*, 1:374–376. These lines are from Liu Yiqing's *Shishuo xinyu*, 1:385–386, which records the popular song then circulating about him. Line 4 is a direct citation.

30. Several generations of critics have associated wine with Li Bo's "Romantic" spirit, a position best summed up by Wang Yunxi in part 3 of his preface (*LBJJZ*, 1:13–20).

31. Guo Moruo, 134–155.

32. In "Drinking Wine, #7" Tao Yuanming uses the expression, "the stuff that makes one forget sorrows" *(wangyou wu)*. (*Tao Yuanming ji jiaojian*, 3.224).

33. *LBJJZ*, 2:1352.

34. Ibid., 1340.

35. *Maoshi zhengyi*, 2:434.

36. Ibid., 1:191.

37. Ibid., 2:547. From the "Airs of Tang," "Bao yu."

38. Ibid., 3:889. From the "Lesser Elegantiae," "Ju gong."

39. According to Zhan Ying (1:270), this line actually means (in keeping with the legend) that Yao had to cede to Shun, and Shun had to cede to Yu.

40. *LBJJZ*, 1:191.

41. Fan Peng, "Li Hanlin shi," *j.* 1, in *LBZLHB*, 1:64.

42. Weng Fanggang, *Shizhou shihua*, *j.* 1, in *QSHXB*, 2:1372.

43. See chapter 1, n. 26, and Ying-shih Yü, "Intellectual Breakthroughs in the T'ang-Sung Transition."

44. For an account of this and the related events of the period mentioned here, see Twitchett, *Cambridge History of China*, 3:453–463.

45. *LBJJZ*, 1:195–196.

46. Indeed, Chen (147–148) considers that this poem not only prefigures Bo Juyi's celebrated "Song of Everlasting Sorrow" ("Chang hen ge"), but—perhaps because of its skillful intertwining of the hidden and the manifest, the empty and the substantive—far surpasses it: "One thousand words of the 'Song of Everlasting Sorrow' cannot attain [the quality of] one verse of 'Parted Far Away.'"

47. Ono, 619–620. For excerpts from a wide variety of interpretations, see Zhan Ying, 1:276–281.

48. For a brief account of this extremely controversial event, which led to Li Bo's imprisonment in 757, see Owen, *Great Age*, 115–116.

49. Yin Fan, *Heyue yingling ji*, omits this line.

50. Guo Maoqian, 3:1016–1027.

51. Ibid., 1016.

52. Hawkes, 104–106.

53. *Wenxuan*, 29.1b–2a.

Chapter 6 Epilogue

1. *LBJJZ*, 2:1354.

2. In his *Canglang shihua*, Yan Yu famously responds to what is clearly an already established notion of pairing Li Bo and Li He by saying, "People say that Taibai is an 'immortal genius' *(xiancai)* and that Changji [Li He] is a 'demonic genius' *(guicai)*. This is not the case. It is simply that Taibai's are the lyrics of a 'heavenly immortal' *(tianxian),* and Changji's are those of a 'demonic immortal' *(guixian)*." Guo Shaoyu provides an extensive comment in which he traces previous usages of these and related terms in reference to the two poets, followed by Pan Deyu's subsequent objections that he finds this particular discourse incomprehensible. Guo sagaciously concludes that it is best not to try to pin these metaphors down with too much precision; rather, one should appreciate the underlying sensibility they clearly reflect. For both Yan Yu's remark and Guo Shaoyu's comment, see Yan Yu, *Canglang shihua,* 179.

3. *LBJJZ*, 2:1311.

4. Susan Stewart, "Proust's Turn from Nostalgia," 82, 90.

5. Stewart, 94.

6. There are, of course, some exceptions. Poems that were composed upon visiting a specific place associated with Li Bo tend to be both more subtle and more personal. One of the most moving is Long Tianxi's "Guo Chiyang you huai Tang Li Hanlin" [Passing by Chiyang, I was missing Li Hanlin of the Tang], in *LBJJZ*, 2:1846.

7. *LBJJZ*, 2:1844.

8. See, for example, Qian Qi's "Jiang xing wuti" [Traveling on the river: untitled]. In *LBJJZ*, 2:1841.

9. From Xu Ji's "Li Taibai zayan" [Some words on Li Taibai]. In *LBJJZ*, 2:1844.

10. You Tong, "Qi si" [Seven longings]. In *LBJJZ*, 2:1852.

11. *LBJJZ*, 2:1836.

12. *LBJJZ*, 2:1842.

13. "People of this world would all like to kill him, / I alone tend to cherish his genius." In *LBJJZ*, 2:1837.

14. In his poem "Zeng Wang Lun" [For Wang Lun]:

Li Bo mounts his boat about to take his leave,
Suddenly hears, upon the shore, the sound of the "Stamping Song."

The water of Peach Blossom Pond a thousand meters deep,
Is not as deep as Wang Lun's feelings as he sends me off. (LBJJZ, 1:820).

CHARACTER GLOSSARY

Proper Names (not listed separately in bibliography)

Cao Xueqin	曹雪芹	Jia Yi	賈宜
Cao Zhi	曹直	Jiang Yan	江淹
Cen Shen	岑參		
Chen Fan	陳蕃	Liang Jianwen	梁簡文
Chen Guangpu	陳廣溥	Li Bo/Li Bai	李白
Chen Heshu	陳和叔	Li Hanlin	李翰林
Chen Yi	陳繹	Li Qinglian	李青蓮
Chen Yiceng	陳繹曾	Li Taibo/Li	李太白
Chen Zi'ang	陳子昂	Taibai	
Chu Guangxi	儲光羲	Li Dongyang	李東陽
Cui Bao	崔豹	Li Lian	李濂
		Li Ling	李陵
Ding Guyun	丁古雲	Li Shangyin	李商隱
Dou Tao	竇滔	Li Wang	李旺
Du Fu	杜甫	Li Yangbing	李陽冰
Du Zimei	杜子美	Li Zhaoyuan	李兆元
Du Shaoling	杜少陵	Liu Xiaowei	劉孝威
Du Gongbu	杜工部	Liu Yong	柳永
Du Mu	杜牧	Liu Zongyuan	柳宗元
		Liu Zihou	柳子厚
Fan Peng	范梈	Lu Qiong	陸瓊
Fan Deji	范德機	Lu You	陸游
Fu Qiu Gong	浮丘公		
Fu Xuan	傅玄	Meng Haoran	孟浩然
Gao Shi	高適	Qian Qi	錢起
Guanxiu	貫休	Qian Shirui	錢世瑞
Jiang Deyin	姜德隱	Qiu Hu	秋胡
Guo Pu	郭璞	Qiu Jie	秋潔
He Zhizhang	賀知章		
Huang Luzhi	黃魯直	Ruan Ji	阮籍

Sa Tianxi	薩天錫	Wang Zhideng	王志登
Shan Tao	山濤	Wu Jun	呉均
Shen Yue	沈約	Wu Qiao	吳喬
Shen Xiuwen	沈休文		
Shi Runzhang	施閏章	Xie Tiao	謝朓
Sima Chengzhen	司馬承禎	Xu Ji	徐積
Sima Ziwei	司馬子微	Xu Zhongju	徐仲車
Sima Xiangru	司馬相如	Xu Zhusu	許竹素
Su Hui	蘇蕙		
Su Shi	蘇軾	Yan Jiuneng	嚴久能
Su Dongpo	蘇東坡	Yang Wanli	楊萬里
Su Zizhan	子瞻	Yang Chengzhai	楊誠齋
		Yao Xuan	姚宣
		Ying Shi	應時
Wang Anshi	王安石	You Tong	优同
Wang Jiefu	王介甫	Yu Xin	臾信
Wang Can	王粲	Yuan Hongdao	袁宏道
Wang Changling	王昌齡	Yuan Mei	袁枚
Wang Chong	王充	Yue Shi	樂史
Wang Dingguo	王定國		
Wang Guowei	王國維	Zhang Ji	張籍
Wang Jian	王建	Zhao Fang	趙汸
Wang Taiqing	王臺卿	Zhong Rong	鍾嶸
Wang Wei	王維	Zhou Jing	周景
Wang Mojie	王摩詰	Zhuangzi	莊子
Wang Xizhi	王羲之	Zhuang Zhou	莊周
Wang Yangming	王陽明		
Wang Yun	王筠		

Titles of Literary Works (not listed separately in bibliography)

"Bingju xing"	兵車行	Ganxing	感興
"Bu jian"	不見	Ganyu	感遇
		Guangyiji	廣異記
Caotang ji	草堂集	Gufeng	古風
"Chang xiangsi"	長相思	"Gui qu lai ci"	歸去來詞
Chang Xingxing zhai wenji	常醒醒齋文集	Gujin zhu	古今注
		"Gu libie"	古離別
"Dan Weng"	滄翁	"Guo Chiyang you huai Tang Li Hanlin"	過池陽有懷唐李翰林
"Daren"	大人		
"Deng chishang lou"	登池上摟		
"Deng lou fu"	登樓賦	Hongloumeng	紅樓夢
Dunzhai xianlan	遯齋閑覽	"Huama xing"	畫馬行
"Du zuo Jingting shan"	獨坐敬亭山	"Jiang Han"	江漢
		"Jiang xing wuti"	江行無題

Li Du shiwei	李杜詩緯	*Taibai yishi*	太白遺史
Liexian zhuan	列仙傳		
"Li Hanlin yi fu yiqi	李翰林一負逸	*Wen jian lu*	聞見錄
bi you zhenfang,	氣必有真放,	"Wuse"	物色
yi Li Hanlin wei	以李翰林為		
zhenfang yan"	真放焉	"Xie Gong ting"	謝公亭
Li shi wei	李詩緯	"Xing Lu Nan"	行路難
		"Xinhun bie"	新婚別
"Moshang sang"	陌上桑	"Xuanzhou Xie Tiao	宣州謝朓樓餞
		lou canbie jiaoshu	別校書叔雲
"Qian li si"	千里思	Shuyun"	
"Qiuxing"	秋興		
		"Yan'ge Luofu xing"	豔歌羅敷行
"Shan Gong"	山公	*Yijing*	易經
Shi'er bi fang zalu	十二比舫雜錄	*Yi tong zhi*	一統志
Shijing	詩經	*Yonghuai*	詠懷
Shipin	詩品	"You xian"	遊仙
Shiping	詩評	Yuan Ang Chao	袁盎晁錯列傳
Shipu	詩譜	Cuo liezhuan	
"Shudao nan"	蜀道難	"Yuan bieli"	遠別離
Shui jing zhu	水經注	"Yuan you"	遠遊
"Shu qing ji congdi	書情寄從弟邠	"Yu fu pian"	漁父篇
Binzhou	州長史昭	"Yujie yuan"	玉階怨
Changshi Zhao"		"Zhao yin"	招隱

Specialized Terms and Quoted Phrases

baihua	白話	chenzhong	沉重
bense	本色	chi tang sheng chun	池塘生春草
bi	比	cao	
bianfeng bianya	變風變雅	chuangzuo	創作
biejia	別駕	ci	詞
bieli	別離	cishi	刺使
biequ	別趣	ci wu he zu gong /	此物何足貢／
bing	病	dan gan bie jing	但感別經時
bukexue/kexue	不可學／可學	shi	
buran	不染	congrong	從容
cai	才	dajia	大家
cai/xue	才／學	daoxue	道學
cai ju dong li xia,	採菊東籬下	diandao shishi	顛倒事實
you ran jian nan	悠然見南山		
shan		er	而
chang	長		
cha zhi hao li, liao	差之毫釐	fa	法
yi qian li	謬以千里	fadu	法度
chenyu	沉鬱		

fei fanran zhi zuo	非泛然之作	ling	靈
feng (wind/airε)	風	lingmiao	靈妙
feng (phoenix)	鳳	liu (detain/willow)	留／柳
fengge	風格		
fengyun	風韻	meigan	美感
fu	賦	mianmu	面目
fugu	復古	miao	妙
		mili	迷離
gaoyi	高逸	mingyi	命意
gewu	格物		
gong	工	nigu	擬古
gouzao jingjie	構造境界		
gu	古	peng	鵬
guicai	鬼才	piaopiao	飄飄
guixian	鬼仙	piaoyi	飄逸
guti shi	古體詩		
guwen	古文	qi (strange, extraordinary)	奇
		qi (air, vital force)	氣
hanxu	含畜	qiao	巧
haofang piaoyi	豪放飄逸	qiguai	奇怪
haojun	豪俊	qi gujin	奇古今
haomai	豪邁	qing	情
haoyi	豪逸	qing jing jiao rong	情景交融
huaigu	懷古	qingyi	清逸
huo duan huo xu	或斷或續	qingyun	情韻
		qing yun yi xi bai ni shang	青雲衣兮白霓裳
jian ren suo du zhuan	兼人所獨專	qingzhen	清真
jie	接	qi qi cai	奇其材
jing	經	qiu	遒
jingqi	精奇	qixiang	氣象
jinti shi	近體詩	qiyi	奇臆
jueju	絕句	qiyu	奇語
		qi zhi youqi	奇之又奇
kaozhengxue	考證學	qu	趣
kong	空		
kongling	空靈	ren bu dai	人不逮
kongyan	空言		
		shen	神
lan	覽	shen/gong	神／工
langman	浪漫	sheng	笙
langmanpai wenxue	浪漫派文學	shengqing	聲情
li	理	shenjing	神境
liangzhi	良知	shenmixing	神秘性
libie	離別	shen qing heng yi	神情橫逸
Li-Du youlie	李杜優劣		

shensi	深思	xiangxiangli	想象力
shenyou	神遊	xianshi	現實
shenyun	神韻	xianyu	仙語
shen yu shi zhe	神於詩者	xiao	傚
shi (events/facts)	事	xiaogu	傚古
shi (knowledge/ judgment)	識	xing	性
		xing (stimulus, incitation)	興
shi (poem)	詩		
shi (substance)	實	xingling	性靈
shi bu gao	識不高	xingxiang	興象
shi du shen qian	識度甚淺	xiongyi	雄逸
shigan	實感	xu	虛
shihua	詩話	xuwu	虛無
shijian	識見	xue	學
shijing	實景	xueli	學力
shisheng	詩聖	xuewen	學問
shishi	詩史		
shiwang	詩王	yi (intent, meaning, idea, governing concept)	意
shi yan zhi	詩言志		
shuairan er cheng	率然而成		
si (longing, thoughts)	思	yima qianyan	倚馬千言
		yin shi	吟詩
si (silk thread)	絲	yiqu	意趣
		yiyi	意義
tian	天	you you	悠悠
tiancai	天才	yuan	遠
tianxian	天仙	yuefu	樂府
tishi	體勢	yun	韻
		yuyan	寓言
wangyou wu	忘憂物		
wan shu	萬殊	zaqu geci	雜曲歌詞
wei (false)	偽	zhanghuang qishi	張皇氣勢
wei (savoriness)	味	zheng	正
wen/zhi	文／質	zhengzong	正宗
wu (enlightenment/ realization)	悟	zhexian	謫仙
		zhi	質
wu (false)	誣	zhiyan	質言
		zhiyin	知音
xiang	相	zhuo	拙
xiang	想	ziran	自然
xianguai	險怪	zongyi	縱逸
xiangwai	象外	zongzhi	宗旨
xiangxiang	想像	zongzi buji	縱恣不羈

BIBLIOGRAPHY

Primary Sources and Poetry Anthologies

Ban Gu 班固. *Han shu* 漢書. 12 Vols. 1962. Reprint, Beijing: Zhonghua shuju, 1975.

Bao Zhao 鮑照. *Bao shi ji* 鮑氏集. Vol. 432 of *SBBY*.

Bo Juyi 白居易. *Bo Juyi ji*. 4 vols. Beijing: Zhonghua shuju, 1979.

Chen Hang 陳沆. *Shi bi xing jian* 詩比興箋. Shanghai: Shanghai guji, 1981.

Chen Hongxu 陳弘緒. *Chen Shiye xiansheng ji/Shizhuang chuji* 陳士業先生集／石莊初集. In *Siku quanshu cunmu bubian*, vol. 54. Jinan: Qi Lu shushe, 1997.

Chen Shan 陳善. *Menshi xinhua* 捫蝨新話. In *Congshu jixuan* 叢書集選, vol. 52. Taipei: Xinwenfeng chuban, 1984.

Chen Tingzhuo 陳廷焯. *Baiyuzhai cihua* 白雨齋詞話. Shanghai: Shanghai guji, 1984.

Chen Zilong 陳子龍. *Chen Zhongyu ji*. 4 vols. In *Qian kun zheng qi ji* 乾坤正氣集, edited by Pan Xi'en 潘錫恩. Taipei: Huanqiu shuju, 1966.

Congshu jicheng chubian 叢書集成初編 *[CSJCCB]*. 4,000 vols. Edited by Wang Yunwu 王雲吾. Shanghai: Shangwu, 1935–1939.

Congshu jicheng xinbian 叢書集成新編 *[CSJCXB]*. 120 vols. Taipei: Xin wen feng, 1985.

Congshu jicheng xubian 叢書集成續編 *[CSJCXB2]*. 180 vols. Shanghai: Shanghai shudian, 1994.

Dai Qinli, ed. 逯欽立. *Xian Qin Han Wei Jin Nanbeichao shi* 先秦漢魏晉南北朝詩. Beijing: Zhonghua shuju, 1983.

Du Fu 杜甫. *Du shi jing quan* 杜詩鏡銓. 2 vols. Edited and annotated by Yang Lun. 1969. Reprint, Shanghai: Shanghai guji, 1980.

———. *Qian zhu Du shi* 錢注杜詩. 2 vols. Edited and annotated by Qian Qianyi. 1958. Reprint, Shanghai: Shanghai guji, 1979.

Fang Dongshu 方東樹. *Zhaomei zhanyan* 昭昧詹言. Beijing: Renmin wenxue, 1961.

Fang Hongjing 方弘靜. *Qian yi lu* 千一錄. 12 vols. China: s.n., 1573–1620.

Gao Bing 高柄. *Tangshi pinhui* 唐詩品彙. 2 vols. Shanghai: Shanghai guji, 1982.

Gao Buying 高步瀛, ed. *Tang Song wen juyao* 唐宋文舉要. 3 vols. Beijing: Zhonghua, 1963.

Ge Hong 葛洪. *Baopuzi neipian jiaoshi* 包朴子內篇校釋. 2 vols. Edited by Wang Ming 王明. Beijing: Zhonghua, 1985.

———. *Shenxian zhuan* 神仙傳. In *CSJCXB*, 100:279–329.

Ge Lifang 葛立方. *Yunyu yangqiu* 韻語陽秋. Shanghai: Shanshi, 1889.

Guan Shiming 管世銘. *Du xue shan fang Tangshi xu li* 讀雪山房唐詩序例. In *QSHXB*, 2:1537–1567.

Guo Maoqian 郭茂倩. *Yuefu shiji* 樂府詩集. 4 vols. Beijing: Zhonghua shuju, 1979.

Han wudi neizhuan 漢武帝內傳. In *Zhengtong daozang* 正統道藏, 61 vols. Taipei: Yiwen yinshuguan yinhang, 1977.

Han Yu 韓愈. *Han Yu quanji jiao zhu*. Edited by Qu Shouyuan 屈守元 and Chang Sichun 常思春. 5 vols. Chengdu: Sichuan daxue chubanshe, 1996.

He Jing 郝經. *He Wenzhong gongji* 郝文忠公集. In Pan Xi'en, *Qian kun zheng qi ji, j.* 111.

He Yisun 賀貽孫. *Shifa* 詩筏. In *QSHXB*, 1:135–202.

Hong Mai 洪邁. *Rongzhai suibi* 容齋隨筆. Changchun: Jilin wenshi, 1995.

Hu Yinglin 胡應麟. *Shisou* 詩藪. Shanghai: Shanghai guji, 1979.

Hu Zhenheng 胡震亨. *Tangyin guiqian* 唐音癸籤. Shanghai: Gudian wenxue, 1957.

Hu Zi 胡仔. *Tiaoxi yuyin conghua* 苕溪漁隱叢話. Vols. 608–609 of *SBBY*.

Huainanzi 淮南子. Vol. 7 of *ZZJC*. 1954. Reprint, Beijing: Zhonghua, 1993.

Huang Che 黃徹. *Gongxi shihua* 碧溪詩話. Edited by Tang Xinxiang 湯新祥. Beijing: Renmin wenxue, 1986.

Huang Tingjian 黃庭堅. *Huang Tingjian xuanji* 黃庭堅選集. Edited by Huang Baohua 黃寶華. Shanghai: Shanghai guji, 1991.

Huang Zongxi 黃宗. *Mingwenhai* 明文海. Vol. 1455 of *SKQS*.

Hui Hong 惠洪. *Lengzhai yehua* 冷齋夜話. Beijing: Zhonghua shuju, 1988.

Ji Yougong 計有功. *Tangshi jishi jiaojian* 唐詩紀事校箋. 2 vols. Edited by Wang Zhongyong 王仲鏞. Chengdu: Bashu shushe, 1989.

Jin Shengtan 金聖歎. *Du shi jie* 杜詩解. Shanghai: Shanghai guji, 1984.

Jinshu 晉書. Edited by Fang Xuanling 房玄齡. 10 vols. Beijing: Zhonghua, 1974.

Jiu Tangshu 舊唐書. Edited by Liu Xu 劉昫. 16 vols. Beijing: Zhonghua, 1975.

Li Bo 李白. *Li Bo ji jiaozhu* 李白集校注 *[LBJJZ]*. 2 vols. Edited by Ju Tuiyuan 瞿蛻園 and Zhu Jincheng 朱金城. Shanghai: Shanghai guji chubanshe, 1980.

———. *Li Taibai quanji* 李太白全集 *[LTBQJ]*. 3 vols. Edited by Wang Qi 王琦. Beijing: Zhonghua shuju, 1985.

Li Bo ziliao huibian: Jin Yuan Ming Qing zhi bu 李白資料彙編 *[LBZLHB]*. 3 vols. Edited by Pei Fei 裴斐 and Liu Shanliang 劉善良. Beijing: Zhonghua shuju, 1994.

Li Diaoyuan 李調元. *Tongshan wenji* 童山文集. Vols. 2515–2517 of *CSJCCB*.

———. *Yucun shihua* 雨村詩話. In *QSHXB*, 2:1515–1536.

Li Dongyang 李東陽. *Huailutang shihua* 懷麓堂詩話. Shanghai: Yixue shuju, [1916?].

Li Gang 李綱. *Liang Xi xiansheng wen ji* 梁溪先生文集. 1834.

Li Zhi 李贄. *Fenshu, Xu Fenshu* 焚書, 續焚書. Beijing: Zhonghua, 1975.

Liang Qichao 梁啟超. *Yinbingshi wenji* 飲冰室文集. 10 vols. Shanghai: Zhonghua shuju, 1926.

Lidai shihua 歷代詩話 *[LDSH]*. 2 vols. Compiled by He Wenhuan 何溫煥. Beijing: Zhonghua shuju, 1981.

Lidai shihua xubian 歷代詩話續編 *[LDSHXB]*. 3 vols. Compiled by Ding Fubao 丁福保. Beijing: Zhonghua shuju, 1983.

Lienü zhuan jinzhu jinshi 列女傳今註今釋. Edited and annotated by Zhang Jing 張敬. Taipei: Taiwan shangwu yinshuguan, 1994.

Liexian zhuan 列仙傳. In *Sengaikyo; ressenden* 山海經／列仙傳, edited by Maeno Naoaki 前野直彬. Tokyo: Shueisha, 1975, 637–732.

Liexian zhuan jiaojian 列仙傳校箋. Edited by Wang Shumin 王叔岷 and Liu Xiang 劉向. Taipei: Zhongyang yanjiu yuan, zhongguo wenzhe zhuankan, 1995.

Liezi zhu 列子注. Edited by Zhang Kan 張湛. Vol. 3 of *ZZJC*.

Lin Changyi 林昌彝. *Haitian qinsi lu* 海天琴思錄. 4 vols. China: s.n., 1864.

Liu Ban 劉攽. *Zhongshan shihua* 中山詩話. Vol. 1478 of *SKQS*.

Liu Lu 劉履. *Feng ya yi* 風雅翼. Vol. 1370 of *SKQS*.

Liu Xie 劉勰. *Wenxin diaolong* 文心雕龍. Edited by Zhou Zhenfu 周振甫. Beijing: Renmin wenxue, 1983.

Liu Xu 劉昫, ed. *Jiu Tangshu* 舊唐書. 16 vols. Beijing: Zhonghua, 1975.

Liu Yiqing 劉義慶. *Shishuo xinyu jiaojian* 世說新語校箋. 2 vols. Edited by Xu Zhene 徐辰堮. 1984. Reprint, Beijing: Zhonghua shuju, 2000.

Lu Ji 陸機. "Wenfu" 文賦. In *Wenxuan*, 17.1a–10a.

Lu Shiyong 陸時雍. *Shijing zonglun* 詩鏡總論. Shanghai: Yixue shuju, 1916.

Lu You 陸游. *Lao xue an biji* 老學庵筆記. Shanghai: Shanghai shudian, 1990.

Luo Dajing 羅大經. *Helin yulu* 鶴林玉露. Beijing: Zhonghua, 1983.

Ma Duanlin 馬端臨. *Wenxian tongkao* 文獻通考. Beijing: Zhonghua, 1986.

Maoshi zhengyi 毛詩正義. 6 vols. Hong Kong: Zhonghua shuju, 1964.

Meng Qi 孟棨. *Benshishi* 本事詩. In vol. 1 of *LDSHXB*.

Ouyang Xiu 歐陽修. *Ouyang Xiu quanji* 歐陽修. 2 vols. Hong Kong: Guangzhi shuju, 1974.

Pan Deyu 潘德輿. *Yangyizhai shihua* 養一齋詩話 [Includes his *Li Du shihua*, 3 *juan*]. 4 vols. China: s.n., 1836.

Pan Xi'en 潘錫恩. *Qian kun zheng qi ji* 乾坤正氣集. Taipei: Huanqiu shuju, 1966.

Pi Rixiu 皮日休. *Pizi wen sou* 皮子文籔. Shanghai: Shanghai guji, 1981.

Qian Qianyi 錢謙益. *Muzhai youxue ji* 牧齋有學集. Vols. 115–116 of *Siku jinhuishu congkan* 四庫禁燬書叢刊. Beijing: Beijing chubanshe, 1997.

Qiao Songnian 喬松年. *Luomoting zhaji* 蘿藦亭扎記. Vol. 93 of *CSJCXB2*.

Qiao Yi 喬億. *Jianxi shuoshi* 劍溪說詩. Vol. 2 of *QSHXB*.

Qing shihua 清詩話. 2 vols. Shanghai: Shanghai guji, 1982.

Qing shihua xubian 清詩話續編 *[QSHXB]*. 2 vols. Edited by Guo Shaoyu 郭紹虞. Shanghai: Shanghai guji, 1983.

Quan Han Sanguo Jin nanbeichao shi 全漢三國南北朝詩. Edited by Ding Zhonggu 丁仲祜. 3 vols. Taipei: Yiwen yinshuguan, 1968.

Quan Tangshi 全唐詩 *[QTS]*. 12 vols. Taipei: Wen shizhe chubanshe, 1978.

Ruan Ji 阮籍. *Ruan Bubing* Yonghuai *shi zhu* 阮步兵詠懷詩註. Edited by Huang Jie 黃節. Taipei: Yiwen yinshuguan, 1971.

Shen Deqian 沈德潛. *Gushi yuan* 古詩源. Beijing: Zhonghua shuju, 1963.

———. *Shuo shi zui yu* 說詩晬語. In vol. 67 of *SBBY*.

———, ed. and ann. *Guiyu wen chao* 歸愚文鈔. Vols. 9–18 of *Shen Guiyu shiwen quanji* 沈歸愚詩文全集. [China:] Chiao chung tang, 1759–1767.

———. *Qi zi shi xuan* 七子詩選. 4 vols. China: s.n., [1767?].

———. *Tangshi biecai ji* 唐詩別材集. Hong Kong: Zhonghua shuju, 1977.

Shi Runzhang 施閏章. *Shi Yushan ji* 施愚山集. Edited by He Qinshan 何慶善 and Yang Yingqin 揚應芹. Hefei: Huangshan shushe, 1992.

Shi Shan 施山. *Jianglu'an zaji* 薑露盦雜集. 2 vols. Shanghai: Shenbao guan, [1879?].

Sima Qian 司馬遷. *Shiji* 史記. 10 vols. Beijing: Zhonghua, 1959.

Su Che 蘇轍. *Luancheng ji* 欒城集. 3 vols. Shanghai: Shanghai guji, 1987.

Su Shi 蘇軾. *Su Dongpo ji* 蘇東破集. 3 vols. Shanghai: Shangwu yinshu guan,1933.

———. *Su Shi lun wenyi* 蘇軾論文藝. Edited by Yan Zhongqi. Beijing: Beijing chubanshe, 1985.

———. *Su Shi wenji* 蘇軾文集. Edited by Kong Fanli 孔凡禮. 1986. Reprint, Beijing: Zhonghua, 1992.

Sunzi 孫子. *Sunzi shijia zhu* 孫子十家注. Vol. 6 of *ZZJC*.

Taiping guangji 太平廣記. Edited by Li Fang 李昉. 10 vols. Beijing: Zhonghua, 1961.

Taiping yulan 太平御覽. Edited by Li Fang 李昉. 4 vols. 1963. Reprint, Beijing: Zhonghua, 1998.

Tang Guizhang 唐圭璋. *Cihua congbian* 詞話叢編. Beijing: Zhonghua, 1986.

Tao Qian 陶潛. *Tao Yuanming ji jiaojian* 陶淵明集校箋. Edited by Gong Bin 龔斌. Shanghai: Shanghai guji, 1996.

Tian Wen 田雯. *Guhuantang ji* 古懽堂集. *QSHXB*, 2:689–724.

Tu Long 屠隆. *Hongbaoji* 鴻苞集. Edited by Mao Yuanyi 茅元儀. China: s.n., 1610.

———. *Youquanji* 由拳集. Vol. 180 of *Siku quanshu cunmu congshu* 四庫全書存目叢書. Jinan: Qilu shushe, 1997.

Wang Chong 王充. *Lunheng* 論衡. In vol. 7 of *ZZJC*.

Wang Fuzhi 王夫之. *Jiangzhai shihua* 薑齋詩話. Edited by Guo Shaoyu. Beijing: Renmin wenxue, 1961.

———. *Tangshi pingxuan* 唐詩評選. Beijing: Wenhua yishu chubanshe, 1997.

Wang Shizhen 王士禎. *Daijingtang shihua* 帶經澄詩話. 2 vols. Edited and annotated by Dai Hongseng. Beijing: Renmin wenxue, 1982.

Wang Shizhen 王世貞. *Yiyuan zhiyan* 藝苑巵言. In *LDSHXB*.

Weng Fanggang 翁方綱. *Fuchuzhai wenji* 復初齋文集. Annotated by Li Yenchang. 4 vols. China: s.n., 1877.

Wenxuan 文選. Edited by Xiao Tong 蕭統. 3 vols. Annotated by Li Shan 李善. 1977. Reprint, Beijing: Zhonghua, 1981.

Wu Jing 吳兢. *Yuefu jieti* 樂府解題. In *Shuo fu* 說郛. China: Wanweishantang, 1646, *j*. 102.

Wu Qiao 吳喬. *Weilu shihua* 圍爐詩話. In *CSJC,* 2609.

Wu Yue chunqiu jijiao huikao 吳越春秋輯校彙考. Edited by Zhou Shengchun 周生春. Shanghai: Shanghai guji, 1997.

Xie Zhen 謝榛. *Siming shihua* 四溟詩話. Beijing: Renmin, 1961.

Xu Shen 許慎, comp. *Shuowen jiezi zhu* 說文解字注. Taipei: Liming wenhua, 1989.

Yan Junshou 延君壽. *Laosheng changtan* 老牛常談. In vol. 159 of *CSJCXB.*

Yan Yu 嚴羽. *Canglang shihua jiaoshi* 滄浪詩話校釋. Edited and annotated by Guo Shaoyu. Beijing: Zhonghua shuju, 1983.

Yang Shen 楊慎. *Zongzuan Sheng'an heji* 總纂升菴合集. Edited by Zheng Baoshen 鄭寶深. China: Wang Hong wen tang cangban 王鴻文堂藏板, 1882.

Yao Ying 姚瑩. *Dongming waiji* 東溟外集. In vol. 4 of *Zhongfutang quanji,* 10 vols. China: n.s., 1867.

Ye Xie 葉燮. *Yuanshi* 原詩. In *Qing shihua,* 2:563–615.

Yin Fan 殷璠. *Heyue yingling ji* 河嶽英靈集. In vol. 93 of *SBCK.*

Yiwen leiju 藝文類聚. Compiled by Ouyang Xun 歐陽詢 et al. 4 vols. Hong Kong: Zhonghua shuju, 1973.

You Tong 尤侗. *Xitang zazu* 西堂雜俎. Taipei: Guangwen shuju, 1970.

Yuan Hongdao 袁宏道. *Yuan Zhonglang quanji* 袁中郎全集. Hong Kong: Guangzhi shuju, 195?.

Yuan Ke 袁珂, ed. *Shanhaijing jiaozhu* 山海經校注. Shanghai: Shanghai guji, 1980.

Yuan Zhen 元稹. *Yuan Changqing ji* 元長慶集. Shanghai: Shanghai guji, 1994.

Yuxuan Tang Song shichun 御選唐宋詩醇. Edited by the Qianlong emperor. 8 vols. Shanghai: Hongwen shuju, 1895.

Zeng Guofan 曾國藩. *Zeng Wenzheng gong wenji* 曾文正公文集. Changsha: Zhuangzhong shuju, 1874.

Zeng Jili 曾季貍. *Tingzhai shihua* 艇齋詩話. In *LDSHXB.*

Zhang Dai 張岱. *Langhuan wenji* 瑯嬛文集. Changsha: Yuelu shushe, 1985.

Zhang Xuecheng 章學誠. *Wenshi tongyi bubian* 文史通義補編. In *CSJC,* 5:608–617.

———. *Wenshi tongyi jiaozhu* 文史通義校注. Annotated by Ye Ying 葉瑛. 2 vols. Beijing: Zhonghua shuju, 1985.

Zhao Cigong 趙次公. *Du Gongbu Caotang ji* 杜工部草堂記. In *Chengdu wenji* 成都文集, edited by Hu Zhongrong 扈仲榮 and Cheng Yusun 程遇孫, *j.* 42 (*SKQS,* vol. 1354).

Zhao Yi 趙翼. *Oubei shihua* 甌北詩話. Compiled and annotated by Huo Songlin 霍松林 and Hu Zhuyou 胡主佑. Beijing: Renmin wenxue, 1981.

Zhong Rong 鍾嶸. *Shipin* 詩品. In *LDSH,* 1:1–24.

Zhou Ting 周珽. *Tangshi xuanmai huitong* 唐詩選脈會通. In *Siku quanshu cunmu congshu bubian* 四庫全書存目叢書補編, additional vol. 26. Jinan: Jilu shushe, 1997.

Zhou Zhongfu 周中孚. *Zheng tang zha ji* 鄭堂札記. In *Yangshi qianqibai ershijiu he zhai congshu* 仰視千七百二十九鶴齋叢書. Edited by Zhao Zhiqian 趙之謙. Shaoxing: Moruntang shuyuan, 1929.

Zhu Xi 朱熹. *Chuci jizhu* 楚辭集注. Hong Kong: Zhonghua shuju, 1987.

———. *Jin si lu* 近思錄. Vols. 630–633 of *CSJCCB.*

――――. *Zhuzi yishu* 朱子遺書. 12 vols. Taipei: Yiwen yinshuguan, 1969.

. *Zhuzi yulei* 朱子語類. 8 vols. 1962. Reprint, Taipei: Zhongwen chubanshe, 1973.

Zhu Yao 祝堯. *Gufu bianti* 古賦辨體. In vol. 1366 of *SKQS*.

Zhuangzi 莊子. *Zhuangzi jijie* 莊子集解. Edited by Wang Xianqian 王先謙. In vol. 3 of *ZZJC*.

Zhuzi jicheng 諸子集成. 8 vols. 1954. Reprint, Beijing: Zhonghua, 1993.

Secondary Sources

Allen, Joseph. *In the Voice of Others: Chinese Music Bureau Poetry*. Ann Arbor: Center for Chinese Studies, University of Michigan Press, 1992.

Bakhtin, Mikhail. *The Dialogic Imagination: Four Essays by M. M. Bakhtin*. Edited by Michael Holquist and translated by Caryl Emerson and Michael Holquist. Austin: The University of Texas Press, 1981.

Birch, Cyril, ed. *Anthology of Chinese Literature*. 2 vols. New York: Grove, 1965.

Birrell, Anne. *Popular Songs and Ballads of Han China*. London: Unwin Hyman, 1988.

Bloom, Harold. *The Anxiety of Influence: A Theory of Poetry*. New York: Oxford University Press, 1973.

Bol, Peter K. *"This Culture of Ours": Intellectual Transition in T'ang and Sung China*. Stanford: Stanford University Press, 1992.

Bollas, Christopher. *Being a Character: Psychoanalysis and Self-Experience*. New York: Hill and Wang, 1992.

Bryant, Daniel. "On the Authenticity of the Tz'u Attributed to Li Po," *Tang Studies* 7 (1989):105–136.

Budick, Sanford, and Wolfgang Iser, eds. *Languages of the Unsayable: The Play of Negativity in Literature and Literary Theory*. Stanford: Stanford University Press, 1987.

Bush, Susan, and Christian Murck, eds. *Theories of the Arts in China*. Princeton: Princeton University Press, 1983.

Cai Zongqi. "Dramatic and Narrative Modes of Presentation in Han Yüeh-fu." *Monumenta Serica* 44 (1996):101–140.

――――. *The Matrix of Lyric Transformation: Poetic Modes and Self-Presentation in Early Chinese Pentasyllabic Poetry*. Ann Arbor: Center for Chinese Studies, University of Michigan Press, 1996.

――――. "*Wenxin diaolong* yu chuantong wenxueguan kuangjia he chuantong wenlun de xitongxing" [The *Wenxin diaolong* and the systematic nature of traditional literary frameworks and traditional literary discourse]. *Wenxin diaolong yanjiu* 2 (September 1996):326–345.

Chang, Hao. *Chinese Intellectuals in Crisis: Search for Order and Meaning (1890–1911)*. Berkeley: University of California Press, 1987.

――――. *Liang Ch'i-ch'ao and Intellectual Transition in China, 1890–1907*. Cambridge: Harvard University Press, 1971.

Chang, Kang-i Sun. *The Late-Ming Poet Ch'en Tzu-lung*. New Haven: Yale University Press, 1991.

――――. *Six Dynasties Poetry*. Princeton: Princeton University Press, 1986.

Chaves, Jonathan. "The Expression of Self in the Kung-an School: Non-Romantic Individualism." In *Expressions of Self in Chinese Literature*, edited by Robert Hegel and Richard C. Hessney, 123–150. New York: Columbia University Press, 1985.

———. "The Panoply of Images: A Reconsideration of the Literary Theory of the Kung-an School." In *Theories of the Arts in China*, edited by Susan Bush and Christian Murck, 341–364. Princeton: Princeton University Press, 1983.

Ch'en, Yu-shih. "The Literary Theory and Practice of Ou-yang Hsiu." In *Chinese Approaches to Literature*, edited by Adele Rickett. Princeton: Princeton University Press, 1978.

Cheng, François. *Vide et plein: le langage pictural chinois.* 1979. Reprint, Paris: Seuil, 1991.

Chodorow, Nancy. *The Power of Feelings: Personal Meaning in Psychoanalysis, Gender, and Culture.* New Haven: Yale University Press, 1999.

Chou, Chih-p'ing. *Yüan Hung-tao and the Kung-an School.* Cambridge: Cambridge University Press, 1988.

Chou, Eva Shan, "Beginning with Images in the Nature Poetry of Wang Wei." *HJAS* 42/1 (June 1982):117–137.

———. *Reconsidering Tu Fu: Literary Greatness and the Cultural Context.* Cambridge: Cambridge University Press, 1995.

Chow, Tse-tsung. *The May Fourth Movement: Intellectual Revolution in China.* Cambridge: Harvard University Press, 1960.

Culler, Jonathan. "On the Negativity of Modern Poetry: Friedrich, Baudelaire, and the Critical Tradition." In *Languages of the Unsayable: The Play of Negativity in Literature and Literary Theory*, edited by Sanford Budick and Wolfgang Iser, 189–208. Stanford: Stanford University Press, 1987.

Davis, A. R. "The Double Ninth Festival in Chinese Poetry: A Study of Variations upon a Theme." In *Wen Lin*, edited by Chow Tse-tsung, 45–64. Madison: University of Wisconsin Press, 1968.

Eide, Elling. "On Li Po." In *Perspectives on the T'ang*, edited by Arthur F. Wright and Denis Twitchett, 367–403. New Haven: Yale University Press, 1973.

Faure, Bernard. "Space and Place in Chinese Religious Traditions." *History of Religions* 26/4 (May 1987):337–356.

Fingarette, Herbert. *Confucius—The Secular as Sacred.* New York: Harper and Row, 1972.

Fisher, Philip. *Wonder, the Rainbow, and the Aesthetics of Rare Experiences.* Cambridge: Harvard University Press, 1998.

Fisk, Craig. "Literary Criticism." In *The Indiana Companion to Traditional Chinese Literature*, edited by William H. Nienhauser Jr., 49–58. Bloomington: Indiana University Press, 1986.

Francis, Mark E. "Canon Formation in Traditional Chinese Poetry: Chinese Canons, Sacred and Profane." In *China in a Polycentric World: Essays in Chinese Comparative Literature*, edited by Yingjin Zhang, 50–70. Stanford: Stanford University Press, 1998.

Frankel, Hans H. "The Development of the Han and Wei Yueh-fu as a High Literary Genre." In *The Vitality of the Lyric Voice: Shih Poetry from the Late Han to the T'ang,* edited by Shuen-fu Lin and Stephen Owen, 255–286. Princeton: Princeton University Press, 1986.

———. "The Relation between Narrator and Characters in *Yuefu* Ballads." *CHINOPERL Papers* 13 (1984–1985):107–127.

Fuller, Michael. "Pursuing the Complete Bamboo in the Breast: Reflections on a Classical Image for Immediacy." *HJAS* 53/1 (1993):5–23.

Gadamer, Hans-Georg. *Truth and Method.* 1975. Reprint, New York: Crossroad, 1989.

Gálik, Marián. *The Genesis of Modern Chinese Literary Criticism (1917–1930).* London: Curzon Press, 1980.

Gardner, Daniel K. *Chu Hsi: Learning to Be a Sage.* Berkeley: University of California Press, 1990.

Ge Jingchun 葛景春. *Li Bo yu Tangdai wenhua* 李白與唐代文化. Zhengzhou: Zhongzhou guji, 1994.

Genette, Gérard. *Palimpsestes: la litterature au second degré.* Paris: Seuil, 1982.

Gibbs, Donald. "Notes on the Wind: The Term 'Feng' in Chinese Literary Criticism." In *Transition and Permanence: A Festschrift in Honor of Dr. Hsiao Kung-ch'üan,* edited by David C. Buxbaum and Frederick W. Mote, 285–293. Hong Kong: Cathay Press, 1972.

Gong Shu, "The Function of Space and Time as Compositional Elements in Wang Wei's Poetry: A Study of Five Poems," *Literature East and West* 16/4 (April 1975):1168–1193.

Guang Sheng. "Zhongguo guominxing ji qi ruodian" 中國國民性及其弱點, *Xin qingnian* 新青年 2/6 (1917):495–505.

Guha, Ranajit, and Gayatri Chakravorty Spivak, eds. *Selected Subaltern Studies.* London: Oxford University Press, 1988.

Guo Moruo 郭沫若. *Li Bo yu Du Fu* 李白與杜甫. Beijing: Renmin wenxue, 1972.

Guo Shaoyu 郭紹虞. *Zhongguo wenxue pipingshi* 中國文學批評史. Hong Kong: Hongzhi shudian, 1956.

Gu Yisheng 顧易生, Jiang Fan 蔣凡, and Liu Mingjin 劉明今. *Song Jin Yuan wenxue pipingshi* 宋金元文學批評史. 2 vols. Shanghai: Shanghai guji, 1996.

Hamlin, Cyrus. *Hermeneutics of Form: Romantic Poetics in Theory and Practice.* New Haven: Henry R. Schwab, 1998.

Hanabusa, Hideki. *Rihaku kashi sakuin* 李白歌詩索引. Kyoto: Kyoto Daigaku jinbun kagaku kenkyujo sakuin henshu iinkai, 1957.

Hartman, Charles. *Han Yü and the T'ang Search for Unity.* Princeton: Princeton University Press, 1986.

Henderson, John B. *Scripture, Canon, and Commentary: A Comparison of Confucian and Western Exegesis.* Princeton: Princeton University Press, 1991.

Herrnstein Smith, Barbara. "Contingencies of Value." In *Canons,* edited by Robert von Hallberg, 5–39. Chicago: Chicago University Press, 1984.

Hightower, James R. "Allusion in the Poetry of T'ao Ch'ien," *HJAS* 31 (1971):5–27.

Hightower, James R., and Florence Chia-ying Yeh, eds. *Studies in Chinese Poetry*. Cambridge: Harvard University Press, 1998.

Holzman, Donald. *Poetry and Politics: The Life and Works of Juan Chi (210–263)*. Cambridge: Cambridge University Press, 1976.

Huang Baozhen 黃寶真 et al., eds. *Zhongguo wenxue lilun shi* 中國文學理論史. 4 vols. Taipei: Hongye wenhua chubanshe, 1994.

Hucker, Charles O. *A Dictionary of Official Titles in Imperial China*. Stanford: Stanford University Press, 1985.

Jia Jinhua 賈晉華. "Li Bo *Gufeng* xinlun" 李白古風新論. In *Zhongguo Li Bo yanjiu* 中國李白研究, 130–140. Jiangsu: Jiangsu guji chubanshe, 1993.

Jiang Guangdou 姜光斗. "Lun Li Bo dui Han Yu qixian shifeng de yingxiang" 論李白對韓愈奇險詩風的影響. In *Zhongguo Li Bo yanjiu*, 142–148. Jiangsu: Jiangsu guji, 1990.

Jullien, François. *Eloge de la fadeur*. Paris: Picquier, 1991.

———. *Procès ou création: une introduction à la pensée chinoise: essai de problématique interculturelle*. Paris: Seuil, 1996, 1989.

———. *La propension des choses: pour une histoire de l'efficacité en Chine*. Paris: Seuil, 1992.

Kao, Yu-kung. "The Aesthetics of Regulated Verse." In *The Vitality of the Lyric Voice: Shih Poetry from the Late Han to the T'ang*, edited by Shuen-fu Lin and Stephen Owen, 332–385. Princeton: Princeton University Press, 1986.

Kao, Yu-kung, and Tsu-lin Mei. "Meaning, Metaphor, and Allusion in T'ang Poetry," *HJAS* 38/2 (December 1978):281–356.

Knechtges, David R. *The Han Rhapsody: A Study of the Fu of Yang Hsiung (53 B.C.–A.D. 18)*. Cambridge: Cambridge University Press, 1976.

Kwong, Charles Yim-Tze. *Tao Qian and the Chinese Poetic Tradition: The Quest for Cultural Identity*. Ann Arbor: University of Michigan Press, 1994.

Lattimore, David. "Allusion in T'ang Poetry." In *Perspectives on the T'ang*, edited by Arthur F. Wright and Denis Twitchett, 405–439. New Haven: Yale University Press, 1973.

Lee, Leo Ou-fan. *The Romantic Generation of Chinese Writers*, Cambridge: Harvard University Press, 1973.

Levenson, Joseph R. *Liang Ch'i-ch'ao and the Mind of Modern China*. Berkeley: University of California Press, 1967.

Li Bo. *The Selected Poems of Li Po*. Translated and edited by David Hinton. New York: New Directions, 1996.

Li, Wai-yee. "The Rhetoric of Spontaneity in Late-Ming Literature," *Ming Studies* 35 (August 1995):32–49.

Li Yuegang 李曰岡. *Cifu liubian shi* 辭賦流變史. Taipei: Wenjin chubanshe, 1987.

Liu Hsieh. *The Literary Mind and the Carving of Dragons*. Translated and annotated by Vincent Yu-chung Shih. New York: Columbia University Press, 1959.

Liu I-ch'ing, *Shih-shuo Hsin-yü: A New Account of Tales of the World*. Translated and annotated by Richard B. Mather. Minneapolis: University of Minnesota Press, 1976.

Liu, James J. Y. *Chinese Theories of Literature*. Chicago: University of Chicago Press, 1975.

Liu, Lydia H. *Translingual Practice: Literature, National Culture, and Translated Modernity. China, 1900–1937* Stanford: Stanford University Press, 1995.

Liu, Wu-chi, and Irving Yucheng Lo, eds. *Sunflower Splendor: Three Thousand Years of Chinese Poetry.* Bloomington: Indiana University Press, 1975.

Luo Zongqiang 羅宗強. *Li Du lun lüe* 李杜論略. Hohhot: Nei Menggu renmin chubanshe, 1980.

Lynn, Richard John. "Alternate Routes to Self-Realization in Ming Theories of Poetry." In *Theories of the Arts in China,* edited by Susan Bush and Christian Murck, 317–340. Princeton: Princeton University Press, 1983.

———. "Orthodoxy and Enlightenment: Wang Shih-chen's Theory of Poetry and Its Antecedents." In *The Unfolding of Neo-Confucianism,* edited by W. T. deBary, 217–269. New York: Columbia University Press, 1975.

———. "The Talent-Learning Polarity in Chinese Poetics" *CLEAR* 5/2 (1983):157–184.

Martin, Helmut. "A Transitional Concept of Chinese Literature, 1897–1917: Liang Ch'i-ch'ao on Poetry-Reform, Historical Drama, and the Political Novel," *Oriens Extremus* 20 (1973):175–217.

Masuda, Kiyohide 増田清秀. *Gakufu no rekishiteki kenkyu* 樂府の歴史的研究. Tokyo: Sobunsha, 1975.

Matsuura Tomohisa 松浦友久. *Rihaku kenkyū—sōsei no koso* 李白研究: 抒情の構造. Tokyo: Sanseito Press, 1975.

———. *Rihaku—shi to shinshō* 李白: 詩と心象. Tokyo: Shakai shisōsha, 1984.

McDougall, Bonnie S. *The Introduction of Western Literary Theories into Modern China, 1919–1925.* Tokyo: Centre for East Asian Cultural Studies, 1971.

McMullen, David L. "Historical and Literary Theory in the Mid-Eighth Century." In *Perspectives on the T'ang,* edited by Arthur F. Wright and Denis Twitchett, 307–342. New Haven: Yale University Press, 1973.

Mei, Tsu-lin, and Yu-kung Kao. "Tu Fu's 'Autumn Meditations': An Exercise in Linguistic Criticism," *HJAS* 28 (1968):44–80.

Miao, Ronald, and Marie Chan, eds. *Studies in Chinese Poetry and Poetics.* San Francisco: Chinese Materials Center, 1978.

Mote, Frederick W. *Imperial China, 900–1800.* Cambridge: Harvard University Press, 1999.

Ng, On-cho. "A Tension in Ch'ing Thought: 'Historicism' in Seventeenth- and Eighteenth-Century Chinese Thought," *Journal of the History of Ideas* 54/4 (October 1993):561–583.

Nienhauser, William H., Jr., ed. and comp. *The Indiana Companion to Traditional Chinese Literature.* Bloomington: Indiana University Press, 1986.

Nienhauser, William H., Jr., et al. *Liu Tsung-yuan.* New York: Twayne Publishers, 1973.

Ono Jitsunosuke 大野實之助, trans. and ann. *Ritaihaku shika zenkai* 李太白詩歌全解. Tokyo: Waseda University Press, 1981.

Owen, Stephen. *The End of the "Middle Ages": Essays in Mid-T'ang Literary Culture.* Stanford: Stanford University Press, 1996.

———. *The Great Age of Chinese Poetry: The High T'ang*. New Haven: Yale University Press, 1981.

———. *The Poetry of Meng Chiao and Han Yü*. New Haven: Yale University Press, 1975.

———. *Readings in Chinese Literary Thought*. Cambridge: Council on East Asian Studies, Harvard University Press, 1992.

———. *Remembrances: The Experience of the Past in Classical Chinese Literature*. Cambridge: Harvard University Press, 1986.

———. "Ruined Estates: Literary History and the Poetry of Eden," *CLEAR* 10 (1988):21–41.

———. *Traditional Chinese Poetry and Poetics: Omen of the World*. Madison: University of Wisconsin Press, 1985.

Palumbo-Liu, David. *The Poetics of Appropriation: The Literary Theory and Practice of Huang Tingjian*. Stanford: Stanford University Press, 1993.

Peterson, Willard J. "Squares and Circles: Mapping the History of Chinese Thought," *Journal of the History of Ideas* 49/1 (1988):47–60.

Peterson, Willard J., Andrew H. Plaks, and Ying-shih Yü, eds. *The Power of Culture: Studies in Chinese Cultural History*. Hong Kong: Chinese University Press, 1994.

Plaks, Andrew H. *Archetype and Allegory in* Dream of the Red Chamber. Princeton: Princeton University Press, 1976.

Pohl, Karl-Heinz. "Ye Xie's 'On the Origin of Poetry' *(Yuan Shi):* A Poetic of the Early Qing," *T'oung Pao* 78 (1992):1–32.

Qiao Xiangzhong. "Li Bo *Gufeng* kaoxi" 李白古風考析. In *Li Bo lun* 李白論, edited by Qiao Xiangzhong, 4–21. Shandong: Qilu shushe, 1986.

Qu Yuan et al. *Songs of the South,* translated and edited by David Hawkes. Harmondsworth Middlesex: Penguin, 1985.

Rickett, Adele Austin. "The Anthologist as Literary Critic in China," *Literature East and West* 19 (1975):145–165.

Robertson, Maureen. "... To Convey What Is Precious: Ssu-k'ung Tu's Poetics and the *Erh-shih-ssu Shih P'in*," in *Transition and Permanence: A Festschrift in Honor of Dr. Hsiao Kung-ch'üan*, edited by David C. Buxbaum and Frederick W. Mote, 323–357. Hong Kong: Cathay Press, 1972.

Ruan Tingyu 阮廷瑜. *Li Bo shi lun* 李白詩論. Taipei: Guoli bianyi guan, 1986.

Rushton, Peter. "The Daoist's Mirror: Reflections on the Neo-Confucian Reader and the Rhetoric of *Jin Ping Mei*," *CLEAR* 8 (1986):63–81.

Saussy, Haun. *The Problem of a Chinese Aesthetic*. Stanford: Stanford University Press, 1993.

Scarry, Elaine. *On Beauty and Being Just*. Princeton: Princeton University Press, 1999.

Schneider, Laurence. *A Madman of Ch'u: The Chinese Myth of Loyalty and Dissent*. Berkeley: University of California Press, 1980.

Schwartz, Benjamin I. "Some Polarities in Neo-Confucian Thought." In *Confucianism in Action*, edited by David S. Nivison and Arthur F. Wright, 50–62. Stanford: Stanford University Press, 1959.

———. *The World of Thought in Ancient China*. Cambridge: Harvard University Press, 1985.

Stewart, Susan. "Proust's Turn from Nostalgia," *Raritan* 19/2 (Fall 1999):77–94.

Takashima Toshio 高島俊男. *Ri Haku to To Ho; sono kodo to bungaku* 李白と杜甫; その行動と文学. Tokyo: Hyoronsha, 1972.

Tu, Ching-I. "Neo-Confucianism and Literary Criticism in Ming China: The Case of T'ang Shun-chih (1507–1560)," *Tamkang Review* 15 (1984–1985):547–560.

Twitchett, Denis. *The Cambridge History of China*. Vol. 3. Cambridge: Cambridge University Press, 1979.

Van Zoeren, Steven. *Poetry and Personality: Reading, Exegesis, and Hermeneutics in Traditional China*. Stanford: Stanford University Press, 1991.

Varsano, Paula. "Immediacy and Allusion in the Poetry of Li Bo," *HJAS* 52/1 (June 1992):225–261.

———. "Transformation and Imitation: The Poetry of Li Bai." Ph.D. diss., Princeton University, 1988.

Wang Chong. *Lun-heng*. Translated and annotated by Alfred Forke. 2 vols. New York: Paragon, 1962.

Wang Yunxi 王運熙. "Handai suyue he min'ge" 漢代俗樂和民歌. In *Yanjiu yuefu shi lunwen ji* 研究樂府詩論文集, 27–42. Beijing: Zuojia chubanshe, 1957.

———. "Han Wei Liuchao yuefu dui Li Bo de yingxiang" 漢魏六朝樂府對李白的影響. In Yu Pingbo, *Li Bo shiluncong*, 80–100. Hong Kong: Xianggang wenyuanshu, 1972.

———. "Liang 'Tangshu' dui Li Bo de bu tong pingjia" 兩唐書對李白的不同評價. In *Zhongguo Li Bo yanjiu*, 83–89. Jiangsu: Jiangsu guji, 1991.

———. "Tan Zhongguo gudai wenlun zhong de bi xing shuo" 談中國古代文論中的比興說. In *Wenyi luncong* 4 (1978):42–58.

Warren, Robert Penn. "Pure and Impure Poetry." In *Critiques and Essays in Criticism, 1920–1948: Representing the Achievement of Modern British and American Critics,* edited by R. W. Stallman, 85–104. New York: Ronald Press, 1949.

Wixted, John Timothy. "The Nature of Evaluation in the *Shih-p'in*." In *Theories of the Arts in China,* edited by Susan Bush and Christian Murck, 225–264. Princeton: Princeton University Press, 1983.

Wright, Arthur F., and Denis Twitchett, eds. *Perspectives on the T'ang*. New Haven: Yale University Press, 1973.

Wu Guoping 鄔國平. "Li Du shige bijiao pingshu" 李杜詩歌比較評述. In *Zhongguo Li Bo yanjiu*, 101–121. Jiangsu: Jiangsu guji, 1991.

Xiao Tong. *Wen Xuan or Selections of Refined Literature*. Translated and annotated by David Knechtges. 2 vols. Princeton: Princeton University Press, 1982, 1987.

Xu Fuguan 徐復觀. "Shi shi de bixing: chong xin dianding Zhongguo shi de xinshang jichu" 釋詩的比興—重新奠定中國詩的欣賞基礎. In Xu Fuguan, *Zhongguo wenxue lun ji* 中國文學論集, 91–117. Taipei: Xuesheng shuju, 1985.

Yeh Chia-ying and Jan Walls, "Theory, Standards, and Practice of Criticizing Poetry in Chung Hung's *Shih-p'in*." In *Studies in Chinese Poetry and Poetics*, edited by Ronald Miao, 1:43–79. San Francisco: Chinese Materials Center, 1978.

Yeh, Florence Chia-ying, "Ch'en Tzu-lung and the Renascence of the Song Lyric." In *Studies in Chinese Poetry*, edited by James R. Hightower and Florence Chia-ying Yeh, 412–438. Cambridge: Harvard University Press, 1998.

Yeh, Michelle. *Modern Chinese Poetry: Theory and Practice since 1917*. New Haven: Yale University Press, 1991.

Yoshikawa Kojiro. *An Introduction to Song Poetry*. Translated by Burton Watson. Cambridge: Harvard University Press, 1967.

You Guo'en 游國恩. *Zhongguo wenxueshi* 中國文學史. 2 vols. Beijing: Zhongguo tushukan xingshe, 1986.

Yu Guanying 余冠英. *Han-Wei Liuchao shi luncong* 漢魏六朝詩論叢. Shanghai: Tangdi chubanshe, 1952.

Yu, Pauline. "Poems in Their Place: Collections and Canons in Early Chinese Literature," *HJAS* 50/1 (1990):163–196.

―――. *The Poetry of Wang Wei: New Translations and Commentary*. Bloomington: Indiana University Press, 1980.

―――. *The Reading of Imagery in the Chinese Tradition*. Princeton: Princeton University Press, 1987.

―――. "Ssu-k'ung T'u's *Shih-p'in*: Poetic Theory in Poetic Form." In *Studies in Chinese Poetry and Poetics*, edited by Ronald Miao, 81–103. San Francisco: Chinese Materials Center, 1978.

Yu Pingbo 俞平伯. *Li Bo shiluncong* 李白詩論叢. Hong Kong: Xianggang wenyuanshu, 1962.

Yu Xianhao 郁賢皓. "Lun Li Bo 'Gufeng' wushijiu shou" 論李白古風五十九首. In *Zhongguo Li Bo yanjiu*, edited by Zhu Jincheng. Ma'anshan: Jiangsu guji chubanshe, 1990.

Yü, Ying-shih, "Intellectual Breakthroughs in the T'ang-Sung Transition." In *The Power of Culture*, edited by Willard J. Peterson, Andrew H. Plaks, and Ying-shih Yü, 158–171. Hong Kong: Chinese University Press, 1994.

Yuan Xingpei 袁行霈. "Li Bo de yuzhou jingjie" 李白的宇宙境界. In *Zhongguo Li Bo yanjiu*, 37–50. Jiangsu: Jiangsu guji, 1991.

―――. "Li Du shige de fengge yu yixiang" 李杜詩歌的風格與意像. In *Zhongguo shige yishu yanjiu* 中國詩歌藝術研究, 241–260. Beijing: Beijing University Press, 1987.

Zeitlin, Judith. *Historian of the Strange: Pu Songling and the Chinese Classical Tale*. Stanford: Stanford University Press, 1993.

Zhang Baoquan 張保全, ed. *Zhongguo gudai shihua cihua cidian* 中國古代詩話詞話詞典. Guilin: Guangxi shifan daxue chubanshe, 1992.

Zhang Shaokang 章少康 and Liu Sanfu 劉三富, *Zhongguo wenxue lilun piping fazhan shi* 中國文學理論發展史. Beijing: Beijing daxue chubanshe, 1995.

Zhan Ying 詹英. *Li Bo quanji jiaozhu hui shi jiping* 李白全集校注匯釋集評. 8 vols. Tianjin: Baihua wenyi chubanshe, 1996.

Zhou Shaoxian 周紹憲. *Lun Li Du shi* 論李杜詩. Taipei: Chung Hwa Book Company, 1975.

Zhu Xi. *Reflections on Things at Hand*. Translated by Wing-tsit Chan. New York: Columbia University Press, 1967.

Zhuangzi, *Chuang Tzu: Basic Writings*. Translated by Burton Watson. New York: Columbia University Press, 1964.

INDEX

This index includes the titles of all of Li Bo's poems that are mentioned or translated in this book. Poems by other poets (translated only) are included under the name of the poet.

ABOUT THE AUTHOR

PAULA VARSANO received her Ph.D. in classical Chinese literature from Princeton University. She has published numerous articles and essays on Chinese poetics and Tang poetry. This is her first book.